Dr. Macintosh®   Second Edition

How to Become a
Macintosh Power User

Dr. Macintosh® Second Edition
How to Become a Macintosh Power User

Bob LeVitus

with Laurie Miller Love

Addison-Wesley Publishing Company, Inc.
Reading, Massachusetts   Menlo Park, California   New York
Don Mills, Ontario   Wokingham, England   Amsterdam   Bonn
Sydney   Singapore   Tokyo   Madrid   San Juan
Paris   Seoul   Milan   Mexico City   Taipei

Many of the designations used by manufacturers and sellers to distinguish their products are claimed as trademarks. Where those designations appear in this book and Addison-Wesley was aware of a trademark claim, the designations have been printed in initial capital letters.

The authors and publisher have taken care in preparation of this book, but make no expressed or implied warranty of any kind and assume no responsibility for errors or omissions. No liability is assumed for incidental or consequential damages in connection with or arising out of the use of the information or programs contained herein.

Library of Congress Cataloging-in-Publication Data

LeVitus, Bob.
    Dr. Macintosh : how to become a Macintosh power
    user / Bob LeVitus with Laurie Miller Love.— 2nd ed.
        p.   cm.
    Includes index.
    ISBN 0-201-57050-5
     1. Macintosh (Computer) I. Love, Laurie Miller. II. Title.
  III. Title: Doctor Macintosh : how to become a Macintosh power user
    QA76.8.M3L48 1992
    004.165—dc20   91-45448
                                            CIP

Sponsoring Editor: David Rogelberg
Technical Reviewer: Raines Cohen
Project Editor: Joanne Clapp Fullagar
Cover Design: Jean Seal
Cover Illustrations: Berkeley Breathed
Set in 11-point Palatino by ST Associates

ISBN 0-201-57050-5

1 2 3 4 5 6 7 8 9–MW–9695949392
First printing, March 1992

For Lisa and Allison

Acknowledgments

First, and foremost, thanks to my wife, Lisa, who tirelessly proofread, called manufacturers, checked facts, took care of our 3-year-old daughter, cooked, got pregnant again, and rubbed my shoulders. Without her this book could never have been finished.

Special thanks to my collaborator, Laurie Miller Love. She did most of the hard stuff, much of the writing, and at least half of the agonizing.

Big-time thanks to technical editor, Raines Cohen. His handwriting is totally illegible, but he knows Mac stuff cold. Any errors you find are mine and mine alone.

Thanks to everyone at Addison-Wesley. Your input was invaluable; your support endless. Thanks to Wayne Matthews, at Wallace Engraving in Austin, TX, for the tips about service bureaus in Chapter 8. And thanks to super-agent Bill Gladstone, for coming up with the original concept for this book.

Most of all, I want to thank each of the power users who contributed to a tip to Chapter 11. If you really want to master the Mac, read this chapter carefully. They know what they're talking about—the tips they submitted are, in my humble opinion, the best part of the book.

B.L.
Winter, 1991

Contents

Introduction

What Will This Book Do for You?

This book is about learning to use your Mac better, whether you are a new or *power* Mac user.

Though the Mac is the easiest personal computer to learn and master, you can learn hundreds (thousands?) of shortcuts, secrets, hints, and tips to make using it even easier. I ought to know—I've spent the last five years seeking them out. In this book, I'll do my best to share the best of them with you.

So what is a power user, and why do I want to help you become one? Well, according to the Dr. Macintosh Dictionary at the end of this book:

Definition

> *Power User* (pou'er yoo'zer) n. **1.** Someone who uses a Macintosh better, faster, or more elegantly than you do. **2.** Someone who can answer Macintosh-related questions you can't.

Being a power user means finding faster, easier, and better ways of doing things. And knowing what to do in an emergency. To become a power user, you need absolutely no knowledge of programming. In fact, many power users, myself included, don't know how to program. Being a power user is about *using* your Mac, not programming it! I guarantee that, after reading this book, you'll be more productive every time you sit down in front of your Mac.

I've been doing this for a long time. I can't tell you how many times I've done something the same way for months, only to have someone show me a better way—one that takes less time or effort. This book will save you from having to reinvent the wheel.

How I Learned What I Know

I live and breathe Macintosh. For almost three years I served as editor-in-chief of *MACazine*, one of the first, and always the most outspoken, of the Macintosh publications. Known as the *Village Voice* of Macintosh computer magazines, *MACazine* had a hard-hitting, no-holds-barred policy that made us popular with our readers. We weren't afraid to tell them about the bugs, but we were just as likely to gush enthusiastically about a product that worked well. Unfortunately, *MACazine* ceased publication early in 1989, a victim of the economics of being a small independent in a marketplace dominated by efficient megacorporations.

Since that time, I have written several books—the first and second editions of *Dr. Macintosh*, *Stupid Mac Tricks*, and *Son of Stupid Mac Tricks*. I'm also a contributing editor for *MacUser*; I write the Help Folder question-and-answer column and the Beating the System column about System software.

So you could say that my job for the past five years has been to find information that will help people get more from their Macs. And the job has wonderful perks. I have the tremendous opportunity to examine more software in a month than most people will use in a lifetime.

Needless to say, I've spent a good part of the past few years hunched over in front of one of my Macs (I have several—a IIci, and an LC right this second, with a Quadra 900 and a Power-Book 170 on order!) and labor from dawn to dusk, and often long into the night. If I'm not testing new software or hardware,

I'm writing or preparing camera-ready copy. Or I'm using my modem to gather information and keep in touch with friends and business acquaintances. Because I use my Mac for almost everything—writing, schedules, graphics, communications, household finance, and more—I like nothing better than discovering a method of doing something better, faster, or more elegantly. And, in the true Macintosh spirit, I love being able to share it with other Macintosh users.

I spend a lot of time trying to discover the best or most convenient way of doing something. I think of my job as knowing what is going on in the Macintosh community—what is hot and what is not. I read everything out there about the Macintosh. And I mean *everything*; I read every issue of *Macworld, MacUser, MacWeek, InfoWorld, PC Week, Personal Computing, Home Office Computing, Publish,* and *Personal Publishing* from cover to cover. Then I read about twenty user group newsletters. (Some of the best information, hints, and tips appear in user group newsletters. User group members join because they want answers. Many of them are already power users. Check the dictionary in the back of the book if you don't know what a user group is.)

In addition, as if all that reading doesn't keep me busy enough, I'm a modem rat too. I prowl CompuServe and America Online's Macintosh boards most nights, and drop in on GEnie about once a week.

This book contains the best of what I've picked up over the years through my experiences as a Macintosh lover, beta-tester, editor, modem rat, advice counselor, consultant, author, and general all-around Macaholic.

What's New in the Second Edition

There are three major differences between the first Dr. Mac book and this second edition.

First, this book has been updated to be System 7–friendly, meaning that we've upgraded it to cover the special features of

System 7. In fact, two new chapters have been added: "Getting to Know the Finder" and "Customizing Your Mac," which give details on doing both under System 7 as well as System 6. Throughout the rest of the book, we describe how to use a particular piece of software or how to do a given task under both System 7 and System 6. However, in general, the slant of the book is toward System 7, because it is the latest and greatest System software release on the market at this writing.

Second, we've enhanced existing chapters to provide more complete information for beginning users. If you are a beginning user, someone who just bought a Macintosh and has no idea of what to do with it, you can pick up *Dr. Macintosh, Second Edition*, and learn everything you need to know. By the time you finish this book, you'll be a power user.

Third, you'll find updated information on all products mentioned and recommended in the book, covering the latest versions at this writing, how they work under System 7, and any other new features.

How the Book Is Organized

The chapters in this book are organized logically by topic. Each includes an introduction followed by a detailed discussion. The chapters also include tutorials and specific hints and tips. Each ends with a summary and recommendations: my insights and purchase suggestions. Product recommendations are listed alphabetically and include product name, publisher, address, phone number, and approximate list price.

The book is made up of the following chapters:

Chapter 1: In the Beginning... This chapter covers everything you should know about Macintosh System software. You'll learn what the System and Finder do and how to upgrade your System software. You'll also find System and Finder tips and general timesaving hints.

Chapter 2: Getting to Know the Finder This chapter is rich with all the information you need to work in the Finder. The first section covers the basics of the Macintosh desktop. The second section gives you detailed instructions on how to use every command in the Finder 6 menus. The third section gives a similar treatment to Finder 7 menus and commands, highlighting the major differences between System 6 and System 7. Discussions include how to use System 7's file sharing and the publish and subscribe features. You'll also find a plethora of Finder shortcuts, tips, and hints in this chapter.

Chapter 3: Customizing Your Mac In this chapter, you will learn how to use desk accessories, fonts, startup documents, control panels, FKEYs, and sounds to customize and personalize your Macintosh environment. Included are discussions of how working with desk accessories, fonts, sounds, and control panels differs between System 6 and System 7.

Chapter 4: The Care and Feeding of Hard Disks In this chapter, you'll find out what a hard disk is, what it does, how it works, and why you want one. You'll learn how to go about selecting the right hard disk for you and how to organize it once you've got it. The chapter also provides hints and tips for setting up your hard disk and keeping it running smoothly.

Chapter 5: Protecting Your Work This chapter includes the hows and whys of disk backup, some strategies for avoiding disaster, and tips on the best software and hardware for your needs.

Chapter 6: File and Disk Recovery This chapter may be the most important one in the book: It tells you how to prevent disk crashes and data loss, and what to do when either of these disasters occur. In addition to providing complete instructions for creating your own Disaster Disk, this chapter tells you what to do in the following situations:

- When your hard disk doesn't boot
- When nothing happens when you turn on your Mac
- If you're asked if you want to initialize your hard disk (say "no")
- If you have a startup document conflict.

Chapter 7: Hardware Upgrades This chapter provides everything you need to know about the three most effective hardware upgrades for enhancing productivity: memory upgrades, accelerator boards, and large-screen monitors. You'll also be given a logical strategy for justifying the expense of these upgrades.

Chapter 8: Printing In this chapter, you'll learn how to get the best results no matter which printer you're using. The text includes specific hints for using ImageWriters, LaserWriters, and Linotronic typesetters, as well as a discussion of PostScript versus non-PostScript printers.

Chapter 9: Telecommunication In this chapter, you'll find out what a modem is, why a modem is like a magic carpet, and lots of good reasons to telecommunicate with fellow Mac users. This chapter gives advice on selecting the proper hardware and software for your needs. Descriptions of many places your modem can take you are also provided.

Chapter 10: Utility Software This chapter includes a complete discussion of the power user's best friend: utility software—software that owes its usefulness to the computer. A utility would be meaningless without a computer to run it on. Word processors and spreadsheets are not utilities; disk backup programs, macro recorders, and screen savers are. The essential must-buy utilities are examined, as are several productivity-enhancing add-ons that are highly recommended if you have the budget for them.

Chapter 11: What Other Power Users Think You Should Know This chapter offers an incredible collection of tips and hints from other power users all across the country. These tips have been gathered via several on-line services, including CompuServe, America Online, and GEnie.

Information about the products mentioned in each chapter appears in the "Recommendations" section found at the end of each chapter.

The book concludes with an appendix containing all you need to know about virus protection; "The Doctor's Office," a look at the hardware and software I use every day; and "The Dr. Macintosh Dictionary," which explains in plain English many commonly used computer terms (RAM, ROM, INIT, AppleTalk, crash, and so forth). A comprehensive index is also provided.

How To Use the Book

The best way to use this book is to read it from cover to cover. If you are an intermediate to advanced Mac user, skim over the things you already know, but read every chapter. A lot of good hints and tips are scattered throughout. If you read only part of the book, you run the risk of missing something that could save you time or trouble someday.

If you come across a term you don't understand, check the Dr. Macintosh Dictionary, which appears at the end of the book. New terms are usually defined the first time they appear in text. If you're looking for information about a specific topic, try either the dictionary or the index. I've tried to make both the index and the dictionary as comprehensive as possible.

I'd appreciate your comments. If you don't have a modem, I can be reached in care of my publisher, Addison-Wesley Publishing Company, 1 Jacob Way, Reading, MA 01867. For those of you with modems, my electronic addresses are as follows:

- CompuServe: 76004,2076
- America Online, MCI, and AppleLink: LEVITUS
- GEnie: R.LEVITUS

I'm particularly interested in suggestions for how I could make the third edition of this book more helpful to you. Of course, if you've got any hints or tips of your own, I'd love to know about them.

This book has been a pleasure to write. I hope you have as much fun reading it as I had writing it!

1

In the Beginning…

An introduction to your Macintosh System software plus some general hints and tips for using your Mac more effectively.

Long, long ago, when I bought my first Mac, I thought it would take me only a few days to master. After all, the manuals were short and the interface intuitive. And, within a few days, I had indeed reached a level of proficiency. I could double-click, save, and use the trash. I knew what startup and data disks were. I knew the difference between an application and a document. I knew about something called the Font/DA Mover. That, I thought, was all I needed.

Over the next few months I came to realize that there are hundreds of ways you can customize your Mac to control the way it does things. And there are thousands of shortcuts, both documented and

Definition

> *Font/DA Mover* is the application supplied by Apple with System software prior to System 7 for installing and removing fonts and desk accessories.

undocumented, waiting to be discovered. Not to mention all of the things you should try when things aren't working just right.

Around the same time, I became editor-in-chief of MACazine, *and after that, a contributing editor for* MacUser. *So for the past five years, my job has been discovering and sharing information that helps Macintosh owners use their machines better, faster, and more elegantly. I'm not ashamed to admit that I'm still learning, because it's true, but I must say I've learned an awful lot in these past five years.*

The Macintosh is an extremely powerful tool, contained in a deceptively easy-to-use wrapper. Even someone who knows almost nothing about it can be productive on a Mac. But a power user, one who knows tips and shortcuts and a bit about what to do in an emergency, may be twice as productive.

That's what it's all about: doing more in less time, finding easier ways of doing things, and knowing what to do in an emergency.

This chapter covers the basics of Macintosh System software. The reason this material appears in the first chapter should be obvious: Although every reader may not need or want a hard disk or high-powered software, anyone who uses a Mac must use the System and Finder and other System software. The information in this chapter, along with its hints and techniques, should help each of you coax more performance out of your Mac.

Before you start reading this chapter, you should be familiar with the Apple **Owner's Guide** *that came with your Mac, as well as the documentation that comes with Apple System software releases. These two document sets go a long way toward explaining the mysteries of System software. So if you only glanced at them when you got your computer, you should probably give them another look. Go ahead, I'll wait. This chapter also assumes you have installed the System software—version 6.0.x or 7—on your Mac. (Most Macs come with System software installed already.)*

Definition

6.0.x means any version of System 6—System 6.0. through System 6.0.8. If you are using System 6, you should be using version 6.0.4 or later, as these are generally regarded as more stable than earlier versions.

The System and Finder (System Software)

The System and Finder are the programs containing the instructions that make your Mac work. The System and Finder, along with other software your Mac uses to start up and operate, comprise System software. System software differs from application software, such as MacWrite and MacPaint, in that it manages memory and communicates with input and output devices, such as printers and scanners. System software is always kept in a special folder called the System Folder.

The System

The System is a file used by the Mac to start up and provide system-wide information. The System file contains some of the instructions your Mac needs to run, plus information that adds to or modifies the remainder of the operating instructions. (Other operating instructions are stored in read-only memory, which resides on a chip inside your Mac.) The System file also holds your fonts and sounds. In System 6, the System file holds your desk accessories in addition to your fonts and sounds.

Definition

Read-only memory (ROM) is nonvolatile memory that resides on a chip inside your Mac. It contains parts of the Macintosh Operating System. It can never be erased or changed.

The Finder

The Finder, which starts automatically when you turn on your Mac, contains the information that draws and manages the Macintosh desktop. You use the Finder to manipulate icons on the desktop, to launch applications and utilities, to customize your Mac, and to organize your files into folders. It's like your home base—you start up and shut down at, the Finder. The Finder is also in charge of copying, ejecting, and erasing disks, and of the Apple menu. Read Chapter 2, and you'll discover just about everything you need to know about using the Finder in both System 6 and System 7.

System Folder

A special folder, called the System Folder, contains the System software (System and Finder), the Clipboard file, the Scrapbook file, and other software your Mac needs to operate.

Figure 1-1 shows a typical System Folder under System 7. Your System Folder will probably look different from this one.

System 7 uses several special folders within its System Folder—Control Panels, Extensions, Startup Items, Apple Menu Items, and Preferences—to help you organize, manage, and customize your Mac environment. These folders go a long way toward reducing System Folder clutter that can easily develop under System 6, where items of these types were left loose in the System Folder. In addition, the System 7 System Folder recognizes the types of files it uses and automatically places those files in the appropriate folders when you drag them onto the System Folder's icon. Chapter 3 goes into greater detail on how to use the files and documents inside these special folders.

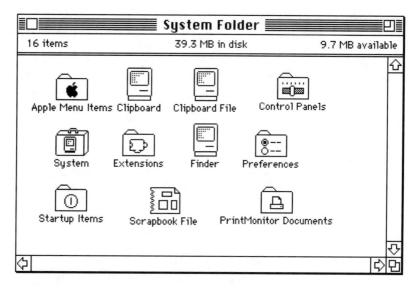

Figure 1-1.   Typical System 7 System Folder

For your Mac to start up properly, at least one disk with a System Folder containing the System and Finder must be available when you turn on the Mac. This is called a startup disk. After you turn on your Mac, the System and Finder are loaded into your Mac's memory.

Because System and Finder are always running, one important thing to remember is that there is a greater chance of their becoming damaged than there is for application software (your programs, such as MacWrite and MacPaint). So in Chapter 6, I'll teach you how to replace your System and Finder at the first sign of trouble. Even when things are running fine, I replace the System and Finder on my hard disk every couple of months, just in case.

For now, just remember that because these files are always in use, they stand a greater chance of becoming damaged than application software, and they should be the first thing you suspect if things start acting funny.

Apple System Software Updates

Apple issues new System software periodically. Apple System software updates are multiple-disk sets that include the latest System, Finder, extensions, control panels, and so on. Table 1-1 lists all the files and programs that come with System 6 and System 7.

Definition

Extensions are a type of file that load into memory when you start up your Mac. Extensions are usually drivers, which allow the Mac to direct the operation of a peripheral device (such as a printer or scanner), or INITs (startup programs), which launch automatically when you start your Mac.

Control panels, also known as *CDEVs* (**C**ontrol panel **DEV**ices), are miniprograms that let you control many Macintosh features, such as sound, mouse movements, the internal clock, memory usage, labels, and so on. Many third-party utilities, such as screen savers and spelling checkers, are control panels. Under System 6, you use the Control Panel desk accessory to access them; under System 7, they're stored in the Control Panels folder.

Each System software update fixes bugs and adds features to the previous releases. To ensure that your Mac always operates at peak performance, always use the latest System software (unless you're a Mac 512 or 512Ke owner, in which case you should be using the latest version for those machines, version 4.1).

To find out what version you're currently using, choose About This Macintosh from the Apple menu (shown in Figure 1-2) in System 7. At this writing, the latest version is System 7.0. In System 6, choose About the Finder from the Apple menu. You can use this same method to determine the current version of an application program you are running. For example, if you are running Word, choose About Microsoft Word from the Apple menu to see the version number.

Table 1–1.   System Software Files

System 6		System 7	
File	**Type**	**File**	**Type**
System	System	System	System
Finder	System	Finder	System
ImageWriter	Driver	Clipboard	System
Clipboard	System	Scrapbook	System
Scrapbook	System	ImageWriter	Extension
LaserWriter	Driver	LaserWriter	Extension
Laser Prep	Driver	AppleTalk ImageWriter	Extension
AppleTalk ImageWriter	Driver	Personal LaserWriter SC	Extension
General	Control Panel	AppleShare	Extension
Key Layout	System	File Sharing	Extension
Keyboard	Control Panel	DAL	Extension
Mouse	Control Panel	Network	Extension
Monitors	Control Panel	Finder Help	Extension
Sound	Control Panel	Apple Menu Items	Folder
Startup Device	Control Panel	Control Panels	Folder
Easy Access	System	Extensions	Folder
Color	Control Panel	Preferences	Folder
DA Handler	Document	Startup Items	Folder
MultiFinder	System	Brightness	Control Panel
Backgrounder	System	Color	Control Panel
PrintMonitor	Application	Easy Access	Control Panel
LQ ImageWriter	Driver	File Sharing Monitor	Control Panel
LQ AppleTalk ImageWriter	Driver	General	Control Panel
LaserWriter IIsc	Driver	Keyboard	Control Panel
		Labels	Control Panel
		Map	Control Panel
		Memory	Control Panel
		Monitors	Control Panel
		Mouse	Control Panel
		Portable	Control Panel
		Sharing Setup	Control Panel
		Sound	Control Panel
		Startup Disk	Control Panel
		Users & Groups	Control Panel
		Views	Control Panel
		LQ AppleTalk ImageWriter	Driver
		LQ ImageWriter	Driver
		TeachText	Application
		PrintMonitor	Extension

Source: Macintosh System Software User's Guide

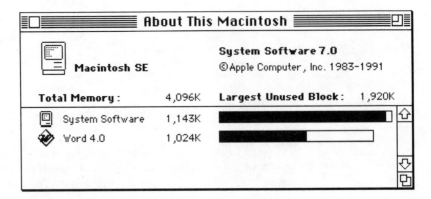

Figure 1-2.   About This Macintosh from System 7.0

You'll notice that, in addition to the System software version, the About box also provides information about memory (RAM) usage. Figure 1-2 shows a Macintosh SE running System 7.0 with 4Mb (4,096K) of RAM. Microsoft Word is using 1Mb (1,024K), and the System software is using 1,143K, which leaves 1,920K available for other applications.

Definition

RAM is an acronym for random-access memory, the temporary memory in which a Mac stores information while it's running. Information in RAM, such as anything you've cut or copied to the Clipboard or documents you haven't saved to disk, disappears when your Mac is shut down or restarted.

Updating Your System Software

You should remember two things when you update your System software:

- Before you update, back up your entire hard disk.
- Always use the Installer.

Definition

> The *Installer* is an Apple-supplied program that installs or updates your System software and lets you add additional resources, such as networking software or printer drivers.

Back Up Your Entire Hard Disk   The safest thing to do is to back up your hard disk to floppy disks before using the Installer to update. (If you don't understand, Chapter 5 contains instructions and strategies for backing up your hard disk.) If you don't want to back up your entire hard disk, at least back up your old System Folder. That way, if something doesn't work properly with the new System software, you can easily change things back to the way they were by deleting the new System Folder and replacing it with the old one from the backup.

Do not, under any circumstances, store backup copies of the System or Finder on your hard disk. You should *never* have more than one System and Finder on a disk. Never. The reason for this is simple: The Mac expects to find only one System Folder, containing exactly one System and Finder, on any disk or volume. When more than one exist, the Mac gets confused and acts unpredictably. Crashes and System errors will occur.

Definition

> A *volume* is the term used to refer to a storage device, such as a hard disk or a file server. Volume can refer to an entire disk or part of a disk. (See *partition* in the Dr. Macintosh Dictionary.)

If you suspect you have inadvertently gotten a second System or Finder on your hard disk, you'll find the procedure for removing them in Chapter 4.

Tip

If an application or desk accessory doesn't work with a new version of System software, the publisher of the program or desk accessory will usually release an update. If you're having problems with any piece of hardware or software after installing new System software, contact its manufacturer to describe the problem, then go back to using the older System software until the hardware or software has been updated by the manufacturer. Or, postpone using that software until you receive the update.

Use the Installer After backing up your old System Folder, use the Installer program to update your system. Doing so ensures that you'll be updating only the things your specific system needs.

The Installer is provided with Apple System software updates. It's an application that automatically copies everything you need from the upgrade floppy disks to whatever disk you choose. You should always use the Installer to update System software. Never just drag the files—doing so does not guarantee that the System software is properly installed. The Installer knows which model of Mac you're using and installs only the items that Mac needs. Just follow the directions in the Read Me file provided with the Installer and you'll be fine.

Tip

If you suspect any corruption or damage to your present System and Finder, start up your Mac with any startup disk and delete the suspect System and Finder before running the Installer. This makes the Installer put a brand new System and Finder on the disk you select instead of updating your old ones and preserving the corruption in them. Before deleting the System file, make sure you have copies of any fonts, desk accessories (DAs), or sounds you have installed in the system. (Refer to Chapter 3 for information on DAs and fonts and Chapter 6 for information about corruption or damage to your System software.)

Obtaining System Software

There are three ways to obtain the latest System software:

- From an Apple dealer
- From a user group
- From an on-line information service (CompuServe, America Online, or GEnie)

Apple dealers usually have the latest version of the System software. The System 7 Personal Upgrade Kit lists for $99. Dealers are not *required* by Apple to make you purchase the complete package of disks and manuals—they are *permitted* to let you copy the software (but not the documentation) to your own disks. Most dealers do not allow you to do this, however; they insist that you purchase the package. If you happen upon a dealer who *does* allow you to make copies of the software, you're very lucky. Don't forget it when you need to buy something later on—a good Apple dealer is hard to find.

If you're a member of a user group, you usually can pick up copies of the latest System software for no more than the cost of the disks. This method gets you only the software, and perhaps some on-disk release notes. If you want complete printed documentation, you must purchase the full update from an authorized Apple dealer.

If you elect to get your System software updates via modem, you only pay the cost of the connection time for the download. Again, you get only the software, and perhaps some release notes.

If you've never upgraded your System software, I suggest you purchase the upgrade and documentation from a dealer and follow the instructions. It's easy.

If you've updated your System software before, you may not need the documentation. You'll save yourself a few bucks if you get the update without printed documentation from a friendly dealer, user group, or on-line service. However, System 7 contains so many new and improved system features that it is well worth it for you to acquire the System 7 documentation. The *Macintosh Reference*, which comes with the System 7 Personal Upgrade Kit, is a particularly handy manual to have around.

General Hints

The following sections provide some general hints to help you get the most out of your Macintosh.

Read the Manual

An old saying goes, "Power users don't read manuals." Don't believe it. Much of the power of today's Macintosh software is concealed. If you don't read the documentation, you will no doubt miss out on powerful features that aren't in the menus.

Read about the Macintosh

You can never stop learning about the Mac. Read everything you have time for. Publications worth investigating include *Macworld*, *MacUser*, and *MacWeek*.

These publications will help you keep up to date on Mac technology. I think *MacUser* is the most useful, but that shouldn't surprise you since I'm a contributing editor. Even so, I think you'll find it packed with useful tips, hints, product reviews, and comparisons.

Improve Your Typing Skills

If you're not typing at least 40 words per minute, you're wasting time. Possibly the easiest way to get more done in less time is to become a better typist. Lots of inexpensive programs can help— Type! or Typing Instructor Encore are a couple of pretty good ones.

When I bought my first Mac, I couldn't type at all. Now I can type about 60 words per minute, with relatively few mistakes. And the mistakes I make are caught by Thunder 7, by far the best Mac spelling checker/thesaurus.

Customize Your Working Environment

Many users forget that many aspects of the Macintosh work environment can be changed with control panels. This is especially true with System 7, which comes with 17 different control panels (see Table 1-1). You can change the desktop pattern, rate of insertion point blinking, menu blinking, sound volume, RAM cache setting, and internal clock settings.

To change any of these settings:

System 7
1. Choose Control Panels from the Apple menu. If you are working in an application, the Mac switches you to the Finder and opens the Control Panels window.
2. In the Control Panels window, double-click the General Controls icon.
3. Make any changes you want to the settings shown.
4. Click the close box to save your changes. In System 7, most control panel changes take effect immediately.

System 6
1. Choose Control Panel from the Apple menu.
2. In the Control Panel box, click the General icon.
3. Make any changes you want to the settings shown.
4. Click the Control Panel's close box to save your changes.
5. You may have to restart your Mac for your changes to take effect.

Figure 1-3 shows the General control panel settings in System 7. The General settings are similar in System 6. Chapter 3 covers using control panels in greater detail, including how to change the sensitivity of your keyboard or mouse, and how to choose a different beep sound. For now, just keep in mind that control panels give you a quick way to customize many facets of your everyday work environment. Play around with the different settings until you find the ones that are best for you.

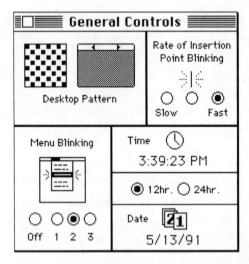

Figure 1–3.   General control panel in System 7

Develop Mouse Independence

Another way to get things done faster is to reduce your dependence on the mouse. Use Command-key equivalents (sometimes called keyboard shortcuts), which are a combination of keypresses involving the Command key and one or more keys that choose commands from menus without using the mouse. For example, when you need to create a new folder in the Finder, get into the habit of using the shortcut Command-N instead of grabbing the mouse, pulling down the File menu, and selecting New Folder.

Almost every Macintosh program has Command-key equivalents for some menu choices. Learn them and use them.

Once you get into the habit of using them, grabbing the mouse to pull down a menu will seem archaic.

You'll learn more about the Command key and Command-key equivalents in Chapter 2.

Unfortunately, many programs don't offer Command-key equivalents for frequently performed actions. To get around this, purchase a keyboard enhancer or macro program such as QuicKeys2 or Tempo II Plus (or even the less powerful Macro-Maker, which is included with System 6).

Definition

> A *macro* is a sequence of keyboard or mouse actions defined by the user to automate repetitive tasks.

With one of these programs you can, with a single keystroke:

- Launch applications or documents
- Open desk accessories
- Create your own Command-key equivalents in any program or in the Finder
- Scroll, close, or resize windows
- Type any text you like (boilerplate text)
- Type the time and/or date
- Restart/Shut Down
- And much more

You'll learn more about macro programs in Chapter 10.

Don't Be Afraid to Use Technical Support

When you buy software, you're usually entitled to some kind of technical support from the publisher. Generally, the publisher provides you with a specific telephone number you can call to talk to a technical representative. Many publishers also provide a fax number, a bulletin board, or an on-line service address where you can post your product questions. Most of the time, these services are free, particularly if you register your software; however, some publishers may charge you for various kinds of extended support.

Nonetheless, if you're having trouble getting something done, or if a feature doesn't seem to work properly, you should call for help. But before making the call, check the manual. There's nothing more embarrassing than calling for help and having the voice on the phone tell you the solution is on page 5 of the manual.

Try to be helpful when you call. Know what version of the program you are using and what System version you're running by checking the About box. If you've installed any INITs (Extensions) or control panels, be sure to mention them when you call.

Try to explain exactly what happened just before the problem occurred, and describe it carefully to the support representative. See if you can duplicate the problem before calling. If it occurs repeatedly, it will be much easier to resolve than if it only happens sporadically.

Being prepared when you call for technical support saves both you and the tech support representative time, and goes a long way toward helping the technician solve your problem.

Join a User Group

One of the best ways to learn about the Mac is to join a user group. User groups are made up of people just like you—people who want to learn how to use their Mac more effectively. They hold regular meetings, demonstrate the latest software, exchange shareware and public-domain software, and publish informative newsletters. There are over 1,000 user groups in the U.S. alone! If you're not involved with a user group, you're really missing out.

Apple provides a toll-free hot line to find out about the user group nearest you. If you want to know how to contact them, call 800–538–9696, extension 500.

Experiment

Don't be afraid to experiment. Try anything and everything. One of my favorites is to hold down the Option key and select items from menus or tools from a palette. Try this in Excel or Adobe Illustrator. You'll be surprised what pops up! All kinds of hidden dialog boxes and controls are available. Of course, if you read the manual, you'd know all about these "secret" features.

Poke around, try everything! It's impossible to hurt your Mac by playing with software. Just remember to back up important files before you begin to play.

Buy What You Need to Be Productive

Even though most products I recommend in this book are inexpensive, the question "When should I spend money on something?" has probably crossed your mind already.

The items I recommend throughout the book range from shareware that requests a donation of only a few dollars to hard disks and accelerator cards that cost several thousand dollars.

When faced with any cash outlay, you have to ask yourself: "How much time will it save me each day?" Divide the cost of the product by whatever you think your time is worth.

It hardly makes sense to perform this calculation for inexpensive software. But let's assume that you want to justify a *major* purchase, such as a tape backup unit for $600.

Right now, backing up to floppy disks is taking 20 minutes a day. You have to sit there and swap disks, so it can't be done unattended. If you buy the tape drive, you will be able to perform an incremental backup in less than 10 minutes, unattended. That means you can do something else—like go to lunch or go home for the evening. When you return, the backup is complete. So let's say it saves you the full 20 minutes a day.

If your time is worth $20 an hour, you're saving $6.66 a day. So, assuming you back up every day (as well you should!), in three months, the tape drive will pay for itself. ($600 divided by $6.66 equals 90 days.)

This approach works beautifully on your boss when you've got your eye on a new piece of hardware or software.

Look at purchases for your Mac as investments in productivity. Evaluate potential purchases based on the amount of time they'll save you. You'll be surprised at how affordable things become when viewed in this light.

The Doctor's
Opinion
☎

If that doesn't work, but you can't live without it, buy it anyway.

Recommendations

Information on obtaining Apple System software and other products I recommend is listed below.

Apple System Software Updates (includes Installer, Teach-Text, System, Finder, and more)

- Shrink-wrapped packages, with disks and printed documentation, are available only from authorized Apple dealers for approximately $99.

System software files without documentation are available from:

- User groups at variable cost. Some groups provide it free if you bring your own disk.
- On-line services such as CompuServe, GEnie, and America Online at the cost of connection time only.
- Some Apple dealers. Apple dealers are not *required* to sell you the $99 package. Many, particularly dealers that value their customers, will let you come in when things

aren't too busy and copy the files. It's considered polite to purchase the blank floppy disks you use from the dealer.

MacUser

Subscription Information
P.O. Box 56986
Boulder, CO 80322
800–627–2247

MacWeek

P.O. Box 1766
Riverton, NJ 08077–9766
609–461–2100

Macworld

Subscriber Services
P.O. Box 54529
Boulder, CO 80322–4529
800–288–6848

QuicKeys 2

CE Software
P.O. Box 65580
West Des Moines, IA 50265
800–523–7638
515–224–1995
Approximately $150

My favorite macro program.

Tempo II Plus
> Affinity Microsystems
> 1050 Walnut Street, Suite 425
> Boulder, CO 80302
> 800–367–6771
> 303–442–4840
> Approximately $170

Another powerful macro program. Chapter 10 has a more detailed report on macros and macro software.

Thunder 7
> Baseline Publishing, Inc.
> 1770 Moriah Woods Boulevard, Suite 14
> Memphis, TN 38117–7118
> 800–926–9677
> 901–682–9676
> Approximately $100

The best spelling checker/thesaurus program around.

Type!
> Brøderbund
> P.O. Box 6125
> Novato, CA 94948–6125
> 800–521–6263
> 415–382–4400
> Approximately $30

A fine program for learning typing or improving your typing speed. Includes a game, Type!-athlon.

Typing Instructor Encore
>   Individual Software
>   5870 Stoneridge Drive, #1
>   Pleasanton, CA 94588
>   800–822–3522
>   415–734–6767
>   Approximately $30

Another good program to help you learn or improve your typing. Includes a game, Lobster Sea Adventure. Also allows you to create your own tests, or order inexpensive optional Type 'N Discover disks, filled with additional tests on subjects such as Business, Entertainment, History, or Sports.

Summary

This chapter introduced you to Macintosh System software, the System, and the Finder. Here are some of the more important things you should remember.

Because they're always running, your System and Finder are the first things you should suspect when your Mac acts up. If replacing them doesn't clear things up, read Chapter 6, even if your disks seem to be all right. Many of the techniques used in recovery can also be used to clear up problems *before* they damage your files or disks.

Use the Installer whenever you upgrade your System software, and always keep a backup of your old System Folder until you're sure the update isn't causing any problems. And don't forget: Never keep more than one System and Finder on any hard disk.

Try to reduce your use of the mouse. Sure, it's easy to grab the mouse, but Command-key shortcuts save time. Get into the habit of using them. And don't forget to brush up on your typing. This might be the easiest thing you can do to accomplish more in less time.

Never stop learning about the Mac. Be hungry for new knowledge. Read magazines, go on-line, or join a user group— do all three if you can. Remember, you can never know too much.

Experiment whenever you can. Try new techniques. Only you know what will save you time. If you have a hunch, check it out. You can't break your Mac. Just remember, if you're trying anything that seems even remotely dangerous, make sure you have backup copies of anything important.

In the next chapter, you will find out everything you always wanted to know about working in the Finder.

2

Getting to Know the Finder

The Finder is the soul of your Macintosh. Knowing all you can about it will make using your Mac a much more satisfying experience.

The Finder, sometimes referred to as the desktop, is the heart and soul of your Macintosh. Much of your time spent using the Mac is actually time spent using the Finder. So in this chapter, you'll learn how it works, and I'll do my best to provide you with a wealth of hints, tips, and shortcuts to help you use it better.

The first section provides a general overview of the Macintosh desktop. This information is useful for the beginning Mac user. If you are already a seasoned Mac user, you can skip the first section.

The second section covers Finder features by detailing the Finder's menus and commands. Described first are menus and commands specific to Finder 6. This information becomes the basis for the second part, which describes Finder 7 menus and commands that are different from or new since Finder 6.

The last section is a treasury of Finder tips, tricks, and shortcuts for all flavors of System software.

If you are new to the Macintosh, you should read all three sections. If you have used System 6 but are new to System 7, you can skip the first section and the first part of the second section, and go right to "Finder 7 Menus and Commands." EVERYONE should read the "General Finder Hints and Tips" section.

The Macintosh Desktop

When you turn on your Mac, you see the Macintosh desktop, shown in Figure 2-1. You see icons and windows and the menu bar.

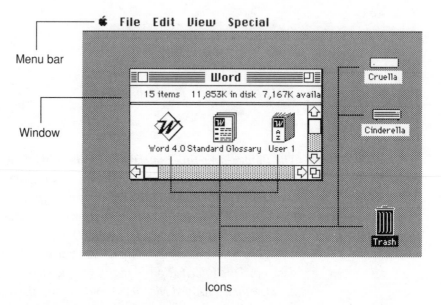

Figure 2-1.   The Macintosh desktop (System 6 shown; System 7 looks slightly different)

Icons

Icons are small pictures that represent documents, file folders, applications, disks, and other tools you work with as you use your Mac. Every icon has a name; application icons have the name of the application, and other icons bear the names you provide when you create folders and documents or initialize disks. You select icons by clicking once on them; you open most icons by double-clicking.

You can rename an icon by clicking once to select it, then typing the new name. Under System 6, you can click anywhere on the icon or its name; under System 7, you must click directly on the name, or click on the icon itself and then press the Return or Enter key.

Document and folder names can be up to 31 characters long; disk names can be 27. You cannot give two icons in the same folder or disk the same name. If you do, you see an alert message. Also, never use colons (:) when naming documents, folders, applications, or disks; the Mac uses colons internally to track path names. The Finder won't let you use a colon in a file name, but a few programs will let you save a file with a colon in its name. Be careful.

Another desktop element appearing as an icon is the Trash. You use the Trash to remove documents, folders, and applications from your disks. To use the Trash:

1. Click once to select the document, folder, or application you want to discard.
2. Drag your selection to the Trash icon, until it is highlighted.
3. Release the mouse button to move your selection into the Trash.

The Trash icon bulges to indicate that it contains something. To permanently remove the items in the Trash, choose Empty Trash from the Special menu. More information about the Trash, and a discussion about its differences in System 6 and System 7, appears later in this chapter.

Windows

When you open a disk or folder, you'll see a window called a *directory* that enables you to view the contents of that disk or folder. The Finder automatically creates a directory every time you create a new folder or initialize a disk. Each time you add a document to a folder, rename an icon, or remove an icon from a folder or disk, the directory gets updated.

You can view the contents of a disk or folder in the window either by icon (large or small) or as a list. List views allow you to arrange window contents chronologically by date, alphabetically by name, and so on. To get a different view of the active window, choose a different command from the View menu (described later in this chapter).

Inherent to the Mac is the Hierarchical File System (HFS), a feature that lets you use folders to organize documents, applications, and other folders on a disk. You can nest a folder in other folders to create as many levels as you need (up to twelve levels). You can create a hierarchy of folders within folders, arranging your work in a way that makes sense to you. Chapter 4 offers numerous suggestions for using folders to organize your hard disk.

The Menu Bar

Across the top of the desktop is the menu bar, showing the titles of Finder menus. You position the pointer on a menu title and hold down the mouse button to pull down a menu. A menu contains a list of actions (called *commands*) from which you choose. The commands listed in each Finder menu operate on icons (files, folders, and/or disks) in Finder windows and on the desktop.

To choose a menu command, pull down the menu and, without releasing the mouse, drag the pointer to the command you want. When it is highlighted, release the mouse button.

Many Finder commands have shortcuts called Command-key equivalents, which give you the option of choosing a menu command from the keyboard, rather than using the mouse to pull down the menu and choose a command. To use a Command-key equivalent, hold down the Command key and press the appropriate key at the same time. For example, if you want to use the Finder's Open command, hold down the Command key and type the letter *O*.

Definition

> The *Command* key is the one with the little pretzel on it, usually located next to the spacebar; on some keyboards it also has a little apple on it.

Sometimes commands appear dimmed in a menu, which means the command is not available to you. For example, if a hard disk is your startup disk and you have no floppy disk in the internal drive, the Eject Disk command in the Special menu is dimmed (under System 6, it's the Eject command in the File menu). It's dimmed because you cannot eject your hard disk.

Some menu commands are followed by an ellipsis (...). The ellipsis indicates that selecting this command opens a dialog box, allowing you to give more specific instructions about the particular action(s) you want the Finder to take.

Dialog boxes have radio buttons, check boxes, and text-entry areas (collectively called *controls*) that you use to specify the options you want. In addition, dialog boxes always provide a highlighted button (usually the OK button) indicating the preset action to take.

For example, in the Page Setup dialog box (see Figure 2-2), you can set a variety of options by clicking radio buttons (US Letter, A4 Letter, and so on), choosing check boxes (Font Substitution, Text Smoothing, and so on), or typing in text-entry areas (Reduce or Enlarge).

Definition

A *dialog box* is a box that appears on the screen and contains a message, often requesting more information from you or allowing you to select more options.

A *radio button* is a type of button, usually found in dialog boxes, that you click to select one of several options. Radio-button options are mutually exclusive.

A *check box* is a small box associated with an option in a dialog box or window that you click to select one or more options. An option is turned on when you see an X in the check box.

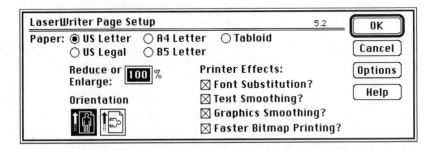

Figure 2-2. The Page Setup dialog box shows typical dialog box controls

In any dialog box, the Cancel button always gives you an opportunity to change your mind—it closes the dialog box and restores all controls to the state they were in before the dialog box opened.

Many dialog boxes offer keyboard shortcuts, although they are not usually shown on the screen. The two most important are as follows:

- Enter or Return: Shortcut for clicking the highlighted button
- Command-. (period): Shortcut for clicking the Cancel button

Finder 6 Menus and Commands

Finder 6 menus are Apple, File, Edit, View, and Special (see Figure 2-3). If you have a color monitor, you will also see the Color menu.

 File   Edit   View   Special

Figure 2-3.   Finder 6 menu bar

The Apple Menu

The Apple menu (shown in Figure 2-4) is where you'll find the desk accessories (DAs) installed in your System. Chapter 3 gives detailed info on desk accessories and how to install and use them. If you're running MultiFinder (discussed in Chapter 7), the bottom of the Apple menu lists all the applications that are currently open.

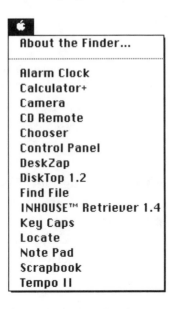

Figure 2-4.   The Apple menu

At the top of the Apple menu is the About command, discussed in Chapter 1. When you choose About, you get information about the System you are currently running and about memory usage.

You launch desk accessories by choosing them from the Apple menu. You can launch desk accessories at any time, either in the Finder or while another application is running.

The File Menu

You use commands in the File menu (shown in Figure 2-5) to work with icons.

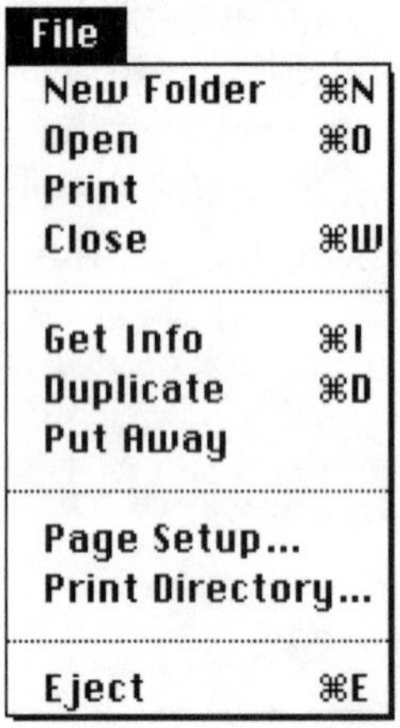

```
┌─────────────────────────┐
│ File                    │
├─────────────────────────┤
│ New Folder        ⌘N    │
│ Open              ⌘O    │
│ Print                   │
│ Close             ⌘W    │
│.........................│
│ Get Info          ⌘I    │
│ Duplicate         ⌘D    │
│ Put Away                │
│.........................│
│ Page Setup...           │
│ Print Directory...      │
│.........................│
│ Eject             ⌘E    │
└─────────────────────────┘
```

Figure 2-5.   The File menu

Creating a New Folder Choosing New Folder creates a new, empty folder in the folder or disk that is currently active. The new folder icon appears highlighted with the preset name Empty Folder. Begin typing immediately to rename the folder; press Return, or click anywhere else, to have the name take effect.

Opening an Icon You use the Open command to open a folder, disk, or volume, to launch an application, or to open a document. Select the icon or the name of the folder, disk, file, or application you want to open, and choose Open. Using the Open command on a selected icon is the same as double-clicking it.

Printing Documents at the Finder The Print command lets you print documents from the Finder. You can print one or more documents, but they must all have been created by the same application. Before you use the Print command, make sure the proper printer has been selected in the Chooser by following these steps:

1. Choose Chooser from the Apple menu.
2. In the Chooser window (see Figure 2-6), click the type of device you want from the choices on the left, such as LaserWriter.

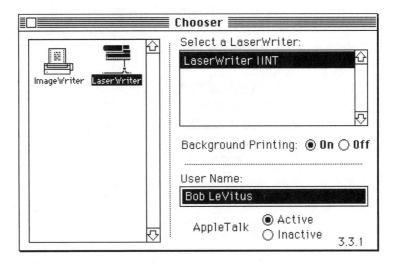

Figure 2-6.   The Chooser window

3. If you are connected to more than one printer of the selected type, click the printer you want to use from the list that appears on the right. You may need to scroll through the list to find the one you want.
4. Click the Chooser's close box.

If you want to set paper size, reduction or enlargement percentages, or other printing options for Finder windows you plan to print, choose Page Setup from the File menu and make your selections in the dialog box. Now you are ready to print documents from the Finder:

1. Select the document(s) you want to print by dragging the selection rectangle around the icons. If you want them to print in a specific order, click on the icon of the first file you want to print, then hold down the Shift key and click the rest of them in the order you want them to print.
2. Choose Print from the File menu.
3. In the Print dialog box, select the printing options you want, and click Print.

Closing Windows   Choosing Close Window from the File menu (Command-W) closes the active folder or disk window. You can also close a window by clicking its close box (see Figure 2–7).

Figure 2-7.   Clicking the close box

You have several ways to close *all* Finder windows:

- Click the close box of any window while holding down the Option key.

- Choose Close from the File menu while holding down the Option key.
- Press Command-Option-W.
- Hold down the Option key when you quit any application. This returns you to the Finder with all windows closed. (This technique does not work under MultiFinder or System 7.)

Getting Info Choosing the Get Info command opens a window showing information about the selected icon or name. You can get info on files, folders, applications, disks, volumes, and the Trash. To open the Get Info window and view information about any icon on the desktop:

1. Click an icon once to select it.
2. Choose Get Info from the File menu.

The Get Info window opens and displays the following information (see Figure 2-8):

- File name
- Icon
- Type of file (document, folder, or application); if it's a document, includes what type of application was used to create it
- Size in kilobytes (K) on disk, and the number of bytes used
- Disk the file resides on
- Date and time it was originally created
- Date and time it was last modified
- Version number (for applications)
- Comments area where you can type notes about the document
- Lock status, when checked, indicates the document cannot be modified or deleted

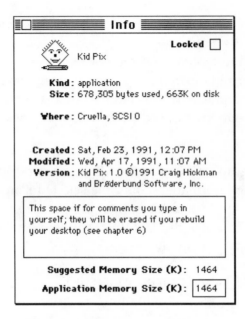

Figure 2-8.   An application's Get Info box

The Get Info window also tells you whether the selected item is locked. When a document or application is locked, no one can rename, modify, or remove it without unlocking it first. Locked items have a small padlock icon next to their names in list views.

Another thing you can do in the Get Info window is to change the amount of memory allocated to an application (under MultiFinder only). This is useful when the application won't let you open large documents such as a large spreadsheet, 24-bit color picture, or large TIFF file. If you try opening a document and see a message telling you there is not enough memory, try setting the application memory size a bit higher:

1. Quit the application and return to the Finder.
2. Select the application's icon.
3. Choose Get Info from the File menu.
4. In the Application Memory Size box, type a number to change the size. Try increasing it about 10 percent. If

that's not enough, and you're still getting "not enough memory" messages, increase it 10 percent more. Keep doing this until you can successfully open the document in question. To revert to the preset (suggested) memory size, leave the Application Memory Size box blank.

5. Click the Get Info window's close box.

IMPORTANT: Make sure your system has enough RAM to handle an increase in application memory size. If you have only 1 or 2Mb of RAM, you probably shouldn't fiddle with this. Another thing: It's usually not a good idea to set the application memory below the suggested memory size. If you do, the application may behave unpredictably, if it works at all.

Duplicating Icons Choosing the Duplicate command from the File menu creates an exact copy of the document, folder, or application you select in the Finder. Once the selected icon is duplicated, it has the name Copy of ____ .

Putting Away Desktop Items Many times, it's convenient to drag a file or application icon out of a folder and place it on the gray desktop for easy access. When you want to put the file or application back into its original folder or disk, choose Put Away from the File menu.

Page Setup After you choose a printer or other output device from the Chooser and before you print a document or window, you can set various printing options by choosing Page Setup from the File menu. The Page Setup dialog box appears, listing printing options that are specific to the type of printer or output device you are using. Figure 2-2 shows the Page Setup dialog box for a LaserWriter II NTX.

Printing a Window You can print the directory of a window on the desktop by choosing Print Directory from the File menu. When you do so, the Print dialog box appears (see Figure 2-9), offering you various printing options. The resulting printout shows the entire contents of the active window, exactly as it appears on the screen. Read more about printing in Chapter 8.

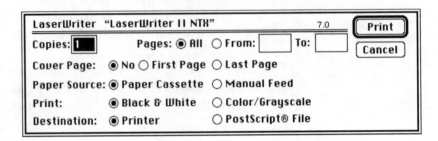

LaserWriter "LaserWriter II NTX" 7.0				

Figure 2-9.   The Print dialog box

Ejecting Disks To eject a floppy disk from a disk drive, select the disk's icon and choose Eject from the File menu, or press Command-E. When a disk is ejected this way, the disk's icon remains dimmed on the desktop. Although the disk has been ejected, we say that it is still *mounted*. If the disk window is open when you choose the Eject command, the window's contents remain on the screen and are also dimmed. Even though the disk is not in your drive, you can still double-click the dimmed disk icon, or any of the dimmed icons in its windows. If you do, your Mac will ask you to reinsert the disk.

Another way to eject disks is to use the Mac's built-in Eject keyboard shortcuts, Command-Shift-1 (internal drive) and/or Command-Shift-2 (external drive, or second internal drive if you have two internal floppy drives).

Tip

Many applications give you the option of ejecting a disk, via an Eject button, when you use the Open, Save, or Save As dialog box.

Most of the time you *don't* want the dimmed icon to remain on the desktop. In these cases, you must eject and *dismount* the disk. Dismounting a disk means ejecting it and removing its dimmed-out icon from the desktop. You have three ways to do this:

1. Drag the disk's icon to the Trash. (Click the disk icon once to select it, then drag the disk icon to the Trash, until the Trash icon is highlighted.) The disk is ejected from the drive and its image disappears from the desktop.
2. Hold down the Option key, then choose Eject from the File menu.
3. Use the keyboard shortcut Command-Option-E.

The Edit Menu

The commands in the Edit menu (see Figure 2-10) let you edit text in the Finder, such as names of icons or comments in the Get Info window.

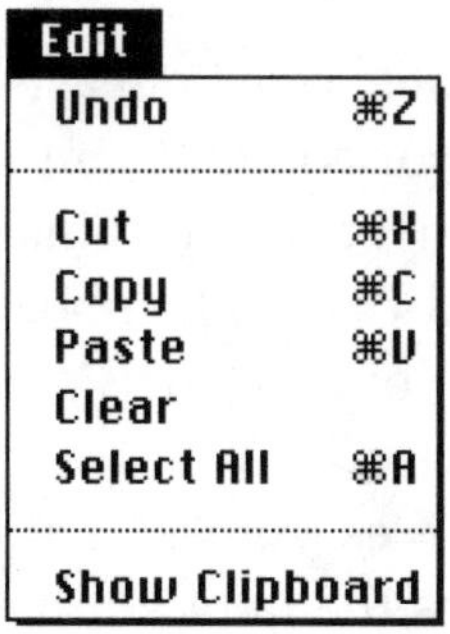

```
┌──────────────────────┐
│ Edit                 │
├──────────────────────┤
│  Undo          ⌘Z    │
│ .................... │
│  Cut           ⌘H    │
│  Copy          ⌘C    │
│  Paste         ⌘U    │
│  Clear               │
│  Select All    ⌘A    │
│ .................... │
│  Show Clipboard      │
└──────────────────────┘
```

Figure 2-10.   The Edit menu

The Undo, Cut, Copy, Paste, and Clear commands are standard to all Macintosh applications. You use Undo to reverse the most recent action you took, whether it was deleting text, moving an icon, or whatever. (Unfortunately, the Undo command is not always available, and it seems that the times it's not are the times you need it most. For example, if you copy a file from one disk to another, you can't undo it. So don't become too reliant on Undo.)

You use the Cut, Copy, and Paste commands to interact with the Clipboard. When you cut or copy something to the Clipboard, it is available in memory for pasting anywhere you like. You can cut, copy, and paste text or graphics. To view the contents of the Clipboard, choose Show Clipboard from the Edit menu.

Definition

The *Clipboard* is a special area in your Mac's memory that temporarily holds the last item you copied or cut. The contents of the Clipboard are replaced with the new item each time you copy or cut text or graphics. Due to the Clipboard's temporary nature, its contents disappear completely when you restart or shut down your Mac.

The Clipboard holds only one item at a time—the last piece of text or graphics you cut or copied (item A). When you cut or copy something new (item B), the original item (item A) disappears, and it is replaced on the Clipboard by the new item (item B). At this point, if you use the Paste command, item B appears.

Unlike Cut, which places your selection in the Clipboard, Clear permanently removes the item you have selected without placing it in the Clipboard.

The Select All command selects (highlights) everything in the active window or document.

Tip

Be careful when you clear something—you cannot undo a Clear.

The View Menu

The Finder's View menu (shown in Figure 2-11) is where you find a variety of ways to view the contents of windows, folders, and disks. When you initially create a new folder, its contents are preset to be viewed by icon.

Figure 2-11.   The View menu

List views—the By Name, By Size, By Kind, and By Date choices—show a window's contents in a text list, in order by the appropriate choice. For example, if you choose By Date, the contents of the active window appear in a chronological list, from the most recently modified document, folder, and so on, to the earliest modified item, as shown in Figure 2-12.

Name	Size	Kind	Last Modified	
Home	24K	HyperCard document	Tue, Feb 19, 1991	5:04 PM
Version 1.2 Release Notes	83K	HyperCard document	Thu, Jan 26, 1989	3:42 PM
HyperCard	392K	application	Tue, Nov 8, 1988	9:28 AM
Phone	18K	HyperCard document	Mon, Oct 3, 1988	10:49 PM
Clip Art	29K	HyperCard document	Mon, Apr 25, 1988	2:29 PM
Area Codes	37K	HyperCard document	Mon, Apr 25, 1988	2:22 PM
Documents	13K	HyperCard document	Mon, Apr 25, 1988	12:49 PM
Slide Show	63K	HyperCard document	Mon, Apr 25, 1988	12:49 PM
Address	13K	HyperCard document	Mon, Apr 25, 1988	12:49 PM

Hyper

Figure 2-12.   A System 6 window in list view

A small icon appears next to each item in the list to indicate whether it is a document, folder, or application. To view the contents of a listed folder, double-click the folder icon. Another window opens showing that folder's contents. To select two or more items in a list view, hold down the Shift key and click them one at a time. (In icon views, you can drag the selection rectangle around icons to select them.)

If you are using a color system, you can choose to view window contents by color. This is practical only if you have previously assigned different colors to items in the window using the Color menu. When you choose By Color, the window contents appear as a list in the same order as colors appear in the Color menu (from orange to black), and the small icons next to the icon names retain the colors you previously assigned. If you choose By Color and you have not assigned colors to the icons, the list appears in alphabetical order (same as the By Name option).

If you're not familiar with the Macintosh's views, take a few minutes to experiment with them.

The Doctor's
Opinion

If you're like me, you'll probably find the list views more useful than the icon views. Icon views are prettier, but list views show more information in less space.

The Special Menu

The Special menu is where you find special system maintenance commands (see Figure 2-13).

Cleaning Up Clean Up is available only when you are viewing windows by icon or by small icon (View menu).

When you are viewing a window by icons, the command is called Clean Up Window, and it arranges the icons in neat rows and columns along an invisible grid.

Figure 2-13.   The Special menu

If you select one or more icons by Shift-clicking or drag-selecting, the command becomes Clean Up Selection. Choosing it arranges the selected icons in the nearest available cells on the invisible grid.

If you don't have any windows open and active on the desktop, and you haven't selected any objects on the screen, the command is Clean Up Desktop. Choosing it arranges the desktop icons in a neat, orderly grid.

Holding down the Option key when you pull down the Special menu causes this command to change to just plain Clean Up (instead of Clean Up Window, Clean Up Selection, or Clean Up Desktop). This method cleans up everything in a window regardless of whether an icon is selected, and it works much faster than any of the other Clean Up commands.

Tip

If you hold down the Command key when you drag any icon, it snaps to the nearest invisible grid point.

If you're not familiar the Clean Up commands, open a window, and choose By Icon or By Small Icon from the View menu. Now spend a few minutes playing with its various flavors. Also try dragging icons while holding down the Command key.

Emptying Trash You use the Empty Trash command to permanently remove the contents of your Trash. For example, to
remove a file from your hard disk, select the file's icon and drag
it to the Trash until the Trash icon highlights (see Figure 2-14).
To permanently delete the contents of a folder:

1. Shift-click or drag-select to select the folder's contents.
2. Drag the selected icons to the Trash. You can also drag
   the folder's icon to the Trash.
3. Choose Empty Trash from the Special menu.

If there is nothing in the Trash, the Empty Trash command
is dimmed.

Under System 6, the Trash is automatically emptied when
you launch an application, restart, or shut down.

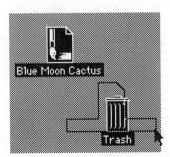

Figure 2-14.   Document being dragged to the Trash

Erasing a Disk To erase a disk, choose the Erase Disk command
from the Special menu. Erase Disk not only erases but also
initializes the selected disk. When you choose Erase Disk, a
dialog box appears with the message shown in Figure 2-15.

You have the choice of canceling the erase operation, or
initializing the selected disk as either one- or two-sided. (By the
way, if you insert an uninitialized disk or a non-Macintosh disk
in a floppy drive, the same dialog box appears, allowing you to
immediately format that disk.)

Figure 2-15.   The Erase Disk dialog box

If you have a Mac with a 1.4Mb floppy drive and you want to erase a 1.4Mb floppy disk, you'll see a slightly different dialog box; the Mac automatically formats 1.4Mb disks properly.

If there is no other disk besides your startup disk, the Erase Disk command is dimmed because your Mac won't let you erase the startup disk.

Setting the Startup Disk   The Set Startup command opens a dialog box (see Figure 2-16) that lets you switch between Finder and MultiFinder and set applications, desk accessories, folders, or documents to open automatically when you boot from that startup disk.

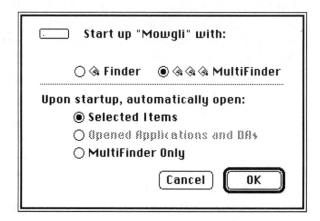

Figure 2-16.   The Set Startup dialog box

Recall that the startup disk is the disk that contains the System and Finder. If you have more than one disk containing the System and Finder, you can set a different startup disk by following these steps:

1. Choose Control Panel from the Apple menu.
2. In the Control Panel window, click the Startup Device icon. If this icon is not visible, scroll the list of icons on the left until it is.
3. In the right side of the window, click once on the icon of the disk you want to make the startup disk.
4. Click the Control Panel's close box.

The next time you start your Mac, the new disk will be the startup disk.

Now you can use Set Startup to set different applications to launch when you start up the given disk. When you choose Set Startup, the name of your designated startup disk appears at the top. For example, in Figure 2-16, my startup disk is Mowgli.

You can set your disk to start up running the Finder or running MultiFinder. When MultiFinder is selected, you have the option of selecting one or more applications, documents, or folders to open automatically at startup. This is great if you use the same applications and folders every day. You can do this in two ways. First, you can select multiple icons in a window at the desktop. All the selected icons must be in the same window for this method to work. For example, to automatically launch Word and open the document called To Do List (both of which are in the Word folder):

1. Shift-click or drag to select the Word application icon and the To Do List document icon.
2. Choose Set Startup from the Special menu.
3. Click MultiFinder, if not already selected.
4. Click the Selected Items option, and click OK.

If you just want to launch Word, or another application, simply select its icon in step 1 above. The selected application's name appears instead of Selected Items in the dialog box.

The second method involves opening all the applications and desk accessories you want automatically opened at startup before choosing Set Startup.

1. Open the application(s) and desk accessories you want to launch at startup.
2. Go to the Finder, and choose Set Startup from the Special menu.
3. In the dialog box, make sure MultiFinder is selected, and click the Opened Applications and DAs option (see Figure 2-17).
4. Click OK.

The changes you set remain in effect until you change them again.

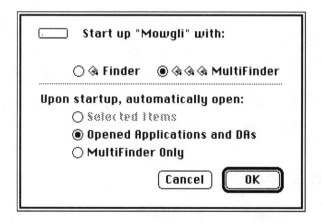

Figure 2-17.   Setting the startup disk to automatically open the selected applications and desk accessories

Restarting and Shutting Down The Restart and Shut Down commands in the Special menu are self-explanatory. You choose Restart to turn off your Mac and immediately turn it back on again. Restart ejects any floppy disks, quits any open applications, gives you the option of saving any open files, and restarts your Mac. Restart also empties the Trash without asking you if it's OK to do so.

You have to restart your Mac when you change most control panel options, add fonts or desk accessories to your System, or make similar modifications.

Choosing Shut Down is the same as choosing Restart, except your Mac doesn't start up again. On Mac II machines, choosing Shut Down automatically turns off the computer. On other Mac models, you see a message that tells you it is safe to turn off your computer.

The Color Menu

The Color menu is a pull-down palette of colors. The kind and number of colors shown in the palette depends on the number of colors supported by your system.

You use the Color menu to assign colors to selected icons, giving you another way to arrange and identify items on the desktop.

The Color menu is available only if you're using a Mac that supports color monitors.

Finder 7 Menus and Commands

In general, Finder 7 menus and commands build on those from Finder 6, offering new commands as well as enhancements to old ones. As a result, this section describes those menus and commands of Finder 7 that are new since or different from Finder 6.

In addition to the Apple, File, Edit, View, and Special menus found in Finder 6, Finder 7 adds the Label menu. The Label menu replaces the old Color menu, and it appears on both color and black-and-white Macs.

Also new are the Help and Application menus, each represented by an identifying icon at the right of the menu bar. Figure 2-18 shows the Finder 7 menu bar.

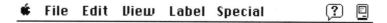

Figure 2-18.   Finder 7 menu bar

Balloon Help

It's important to talk about System 7's new Balloon Help before discussing other features of Finder 7, because you can use it to get more information about the Finder. This is particularly useful for new Mac users.

To turn on Balloon Help, choose Show Balloons from the Help menu, as shown in Figure 2-19. With Balloon Help turned on, information pops up in a balloon (like a voice balloon in a comic strip) when you point to any object on the screen. You can get help on menus, commands in menus, dialog boxes, dialog box options, folders, disks, and so on. To turn Balloon Help off, choose Hide Balloons from the Help menu.

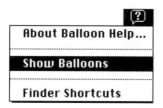

Figure 2-19.   Turning on Balloon Help

System 7 has over 1300 Balloon Help items built right into it, and almost every software publisher plans to incorporate Balloon Help in future releases of their software. It's particularly useful in programs you don't use every day; you can turn the balloons on, and quickly find out what every menu selection, dialog box, and tool does.

Finder Shortcuts, which appears in the Finder 7 Help menu, gives a host of useful keyboard shortcuts and other tips for navigating around the Finder. See "Finder 7 Keyboard Shortcuts" later in this chapter for more information.

Tip

Study the Finder Shortcuts screens carefully, and use the shortcuts often. One of System 7's best features is the degree of keyboard control it offers in the Finder.

The Application Menu

Under System 6, you can optionally turn on and use MultiFinder to run multiple applications simultaneously. System 7 has this capability built into it; multitasking is always up and running. The new Application menu (shown in Figure 2-20), at the far right of your menu bar in System 7, lets you switch between the applications you have running at one time.

Figure 2-20.   The Application menu

I always hated the fact that you can't "hide" an active application's windows under System 6. If you typically used MultiFinder under System 6 to run several applications at once, you remember that your screen would quickly become cluttered with windows that weren't being used. System 7's flexible Hide/Show feature fixes that nicely. You can hide or show any combination of windows using the commands at the top of the Application menu. There are also several less obvious ways to use the Hide/Show feature, revealed in the "Miscellaneous Secrets" section later in this chapter.

Hiding an application and its windows does not close the application; it just temporarily removes them from your screen so you can focus on other application windows.

The Apple Menu

The Apple menu in Finder 7 is where you'll find items contained in your Apple Menu Items folder. It also includes control panels.

Figure 2-21.   The Apple menu in Finder 7

Apple Menu Items Folder The Apple Menu Items folder, which resides in the System Folder, contains the Chooser, an alias for the Control Panels folder, and any desk accessories you designate. You can launch any program or open any folder or file that's listed in your Apple menu either by choosing it from the Apple menu, or by double-clicking it in the Apple Menu Items folder. (By contrast, under System 6, the Apple menu could contain only desk accessories—you weren't able to include folders, applications, or documents in the Apple menu.)

You can put anything in the Apple Menu Items folder, including applications you use frequently, folders, and aliases. If you place a folder (or an alias of a folder) in the Apple Menu Items folder and then choose the folder from the Apple menu, that folder pops open. This is particularly useful if that folder is nested several folders deep. Placing an application's alias in the Apple Menu Items folder is a convenient way to launch the application; you simply choose the alias from the Apple menu, rather than searching through nested folders to find the application.

Definition

An *alias* is a tiny file that opens a document, folder, program, or disk. When you double-click one, or choose it from the Apple menu, it automatically opens the file or folder it's associated with. Aliases occupy only 1 or 2K of disk space. You'll find out more about aliases in a few pages.

To add a file, folder, application, disk, or alias to the Apple menu:

1. Double-click the System Folder icon to open it. (You can keep an alias of the Apple Menu Items folder on the desktop if you like, and save this step.)
2. Drag the icon of the item (or an alias of it) into the Apple Menu Items folder, which is inside the System Folder.

Tip

In most cases, you are better off placing an alias of an item in the Apple Menu Items folder than the item itself. The logic for this is simple. Let's say you want your word processor, MacWrite, to appear in the Apple menu. And let's say you store MacWrite, its dictionaries, and all your MacWrite templates in a folder called MacWrite folder, which is inside a folder called Applications. If you make an alias of the MacWrite application icon, then place the alias in the Apple Menu Items folder, you don't have to move the actual MacWrite application from its rightful place, inside the MacWrite folder, which is inside the Applications folder.

You don't need to restart your Mac to use the new item from the Apple menu. If you want to remove the item from the Apple menu, simply reverse the previous steps to drag the item out of the Apple Menu Items folder.

Items in the Apple menu appear in alphabetical order. You can change the order by preceding an item's name with as many special characters as you like, including asterisks, plus and minus signs, or even spaces. Because the menu list is sorted alphabetically, spaces and special characters come before *a* (see Figure 2-22). To do this:

1. Double-click the Apple Menu Items folder to open it.
2. Click the name of the desired item to select it.
3. Type the special characters you want, or type spaces, in front of the item's name.

Tip

You can use this technique with items in any folder, not just the Apple Menu Items folder. It is also useful for placing those items you use most at the top of the list in a standard directory dialog box.

Definition

The *standard directory dialog box* is the dialog box you use to locate files and change disks from within an application. A directory dialog box appears whenever you choose the Open or Save As command from within an application. Sometimes referred to as the GetFile or PutFile dialog box.

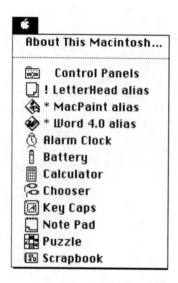

Figure 2-22.   Customize the order in which items appear in the Apple menu

Control Panels The Control Panels item in the Apple menu is actually an alias for the Control Panels folder, which is inside the System Folder. The Control Panels folder contains separate documents, called control panels, that you use to customize certain aspects of your Mac environment. Control panels are covered in more detail in Chapter 3.

The File Menu

The File menu in Finder 7 (see Figure 2-23) is where you'll find some of the most significant improvements in System 7, including file sharing, the ability to make aliases, and a Finder that actually finds. Enhancements to the Finder 7 File menu from that of Finder 6 include a Get Info window with more muscle, and the addition of more Command-key equivalents. Other subtle differences exist as well.

```
┌─────────────────────────┐
│ ▐ File ▌                 │
├─────────────────────────┤
│  New Folder      ⌘N      │
│  Open            ⌘O      │
│  Print           ⌘P      │
│  Close Window    ⌘W      │
│ ·····················    │
│  Get Info        ⌘I      │
│  Sharing...              │
│  Duplicate       ⌘D      │
│  Make Alias              │
│  Put Away        ⌘Y      │
│ ·····················    │
│  Find...         ⌘F      │
│  Find Again      ⌘G      │
│ ·····················    │
│  Page Setup...           │
│  Print Desktop...        │
└─────────────────────────┘
```

Figure 2-23.   The File menu in Finder 7

New Folder The New Folder command in Finder 7 works the same as that of Finder 6, except the preset name is Untitled Folder instead of Empty Folder, and when you create a new folder, an outline indicates the name is selected so you can immediately change it.

Getting Info Finder 7 gives the Get Info command a lot more muscle than it had before.

One of the greatest things about the new Get Info windows (see Figure 2-24) is the Stationery Pad option. Stationery pads, new in System 7, are templates, or documents with common elements. Typical stationery pads might be your company letterhead, a memo template, an invoice template, and so on. By clicking the Stationery Pad box in a document's Get Info window, you designate that the document is a stationery pad. You can also save a document as a stationery pad, if the application you are using supports this option in the Save As dialog box. When you open a stationery pad, a duplicate of it opens as an untitled document.

Tip

If you use a particular kind of stationery frequently, you may find it convenient to put an alias of it in the Apple Menu Items folder (so it will appear in the Apple menu) or on the gray desktop. Putting an alias in either place makes it easier to launch a fresh piece of stationery than if the stationery's icon only exists in a folder somewhere on your hard disk.

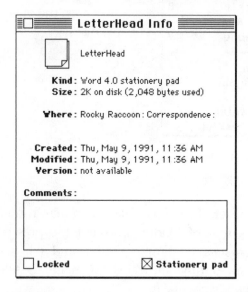

Figure 2-24.   The Get Info window in Finder 7 offers the Stationery Pad option

Another useful feature of the Get Info window is the ability to customize your icons. Finder 7 lets you edit or colorize your icons with nothing more complicated than a paint program. Here's how to do it:

1. In the Finder, select an icon by clicking once.
2. Choose Get Info from the File menu, or press Command-I.
3. In the Get Info window, click the icon once to select it.
4. Choose Copy from the Edit menu, or press Command-C, to copy the icon to the Clipboard.

5. Launch any paint program, and choose New to create a new, blank document.
6. Choose Paste from the Edit menu, or press Command-V, to paste the icon from the Clipboard into the new document.
7. Make any modifications you want to the icon.
8. Select the icon, and choose Copy.
9. In the Get Info window, click the old icon once to select it, and paste the new icon.
10. Close the Get Info window. Your changes take effect immediately.

File Sharing The file sharing feature, which is built into System 7, allows you and other users on an AppleTalk network to share up to ten folders and/or disks without the need for a file server. You can access a folder on someone else's Mac, and vice versa. The sharing feature enables you to set various levels of access others can have to a particular folder or disk. You can decide who can have access and whether they can make modifications to your files. System 7 makes file sharing convenient and affordable for every Mac user, and it's easy to use. All you need is System 7 and an active AppleTalk network.

To make a folder or disk available for other users to share, you first have to turn on the file sharing capability so the network can recognize your Mac. To do this:

1. Choose Control Panels from the Apple menu to open the Control Panels folder.
2. Double-click on the Sharing Setup control panel to open it.
3. In the Sharing Setup dialog box (see Figure 2-25), make up a password and Macintosh name; type these and your name in the appropriate Network Identity boxes.
4. Click Start in the File Sharing area of the dialog box to turn on file sharing. The Start button changes to Cancel, and the adjacent status box informs you that file sharing

is being turned on. To interrupt this process, click
Cancel.

5. When the File Sharing status box indicates that file
   sharing is turned on (as in Figure 2-25), you can then
   select folders and disks to share with other users. Click
   the Sharing Setup window's close box to return to the
   Finder, or click Stop to turn file sharing back off again.

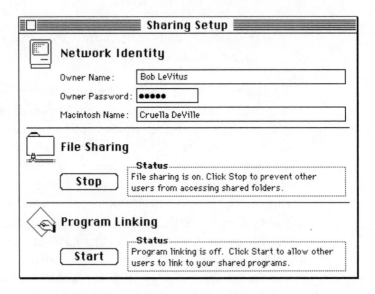

Figure 2-25.   The Sharing Setup dialog box

Once you have turned on file sharing, follow these steps to
make a folder available for other users to access:

1. Click once to select the folder you want others to access.
2. Choose Sharing from the File menu.
3. In the File Sharing dialog box (see Figure 2-26), click the
   box labeled Share This Item and Its Contents.

4. In the access privileges area of the dialog box, specify which users can look at the contents of the folder and the files within it, and which ones can make changes to the folder, by clicking the appropriate options.

5. When you are done, click the window's close box. If you want to save your changes, click Save in response to the message *Save changes to access privileges?*

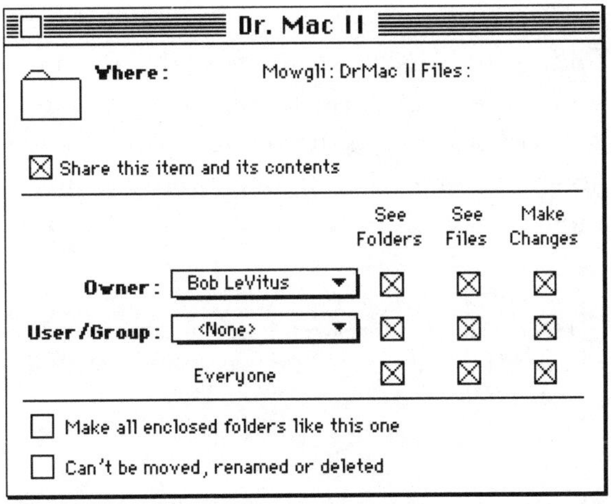

| ≡▢≡≡≡≡≡≡≡ **Dr. Mac II** ≡≡≡≡≡≡≡≡≡ |

Where: Mowgli : DrMac II Files :

☒ Share this item and its contents

		See Folders	See Files	Make Changes
Owner:	Bob LeVitus ▼	☒	☒	☒
User/Group:	<None> ▼	☒	☒	☒
	Everyone	☒	☒	☒

☐ Make all enclosed folders like this one
☐ Can't be moved, renamed or deleted

Figure 2-26.   File Sharing dialog box

After you have set up a folder for sharing, its icon changes to indicate it is available for other users, as shown in Figure 2-27.

Dr. Mac II

Figure 2-27.   Icon of a shared folder

Besides the Sharing Setup control panel, System 7 provides two other control panels that monitor and change various sharing options. The File Sharing Monitor control panel lets you see which folders and disks are set up for sharing and what the current level of access activity is. The Users & Groups control panel lets you change access privileges for individual users and groups of users on the network.

If you want to access a shared folder on another user's Mac, you simply use the Chooser to connect to it, and its icon appears on your desktop.

System 7's file sharing capability does have its drawbacks, however. You can't designate a file by itself as shared (only folders and disks). Also, as with most network configurations, you can expect performance degradation as more users on the network access the shared data. And, there is a limit of ten users accessing one Mac at one time. Finally, file sharing requires more than 200K of RAM; turn it off if you don't need it.

Tip

If you have file sharing turned on, you cannot rename your hard disk or the folders that are set up for sharing. To do so, you must first turn file sharing off.

Duplicating Icons Choosing the Duplicate command from the File menu creates an exact copy of the document, folder, or application you select in the Finder. Once the selected icon is duplicated, it has the name _____ copy. Under System 6, the copy was called Copy of _____. Other than that, the Duplicate command works the same in both versions of System software.

Making Aliases One of the greatest features of Finder 7 is the ability to make aliases of anything—files, folders, or applications, or even remote disks or folders. An alias is a small (usually 2 or 3K) file whose icon acts as a "pointer" to a file, folder, or application. The original can even be a file residing on a different machine on a network.

When you make an alias, you can put it wherever you want; this way, the file, folder, or application—whatever you made an alias of—acts as if it is in two or more places at once.

Opening an alias, by double-clicking it in the Finder or choosing it in an Open dialog box, opens the original file.

To make an alias:

1. Click once on the icon of the item for which you want to make an alias.
2. Choose Make Alias from the File menu. The name of the alias appears in italics, and it is selected so you can rename it if you want (see Figure 2-28).

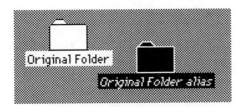

Figure 2-28.   An original folder and its alias

You can use aliases in lots of ways. For example, let's say you create a memo to the marketing department about Joe Client. Do you store it in the Memo folder, the Marketing folder, or the Joe Client folder? That's no longer an issue—just store it wherever you like, and put an alias in the other two folders. Then, you'll be able to find and open it no matter which of the three folders you look in.

Here's another cool way to use aliases: If you're on a network, mount a remote folder or disk on your desktop using the Chooser. Then, create an alias for its icon. From then on, double-clicking the alias mounts that disk or folder automatically, without a trip to the Chooser, and without remembering which machine or zone that file or folder is stored on.

Definition

A *zone* is a small subnetwork within a larger network. Many large networks are divided into zones to enhance their performance.

Finally, you can use aliases to add anything you like—files, folders, documents, disks, applications, folders or volumes on a network, control panels, and so on—to your Apple Menu Items folder. Just make an alias of the item you want to appear in the Apple menu, then put the alias in the Apple Menu Items folder.

Putting Away Desktop Items The Put Away command works the same in Finder 7 as it does in Finder 6—it puts any icon you've moved to the desktop back in the folder you moved it from.

In Finder 7, Put Away has two additional attributes:

- A Command-key shortcut, Command-Y
- The Put Away command now ejects and dismounts a disk

Finding in the Finder The Find and Find Again commands in the File menu let you not only find files, folders, disks, or applications, but these commands also take you to them on the desktop. (Finally, a Finder that finds!) And you can search for files using a wide variety of criteria: by name, size, kind, label, creation or modification date, version number, comments, and lock status. You can narrow down the search even further by specifying that the name, for example, contains, starts with, ends with, is, is not, or doesn't contain the text you are searching for.

To do a simple search, such as searching for a file called Monthly Expense Report:

1. Choose Find from the File menu, or press Command-F.
2. In the Find dialog box (shown in Figure 2-29), type the name of the file you want to find.
3. Click Find to locate the file and go to the folder or disk in which it resides.

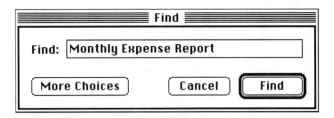

Figure 2-29.   Searching for a file by name

To perform a more complex search, such as searching for a file whose name you have forgotten but you know it starts with *Ad* and it's on the Marketing volume on the network:

1. Choose Find from the File menu.
2. Click More Choices to open the expanded Find dialog box.
3. Leave the Name pop-up menu choice as is. If you wanted to search by label, kind, or other criteria, you would set that here.
4. Click the Contains pop-up menu, and choose Starts With. The choices in this pop-up change according to the selection you make in the Name pop-up.
5. In the entry box, type **Ad**.
6. Choose Marketing (or any other search location) from the Search pop-up menu. (Figure 2-30 shows a sample expanded Find dialog box.)
7. Click Find.

If you want to display your search results all at once, instead of one at a time, click the All at Once box in the Find dialog box. Warning: All at Once may display very slowly if you have a large hard disk.

You can search for the same criteria again by choosing the Find Again command (Command-G) from the File menu.

```
┌─────────────────────────────────────────────────────────┐
│═══════════════════════════ Find ═══════════════════════════│
│  Find and select items whose                               │
│   ┌──────────────┬───┐ ┌──────────────┬───┐ ┌───────────┐ │
│   │   name       │ ▼ │ │ starts with  │ ▼ │ │ Ad        │ │
│   └──────────────┴───┘ └──────────────┴───┘ └───────────┘ │
│  ······································································ │
│      ┌────────────────────────┐                          │
│  Search │ on "Marketing"   ▼ │      ☐ all at once        │
│      └────────────────────────┘                          │
│  ······································································ │
│   ┌──────────────┐              ┌──────────┐ ┌─────────┐ │
│   │ Fewer Choices│              │  Cancel  │ │  Find   │ │
│   └──────────────┘              └──────────┘ └─────────┘ │
└─────────────────────────────────────────────────────────┘
```

Figure 2-30.   Using the expanded Find dialog box with complex search
criteria

The Find feature in Finder 7 replaces the Find File desk accessory that comes with System 6. It really is a great improvement and a timesaver when you can't remember where you put a file.

Page Setup The Page Setup dialog box in Finder 7 is identical to that of Finder 6, with one exception: A pop-up menu now offers a set of choices for special paper sizes (see Figure 2-31).

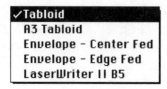

Figure 2-31.   New paper size options in the Page Setup dialog box

Printing a Window In Finder 7, you print a window from the desktop by choosing Print Window. (In Finder 6, the command is Print Directory.) When you do so, the Print Window dialog box appears (see Figure 2-32), so you can set various printing options. A new option in System 7 is the ability to print to a Post-Script file, which is handy for saving files to print to a Laser-Writer or other PostScript device later.

Definition

> *PostScript* is a device-independent page description language created by Adobe Systems, and used by the LaserWriter, Linotronic and other printing and imagesetting devices.

```
┌─────────────────────────────────────────────────────────────┐
│ LaserWriter  "LaserWriter II NTX"              7.0   ┌─Print──┐│
│ Copies:[1▮]        Pages: ◉ All ○ From:[   ] To:[  ] │        ││
│                                                      ┌─Cancel─┐│
│ Cover Page:    ◉ No ○ First Page ○ Last Page                  │
│ Paper Source:◉ Paper Cassette  ○ Manual Feed                  │
│ Print:         ◉ Black & White   ○ Color/Grayscale            │
│ Destination:   ◉ Printer         ○ PostScript® File           │
└───────────────────────────────────────────────────────────────┘
```

Figure 2-32.   The Print Window dialog box

The Edit Menu

The Edit menu in Finder 7 has the same commands as the Edit menu in Finder 6. In addition to using Cut, Copy, and Paste to move items in and out of the Clipboard, System 7 introduces another copy-and-paste feature that is accessible through the Edit menu in System 7-friendly applications. This feature is called publish and subscribe.

Definition

> *System 7-friendly applications* are programs that take advantage of System 7 features and changes to the System software.

Publish and Subscribe You won't see Publish or Subscribe in the Finder's Edit menu; these options appear only in the Edit menus of applications that are System 7-friendly. Although the publish and subscribe feature is not Finder-specific, it is worth mentioning at this point because you use it by choosing the Publish and Subscribe commands from the Edit menu of System 7-friendly programs.

Sometimes called "live" or "smart" copy-and-paste, publish and subscribe lets you *publish* text or graphics, or even an entire document, then *subscribe* to it from another document while maintaining a dynamic link to the original (published) file. If you change a word (or picture) in the original file, it automatically updates it in any document that is a subscriber.

Here's how it works: First you determine what material you want to be automatically updated by creating a publisher. The designated material is then saved to a separate file, called an *edition*. Second, you open another document and indicate where you want the edition material to be inserted and updated by subscribing to the edition. You can have as many subscribers to an edition as you need, and the subscribers can be anywhere on the same disk, on another disk, on another Macintosh, or on a file server.

To create a publisher:

1. Within an application that supports publish and subscribe, select the text or graphics you want published.
2. Choose Create Publisher from the application's Edit menu. A dialog box, similar to the Save As dialog box, opens.
3. Type a name for the edition file, and navigate to the folder or disk where you want it saved.
4. Click Publish. The published material gets saved as an edition file.

To create a subscriber to the published material:

1. In the same or a different application, open the document in which you want to insert the edition.
2. Position the insertion point in the document, and choose Subscribe To from the Edit menu. A dialog box, similar to the Open dialog box, opens.
3. In the dialog box, select the edition to which you want to subscribe, and click Subscribe. The edition is positioned at the insertion point in the document.

The dynamic link between documents remains in effect until you cancel it.

Publish and subscribe is available only in applications that are System 7-friendly. Applications that existed before System 7 was released may be upgraded by software publishers to take advantage of the publish and subscribe feature. If you're curious, check with the publishers of your favorite applications to see if they will be supporting publish and subscribe (if they don't already).

Perhaps the most exciting part of publish and subscribe is that it works over a network. So, for example, the Sales department can publish sales projections for the Marketing department to use in documents they create. If Sales later revises those projections, any Marketing document that subscribed to them will be automatically updated to reflect the latest numbers. And you won't need to buy any additional networking software to use it because System 7 includes built-in file sharing (see "File Sharing" earlier in this chapter).

No doubt about it, publish and subscribe is another thing you're going to love about System 7. For more information about publish and subscribe, and their options, read the *Macintosh Reference* manual that comes with System 7.

The View Menu

The Finder 7 View menu offers a new View By Label option. When you give your documents or folders a label using the Label menu commands (described in the next section), you have the choice of viewing the contents of Finder windows by your labels.

Although the ways in which you can view Finder windows are the same in both Systems, the list views are vastly superior in Finder 7. In Finder 7, the list views are hierarchical outlines (see Figure 2-33). There are little triangles to the left of each folder, and if you click one of them, you'll see the items that folder contains in outline form, without opening a new window.

This may not sound like such a big deal, but it presents several timesaving advantages. You can now select items from several different folders at the same time. You can even drag-select items in the list views.

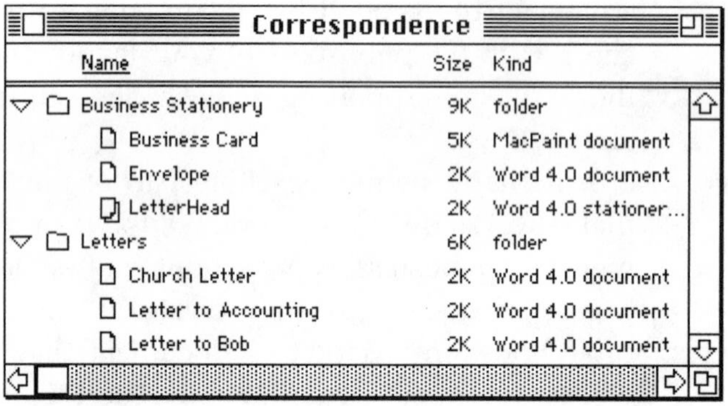

Figure 2-33.   A System 7 window in list view

Tip

To change to a different list view, click one of the column headers, such as Name, Label, Size, and so on. For example, if your current view is By Name, click the Size column header (see Figure 2-34). The view changes to list the window contents by size (from largest to smallest). This feature is so obvious, you wonder why it hasn't been in System software for years. (By the way, third-party utilities, such as DiskTop and DiskTools, have always had it.)

Figure 2-34.   Switching views by clicking a column header

The Label Menu

Finder 7's new Label menu (shown in Figure 2-35) lists text and color labels that you add to the menu using the Labels control panel. You can assign your own labels to each icon on the desktop, which is useful for grouping files together. Then, you can list the files by label in the window by choosing the By Label command from the View menu. If your Mac has color, you can change the color label of icons as well.

Figure 2-35.   The Label menu

Here's how it works. First, create your labels:

1. Choose Control Panels from the Apple menu.
2. In the Control Panels window, double-click Labels to open the Labels control panel (see Figure 2-36).
3. Type the text for each label you want to use. For example, if you want to create a label called Archive for your nonactive files, type **Archive** in one of the label boxes.
4. If you have color, double-click the color labels to change any colors you like.
5. Click the Labels control panel close box to save your changes. Your new labels show up immediately in the Labels menu.

Figure 2-36.   Labels control panel

Now, to add one of your labels to an icon:

1. Click the icon once to select it.
2. Choose the appropriate label from the Labels menu.

Be sure to set the window view to one of the list views (View menu) to see the labels.

The Special Menu

The Special menu in Finder 7 (see Figure 2-37) is virtually the same as under System 6, with subtle differences.

Figure 2-37.   The Special menu

Cleaning Up   The Clean Up command in Finder 7 is pretty much the same as it was under System 6. The Views control panel, discussed in Chapter 3, offers additional control over the invisible grid that aligns icons.

Emptying Trash   Choosing Empty Trash from the Special menu in Finder 7 opens a dialog box with the message shown in Figure 2-38.

Figure 2-38.   The Empty Trash warning message

If you want to empty the Trash in Finder 7, click OK in response to the message. The contents of your Trash are permanently removed, freeing up the disk space that it occupied. Unlike System 6, the Finder never empties the trash without your express permission; the trash is emptied without warning when you launch an application, eject a floppy disk, shut down, or restart using System 6.

You can use the Get Info window of the Trash to turn off the *Warn before emptying* message that appears when you choose Empty Trash from the Special menu. To do this:

1. Click the Trash icon once to select it.
2. Choose Get Info from the File menu (Command-I).
3. In the Get Info window (see Figure 2-39), click the Warn before Emptying check box to deselect the option.
4. Close the Trash Info window.

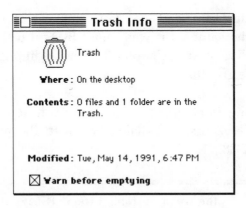

Figure 2-39.   The Trash Info window

After you turn this option off, choosing Empty Trash removes the contents of the Trash without displaying the warning message.

Here are some of the differences between Trash in Finder 6 and Finder 7. When you choose Empty Trash in Finder 6, you don't get any warning; the System just goes ahead and discards whatever files or folders are in the Trash. Finder 7 gives you the chance to change your mind about discarding your files.

Best of all, as I mentioned before, Finder 7 never empties the trash behind your back. In previous System software versions, launching a program, shutting down, restarting your Mac, or ejecting a floppy disk would automatically empty your Trash without any warning. In Finder 7, the Trash works as you'd expect it to: When you throw something in the Trash, it stays there until you choose the Empty Trash command, even if you launch a program, shut down, or restart.

Finally, in Finder 7, the Trash icon stays wherever you put it, even after you restart or shut down. (In Finder 6, the Trash returns to its preset position in the lower right-hand corner of the desktop.)

Tip

You can make an alias of the trash and put it anywhere—even in a folder.

Ejecting Disks To eject a floppy disk, select the disk's icon and choose Eject Disk from the Special menu, or press Command-E.

To eject and dismount a floppy disk, drag its icon to the Trash, or use the Put Away command in the File menu (Command-Y).

Restarting and Shutting Down In Finder 7, the Restart and Shut Down commands in the Special menu work the same as those in Finder 6. However, in Finder 7, Restart does not automatically empty the Trash. After you've restarted the Mac, the contents of the Trash remain the same as before you restarted.

The Startup Items Folder

If you have a sharp eye, you may have noticed that there is no Set Startup command in Finder 7's Special menu. Instead, there's a special folder inside your System Folder, called the Startup Items folder. Any icons in this folder—documents, applications, folders, or aliases of documents, applications, or folders—are automatically opened when you turn on your Mac.

If you make an alias of a folder and put it in the Startup Items folder, when you start your Mac that folder opens automatically; if you put in an individual document or application (or an alias of a document or application), that document or application launches on startup.

Tip

If there's a folder you use every day, especially if it's buried several folders deep and is inconvenient to open the usual way, put an alias of it into the Startup Items folder. Then that folder will be open on the desktop each time you start up your Mac!

I keep aliases of my to-do list and my frequently dialed phone numbers list, as well as an alias of my Apple Menu Items folder (more about that in a few pages) in the Startup Items folder, so they're automatically launched every time I turn on my Mac.

Finder 7 Keyboard Shortcuts

Finder 7 offers significantly more keyboard control than earlier System software. You can see a list of many keyboard shortcuts by choosing Finder Shortcuts from the Help menu. The listed shortcuts fall into these categories:

- Working with icons
- Selecting icons
- Working with windows
- Working with outline views
- Miscellaneous options

Figure 2-40 shows the miscellaneous Finder shortcuts, which is the last of five windows listing shortcuts. Be sure to peruse the other four Finder shortcut windows as well.

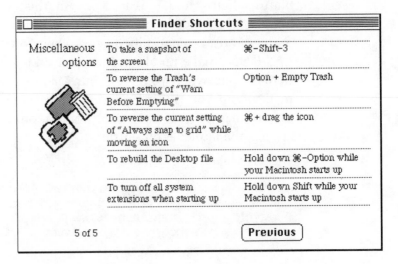

Figure 2-40.   Miscellaneous Finder shortcuts

More Keyboard Shortcuts   You can eject and/or unmount a disk or volume by selecting its icon and typing Command-Y. (Yes, you can also choose Put Away from the File menu, but this is the keyboard shortcut section.)

Holding down the Command-Option-P and -R keys at startup zaps your parameter RAM (PRAM).

Definition

> *Parameter RAM (PRAM)* is the small amount of internal RAM, maintained by battery, that keeps your Mac's clock running and stores things such as serial (modem and printer) port configurations. (Zapping PRAM is discussed in greater detail in Chapter 6.)

Command-Option-Escape forces the active program (or the Finder) to quit. It doesn't allow you to save anything in the program that was active when you froze, and it doesn't always work; but when it does work, it allows you to gracefully exit from the application that froze and to save any documents you have open in other applications. (NOTE: When you use this trick, be sure to restart your Mac as soon as you've saved your work in all other open applications. The freeze indicates that something serious is wrong. If you continue to work without restarting, chances are it will get worse and eventually cause another freeze or crash.)

Finder 7 has drastically improved upon how you can use the keyboard to select and open files and folders. This is GREAT! With Finder 6, you couldn't select or open a file without reaching for the mouse (see "Develop Mouse Independence" in Chapter 1). Finder 7 gives you the option of using either the mouse or keyboard for almost every task. The Finder Shortcuts in the Help menu gives you a complete list of all keyboard shortcuts for working with icons and windows.

Tip

In any window, if you type the first few letters of a file's name, that file is selected. The Tab key selects the next icon and Shift-Tab selects the previous icon alphabetically. The arrow keys can also be used to move from icon to icon.

    If you're used to System 6, which didn't allow you to use the keyboard in the Finder at all, make yourself familiar with these keyboard shortcuts—they're sure to save you time and effort.

General Finder Hints and Tips

Because you'll spend a good part of each Macintosh session in the Finder, you'll want to learn how to do things as quickly as possible. Here are a few of my favorite tips. These apply to both Finder 6 and Finder 7.

Canceling a Double-Click

If you accidentally double-click a document or application that you didn't mean to launch, you can often abort the launch by holding down the Command key and typing a period (.). You have to be quick about it, though. If you wait too long after the double-click, it won't work.

    Many applications also support this method (often called *Command-period*) for aborting an action. Command-period, for example, cancels printing in most applications. Command-period also activates the Cancel button in most dialog boxes.

Temporarily Opening Windows

If you hold down the Option key when you open a folder, that folder will open and the folder that contained it will close automatically. This is convenient when you're looking for something in a folder buried several folders deep. It helps you keep your desktop neat and tidy. Try it, you'll like it!

Fast-Erase for Floppies

If you want to erase a floppy disk quickly, hold down the Option, Command, and Tab keys when you insert it. A dialog box will appear, warning you that you are about to destroy all the information on the disk. This method is faster than inserting a disk, waiting for it to come up, then choosing Erase Disk from the Special menu in the Finder.

Viewing Disk Space in a Window

This tip is useful if you prefer to view windows in one of the list views. When you view window contents by icon or by small icon, information along the top of the windows shows you how much space your disk is occupying and how much disk space is available. You don't see this information if you are viewing windows by name, kind, size, and so on. To determine how much disk space is used and how much is available:

1. Choose New Folder from the File menu to create an empty folder, and rename it as DiskSpace.
2. Choose By Icon or By Small Icon from the View menu.
3. Drag the DiskSpace folder onto the desktop into a position where it will always be visible (such as next to the Trash).
4. Double-click the folder icon to open it, and size the window so just the disk space information at the top of it is visible.
5. Click the close box to close the window.

Now, any time you want to know how much disk space is available on your disk, double-click your DiskSpace icon. Or, you can just leave it open in a suitable location, as shown in Figure 2-41.

Figure 2-41.   DiskSpace window

System 7 provides another way to view disk space in list views. Try this:

1. Choose Control Panels from the Apple menu.
2. In the Control Panels window, double-click the Views control panel to open it.
3. Click the Show Disk Info in Header option in the List Views area of the control panel. (Clicking calculate folder sizes will slow the Finder down—don't turn it on if you can help it.)
4. Click the close box, and your windows in list view will now show disk space information in the window's header (see Figure 2-42).

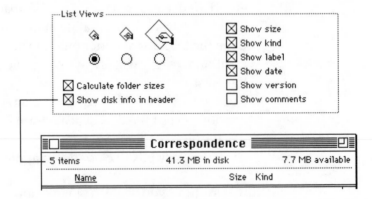

Figure 2-42.   Viewing disk space info in a window header in list view

You'll find a more detailed discussion of the Views control panel in Chapter 3.

Moving a Window without Making It Active

If you simply want to move a window on the desktop without making it active, press and hold down the Command key as you click on its title bar and drag it.

Tip

Finder 7 doesn't activate a window until you release the mouse button, whereas Finder 6 activates windows as soon as you click on any icon in them. So Finder 7 makes it much easier to drag an icon into a partially obscured window. Just remember not to release the mouse too soon.

Moving Quickly up the Hierarchy in Directory Dialog Boxes

If you want to move up through folders, simply click on the volume name (in most cases, the name of your hard disk) in any directory dialog box. (Directory dialog boxes are what you see when you choose Open or Save or Save As.) This moves you up one level of folders. This is a fast way to navigate upward through nested folders. Command–Up Arrow does the same thing.

System 7 changed some of the navigational features of directory dialog boxes over System 6. First, Open and Save dialog boxes include a Desktop button as well as the Desktop level of the hierarchical file system in the pop-up menu above the file list. Just click Desktop, press Command-D, or choose Desktop from the pop-up menu to save a file onto another disk. (Under System 6, you click the Drive button or press the Tab key to switch to another disk drive and to show its contents in the file list. Under System 7, Command–Left Arrow or Command–Right Arrow switches from one disk drive to the next, showing its contents in the file list.)

Second, some directory dialog boxes in System 7–savvy applications have a New Folder button in directory dialog boxes, which means you can create a new folder and save your file in the new folder, all within the dialog box. This really helps to save time and promotes better file organization.

Finder 7 Hints and Tips

Background Copying

Finder 7 lets you copy files in the background. This tip is in the manual, but you may not pick up on it right away. Unlike Finder 6, Finder 7 allows you to continue working while a copy takes place in the background. Just make sure you launch the application you want to work in *before* you begin copying the files. You can't use the Finder (which means you can't launch programs) while you're copying, but you can use any application that is already open. You may notice a slight degradation of performance—a twitchiness similar to background printing—but it's a small price to pay when you've got work to do.

Tip

Technical editor Raines Cohen points out that as a result of this new background copying capability, Finder 7 copies files more slowly than Finder 6. If you do a lot of file copying, consider a utility like DiskTop (see Chapter 10), which copies files much faster than the Finder.

Moving Quickly up the Hierarchy in the Finder

If you're at the Finder and you want to move up through folders, Command-click and hold down on the title of the active window, and you'll see a pop-up menu just like the one you see in directory dialog boxes (as shown in Figure 2-43).

Drag down to highlight the folder or disk you want to open, and the Finder makes that folder or disk active and brings it to the front.

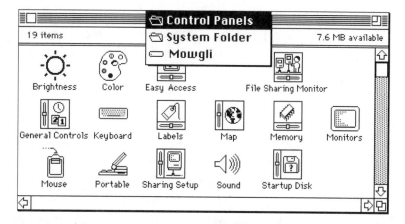

Figure 2-43.   Command-clicking a Finder window's title bar to see a pop-up menu of the enclosing folders and disk

Pasting a List View Outline into a Document

You can paste the outline you see in a Finder window in list view by following these steps:

1. In the Finder, open a window.
2. Choose a list view (By Name, By Date, By Label, By Size, or By Kind) from the View menu.
3. Choose Select All from the Edit menu, or press Command-A, to select the contents of the window.
4. Choose Copy from the Edit menu (Command-C) to copy the selection to the Clipboard.
5. Open a text document in a word processing application.
6. Choose Paste from the Edit menu (Command-V). The outline appears in your document at the current insertion point.

For some reason, Finder 7 limits the number of files or folders you can copy at one time. The exact number depends on the number of characters in the file names, but it's usually between ten and twenty. If you don't get all of the files you copied when you paste, go back to the Finder window and select the files that were omitted, then copy and paste again. Repeat as necessary until all the files in the window have been copied.

Alias Secrets

System 7's new aliases are great, but some of the ways you can use them might not be obvious. Here are some of my favorites.

If you make an alias of a folder—any folder—and put it in the Startup Items folder (in the System Folder), then when you start your Mac, that folder will open automatically. I keep an alias of my Apple Menu Items folder in the Startup Items folder, so the Apple Menu Items folder is always open on my desktop when I turn on my Mac. That gives me two ways to access items in my Apple menu—from the Apple menu itself, or from the Apple Menu Items folder. Although this may sound redundant, in practice it's wonderful because of Finder 7's keyboard short-cuts, which let you select and open folders and files without using the mouse.

Aliases are also great if you're on a network. I love the office-on-a-floppy-disk trick, which lets you access your Mac from any other Mac on the network. Just create an alias for your hard disk, then copy the alias to a floppy disk and shove the floppy in your pocket. As long as File Sharing is turned on, and you have given yourself the proper privileges, you'll be able to mount your hard disk from any Mac on the network by merely inserting the floppy and double-clicking your hard disk's alias.

In a similar vein, if you mount the same remote disk fre-quently, make an alias of its icon. After that, you won't need to use the Chooser to mount it; just double-click the alias. Or, drop the alias in your Apple Menu Items folder and mount the volume by choosing it from the Apple menu. You can even drop the alias in your Startup Items folder, and the volume will be mounted automatically each time you start up your Mac.

Miscellaneous Secrets

You can see exactly how much memory the System software, or any application, is actually using by turning on Balloon Help and pointing to the System Software bar in the About This Macintosh box (see Figure 2-44). Try this:

1. Choose Show Balloons from the Help menu to turn on Balloon Help.
2. Choose About This Macintosh from the Apple menu. Examine the bar graph and determine how much memory is *reserved* for your System software.
3. To see how much memory it is actually *using*, point to the System Software bar.

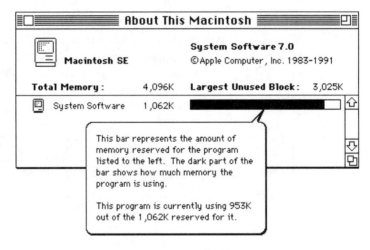

Figure 2-44. Show Balloons to see exactly how much memory the System software is using

Here's another Finder 7 secret worth knowing: You can now drag a document icon onto an application icon, and if the document can be launched by that application, it will be. The way it works is pretty cool—if a document can't be launched by a program, nothing happens when you drag its icon onto the application's icon; if the document can be launched, the application icon inverts when you drag the document over it, and the application launches when you release the mouse button, opening the document.

In a related vein: If you double-click a text or PICT file (PICT is the file format for object-oriented graphics documents created by programs like MacDraw), and you don't have the application that created that file, you no longer get the dreaded *An application can't be found* message you see under System 6. Instead, System 7 asks if you'd like to open the document using TeachText (see Figure 2-45).

Definition

> *TeachText* is a limited word-processing program supplied by Apple with System software.

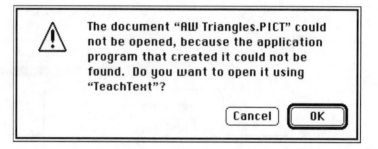

Figure 2-45.   System 7 gives you the option of opening an unknown PICT or text document in TeachText

Under System 6, you can get a screen dump in MacPaint format by pressing Command-Shift-3. (This doesn't work on Mac II machines.) Under System 7, using any Mac, you can create a screen dump by pressing the same key combination, but the file is a PICT-format file (color PICT on machines so equipped). The file is automatically named Picture 1, Picture 2, and so on. If you double-click one of these files, it launches TeachText. You can even use TeachText's selection rectangle to copy part of the picture and paste it somewhere else. And, because you can drag document icons to program icons, you can drag these Picture icons onto the icons of Canvas, PixelPaint, or MacDraw II, if you'd rather edit your screen dumps in one of these applications.

Finder 7's Hide and Show feature, found in the Application menu, is great for keeping the screen uncluttered, particularly if you have several applications open. Here's another way to use it: If you hold down the Option key as you make a choice from the Application menu, the application you're in will be hidden when the application you've chosen becomes active. If you Option-click the desktop area of the Finder, the application you're in will be hidden and the Finder will become active. Finally, if you Option-click any window, the application you're in will be hidden and the window you Option-clicked will become active.

Summary

In this chapter, you learned about the basics of the Macintosh desktop and about working in the Finder, the special "application" that comes with System software. This chapter provided detailed information on Finder 6 and Finder 7 menus and commands.

The Finder is what makes the Macintosh a Macintosh. It has always been intuitive and easy to use. Now, with all of the enhancements that System 7 brings to the Finder, you will fall in love with your Mac all over again.

Get to know your Finder. You spend much of your time using it; mastering it will only make you more efficient.

In the next chapter, you'll examine ways you can customize the Finder, and your Mac in general.

3

Customizing Your Mac

Using desk accessories, control panel devices,
startup documents, FKEYs, fonts, and sounds to
personalize your working environment.

*Once you have worked with your Mac for a while, you will no doubt
want to customize its environment to suit your needs. The Mac's
System software is rich with options for customization, offering you a
great deal of flexibility. The types of tools available for customizing
your Mac include desk accessories (DAs), control panel devices
(CDEVs), startup documents (INITs), fonts, sounds, and function keys
(FKEYs). These tools are often collectively referred to as utilities. Some
tools come with Apple System software, such as the Alarm Clock and
Scrapbook desk accessories, control panel devices such as the Mouse*

and Keyboard, and the System fonts and sounds. Many more are avail-
able from third-party software vendors. (Chapter 10 covers in great
detail the best commercial utilities available and how to use them.)

One of the nicest things about Macintosh computers is that they
are easily customized to suit your wants and needs. The first section
gives you a general overview of the various tools you use to personalize
your Mac. The second section provides information on customizing a
Mac under System 6, and the last section discusses customizing under
System 7.

Desk Accessories

One of the easiest ways to coax more performance out of your
Mac is to enhance your System software by adding productivity
tools called *desk accessories.*

Desk accessories (DAs) are programs that are available no
matter what application is currently running. DAs are available
for every occasion: databases, outline processors, text editors,
graphics editors, spelling checkers, drawing tools, and more are
available in DA form.

Under System 7, there is little difference between desk
accessories and applications. Under System 6, though, DAs
deliver a big advantage—you can access them at any time, even
when you're using an application, with or without MultiFinder.
This enables you to type in your word processor and use a database DA to look up addresses at the same time, even on a
machine with only 1Mb of RAM.

Installing and launching desk accessories differs between
System 6 and System 7. These differences are discussed in detail
later in this chapter. But for now, you should note these main
differences:

System 6:

- You use an Apple-supplied utility called the Font/DA Mover to install and remove DAs from your system.
- You launch DAs by choosing them from the Apple menu.

System 7:

- You make DAs appear in the Apple menu by dragging them to the System Folder (they're automatically placed into the Apple Menu Items folder).

Tip

The System 7 System Folder automatically places some types of files into their proper subfolder—Apple Menu Items, Control Panels, Extensions, and so on—when you drag their icons to the System Folder. In order for this to work, you must drag their icon to the System Folder's icon, not into the open System Folder window.

- You can launch DAs by choosing them from the Apple menu, or by double-clicking their icon as you would any other application.

DAs Included with Both System 6 and 7

Apple provides several desk accessories with the System software. Desk accessories common to both System 6 and System 7 are as follows:

- Alarm Clock
- Calculator
- Key Caps
- Scrapbook
- Notepad
- Puzzle

System 6 also includes the Find File desk accessory, which you use to locate files on disks. This function is integrated into the Finder under System 7.

Alarm Clock   You use the Alarm Clock DA that comes with your System software to sound an alert at a designated time. To set the alarm:

1. Launch the Alarm Clock DA. The alarm clock appears (see Figure 3-1).
2. Click the switch to the right of the current time to expand the Alarm Clock. The highlighted area indicates the item displayed in the middle row of the Alarm Clock—current time, current date, or alarm setting.
3. Click the alarm clock icon (far right at the bottom of the box). The middle row now shows the current alarm setting (12:00 AM in Figure 3-1).
4. To change the alarm time, click the area of the time you want to change, and click the up or down arrows to the right of the alarm time to advance or reverse the alarm time, respectively.
5. When the alarm is set to the time you want it to go off, click the button to the left of the alarm time to turn the alarm on.
6. Click the close box to return to the desktop.

At the designated time, the Alarm Clock will play the System sound you have set.

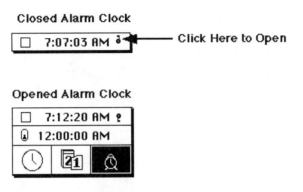

Figure 3-1.   The Alarm Clock DA

Calculator You use the Calculator DA (see Figure 3-2) as you would use a pocket calculator. Click the buttons on the calculator using the mouse, or use the keyboard to type in entries. The Calculator DA is a handy way to perform simple number-crunching operations. If you want, you can copy and paste the calculator's result into other documents or desk accessories.

Figure 3-2.   The Calculator DA

Key Caps The Key Caps DA is used to examine what the set of characters looks like in a font set. It is most useful for determining the keystrokes needed to generate special characters, such as an accented letter (é), a currency symbol (£), a copyright or trademark symbol (© or ™), or a small Apple logo (   ). To use Key Caps:

1. Launch the Key Caps DA. The Key Caps window displays a keyboard template of the preset System font (Chicago).
2. To see a different font, choose the font you want from the Key Caps menu (see Figure 3-3). The Key Caps menu lists all of the fonts currently installed on your system.
3. To see special characters, press the Option, Control, Shift, or Caps Lock key. For example, in most fonts, when you press the Option and 2 keys simultaneously, you'll type a ™ character as shown in Figure 3-3. Characters you type appear in the large box at the top of the Key Caps window; you can copy and paste these characters into any document.
4. Click the close box when you are done.

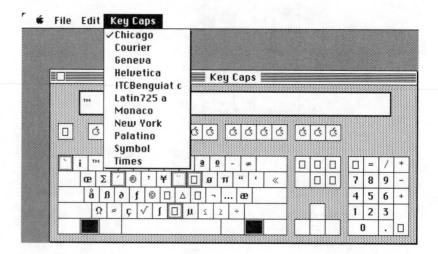

Figure 3-3.   The Key Caps DA and menu

Scrapbook The Scrapbook DA lets you access the Scrapbook file, which resides in your System Folder. The Scrapbook is a handy place for you to store frequently used graphics and text. By pasting a graphic in the Scrapbook, you can copy it into a document whenever you want and as many times as you want. Unlike the Clipboard, which holds only one item—the last graphic or text you cut or copied—the Scrapbook can hold as many images as you want (up to available memory and disk space). For example, your Scrapbook might contain your company's logo, letterhead, a commonly used icon, and so on.

Under System 7, you can also use the Scrapbook to store sounds.

Notepad and Puzzle The Notepad DA is a simple word processor that's useful for jotting down notes to yourself as you're working in another application. The Puzzle is a game for you to play.

Commercial Desk Accessories

Commercial DAs, ones you buy from third parties, include Vantage (word processor), ACTA (outline processor), DeskPaint (graphics), and HyperDA (HyperCard reader). Hundreds of desk accessories are available both commercially and in the public domain as shareware. You'll find more information on the commercial DAs I recommend in Chapter 10.

Definition

HyperCard is a hypermedia application, bundled with the Macintosh, that allows storage and retrieval of text and bitmapped graphics. HyperCard files are called *stacks*.

HyperCard has been included (bundled) with every Macintosh since 1987, but it is rumored that Apple will stop bundling it in 1992.

Control Panel Devices

Control panel devices (CDEVs) let you customize your working environment by setting a variety of preferences—from speaker volume, beep sound, and color settings to startup devices and monitor settings. For example, Chapter 1 described how to use the General Controls window to change the desktop pattern, rate of insertion point blinking, menu blinking, sound volume, RAM cache setting, and internal clock settings.

System 6 lets you access CDEVs through the Control Panel desk accessory on the Apple menu. You open the Control Panel by choosing it from the Apple menu. Once the Control Panel window is open, you click an icon from the left-scrolling list to select the control panel you want. When you select a control panel icon, a set of related features and settings appears at the right.

In System 7, you choose control panels from the Apple menu, which is an alias for the Control Panels folder. (The Control Panels folder resides in the System Folder; the alias you see in the Apple menu resides in the Apple Menu Items folder.) Simply double-click the icon of the CDEV you want to use. Once you open a particular control panel in System 7, its settings and features appear in a window, similar to the features and settings appearing at the right of the System 6 Control Panel window.

Figure 3-4 shows the Control Panel desk accessory in System 6 and the contents of the Control Panels folder in System 7.

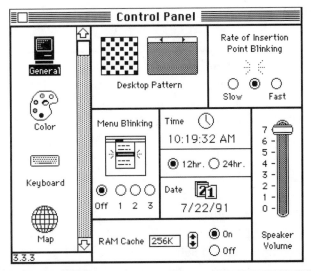

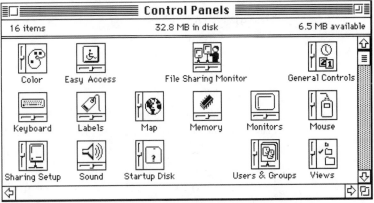

Figure 3-4.   System 6 Control Panel DA (top) and System 7 Control Panels folder (bottom)

Table 3-1 shows the control panels supplied by Apple with System 6 and System 7.

Table 3-1.   System 6 and System 7 Control Panels

	System 6	System 7
General/General Controls	√	√
Color	√	√
Easy Access	√	√
File Sharing Monitor		√
Keyboard	√	√
Labels		√
Map	√	√
Memory		√
Monitors	√	√
Mouse	√	√
Sharing Setup		√
Sound	√	√
Startup Device/Disk	√	√
Users & Groups		√
Views		√

Most control panel devices are loaded into memory automatically at boot time. These CDEVs are said to contain INIT code. Most control panel devices that contain INIT code draw an icon on the screen when you turn on or restart your Mac. The icons are drawn one at a time, in alphabetical order as they are loaded. If you've purchased any commercial CDEVs, you've probably noticed these icons at the bottom of your screen at boot time.

Similar to CDEVs are INITs (startup documents). They too are loaded automatically into memory at boot time. The difference is that INITs just load into memory and remain there until you need them—they don't use the control panel. Think of INITs as invisible CDEVs; they remain quietly in memory until they're needed.

Some INITs, such as the Apple CD-ROM INIT, are truly invisible. Aside from their icon at boot time, and the fact that you can use your CD-ROM player, there's almost no way of knowing they're there.

Tip

> Under System 6, you can see what INITs are in your System Folder by choosing By Kind from the View menu, then looking for Startup Documents. That's what INITs are called.
>   Under System 7, INITs are usually found in the Extensions folder, which resides within your System Folder.

Other INITs, such as Suitcase II or MasterJuggler (both are INITs that let you manage desk accessories and fonts—more about them later in this chapter and in Chapter 10) add a menu item to your Apple menu so you can change its parameters.

INITs and CDEVs can sometimes conflict, or cause problems with other programs or each other. In Chapter 6 you'll learn more about this, and how to avoid problems.

In addition to the CDEVs and INITs that come with your System software (such as Keyboard, Mouse, Color, and so on), you can purchase commercial INITs and CDEVs such as Suitcase II (INIT) or the After Dark screen saver (CDEV).

The installation procedure is the same for INITs and CDEVs—you drag their icon into the System Folder, and restart your Mac to install them. Under System 7, you'll see an alert when you drag these items to the System Folder. It tells you that these items must be stored in special folders—the Control Panels folder for CDEVs, and the Extensions folder for INITs. When you see this alert, click OK and your Mac will automatically place the INIT or CDEV in the proper folder for you.

For what it's worth, there is a trend away from INITs and toward CDEVs. A few years ago there were lots of INITs on the market; today, there are relatively few.

Now let's take a look at how you use control panels to customize your work environment. The control panels discussed in this section are common to both System 6 and System 7. System 7–specific control panels are described later in this chapter in the "Customizing in System 7" section.

Control Panels Included with Both System 6 and 7

Eight control panels are common to System 6 and 7.

General/General Controls Set your Mac's clock, choose a desktop pattern, or adjust cursor and menu blinking rates.

Color If you are using a color monitor, you can choose the color used to highlight selected text, as well as the color in Finder windows, by using the Color control panel and the color wheel dialog box. On a monochrome monitor, the highlight color is always black or gray.

Keyboard To adjust keyboard sensitivity—the rate at which a character repeats when you hold down a key, or the delay before the character begins repeating—use the Keyboard control panel. You can also use the Keyboard control panel to choose options for keyboard layouts, if you have more than one keyboard layout installed in your system (typically, for foreign-language versions of System software). If you purchased your Mac in the United States, the preset keyboard layout is U.S.

Map A handy little map. I haven't used mine in a long time.

Monitors If your system has a color or gray-scale monitor, the Monitors control panel (see Figure 3-5) is where you set the number of colors to display on the screen. This setting depends on the type of video support your monitor has. Check with your monitor's manual to determine the number of colors or grays you can display.

If you have more than one monitor attached to your Mac, use the Monitors control panel to designate the positions of the monitors and to assign one of them to be the main monitor. This setting enables the Mac to determine their relative positions and manage mouse pointer movements between them, as shown in Figure 3-5.

Clicking the Identify button in the Monitors control panel displays the ID numbers on each monitor icon on the screen, so you know which one is the primary monitor, and which are secondary. So, for example, when I press the Identify button, my small monitor (on the left in Figure 3-5) displays a large number 2, and my big monitor (on the right in Figure 3-5) displays a large number 1. If you change monitor positions or set a different main monitor, you must restart the Mac for your changes to take effect.

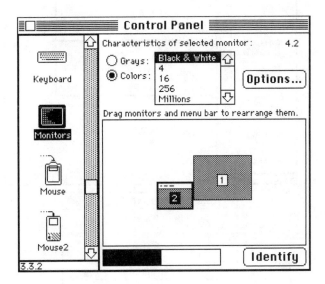

Figure 3-5.   The Monitors control panel

Mouse You use the Mouse control panel to adjust the pointer movement, or *tracking,* and the double-clicking speed of your mouse. Mouse tracking, which refers to the correlation between the distance the pointer moves on the screen to the distance you move the mouse on a mouse pad, is preset to a medium speed.

The Very Slow/Tablet mouse tracking setting (see Figure 3-6) is useful if you are using a graphics tablet to create drawings.

You can also change the double-click speed of the mouse. If your Mac interprets two single-clicks as a double-click, choose a faster speed. On the other hand, if it interprets a double-click as two single-clicks, choose a slower speed. I prefer the fastest settings for both.

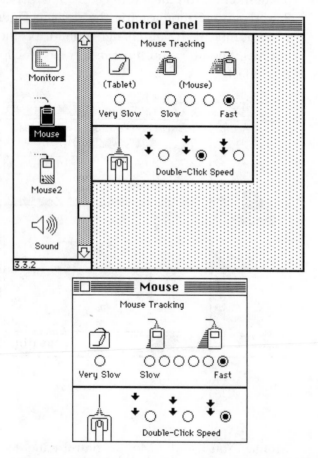

Figure 3-6.   The Mouse control panel in System 6 (top) and System 7 (bottom)

Sound   The Sound control panel is used to adjust your Mac's speaker volume, change the alert sound, and, if you're using System 7, add or remove alert sounds. If your Mac has a built-in microphone, the Sound control panel expands to let you record your own sounds.

Startup Device/Startup Disk   You use the Startup Disk control panel (in System 6 it is called Startup Device) if you have more than one hard disk and you want to set one of them as the startup disk. To do this:

1. Open the Startup Disk control panel.
2. In the window, click the icon of the disk that you want to be the startup disk (see Figure 3-7).
3. Click the window's close box. The next time you restart, your Mac will boot from the new startup disk.

Remember, in order to be a startup disk, the hard disk must have a System Folder. Also, note that this control panel does not work on the Mac Plus or earlier models. On those models the drive with the highest SCSI ID (and a System Folder) will be the startup disk.

Figure 3-7.   The Startup Disk control panel

Fonts

Fonts, more accurately known as *screen* or *bitmapped fonts*, to differentiate them from downloadable PostScript, or printer, fonts (see Chapter 8 for more information), are the character sets you see on the screen. Monaco, Geneva, and Chicago are common examples; Apple provides these with your System software. Like DAs (System 6 only) and sounds, fonts are installed in your System file.

With System 7, Apple has introduced a new outline font technology, called TrueType. Whereas bitmapped fonts consist of a series of dots, outline fonts are math descriptions of typeface designs. Each character in an outline font is a set of coordinate points that describes the boundary of a character's shape. As a result, outline fonts are usually smoother than bitmapped fonts, especially at odd sizes. Most bitmapped fonts look jagged at sizes other than those you've installed. So, for example, if you install the bitmapped font Times in sizes 9, 10, 12, 18, and 24 point, and try to use Times 17 point, it will look bad. Not so with TrueType—every size looks good.

If you are not using System 7, you will probably benefit from using Adobe Type Manager (usually referred to by its acronym, ATM), especially if you are using any QuickDraw printer, such as an ImageWriter or DeskWriter. Adobe Type Manager smooths bitmapped fonts on screen and on printed output by scaling the "jaggies" that often result when you use a large or odd point size. Apple recently made a deal with Adobe to include the ATM technology in future System software releases. You'll find more information on ATM in Chapter 8, as well as more details on printing and getting the best font output.

Many good-looking fonts are available from commercial publishers, and many more are available as shareware.

Adding fonts and dressing up your work is just one more way you can customize your Macintosh environment to suit your needs as well as your personality.

Sounds and FKEYs

Your Mac comes with several sounds preinstalled. If you're using System 6, they are Boing, Clink-Klank, Monkey, and the Simple Beep; under System 7, they are Droplet, Indigo, Quack, Sosumi, Wild Eep, and Simple Beep. You use the Sound control panel to choose which will be used as your System beep, which plays anytime your Mac wants to get your attention.

Speaker volume can be set from 0 (sound off) to 7 (loudest). If you set the speaker volume to 0, the menu bar flashes to alert you instead of making a sound.

Many more sounds are available on-line on bulletin boards or from user groups. If your Mac has a built-in microphone or you have a separate sound input device connected to your Mac, such as Farallon's MacRecorder, you can make your own sounds and install them in your system. If you plan to install a lot of sounds, be aware that they take up quite a bit of RAM and disk space.

FKEYs are another kind of program you can add to your system. They are keyboard shortcuts that are accessed by pressing Command-Shift and a number between 0 and 9. Apple provides FKEYs that are permanently installed in your system and cannot be changed or deleted easily:

- Eject floppy disk (Command-Shift-1 or -2)
- Screen dump to disk (Command-Shift-3)
- Screen dump to ImageWriter (Command-Shift-4)

To eject a floppy disk, click the disk's icon to select it, and press Command-Shift-1. If you have a dual-floppy disk system and the disk you want to eject is in disk drive 2, press Command-Shift-2 instead.

To capture the current contents of the screen and save it to disk as a MacPaint file (System 6) or a PICT file (System 7), press Command-Shift-3. (At the end of Chapter 2, you can find more information about opening a PICT screen dump in System 7.) If you have an ImageWriter, you can print a screen dump by pressing Command-Shift-4. Whatever is currently on your screen is printed on the ImageWriter.

You should be aware of these limitations: Under System 6, Command-Shift-3 does not work on Mac II machines. Also, keep in mind that Command-Shift-4 works only with ImageWriter printers.

Other FKEYs can be assigned to the remaining number keys (5, 6, 7, 8, 9, and 0), to function keys (on extended keyboards), or to Control-key combinations. Most FKEYs come with their own installer, but they can also be installed using ResEdit, one of the shareware installer programs such as Carlos Weber's FKEY Manager, or a commercial product such as Suitcase II or MasterJuggler.

Definition

ResEdit is Apple's resource editing application, which lets experienced users modify the resource fork of Macintosh files.

Among the more useful public-domain and shareware FKEYs are DateKey, which types in the current date at the insertion point when you type Command-Shift-6, and Switch-a-Roo, which allows you to toggle between any two monitor settings (for example, black-and-white and 256 colors) on any color-capable Mac by typing Command-Shift-9. There aren't many commercial FKEYs, but hundreds of useful ones are available as public-domain software or shareware.

You'll learn more about FKEYs in Chapter 10. For now, just remember that FKEYs can save you time and effort.

Customizing in System 6

In System software before System 7, you use Apple's Font/DA Mover to add DAs and fonts to, or remove them from, your

System file. Once DAs are installed under System 6, they are available under the Apple menu at all times.

The Font/DA Mover application comes with the Apple System software in the Font/DA Mover folder on the Macintosh Utilities Disk 2. Also in this folder are two additional files: a desk accessory file and a font file. The desk accessory file consists of the DAs discussed earlier in this chapter (Alarm Clock, Calculator, and so on); and the font file consists of a few fonts to get you started: Courier, Geneva, Helvetica, New York, Symbol, and Times. The Font/DA Mover gets installed when you use the Installer to install System software on your Mac. The sole purpose of the Font/DA Mover is to install or remove fonts and DAs, either those that come with System software or those you purchase separately from software vendors, which are stored in the System file.

The Font/DA Mover works by copying selected DAs or fonts into the System file. When you launch it, the Font/DA Mover is preset to move fonts. To change this so the Font/DA Mover starts up ready to move DAs, press and hold down the Option key while you double-click the Font/DA Mover icon to launch it. Otherwise, click the radio button marked "desk accessory" after the program launches to switch.

Here's how you install a desk accessory with the Font/DA Mover: Let's assume you want to install a DA called Word Finder from the More DAs desk accessory file on Floppy Disk (floppy drive) into the System file on the volume called Mowgli (hard drive).

1. At the Desktop, hold down the Option key as you double-click the Font/DA Mover icon to launch it. (Holding down the Option key is a shortcut to get Font/DA Mover to launch with the desk accessory radio button selected. If you don't hold down the Option key, the Font radio button will be selected instead.)

    When the Font/DA Mover screen appears, notice that Desk Accessory is selected (see Figure 3-8). If you forget to hold down the Option key, click Desk Accessory. The left side of the screen lists the desk accessories installed in the System file of the startup disk.

2. Click the Open button on the right side of the screen, and select the More DAs file on Floppy Disk. In the dialog box, click Open to open the More DAs file. The right side of the screen now lists the DAs installed in the More DAs file; in this case, only Word Finder is listed.

3. Click Word Finder once to select it from the right side, and click Copy. Notice that the directional arrows in the Copy button show you the direction the DA will take, from right to left.

4. When Word Finder is successfully copied to the startup disk's System file, it is listed in the left side of the screen. Click Quit when you are finished.

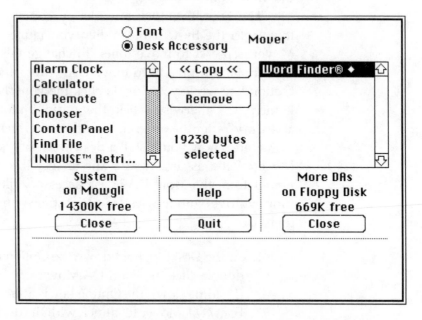

Figure 3-8.   Installing a desk accessory with the Font/DA Mover

Desk accessory files are easy to identify—they have a distinctive icon, commonly known as a *suitcase* (see Figure 3-9). You may need to restart your Mac to use the new DA from the Apple menu.

Word Finder

Figure 3-9.   A desk accessory's distinctive suitcase icon

If you want to remove the DA from the Apple menu, follow the previous steps, selecting the DA you want to remove from the list and clicking the Remove button. An alert message asks you to confirm that you want the DA removed (see Figure 3-10). After removing the DA, you have to restart for your changes to take effect.

Figure 3-10.   An alert message appears when you remove a DA or font

If you want to save a DA that's currently installed in your System file, click the Close button on the right side of the Font/DA Mover, then click the Open button. A standard directory dialog box appears. Click the New button, and a save file dialog box allows you to create and name a new suitcase file. Now, choose the DA (or DAs) you want to save from the list on the left, and click the Copy button. Then, when the copying is completed, click Quit.

To install a font, you follow the same procedure for installing a DA, except don't hold down the Option key when you launch the Font/DA Mover. If you've just installed a DA and now you want to install a font, click the Font radio button in the Font/DA Mover. The left side of the screen lists fonts installed in the System file on the startup disk. Each point size for every font appears separately on the list (see Figure 3-11). As with DAs, if you want to remove fonts, click the Remove button in the Font/DA Mover.

If you have used System 6 for any length of time, you will run into this common problem with DAs: Apple has imposed a limit of fifteen DAs in System 6. If you try installing a sixteenth, Font/DA Mover notifies you that you can't install any more desk accessories. (Incidentally, the number of fonts is also limited, but you are allowed a generous fifty-two fonts, not fifteen as is the case for DAs. In System 7, only the amount of available

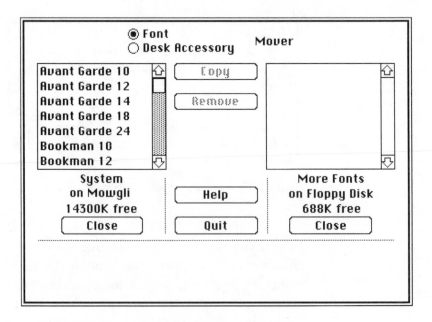

Figure 3-11.   Installing a font with the Font/DA Mover

disk space and RAM limits the number of DAs and fonts you can have in your system.)

Fortunately, you can overcome these limitations with commercial software such as Suitcase II or MasterJuggler. You can then use almost any number of fonts, DAs, FKEYs, and even sounds, without installing them in your System file. The only constraints are disk space and available RAM. Even on a stock Mac Plus, you should easily be able to double or triple the number of desk accessories and fonts you have available. In addition, if you have the disk space, you can store sets of fonts and DAs for occasional use. Figure 3-12 shows an Apple menu containing more than fifteen DAs with Suitcase II installed.

Figure 3-12.   Using Suitcase II to stretch the fifteen-DA limit imposed with System 6

Suitcase II or MasterJuggler also reduce the need to plan ahead—if you need a font, DA, FKEY, or sound, you can access it "on the fly"; without it, you'd have to quit what you were doing, use Font/DA Mover to install it in your system, restart your Mac, then return to what you were doing.

Several other benefits result from using Suitcase II or MasterJuggler instead of installing fonts and DAs directly into your system. First, the System is already a fairly large file. Adding fonts and DAs only makes it larger. This is a bigger problem for users without a hard disk; a system filled with fonts and DAs can easily grow larger than 800K. Installing DAs directly into your system also adds complexity to an already complicated System file. The System file is damaged easily enough without cramming it full of fonts, DAs, sounds, and FKEYs. If your system does become damaged, it is infinitely easier to replace it if it hasn't been extensively customized.

A more complete discussion of both Suitcase II and MasterJuggler appears in Chapter 10.

Customizing in System 7

System 7 does away with the Font/DA Mover, making it much easier for you to install and use desk accessories and fonts. The same is true of other items you can use to customize your system. System 7 gives you a great deal more flexibility in customizing. In general, you customize your Mac in System 7 by dragging desk accessories, fonts, startup documents, sounds, and CDEVs to the System Folder. System 7 automatically places the item in one of the special folders inside the System Folder, as described in Chapter 1.

Once you install desk accessories, CDEVs, sounds, startup documents, and fonts in System 7, you can use them immediately (though you still have to restart before using many CDEVs). And you can open them directly by double-clicking them at the desktop, or by selecting an icon and choosing Open from the File menu. This is also true of the System file. Unlike the System file in System 6, you can double-click the System 7 System file to open it, just as you would open a folder. Once open, the System file window shows the fonts and sounds installed in your system.

Now let's examine some of the more significant differences between customizing your Mac in System 7 and customizing in System 6.

Desk Accessories in System 7

In System 7, desk accessories behave much like ordinary applications. You no longer use the Font/DA Mover to install or remove desk accessories as you do in System 6. Instead, you install DAs by dragging them to any folder or any other location on the desktop. If you prefer, you can still access a desk accessory from the Apple menu. Just drag its icon into the Apple Menu Items folder inside the System Folder. Or, keep the DAs icon in one folder, make an alias of the DA, and drag the alias to the Apple Menu Items folder.

Once you have your DAs installed, you don't need to restart to use them. If you placed them in the Apple Menu Items folder, they immediately appear in the Apple menu, ready for you to use. No matter where you install a DA, you can always open it by double-clicking its icon from the desktop, just as you would open a regular application.

To use desk accessories that are inside suitcase icons, you must first open the suitcase (double-click the suitcase icon), then drag the DA out of the suitcase to another location. Or, you can move the suitcase icon on top of the System Folder icon. You'll see a dialog box asking if you want to put that DA in the Apple Menu Items folder. If you click OK, your Mac automatically removes the DA from the suitcase and moves it to the Apple Menu Items folder.

Unlike System 6 DAs, DAs in System 7 do not have suitcase icons. Rather, they have icons resembling regular applications. Figure 3-13 shows a folder containing several System 7 DAs.

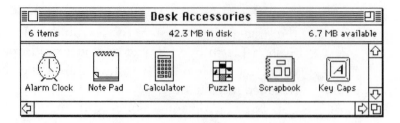

Figure 3-13.   Folder containing DAs in System 7

System 7 Fonts and Sounds

System 7 ships with the new TrueType fonts. TrueType uses a single font outline file to create smooth-looking characters at any point size. Unlike bitmapped fonts, TrueType fonts don't need a separate font for each point size you want to use; unlike PostScript fonts, TrueType fonts don't need a separate printer font file for each font, or Adobe Type Manager (ATM) for smooth screen fonts. With TrueType, a single font file is all you need for both smooth type on the screen and in your output.

Initially, you receive a handful of TrueType fonts with your System software, but almost every third-party font vendor has pledged to provide their libraries in TrueType format. And don't worry about your old fonts—System 7 still supports all your old bitmapped and PostScript fonts; TrueType merely provides a third option. In fact, TrueType fonts can be mixed with bit-mapped and PostScript fonts in the same document.

In System 7, you no longer use the Font/DA Mover to install fonts. To install a font, just drag its icon onto the System Folder's icon, and it automatically gets placed in the System file.

To see a sample of a font:

1. Double-click the System file to open it.
2. In the window, double-click the font whose sample you want to see. The font's window opens, showing you a sample of the font in 9-, 12-, and 18-point sizes (see Figure 3-14).
3. Click the font window's close box when you are done.

Figure 3-14.   Viewing samples of the Courier TrueType font in System 7

You install sounds in System 7 just as you install fonts: by dragging them to the System Folder, where they are placed in the System file. To hear a sound play, double-click the sound's icon. To see which sounds are installed in your system, either double-click the System file itself, or open the Sounds control panel.

System 7 Control Panels

Recall from earlier in this chapter that the Control Panels folder in the System 7 System Folder contains separate documents, one for each control panel. Control panels that are new in System 7 are as follows:

- File Sharing Monitor
- Labels control panel
- Memory control panel
- Sharing Setup control panel
- Users & Groups control panel
- Views control panel

Chapter 2 describes the File Sharing Monitor, Labels, Sharing Setup, and Users & Groups control panels in the "Finder 7 Menus and Commands" section. The Labels control panel is where you set up the text and color labels you want to use to organize the contents of Finder windows. The File Sharing Monitor, Sharing Setup, and Users & Groups control panels are used to customize the file-sharing capability of System 7. In this section, you'll take a look at the Memory and Views control panels.

Memory Control Panel   You use the Memory control panel (see Figure 3-15) to set the size of your Disk Cache, and access System 7's virtual memory and 32-bit addressing features on Macs that support them.

The Disk Cache is a special area of memory (RAM) set aside for frequently accessed data. Because data can be read from RAM far faster than from disk, a cache makes you feel that your computer is running faster.

I advise you to set the Disk Cache to 16K or 32K on Macs with only 2Mb of RAM. At settings below 256K, the effect is

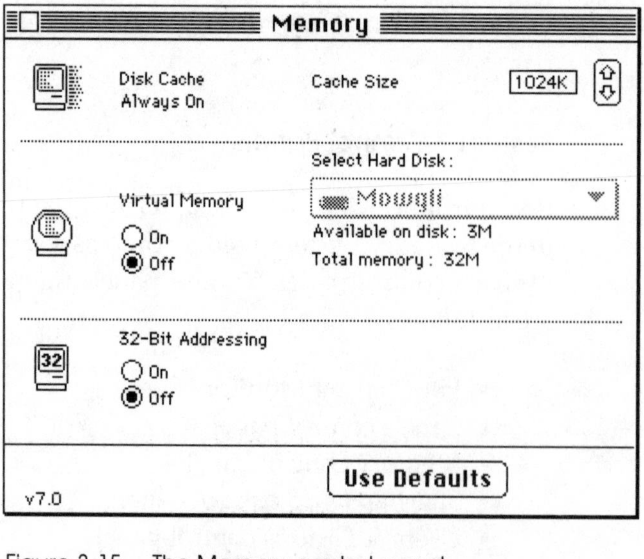

Figure 3-15.   The Memory control panel

barely noticeable, so if you have only 2Mb of RAM, I suggest you waste as little as possible on the Disk Cache. On Macs with 4Mb or more of RAM, try setting the cache to at least 256K; you should see some performance improvement, especially when quitting to the Finder from an application. This is because part of the Finder is usually in the cache at any given time. You'll also see an improvement in the speed of the Find or Search function in many applications with a cache of reasonable size. I keep mine set to 1,024K on my 32Mb IIci. I arrived at this figure through trial and error—if the cache was much smaller, the speed improvement wasn't perceptible. The lowest setting that seemed to make a difference was 1,024K.

If you've got enough RAM, I suggest you try various settings for your cache. You need to reboot between changes for them to take effect. The speed improvement is subtle, so if you don't feel an improvement, return to the Memory control panel, increase the setting, and reboot. If you don't feel a difference after a day or two with the setting at 384K or more, return to the control panel and set the Disk Cache back to 16K or 32K. The amount of RAM you dedicate to the cache is RAM that is unavailable for running your System software or programs, so it's usually wise to use the lowest setting you can, and there's no sense wasting perfectly good RAM on the cache if you don't notice a difference.

Virtual memory is a scheme that lets you treat empty space on your hard disk as additional RAM. So if you've got 4Mb of real RAM, and 4Mb of space on your hard disk, you can use virtual memory to trick your Mac into thinking it's got 8Mb of RAM. This feature is only supported by Macs with 68030 processors, including Mac IIx, IIcx, SE/30, IIci, and IIfx. It is also available if you are using a 68020 machine with a 68851 PMMU chip added. If you've got the horsepower, it's a lifesaver. If you've ever seen a *Not enough memory to...* message, virtual memory and some spare hard disk space will make it a thing of the past.

Unfortunately, virtual memory is significantly slower than real RAM, so if you use several RAM-intensive applications, you might want to add 16, 24, 32, or even more megabytes of real RAM. You can now do so, because System 7 supports 32-bit addressing.

With 32-bit addressing, you can cram up to 128Mb of RAM into your Mac as long as your Mac has so-called "32-bit clean" ROMs—that's the IIci, IIfx, IIsi, and Quadra at this writing. If your Mac has so-called "32-bit dirty" ROMS—that's the II, IIx, IIcx, or SE/30—you need to install a little program called Mode32 before you'll see 32-bit addressing in the Control Panel. (If your Mac isn't capable of using Virtual Memory or 32-bit addressing, those sections won't appear in your Memory control panel.)

Tip

Mode32 was developed by Connectix as a standalone product; Apple acquired an unlimited license to it last September and began distributing it at no charge. Mode32 lets Macs with 32-bit dirty ROMs access up to 128Mb of physical on-board RAM and up to 1 gigabyte of virtual memory using their hard disks. It's available at no charge through user groups, bulletin boards, and dealers.

With 32-bit addressing, you can have up to 128Mb of real RAM. Virtual memory lets you trick your Mac into thinking it's got as much as 1 gigabyte. Between the two you can have more memory—real and virtual—than most people are likely to need in a lifetime!

Views Control Panel You can customize how icons and lists of information are displayed in Finder windows by using the Views control panel (see Figure 3-16). You can specify the following:

- The font and size displayed in Finder windows
- The way icons are aligned in icon and small icon views in windows
- The size of icons and the categories of information displayed in list views

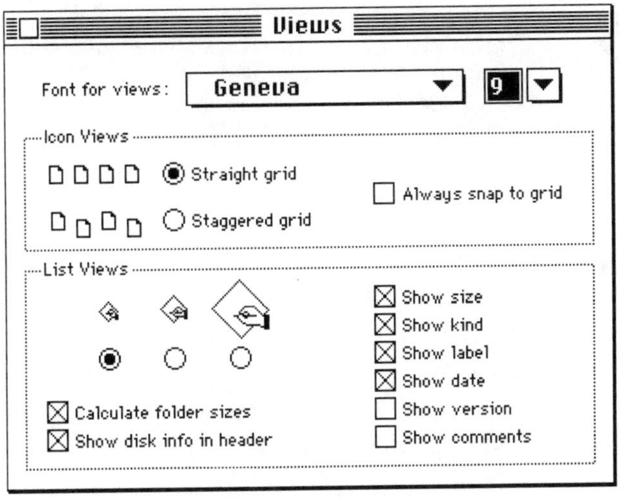

Figure 3-16.   The Views control panel

The font and size options available are those that you have installed in your System file. Pop-up menus for font type and font size let you set the font for icon names and list views.

The options for icon alignment are Straight Grid or Staggered Grid, and Always Snap to Grid. Icon alignment settings take effect when you choose Clean Up from the Special menu. With the Straight Grid and Always Snap to Grid options selected, the Mac arranges icons along an invisible grid in Finder windows (this is the preset alignment). If you'd rather show icons in offset rows, which is good if your icon names are long, choose the Staggered Grid option.

In the List Views area of the Views control panel, you can specify the size of the icon that displays to the left of an item's name in a list window. The preset size is the smallest option. You can also set view windows to calculate and display folder sizes and the amount of disk space available at the top of the window. Additionally, you can customize the type of information that displays in list views according to what suits you. List views are preset to show size, kind, label, and date of each item in the list.

Tip

Checking the Calculate Folder Sizes option slows the Finder down considerably. If you check this option, and the Finder's response seems sluggish to you, uncheck it.

Recommendations

ACTA (ACTA 7)
Symmetry
8603 E. Royal Palm Road, Suite 110
Scottsdale, AZ 85258
800–624–2485
602–998–9106
Approximately $150

An excellent desk accessory outline processor. It includes an outline processing application even more useful than the DA. A fine product.

Adobe Type Manager (ATM)
Adobe Systems, Inc.
1585 Charleston Road
Mountain View, CA 94039–7900
800–833–6687
415–961–4400
Approximately $100

Adobe Type Manager solves the problems of jagged fonts by improving type displays on the screen and output to printers. Especially recommended for users of ImageWriters and other QuickDraw printers. Less useful under System 7, due to TrueType fonts provided with your System software.

ATM will be included at no charge in future Apple System software releases.

After Dark
Berkeley Systems
2095 Rose Street
Berkeley, CA 94709
510–540–5536
Approximately $50

An excellent and entertaining CDEV screen saver.

DeskPaint and DeskDraw
Zedcor
4500 E. Speedway, Suite 22
Tucson, AZ 85712
800–482–4567
602–881–8101
Approximately $200

A desk accessory with more features than the original MacPaint! Includes DeskDraw, a MacDraw-like DA. If you work in MacPaint or MacDraw, you'll love these convenient DAs.

HyperDAII
Symmetry
8603 E. Royal Palm Road, Suite 110
Scottsdale, AZ 85258
800–624–2485
602–998–9106
Approximately $130

The desk accessory that reads HyperCard stacks—an idea so basic I'm surprised Apple didn't think of it. A must if you use HyperCard. Particularly recommended for users with memory constraints (it lets you browse HyperCard stacks on a stock Mac Plus without MultiFinder).

MacRecorder

Farallon Computing, Inc.
2000 Powell Street, Suite 600
Emeryville, CA 94608
510–596–9100
Approximately $200

A hardware and software package that lets you record and input sound into your Mac. It includes the MacRecorder digitizer, and three applications that you can use to record and edit sounds. Compatible with both System 6 and System 7.

MasterJuggler

AlSoft
P.O. Box 927
Spring, TX 77383–0927
800–ALSOFT–1
713–353–4090
Approximately $50

Allows almost unlimited numbers of fonts, DAs, sounds, and FKEYs to be used without having them installed in your System file.

Suitcase II

Fifth Generation Systems
10049 North Reiger Road
Baton Rouge, LA 70809
800–766–7283
504–291–7221
Approximately $80

Allows almost unlimited numbers of fonts, DAs, sounds, and FKEYs to be used without having them installed in your System file.

Thunder 7
>Baseline Publishing, Inc.
>1770 Moriah Woods Boulevard, Suite 14
>Memphis, TN 38117–7118
>800–926–9677
>901–682–9676
>Approximately $100

Thunder 7 is a CDEV spelling checker. It includes a 1.4-million-word thesaurus.

Vantage
>Baseline Publishing, Inc.
>1770 Moriah Woods Boulevard, Suite 14
>Memphis, TN 38117–7118
>800–926–9677
>901–682–9676
>Approximately $100

Vantage is a wonderfully full-featured text-processing desk accessory that can handle most text editing with ease.

Summary

This chapter described how to customize your Macintosh environment using desk accessories, fonts, INITs, CDEVs, and sounds. Customizing your Mac in System 6 generally involves using the Font/DA Mover. On the other hand, System 7 does away with the Font/DA Mover, making the customization process much easier and more flexible.

Now that you have the basics under your belt—what System software is, how to work in the Finder, and how to customize your Mac—it's time to learn about the care and feeding of your hard disk.

4

The Care and Feeding of Hard Disks

What they do, how they work, and how to get the most out of them.

There are at least 20 million reasons to own a hard disk (20 million is the approximate number of bytes in a 20Mb hard disk). If you don't already own one, it's probably the first hardware investment you should make. Nothing else provides so much performance in two all-important areas—speed and storage space—at so low a price. No more hunting for disks or files—everything you need each day is at your fingertips. And a hard disk is significantly faster than a floppy drive. A well-organized hard disk could save you as much as a half hour a day, time you now spend looking at the little watch cursor or searching for floppies.

Another advantage is that you can have all the fonts and desk accessories your little heart desires. And, once you have a hard disk, dozens of utility programs (see Chapter 10) make using it even faster and more convenient. One final advantage—you'll be able to use powerful software that requires a hard disk, such as PageMaker and HyperCard.

Once you've gotten used to a hard disk, working from floppy disks will seem archaic.

When I wrote the first edition of this book, a hard disk was still a bit of a luxury item. In just a few years, things have changed tremendously; most Macintoshes come with a built-in hard disk, and much of today's software requires one.

If you already have one, this chapter will teach you a bit about how it works and how to get the most out of it; if you don't already have one, this chapter should convince you that it's the next investment you should make.

What Is a Hard Disk, and Why Do I Want One?

A hard disk is a giant nonremovable disk that can hold over 20 million bytes. A 20Mb hard disk can hold approximately the same amount of data as twenty-five 800K floppy disks. Hard disks are fast—two or three times faster than floppies. When you use a hard disk, every action that requires disk access—saving, opening a document, and launching or quitting an application—is a whole lot faster. Depending on your needs, you can buy hard disks in sizes ranging in size from 20Mb (≈20,000K) to more than a gigabyte (≈1,000,000K).

The SCSI Chain (Bus)

The SCSI port allows high-speed data transfer to and from your Mac. If you look behind your Mac, the SCSI port is the largest connector—the long, narrow one with two rows of tiny connectors (see Figure 4–1). The proper cable is usually supplied with

Figure 4–1.   The 25-pin SCSI port on the back of your Macintosh

the device. If not, an Apple dealer or a mail-order house such as MacConnection has them for about $25. If you need a cable, be sure to look at the back of your SCSI device and see if the connector is a 25-pin connector (like the one on the back of your Mac) or a 50-pin connector (larger and wider than the one on your Mac). SCSI device manufacturers generally use the 50-pin type, but there are still several who use a 25-pin connector. PowerBooks require a new type of 30-pin SCSI connector known as HDI-30.

Tip

Make sure you pick up the right cable—there's nothing more frustrating than getting the wrong one.

The SCSI interface allows up to six external devices to communicate with your Mac at high speed. You connect each device to the next and connect the last in the chain to your Mac. This is called a *SCSI chain*, and the devices connected to it are said to be connected to the SCSI bus.

Other peripherals besides hard disks can use the SCSI bus to communicate with your Mac. High-speed scanners, CD-ROM drives, and tape or removable-media backup devices are other devices that can share the SCSI bus with your hard disk. Most SCSI devices come with two SCSI connectors, which (unless your manual says otherwise) can be used interchangeably for data coming in and going out. You can connect up to six SCSI devices in a chain, in any order, and they'll all work. (At least in theory. Chapter 6 has further information on termination, SCSI ID numbering, and SCSI cables. If you plan to hook up more than one SCSI device, you should definitely read those sections.)

Hard disks come in many shapes and sizes, ranging from 20Mb to more than a gigabyte (1,000Mb). Some sit under your Mac Plus or SE; others sit vertically alongside it. Still others are mounted inside your Mac—internal drives are available with all Macs in the product line today.

Note: If you decide to install an internal drive in a Mac Plus, be sure to purchase a fan as well. Hard disks run best if they're not allowed to get too hot. In fact, if you have a Plus, you might seriously consider going with an external drive instead. All Macs since the Mac Plus include internal fans.

Some external drives have fans, and others cool themselves by convection; that is, vents near the bottom that allow cool air to enter and rise—the same cooling principle used in the 128, 512, and Plus.

As you can see, there are many choices. But so far, the choices are mostly a matter of preference. Hard disks with fans are usually noisier than those without; but I trust fan-cooled drives a little more than those without. As far as the shape of the case, and horizontal versus vertical orientation, take a look at your desk space. If you have a one-piece Mac (that is, 512, Plus, SE, SE/30, Classic, or Classic II) you might want a drive with zero footprint—one that sits perfectly beneath your Mac. Most current Mac models come with an internal hard disk. If not, you might want to consider one. The SE, Classic, LC, II family, Quadra, Portable, and PowerBook are specifically designed to accommodate internal hard disks. Internal drives have several advantages: They take up no desk space, they can be easily taken with you, and they are somewhat less expensive than external drives. They also have a couple of drawbacks: They must be installed by a technician, and if an internal drive breaks, you will probably lose the use of your Mac until the drive is repaired.

Dozens of manufacturers produce reliable hard disks, with wide differences in performance and price. Before making a decision, perhaps it would be wise to know a bit more about how hard disks work.

How Hard Disks Work

Inside the Box

Your hard disk contains a flat, round, metallic platter, which is either 5.25 or 3.5 inches in diameter, though some newer models use a 2.5-inch platter. The platter is coated with a magnetic recording medium, not unlike the magnetic coating on audio or video tape. The platter is spun by a motor at a constant speed (usually about 3,600 revolutions per minute). A read/write head is suspended micro-inches away from the platter and is moved up and back, using instructions it receives from your computer, to read and write from the spinning platter. The read/write head acts like the record and playback heads of a video or audiocassette player, except that instead of passing the media over the head, hard disks move the head over the spinning media. Information is written and read from tracks, which are concentric circles of data evenly spaced across the surface on the platter.

Because the read/write heads fly next to the platter at a distance closer than the width of a human hair, the head and disk assembly are contained in a sealed casing to protect them against airborne contaminants and accidental jarring. Other components in most hard disks include the following:

- Power supply—To convert the electricity coming out of your wall socket into power that can be used by your hard disk. Almost all electronic devices, including all Macs, have a power supply of some sort.
- SCSI controller board—To translate data into a format that can be sent across the SCSI bus.
- Air filter—To clean the air drawn into your hard disk's case.

Setting the SCSI ID Number

Each device on your SCSI chain must have a unique address (also known as SCSI ID)— a number between 1 and 6.

Definition

> *SCSI ID* – Actually, 7 addresses are available, 0 through 6 inclusive. But 0 is reserved for an internal hard drive; internal drives should always have their SCSI ID set to 0. ID number 7 is reserved for the Mac itself.

Most hard disks also include an external address selector or DIP switches for setting the SCSI ID; a few perform this task with software.

The selector used for choosing SCSI ID numbers is usually found on the back of the drive. For most drives, you select an ID number by clicking a little button until the number you want appears in the little window. If your drive uses DIP switches, consult your owner's manual for instructions. Fortunately, it's not something you do very often, so if your drive uses DIP switches, don't despair. A few drives allow you to set the SCSI ID number from the initialization software. This may be the easiest way of all. (See Chapter 6 for more information on setting the SCSI ID number.)

Interleave

Interleave refers to the order in which the heads read and write the sectors on the hard disk. Many hard disks can work at different interleave values. When you initialize a hard disk, most formatting software automatically selects the proper interleave value for that Mac.

The formatting process creates concentric rings, called tracks. Each track is divided into sectors. Figure 4–2 shows how the platter inside your drive is divided into tracks and sectors when you initialize it.

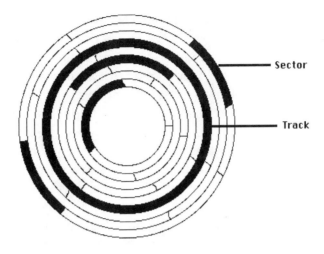

Figure 4–2.   Sectors and tracks

Because each type of computer can send and receive information through the SCSI port at different speeds, the interleave value should be set to optimize the transfer between your computer and your hard disk. (Point of information: The Mac IIfx is capable of rates as high as 3Mb/second, the Mac IIx is capable of about 1.25Mb/second, the Mac SE is capable of about 600K/second, and the Mac Plus is capable of about 300K/second.) Some brands ask you to specify which interleave you want when you first initialize your hard disk, though most automatically select the proper interleave for the model of Mac you're using. My advice: Read the following material as background, and don't mess with interleave unless you're sure of what you're doing. Chances are your initialization software has formatted your disk at the proper interleave for your Mac anyway.

On the other hand, if the interleave on your hard disk is set to a nonoptimized setting for your Mac, you may experience degraded performance. Opening and saving files, launching applications, and other disk-related activities may take longer than they have to if your hard disk's interleave value is not appropriate for the model of Macintosh you're using.

Almost all Mac models newer than the Mac Plus work best with a 1:1 interleave. (A few of the earliest SEs produced require 2:1 or 3:1 interleave—see the Tip on the next page.) The Mac Plus and 512E work best with a 3:1 interleave.

The reason most Mac models utilize disks with a 1:1 interleave is that, because they're fairly fast computers, they can process the data in a sector as fast as the drive can read it, even when the disk reads every sector in consecutive order.

Almost all initialization software (including Apple's HD SC Setup) selects the best interleave automatically, based on which Macintosh it's hooked up to. Some brands of hard disks also allow you to override their interleave settings manually. For example, if you have an Apple hard drive, and use HD SC Setup to format it, you can change the interleave value manually by typing Command-I (see Figure 4–3). For other brands of hard disks, consult the documentation that came with it or call the technical-support phone number.

Using a drive formatted with the wrong interleave for your Mac will degrade performance. For example, if you use a drive formatted at a 3:1 interleave value on a Mac II, your computer

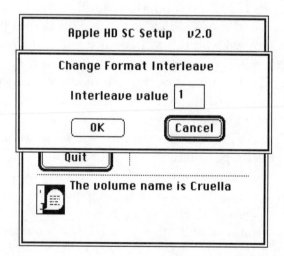

Figure 4–3.   Setting the interleave for Apple hard disks by typing Command-I

will have to wait as two out of three sectors pass under the head. It works the other way, too—if you try using a drive with a 1:1 interleave on an SE, it will be slower than a 2:1 drive. The bottom line is that you want your hard disk to be formatted with the optimum interleave value for the model of Mac you own. And if you're going to use your old hard disk—the one you used with your Mac Plus–with a newer Mac, you should probably back it up, then reinitialize it using the proper interleave factor for your new Mac. Most initialization software automatically chooses the correct interleave for your new Mac.

Tip

> **SE Owners Only!** Some early SEs require 2:1 or 3:1 interleave. If you've got an Apple internal drive, HD SC Setup chooses the proper interleave automatically. But if you're using a third-party hard disk and it asks you what interleave you want to use, here's how to find out: First, quit your third-party initialization utility program and launch Apple's HD SC Setup. Press Command-I. Since HD SC Setup automatically selects the correct interleave for your Mac, the number you see is the interleave you should use. Now quit HD SC Setup and launch your third-party hard drive's initialization software. If it asks you to choose an interleave, use the number you saw in HD SC Setup.

Warning: It's a bad idea to initialize third-party hard drives with HD SC Setup. Always use the software that came with your drive.

If your drive came preformatted, or you don't remember what interleave you used when you first formatted the disk, or you can't figure out how to set the interleave value, call the manufacturer and ask. You paid good money for that drive—you're entitled to a little support.

The best advice: Leave it alone unless you suspect your hard disk has been formatted using the wrong interleave value.

For example, say you had a Mac Plus and used an external hard disk with it. Later, you sold the Plus and bought an SE/30, and you now want to use that external hard disk with it. This situation would require reinitialization to have the drive formatted at the proper interleave for the SE/30. As I said earlier in the chapter, you may not need to do anything more than reinitialize the drive while it's connected to your SE/30—the initialization software should do the rest. Again, if you're not sure, contact the manufacturer.

Interleave Explanation and Demonstration Here's how interleave works. Imagine that each track on your hard disk's platter is divided into 7 sectors. (Note: I picked 7 at random to make the illustration easier to understand. Your hard disk is really divided into more sectors.)

- A 1:1 interleave writes to/reads from each sector in order, taking one revolution to read the entire track.
- A 2:1 interleave writes to/reads from every other sector, taking two revolutions to read the entire track.
- A 3:1 interleave writes to/reads from every third sector, taking three revolutions to read the entire track.

Figure 4–4 illustrates the order in which tracks are read and written using various interleave values.

Now that you know a little bit about how hard disks work, the next section discusses what you need to know about purchasing a hard disk. In general, you need to consider five criteria: size, speed, noise level, bundled software, and brand reliability.

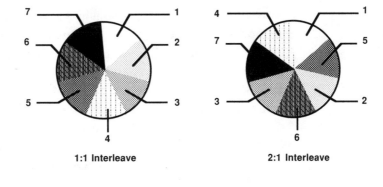

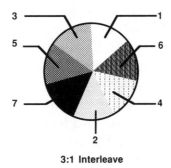

Figure 4–4.   The order in which tracks are read using different interleave values

How to Select Your Hard Disk

Size

When selecting a hard disk, try to figure out how much storage you'll need. Although 20Mb may sound like acres of storage space, you'll be amazed at how quickly you fill it up. Many applications take up several megabytes with their associated files, folders, dictionaries, and tutorials. So, the first rule of selecting your hard disk is: Get the biggest one you can possibly afford.

If you're into desktop publishing, you'll need at least 40Mb, and more will serve you even better. Desktop publishing programs—PageMaker, Quark XPress, DesignStudio, ReadySetGo! —are huge. They each take up several megabytes. Consider the graphics files (which occupy more disk space than text files) you'll find yourself creating and saving on your hard disk, plus the files you create with your desktop publishing program, and you'll find you've quickly filled 10 or 20Mb. A single project can quickly consume a lot of disk space. For example: The data files for this book—not including my page layout program, word processor, or downloadable fonts—take up over 14Mb (see Figure 4–5). And I'm not done yet!

Fonts are another thing that can take up a lot of disk space. If you're planning to use lots of fonts, buy a bigger hard disk than you think you need.

Scanner files—files created using a scanner—also take up gobs of space. A scanner is a hardware device you attach to your Mac. It turns hard copy (such as photographs, drawings, text, and so on) into files you can manipulate with your Mac. Most scanners create files in MacPaint, TIFF, or PICT file

Figure 4–5.   The data files for this book take up more than 14Mb of disk space

formats. If you plan to use a scanner, even 40Mb may not be enough for you. Scanned images can be huge—black-and-white TIFF files can be as big as several megabytes; color scans even bigger. So if you've got scanning on your agenda, you probably want an 80Mb drive. Or bigger!

Definition

TIFF, an acronym for Tagged Image File Format, is a high-resolution bitmap file format that can store gray-scale and/or color information. Most scanners save in TIFF format.

PICT is the file format for object-oriented graphics. PICT files can be written and read by many applications, including the TeachText application that comes with System 7.

When you're trying to estimate your needs, don't forget that you might want to store many other things on your hard disk, and you absolutely have to store your System Folder there. Here's a checklist of some of the things you might want to allow room for:

- System Folder—At least 2Mb. Mine is 24Mb, but it includes tons of CDEVs, INITs, desk accessories, and fonts.
- Utility software—Your backup program, file and disk recovery programs, and so on. See Chapter 5 for more information on backup programs and Chapter 10 for more information on utilities.
- A database—A meg or two for the program itself; more if you plan to create large data files.
- Graphics program or programs—At least 1Mb for each program, plus space for files you create using them.
- Word processor—A meg or two for the program and its dictionaries.

These are only rough guidelines. My estimates may seem a little high; your programs and files may not take as much space. Trust me—data has a way of expanding to fill any available space. You'll quickly come to appreciate having extra space. So, once you've decided how big a disk to get, consider getting an even larger one.

Tip

Shop around. One vendor's 60Mb disk may cost more than another's 80Mb disk. And remember, it's cheaper to buy one big hard disk than two small ones. Plan ahead and get a hard disk big enough to last you several years.

Speed

Manufacturers like to advertise such things as "average access time of only 18 milliseconds." Although average access time forms a relatively accurate basis for comparing different drives, all the specifications in the world won't reveal whether a drive will feel fast enough for you.

Access time is only one measure of a hard disk's speed. It tells how long it takes the drive to locate a particular track. Other benchmarks you may see bandied about include DiskTimer II, SCSI Evaluator, seek, settle, and latency. Don't worry too much about them. You can compare them to get an idea of how one disk compares to another. But for most people, the difference between two drives with similar specifications is unnoticeable in real-world use.

Occasionally magazines use tests, such as how fast a 600K PageMaker file opens and loads, how fast a multimegabyte database opens, and how long it takes to duplicate a file in the Finder. I find these better indicators than the benchmarks mentioned in the previous paragraph. Although none of the tests prove anything absolutely, most of them are good indicators of how fast a drive will "feel" to you.

Yes, it's true that a drive boasting a 10ms (millisecond) average access time will perform noticeably faster than one with a 65ms access time. Files will open faster, and working in the Finder will be quicker. But the difference may not be apparent *to you*. You won't really know unless you sit and try both flavors. The point is that a hard disk that seems slow to one person may be perfectly acceptable for another.

How Important Is Speed, Anyway? Let's put it this way: I love the responsiveness of a 12ms (average access time) drive. That's because I'm sensitive to the speed of my hard disk. Also, I'm using a Mac IIci, which, because of its fast processor, can really milk every ounce of performance out of a fast hard disk. Other people I know don't notice much difference between a 40ms and a 25ms drive.

Macs with faster processors—Mac II series, SE/30, Classic II, and Quadra—benefit most from a fast drive. Attaching a slow hard disk (say 40ms average access time or slower) to a fast Mac will cause it to feel sluggish. If you have a fast Mac, decide how big a hard disk you need, then how much you can afford to spend. Now get the fastest drive in that category.

If you have a Plus, Classic, or SE, speed is of less importance. Your processor can't keep up with a *really* fast hard disk, anyway. On the other hand, if you're planning to get a faster Mac someday, it won't hurt to get it now and use it with your current Mac until that time.

A faster drive may not be worth the extra cost to you. There is a significant cost difference between a 12ms drive and a 25ms drive, but *you* may not be able to notice the difference in performance. In many cases, you'll have to decide between a bigger drive and a faster drive. I think, in most cases, you'll be happier with the bigger one. Remember—the faster the drive, the more expensive it will be. For many people, small differences in speed—5 to 10ms average access time—from one drive to another are almost imperceptible.

In evaluating hard disk speed, the best thing to do would be to go to a dealer and try out several different drives with different specifications. If that's not possible, see if you can get friends with hard disks to let you try theirs and compare the differences. Or check with your local user group; perhaps they know of a place where you can test-drive more than one drive.

Noise Level

Some drives are whisper-quiet; others sound like a jet taking off inches from your ear. In a recent *MacUser* article, the difference between the quietest and loudest drives was over 10dB (decibels), which is a noticeable difference indeed.

Most hard disks make a quiet humming sound when they're running, and emit a different noise—sort of low-pitched squeal or rumble—when they're being accessed (that is, written to or read from). A few are nearly silent—you can hardly hear them at all, even when they're being accessed.

If you're sensitive to noise, be sure to try your drive in a quiet room before you buy it. If the noise it makes is too annoying, consider a different drive.

If you buy from a mail-order vendor (more on that later in this chapter), make sure that they have a money-back guarantee. That way, if their drive is too noisy for your work environment, you can either trade it in on a quieter model from the same manufacturer, or get a refund and buy a quieter drive elsewhere.

For what it's worth, I've usually got three or four external drives piled up on my desk, so my office has a relatively high ambient noise level. I guess I'm just not sensitive to hard disk noise; even the loud ones hardly bother me. Other people I know suffer if even the quietest drive is running in the same room.

Bottom Line: If you're sensitive to noise, make sure your hard disk won't drive you nuts. Try before you buy. Look for drives with a 30-day money-back guarantee if you think noise may bother you.

Bundled Software

The price of your hard disk will usually include some bundled software. All hard disks come with some kind of formatting utility. With some hard disks, that's all you get. Others come with bundled software—working versions of commercially available software, usually utilities, included at no additional cost. You're going to want certain utilities once you have a hard disk, so inquire about each manufacturer's bundle. If you need the software anyway, bundled software lowers the effective price you pay for the drive.

Bundles often include such needed items as:

- A backup utility—Software used to back up the data on your hard disk to a set of floppy disks or some other media. See Chapter 5 for more about specific backup programs.
- Partitioning software—Software that lets you create smaller pseudo-disks out of one big disk. So, for example, you could make an 80Mb drive appear as a pair of 40Mb drives. In Figure 4–6, both Cinderella and Toyland are actually one drive—a Jasmine 100. I've used Jasmine's partitioning software to divide them up into two pseudo–hard disks that appear on the desktop as two separate icons, and act, for all intents and purposes, as though they were two separate hard disks. Cinderella contains applications and utilities, and holds 80Mb; Toyland is filled with games and toys, and holds 20Mb.

The Doctor's Opinion

Since the first edition of this book, Jasmine has been through a bankruptcy and changed ownership. They may very well be out of business by the time you read this. If they're still around, chances are the quality of their service is not anywhere near what it was when I wrote the first edition of this book. After several bad experiences, I no longer recommend Jasmine products; I now deal with APS (Alliance Peripheral Systems) almost exclusively for mail-order hardware. They offer attractive prices, knowledgeable salespeople, and excellent after-sale service.

Figure 4–6.   A single hard disk partitioned into two pseudo–hard disks

The little 4 in the middle of each icon indicates their SCSI ID number. Although two separate hard disks can't have the same SCSI address, partitioned pseudo-hard disks can and do share a single SCSI ID.

Many hard disk manufacturers include partitioning capabilities in the formatting software they supply with each drive.

- Encryption or password protection utilities—Software that allows you to protect your hard disk and/or individual files from unauthorized eyes.

- Disk recovery tools—Programs that help you recover files damaged in a crash, and undelete files you've inadvertently trashed.

- Print spoolers—Lets you print a document while continuing to use your Mac.

- Public domain/shareware—Many manufacturers put 10 to 20Mb of programs, INITs, CDEVs, desk accessories, games, and so on, on their disk for you. If you like to play with new stuff, this might be valuable to you. Be forewarned: Not all manufacturers update their shareware files regularly. Some programs may crash newer Mac models. So use 'em with caution. And make a backup of your entire hard disk before you start to experiment.

Before making a purchase decision, think not only about the software you need today but also about the software you'll need in the future. Be sure to factor in the cost of whatever utilities you'll have to buy if you select a drive that doesn't include that software.

Choosing a Brand

There are many good manufacturers of hard disks. Some, such as Apple and Microtech, are available only through authorized dealers. Others, such as APS (Alliance Peripheral Systems), are available exclusively through mail order. Buying from a dealer may have advantages if your drive breaks, depending on the quality of your dealer's service department. On the other hand, buying from a mail-order vendor is usually less expensive, and they will often repair or replace your drive in less time than a dealer.

Tip

Apple drives are, for the most part, higher priced than their counterparts from independent manufacturers. About the only advantage of buying Apple is that there are a lot of Apple dealers, and it may be easier to get an Apple disk repaired than another brand. Still, I strongly urge you to look at the non-Apple hard disk offerings—you'll almost certainly get more for your money.

Shop around. Compare sizes, speed, noise, price, and bundled software, and consider whether you need local service or if buying by mail from someone such as APS is acceptable to you.

The listings at the end of this chapter represent a few of the manufacturers I recommend. If you're shopping for a hard disk, you'd be well served to start your search with these vendors.

Now that you've selected a hard disk, let's talk about some of the different ways you can keep it organized—to make it easier to find what you need, when you need it.

Organizing Your Hard Disk

Different people organize their hard disk different ways. There is no "right" way to do it. The Macintosh allows you to decide what combination of folders makes sense to you.

I recommend several general strategies for organizing your hard disk. In each of the strategies, some things are constant. For example, no matter how you decide to organize your hard disk, frequently used icons should be stored on the gray desktop. And I like to put all applications in their own folder, which I name Applications.

After a brief discussion of three different strategies, I'll give you a peek at my hard disk and tell you a little about how I keep things organized.

Strategy 1—Organizing by Client/Project

Organizing by client or project works best if you are a consultant or other such business professional who works with several clients or projects simultaneously.

After setting up your System and Applications folders, set up a separate folder for each client or for each project. Its advantage is that everything that has to do with the project or client is

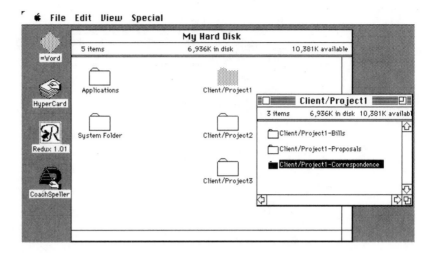

Figure 4–7.   A hard disk organized by client/project

in one folder, where it will be easy to find (see Figure 4–7). If a client calls, or your boss asks about a specific project, you'll be able to find all of the files pertaining to that client or project in their own folder.

If that doesn't suit you, you might prefer Strategy 2…

Strategy 2—Organizing by Task

Another way to organize your hard disk is by task. Documents of the same type go into their own folders. Create one for memos, another for letters, another for proposals, and so on (see Figure 4–8). The advantage here is that if you need to find any letter, regardless of its addressee or purpose, you know it's stored in your Letters folder.

Finally, here's one other way you might organize your hard disk…

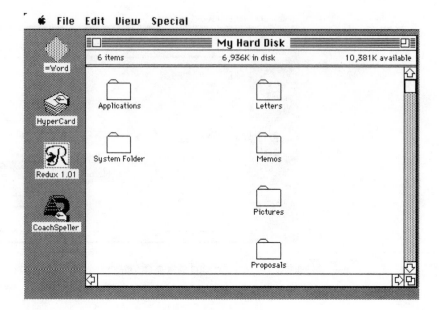

Figure 4–8.   A hard disk organized by task

Strategy 3—Organizing by Application

Some people prefer to organize their files and folders by the application that created the documents. So you'd have a Word folder that contained the Microsoft Word application, all of its associated files (dictionaries, glossary, help file, and so on), and folders containing all of the documents created by Word (see Figure 4–9). Your folder for Adobe Illustrator (a graphics and illustration application) might contain the application plus folders for logos, drawings, ads, and the like.

A Look at My Hard Disk(s)

I'm slightly neurotic about keeping track of stuff on my hard disks. I also arrange my desktop obsessively, so the windows that I use frequently don't overlap.

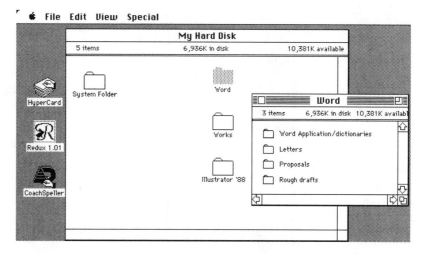

Figure 4–9.   A hard disk organized by application

I have two hard disks—an 80Mb Apple internal (Cruella) and a 210Mb APS external (Cinderella). You can see their disk icons on the right side of Figure 4–10.

My philosophy about what goes where is pretty simple. If it needs to be backed up every day—for example, all of my data files—it's stored on Cruella. If it's a program, utility, clip art, or anything that I've still got a master disk for, it goes in the appropriate folder on Cinderella.

The main reason I organize my Mac this way is that I often take the external drive, Cinderella, on the road when I appear at trade shows and other speaking engagements. (Watch for me—I could be speaking in your town someday soon! And I almost always speak at Macworld Expo—Boston in August; San Francisco in January. C'mon up and say "hi.") All of the programs, utilities, INITs, and CDEVs I use are on Cinderella, so all I have to do is plug her into whatever Mac I'm using and I can demonstrate the software I use most often.

Even though I have master disks for most of what's on Cinderella, I back up both hard disks to DAT tape (more about that in Chapter 5) every night. Better safe than sorry.

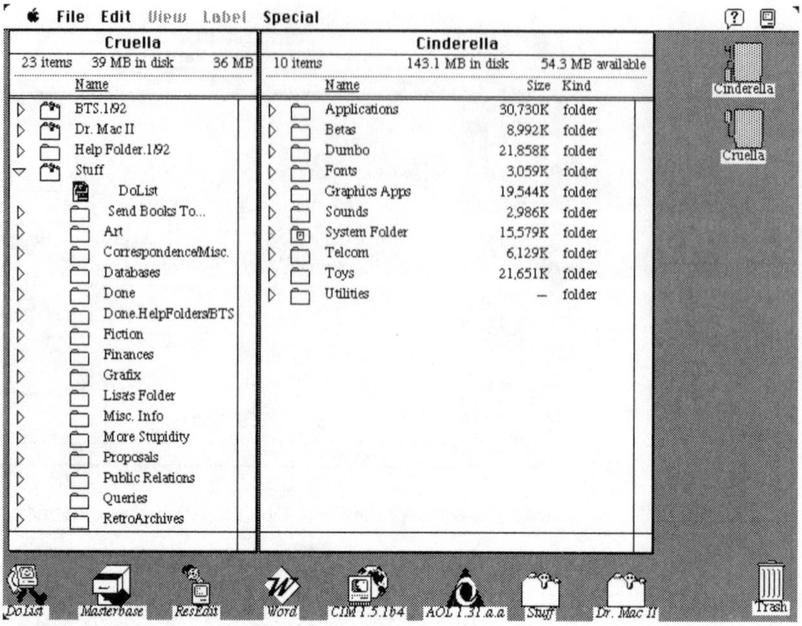

Figure 4–10.   My desktop

All of my data files (documents) are on Cruella. Current projects—things I'm working on this week such as Help Folder 1/92, BTS (Beating the System) 1/92, and Dr. Mac II—are stored at the top level. Everything else goes into one of the folders inside the Stuff folder.

It may not be the most elegant technique in the world, but it works for me. Of course, there are dozens of ways you can organize *your* hard disk. Experiment, and find out what works for you. You may want to combine styles. For example, you could create a folder for each client, then create folders within it for letters, memos, proposals, and so on. Another popular way to keep things organized is to use a file for each month. Within your Letters, Client/Project, and Proposals folders, you would have a folder for each month.

There's no "right" way. Any method that makes it easy for you to find what you're looking for, and back up important files regularly, is a good method.

Whatever method you use to organize your hard disk, you'll probably find it convenient to put frequently used icons (or aliases, if you're using System 7) on the gray desktop. You can see in Figures 4–7, 4–8, and 4–9 (which were originally created for the first edition of this book), and Figure 4–10 (which shows my desktop as it appears these days), that icons for frequently used applications are stored right on the gray desktop area. Here they're easy to find and launch. (Also notice that the icons in Figure 4–10 have their names in italic type because they're aliases.)

Hard Disk Hints and Tips

Choose a Sturdy Surface for Your Hard Disk

If your hard disk is an external model, make sure it is placed on a sturdy surface. If you have an internal hard disk, make sure your Mac itself sits on a sturdy surface. Vibration and shocks can cause the hard disk's head to crash into the spinning disk. You don't want to keep your hard disk (or your Mac, especially one with an internal hard disk) in a place where it's likely to be jarred or bumped.

Have One System and Finder per Hard Disk

Never have more than one System Folder on a hard disk. This is *extremely* important. When you copy applications from the master disk to your hard disk, be careful not to copy the System Folder with the application. Having two or more Systems on a hard disk will cause unpredictable behavior and crashes. Menus may become scrambled, and DAs and INITs will sometimes disappear. That's because you've installed them (or opened them with a utility such as Suitcase II or MasterJuggler) in your System Folder, and now there's another one on the hard disk. If there's more than one System Folder on your hard disk, your Mac won't know which System should be in charge of things.

If you're not sure whether there's an extra System or Finder buried deep within folders on your hard disk, use the Find File DA in System 6, the Find command in System 7, or any desk accessory with a search feature (such as DiskTop) to search for files named System and Finder. If you find more than one, remove all the extra ones and restart your Mac. (See Chapter 1 for more information on removing extra System and Finder files.)

The extra ones are almost certain to be inside another folder. Your real System Folder should always be at root level—that is, at the first level of folders on the disk (as shown in Figure 4–10). If you find a System Folder inside some other folder, it shouldn't be there. For example, in Figure 4-10, if I found a System Folder inside Applications, Betas, Telcom, or any other folder, that would be the one to trash. The one called System Folder with the little System icon on it is the real one.

If you get a message that the file is *In Use* or *Busy* when you try to place it in the Trash, restart and boot from a floppy startup disk. (You can use your Disaster Disk, or any startup disk. Complete instructions for creating a Disaster Disk appear in Chapter 6.) Now you should be able to trash those extra System files.

If you have two hard disks, or if you have partitioned your hard disk, it's fine to have one System Folder on each disk or partition. For example, if you need to have your machine run System 6 some of the time, and System 7 other times, you could install System 6 on one hard disk (or partition) and System 7 on another. Then, to choose between them, use the Startup Disk control panel (called the Startup Device control panel under System 6).

Don't Nest Folders Too Deep

Although the Macintosh allows you to nest folders (that is, place folders within folders) as many levels deep as you like, try not to nest files or folders more than four levels deep. If you have to open four or more folders to get something, it's buried too deep. Create additional folders somewhere else.

If you hate having to double-click your way through folders, as I do, several utilities offer alternate methods of organizing and launching files and folders, a method many power users prefer. (A discussion of file-launching utilities appears in Chapter 10.)

If you're a System 7 user, the problem is less severe, because in list views (such as View by Name), you can see the contents of all folders within one window without having to double-click their icons to open them. (See Chapter 2 for more information on System 7 list views.) Even so, things nested more than five levels deep are inconvenient to get at.

Blessing the System Folder

The System Folder that's in charge of your Mac should show a unique folder icon, which indicates it's the System Folder that is *blessed* (see Figure 4-11).

Figure 4–11.   System Folders blessed and not

If none of the System Folders appear to be blessed, try this little trick with the System Folder that's at the root level:

1. Open the System Folder.
2. Click the System file icon once to select it.
3. Drag the System file icon out of the System Folder (see step 1 in Figure 4–12).
4. Close the System Folder.
5. Drag the System file back into the System Folder (see step 2 in Figure 4-12).

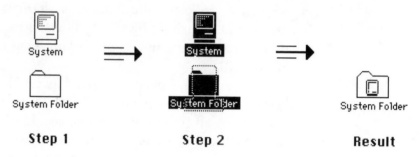

Step 1   **Step 2**   **Result**

Figure 4–12.   Forcing a System Folder to become blessed

Have a Unique SCSI ID for Each SCSI Device

If you have more than one SCSI device, make sure each has a unique SCSI ID number. Every SCSI device has one, and most will allow you to change it. See the manual for your device to find out how to set its SCSI ID (it may also be called a *SCSI address*).

Having two devices with the same ID on the SCSI chain might not damage anything, but it will prevent one or both devices from working. Check to make sure all of your SCSI devices have unique addresses. (See Chapter 6 for more on SCSI IDs and resolving SCSI ID number conflicts.)

Terminate Your SCSI Chain If Necessary

If you have more than one SCSI device connected, make sure your SCSI chain is properly terminated.

Check your owner's manual to find out if your device is internally terminated. External terminators are available from your local Apple dealer. Many hard disk manufacturers include one with the SCSI device. (See Chapter 6 for more information on terminators.)

Changing the Order of SCSI Devices Sometimes Helps

The SCSI chain can even be sensitive to what order devices are connected in. If you have several SCSI devices and are experiencing erratic behavior, one or more devices refusing to mount, frequent crashing when you start up, or even frequent crashing once you're up and running, change the order in which they're connected.

I recently tried connecting several drives to a Mac IIfx, and I found out just how savagely a Macintosh can behave. When I connected them in the order shown in Figure 4–13, I kept crashing at startup. INITs that worked last week, with the same drives hooked up, wouldn't load or would bomb on startup. If the boot process completed, and I actually saw the desktop, almost any action (such as selecting Control Panels from the Apple menu) would cause a System error to occur.

The problem turned out to be the order in which the drives were connected. If they were connected as shown in Figure 4-13, I had horrible problems—my Mac was virtually unusable.

When I reconnected the drives in the order shown in Figure 4–14, everything worked perfectly.

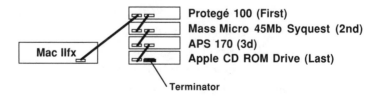

Figure 4–13.   Connecting my SCSI devices in this order caused my Mac to crash

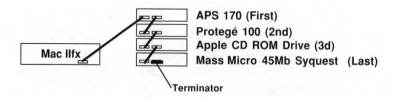

Figure 4–14.   Connected in this order, everything worked perfectly

The moral of the story is that if you have two or more SCSI devices, the order in which they're connected may matter.

This is particularly true if you have a Mac IIfx or newer model. It seems their SCSI busses are even more twitchy than other models—so much so that the IIfx comes with a little form that reads, in part: "If you connect external SCSI devices to your Macintosh IIfx, you must use the new SCSI cable terminator. One of the new terminators is included in the box with your computer. It is black."

And yes, I was using the new black terminator. And I did remove the internal termination from the APS and Mass◊Micro drives (the Protegé and CD-ROM drives have external termination) before firing up the IIfx. Still, I could get the system to work only if the drives were connected in the order shown in Figure 4–14. (APS has since discontinued internally terminated external drives—all of their external drives come with an external terminator these days.)

The Length of Your SCSI Cables Matters

The length of your SCSI cables makes a difference, too. The entire SCSI chain isn't supposed to exceed 18 feet, so you're usually best off using short SCSI cables.

On the other hand, sometimes using a longer cable means the difference between a SCSI chain with several devices working or not. If you're having problems with your SCSI chain, try swapping cables. If you're using a long one, try a short one, and vice versa. Many times this will be all you need to do to get your chain up and running.

Rebuild Your Desktop Periodically

The Macintosh stores an invisible file, called the Desktop, on every disk. The Desktop file is sort of a road map that your Mac uses to keep track of files and folders on that disk. If the Desktop gets bloated with old, obsolete information, or becomes damaged or corrupted in any way, it can slow down your computer. Rebuilding the Desktop guards against these things happening, which is why I consider it routine maintenance and rebuild my Desktop at least once a month whether it needs it or not.

(Detailed information on how and why rebuilding your Desktop is a good idea can be found in Chapter 6.)

Use a Disk Optimizer

Your Macintosh stores your files in pieces on your hard disk. It writes files to any available space on your hard disk, even if that space is not contiguous. As more files are written, different parts of each file are stored in different places on the drive. The drive takes longer to read a file that is written in several places because it has to move its read/write head farther. This phenomenon is called *fragmentation*, and is usually described as a percentage of the total files. So, for example, if 7 percent of the files on your hard disk are written to noncontiguous space, your drive is said to be 7 percent fragmented.

A disk optimizer eliminates fragmentation by taking files that have been written to several different places on your hard disk and rewriting them in a single, contiguous chunk. As a result, your hard disk will run faster, because the amount of head movement has been reduced by putting files back in one place.

In my opinion, the best product for optimizing your hard disk is DiskExpress II. If you're serious about performance, you should optimize your hard disk periodically, and DiskExpress II does the most thorough job of it. Other products rearrange the files on your hard disk and reduce fragmentation, but only

DiskExpress II prioritizes as it optimizes. It's smart enough to write System files and applications to the beginning of the volume, where access is faster. I don't think any other optimizer does that.

The most popular file and disk recovery programs, Symantec Utilities for Macintosh and Norton Utilities for Macintosh, both include a pretty good disk optimizer. (Chapter 6 has more information on both products.)

Important Warning! Never run any disk optimizer unless you have a complete backup of the hard disk you're about to optimize. If the power is interrupted or the Mac is reset while your optimizer is running, the data on your hard disk can be damaged.

Always Turn Off the Mac Properly

Never just reach over and shut off the power on your Mac or peripherals, and never push the programmer's switch unless you're hopelessly crashed.

When you want to turn your Mac off, use the Shut Down command in the Finder's Special menu (see Figure 4-15). For example, if you have a Plus, SE, LC, or Classic:

1. Choose Shut Down from the Finder's Special menu.
2. Wait for the alert that tells you it's okay to turn off your Macintosh safely.
3. Turn off your Mac using the power switch on the back.
4. (Optional) If you have an external hard disk, turn it off now.

Internal hard disks power down automatically when you choose Shut Down.

Mac II users will have little trouble adapting to this: The power-off switch is inconveniently located on the back of the CPU, whereas the power-on switch is on the keyboard. To shut

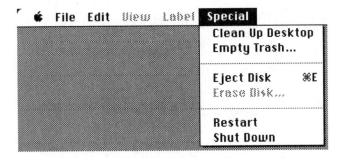

Figure 4–15.   Always use Shut Down or Restart (System 7's Special menu is shown; System 6's looks slightly different)

down a Mac II series computer, just choose Shut Down from the Finder's Special menu. That powers down your Mac, internal hard disk, and monitor.

If you just reach over and turn your hard disk or Mac off without choosing Restart or Shut Down, you run the risk of damaging your directory or Desktop file. Always use Shut Down before turning off a hard disk.

All models of Mac: If you just want to reboot, use the Restart command in the Finder's Special menu. That shuts your computer down momentarily, then starts it back up.

Turn Off the Power Before You Plug or Unplug Cables

Turn off everything before connecting SCSI or ADB (that is, keyboard and mouse) cables. This is a good idea when connecting any type of cable: printer, modem, AppleTalk, and ADB—mouse, keyboard, or trackball. You can do serious damage (such as frying an electrical component or chip) to both your Mac and your peripheral devices if you plug and unplug them with something turned on. If you have more than one SCSI device on the chain, make sure *all* of them are turned off before changing any SCSI connections.

Recommendations

The hard disks I recommend, as well as software for disk management and other products, are listed below.

Hard Drive Manufacturers

There are dozens of manufacturers of hard drives. Many manufacturers include bundles of software, ranging from nothing more than a formatting utility, to a wide range of valuable programs.

Don't take what you read here as gospel. The hard disk manufacturers are always adding products to their bundles, trying to squeeze out a competitive advantage. Before you decide on a hard disk, ask about that bundled software—it can add several hundred dollars in value to your purchase at little or no additional cost to you.

Alliance Peripheral Systems (APS)
2900 S. 291 Highway
Independence, MO 64057
800–223–7550
816–478–8300
Various sizes and prices

Alliance Peripheral Systems is a relatively new mail-order supplier. They have quickly established a reputation for no-frills, fast hard disks, tape drives, and other hardware, at rock-bottom prices. Excellent, fast technical support by toll-free phone.

Warranty: 30-day unconditional money-back; one or two year parts and labor, depending on product.

Apple Computer, Inc.
20525 Mariani Avenue
Cupertino, CA 95014
800–776–2333
408–996–1010
Various sizes and prices

All Apple drives are overpriced, and many are slower than drives from independent manufacturers. About the only thing they have going for them is that they are usually reliable. Because of the price, speed, and warranty differences between Apple and everyone else, I don't recommend Apple drives. Almost any other brand will prove to be a better choice.

Warranty: One year parts and labor.

Micronet Technology, Inc.

20 Mason
Irvine, CA 92718
714–837–6033
Various sizes and prices

Micronet specializes in high-performance hardware. They have a reputation as one of the best and highest-quality suppliers. That's not surprising—Micronet is one of few Macintosh-only developers around. Micronet's president, Charles McConathy, has acquired an excellent reputation among power users for being knowledgeable and pricing his products fairly. Sold only through dealers.

Warranty: One year parts and labor.

Microtech International, Inc.

158 Commerce Street
East Haven, CT 06512
800–325–1895
203–468–6223
Various sizes and prices

Microtech makes a complete line of storage devices—a wide variety of hard disks, plus optical disks, tape drives, and removable hard disks. Available only through dealers.

Warranty: Five years (on many products); call for additional information.

Mail-Order Software and Cables

MacConnection
    14 Mill Street
    Marlow, NH 03456
    800–334–4444
    603–446–7711
    Mail-order discount software and hardware. Mac only.

One of the best resources for software and cables. Offers overnight delivery of most products for $3. If you order before 3:00 AM, you'll get next-day delivery!

Hard Disk Management Software

DiskExpress II
    ALSoft
    P.O. Box 927
    Spring, TX 77383–0927
    800–ALSOFT–1
    713–353–4090
    Approximately $90

The best disk optimizer around. Easily worth the price, if you care about keeping your drives in top shape and coaxing the maximum performance out of them.

DiskTimer II, SCSI Evaluator
Two shareware applications, available from user groups or on-line services, that measure hard disk performance. SCSI Evaluator has more complete tests; DiskTimer II is easier to use and understand.

Symantec Utilities for Macintosh, and Norton Utilities for Macintosh

   Symantec Corporation
   10201 Torre Avenue
   Cupertino, CA 95014
   800–343–4714
   408–252–3570
   Approximately $150 (SUM), $130 (NUM)

Crashed disk and file recovery utilities. Repairs damaged disks, too. Includes numerous handy utilities including a disk optimizer and a fast, flexible file-finding DA.

Summary

A hard disk provides impressive performance improvements and makes life with your Macintosh a lot more convenient. A hard disk will reduce the amount of time you waste each day. There's little question—if you don't already have a hard disk, you want one. If you've never used a Mac with a SCSI hard disk, go out and try one. You won't believe how much faster things go, compared to using floppy disks.

Get the biggest drive you can. You'll be surprised at how quickly you fill up 20Mb. Other things to consider are speed, bundled software, price, and support.

Once you have your drive unpacked and set up, organize it in a way that makes sense to you and that complements the way you work.

Finally, keep your drive healthy. Use the Shut Down and Restart commands, don't plug or unplug cables while the power is on, rebuild your Desktop occasionally, and use an optimizer to keep your hard disk running its best.

In the next chapter, you will discover methods of backing up your hard disks and otherwise protecting your work.

5

Protecting Your Work

Everything you need to know about backing up.

Now that you've learned about hard disks, the next thing you need to do is develop good habits about protecting your valuable work.

Computer equipment, particularly disks and whatever is on them, can fail. Floppy disks ask to be initialized even when you know there is data on them. Hard disks refuse to display their icons in the Finder, or crash every time you mount them. Even the Mac itself can fail. I'd say that most computer equipment is 99 percent reliable. Unfortunately, when it breaks, it's always at the most inopportune and unexpected time.

Which is why backing up was invented. Computers (and hard disks) follow their own kind of Murphy's law—they fail only when you're up against a deadline. Backing up, if you haven't already figured it out, is the process of making copies (backups) of your important files. Restoring, which is the reverse of backing up, is the process of moving files from your backup disk(s) to your working disk or hard disk. Backing up your work protects you from most disasters. Think of it as file insurance. You wouldn't drive without car insurance, would you? Operating your Mac without a reliable backup of your data is almost as dangerous.

Backing up is one of those chores you must remember to do regularly, like brushing your teeth. While both may be inconvenient to do regularly, the consequences of not doing either can be extremely unpleasant. If you don't brush your teeth, they'll rot and fall out; if you don't back up your data, your hard disk will crash and you'll have to re-create all your work.

This chapter will tell you everything you need to know to ensure that your files and disks are safe, no matter what catastrophe should strike.

Why Back Up?

Picture this: You've slaved for days on a project. It's 9:00 in the morning and you're scheduled to present your work in the conference room at 10:00. It's the best thing you've ever done, and you're feeling pretty good as you get ready to print the final draft. You've saved often. Your masterpiece is secure on your hard disk.

All of a sudden, the office lights flicker, then go out for a moment. When the power returns, you hear a comforting "ding" as your Mac comes back to life. You breathe a sigh of relief, but then your heart drops as you stare at the flashing question mark. Your Mac can't tell there's a hard disk connected to it!

After a deep breath, you shut everything off and then restart (powering up the external drive first, to allow it a few seconds to spin up). You cross your fingers as you power up your Mac. Your palms begin to sweat. You haven't backed up in days, and it's now 9:20.

A backup is insurance for your files. If you had backed up your hard disk, you would stride confidently into your presentation. Without a backup—I shudder at the thought.

Backing up can be as simple as copying important files from one disk (hard or floppy) to another in the Finder. This is the easiest and least expensive way to protect your work. Unfortunately, it relies on your remembering to do it, and on your knowing which files need to be backed up. That's a lot to ask, especially if you have a hard disk.

If you're working with floppy disks, the easiest way to back up your work is to end each work session by making a copy of each floppy with data on it. If you want to be really safe, make two copies of anything vital. It's a breeze.

Although backing up floppies is a breeze, backing up a hard disk can be a chore. A large-capacity hard disk can contain thousands of files and folders. Luckily, some utility programs, described later in this chapter, are designed to handle backing up a hard disk with style and grace. With a good backup utility, you can ensure that your files are safe and secure, usually in less than ten minutes a day.

Remember, there are only two kinds of computer users: those who *have* lost data in a crash, and those who *will* lose data in a crash. (I'll probably say that again in the next chapter, but it's that important!) Fortunately, losing data in a crash can be almost painless as long as you have a recent backup. Let's now examine the various backup strategies, as well as the software and hardware available for keeping your work safe and secure.

Backup Strategies

What is the best backup strategy for you? Only you can answer that question. There are lots of ways to back up a hard disk—to a tape drive, removable media such as the Syquest or Bernoulli, or optical drive (each of which acts like a giant floppy disk), or even another hard disk. But even if you can't afford one of these hardware backup devices, you must back up your work. To floppies.

Though there are ways to recover files from crashed hard disks (see Chapter 6), they take time. And they don't always work. I once spent four hours attempting (unsuccessfully, I might add) to recover one important file from a crashed hard disk that hadn't been backed up in several days. I learned a lesson—now I back up my hard disk every night. I even back up twice and keep one of the sets in a different location—in my case, a safe deposit box at the bank. (This is called storing a backup *off-site*. It provides protection against fire and theft, as well as data loss.)

Speaking of which, no matter what your backup technique, storing a backup set off-site is a good idea. If there were a fire or burglary, could your business survive without the contents of your hard disk? Is every copy of your customer list stored in the same room? Some security-conscious firms require backups to be sent off-site every 12 hours, to be stored in fireproof, bomb-proof vaults. That may be overkill for you, but you should at least consider storing a set of backups in another location.

The sections that follow provide some specific backup strategies to use, depending on your hardware and software configuration.

What to Do If You Don't Have Special Backup Software

If you don't have special backup software of some type, I sincerely hope you're not using a hard disk. Backing up a hard disk to floppies without backup software is not a task I'd wish on you.

If you use a hard disk, and if you modify more than a few files a day, you'll have trouble keeping track of which files you've changed and which files need to be backed up. The easiest solution is to consider special software (described later in the chapter) designed to back up your work.

If you don't have backup software, try this: At the end of every day, copy every file you've worked on that day to a backup floppy disk or disks. Here's how:

1. Initialize a floppy disk.
2. Name that disk something meaningful, such as BackupDisk1.
3. Create a new folder on BackupDisk1 and name it Backup-today's date (for example, Backup-1/11/91).
4. Copy all of the documents you've used today from your work disk or disks into the Backup-1/11/91 folder on the floppy disk BackupDisk1.
5. Lock BackupDisk1.
6. Put BackupDisk1 in a safe place.

To be absolutely safe, repeat this process with a different floppy disk. (Call *it* something meaningful, such as BackupDisk1 Offsite.) Then, take this floppy with you wherever you go next. Put it in your car. Or your briefcase. Just store it somewhere other than where you stored BackupDisk1.

Tip

One thing to remember is that floppy disks are magnetic media. That means they're sensitive to magnetic fields. Never store floppies near magnets, or any device that contains magnets. Speakers, for example, contain a magnet.

There's an old story about the guy who couldn't understand why all his floppies were becoming unreadable. It turned out he was storing them by sticking them to the refrigerator with little magnets.

Don't do that!

On subsequent days:

1. Unlock BackupDisk1 and insert it.
2. Create another new folder and name it Backup-today's date and time (for example, Backup- 1/12/91, as shown in Figure 5-1).

3. Copy all of the documents you've used since the last backup from your work disk or disks to BackupDisk1.
4. When you run out of space on BackupDisk1, initialize another floppy, and name it BackupDisk2.
5. Lock all of your backup disks.
6. Put all of your backup disks in a safe place.

Repeat the process with BackupDisk1Offsite to be extra safe, then store BackupDisk1Offsite somewhere offsite.

The key to success using this strategy is to be sure there are two (three, if you use the off-site option) copies of anything important at the end of each work session—one on your work disk or hard disk and another on a backup disk(s). That way, when (notice that I didn't say *if*) an important file becomes damaged, erased, or inaccessible for whatever reason, you calmly reach for your backup copy and continue working.

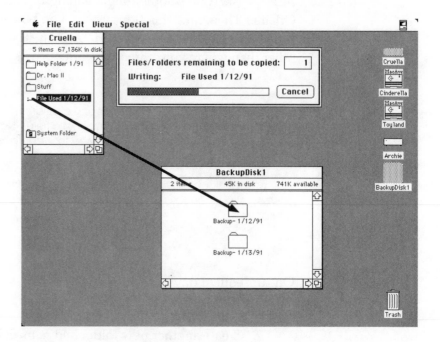

Figure 5–1.   Backing up manually

I caution you: This strategy works only if you're diligent about it. If it seems inconvenient, or like it's too much work, read on. You're a prime candidate for a backup utility that can automate the entire process.

What to Do If You Have a Backup Utility Program

If you have a backup utility program (that is, an application designed to assist you in backing up disks—several are discussed later in this chapter), you can use more sophisticated backup strategies. But first, let me define a few terms you'll need to understand.

Definition

Complete backup—Backup of the entire contents of a disk.

Incremental backup—Backup of only files that have been changed since the last complete or incremental backup.

Backup-style backup—A backup that keeps only one copy of each file in the backup set.

Archive-style backup—A backup that stores all changed versions of each file in the backup set.

All backup software can perform complete and incremental backups. Beyond that, it works one of two ways, either *backup-style* or *archive-style*.

The backup-style creates a complete mirror image of your hard disk the first time you use it. Then, when you perform incremental backups, it replaces files modified since the last backup with the current version. In other words, a backup-style backup set contains only the most recent version of each document. The advantage of this philosophy is that it uses less backup media—usually it means using fewer floppies. The disadvantage is that if you want to retrieve an old version of a document, it won't be in your backup set—only the most recent version will be there.

The archive-style philosophy, on the other hand, adds modified files to the backup set without removing earlier versions. The disadvantage is that you'll need more media—usually more floppy disks. The advantage is that if you decide you liked a document better last week, before you edited it extensively, you can easily find and restore that version. Or, if a file becomes damaged, you can restore an earlier version.

You can usually tell the difference between a program that performs backup-style backups and one that performs archive-style backups—if the program asks you to insert old disks from the backup set, it's probably doing a backup-style backup; if the program asks you to insert new, blank disks, it's probably doing an archive-style backup. Read your manual carefully so you know how your files are being backed up.

Some programs, such as Retrospect, limit you to one style (in its case, archive-style); other programs, such as Redux, allow you to choose between styles.

So it comes down to a choice between safety and convenience. If you're backing up to floppies or expensive removable media (SyQuest and Bernoulli cartridges are not cheap), backup-style saves you time and money. The downside is that there is only one copy of each file in your backup set. Archive-style uses more floppies (or cartridges, or tapes), but lets you restore the most recent version of a file, or any earlier version you choose.

Both backup-style and archive-style backups allow you either to restore your entire hard disk exactly as it was the last time you used the software, or to restore a single file. Some programs, such as Retrospect, even let you restore a group of files that match specified criteria (all files modified since last Monday; all documents; all System files; and so on).

When you first begin your backup regimen, you perform a complete backup. Then, on subsequent days, you perform an incremental backup—the software only backs up files that have been changed since the last backup. If you're using a backup-style program, it replaces the earlier version of the file with the most current version; if you're using an archive-style program, the most current version is added to the backup set (joining all previous versions).

Tip

> Whichever you choose, backup-style or archive-style, one backup set is never enough. If you opt for backup-style, make sure you have several backup sets going simultaneously. If you select archive-style, you still need at least two backup sets to be safe.

Here are three strategies you can use to provide various degrees of protection for the contents of your hard disk. These strategies work regardless of whether you choose backup-style or archive-style backups.

Strategy 1—Maximum Safety and Convenience   Start by performing a complete backup with whatever backup software you've selected. On a 20Mb hard disk this should take under an hour, providing you've initialized all the floppies you'll need first. Now, at the end of each work day, do an incremental backup of the entire hard disk—that is, back up files that have been modified since the last backup. Every backup utility I know of can perform complete and incremental backups automatically. Unless you've made a lot of changes to the files on your hard disk, an incremental backup shouldn't take more than 10 minutes a day. Believe me, it's time well spent.

For maximum protection, alternate between two sets of floppies, always keeping one set offsite. That way, if your office is destroyed by a fire, flood, or other disaster, you'll have everything you need to start working again immediately. Although you'll probably need a new Mac and hard disk, without an offsite backup, not only would you need new hardware, but you would have to re-create everything on your hard disk from scratch. Not fun.

This strategy is the safest because, if your hard disk is damaged in any way, you have two complete backup sets—

applications, System files, and documents—that you can use until your main disk is up and running. The chance of your not having a copy of something in one of the two backup sets is remote as long as you remember to perform your incremental backup each day.

You can color-code the sets and back up to a different set each night. Colored labels are available at most computer or office supply stores. The older set should always be taken off-site at night. That way, if your office is destroyed, you have a complete copy of your hard disk that's no older than one day.

This strategy takes longer than the others, but it ensures that, whatever happens, you have a backup set that's a snapshot (no more than one day old) of your hard disk's contents.

A variation of this strategy is to follow the same regimen but keep only a single backup set. If you elect not to use two backup sets, you might consider taking your backup set with you when you leave the office. Obviously, your level of security is reduced if you keep only one backup set—it's always possible that one or more of the disks in the backup set will become damaged and unusable.

Strategy 2—High Safety, Less-Convenient Crash Recovery
This strategy takes less time than the first—it can reduce the time required to make incremental backups by as much as 50 percent. Using your backup software, follow these steps:

1. Create one backup set of System and Application files only.
2. Then create another backup set and include only documents.
3. To keep both sets current, perform an incremental backup of documents every day, and back up System and application files every week or two.

This strategy saves time, because backup programs decide what to include in an incremental backup based on when the file was last modified. Sometimes certain files—usually applications, System files, or control panels—appear to your backup software as having been modified even if all you did was *use* them. That's because the information in your invisible Desktop file, which is what the backup utility uses to decide which files it should back up, reflects a modification date that is later than the date of your last incremental backup. So they may not really have *changed*, even though your backup software thinks they have.

The reason you can get away with backing up System and application files less frequently is that you *should* have copies of your application and System files on the master disks you keep on your shelf, or better still, in a safe place off-site. If you had to, you could always restore applications or System files from the master disks. Just remember, if you've made any modifications to your System Folder (such as adding fonts, INITs, or other startup items, or changing control panel settings) or to applications (such as updating a user dictionary or changing preferences), and you have to restore the System or applications from the master disks, you'll lose the modifications you made.

Although not as secure as strategy 1, this strategy makes sure the irreplaceable files—your documents—are backed up daily. For added security, you could create two backup sets of each kind—two sets of application and System files and two sets of documents—rotating and storing one set off-site as in strategy 1. You could then rotate the System and application sets off-site once a month and rotate the document sets daily.

Strategy 3—Better Than No Backup Set your backup software to include only documents. (Most backup programs allow this.) Do a complete backup (of only documents) to floppies, then do incremental backups (of only documents) as often as you feel like it.

This strategy assumes that you have copies of your System Folder and applications somewhere on the master disks. Again, if you've made modifications to your System or applications, you'll lose them if you have to restore from your master disks. But at least you'll have all your documents as of the last time you backed up. And that's better than losing everything.

Whatever strategy you adopt, you *must* back up your work. Though hard disks are, for the most part, reliable beasts, they always choose the worst possible moment to die. And although a hard disk can usually be repaired or recovered, that could take hours. Or days. Trust me: Someday it will happen to you. Backing up your hard disk is like dental hygiene—you should feel guilty when you forget it.

Now let's take a look at some of the hardware and software products that make the bothersome-but-essential task of backing up somewhat less painful.

Backup Software

Many disk backup utilities are available. If you own a hard disk and keep anything of any importance on it, you need one. Some hard drives include (bundle) one, and some Apple System software releases prior to System 7 include HD Backup—a bare-bones backup program. Unfortunately, HD Backup is incompatible with System 7 and no update is planned. Apple advises users of HD Backup to purchase third-party equivalents.

If you don't want to spend any additional money, use the utility that came with your drive or, if no utility came with your hard disk, use the drag-copy method I described earlier. (Don't forget, if you use System 6, you can use HD Backup.) Even the generic backup programs that come with off-brand hard disks are better than no backup program at all. Some are just better than others. In a moment, I'll tell you about a couple that I've used extensively and recommend.

All backup software backs up files that have been changed (modified) since the last backup whenever you perform an incremental backup to floppy disks. Backup programs figure this out by checking the last time each file on your hard disk was modified. If you want to know the last time a file was modified, select the file in the Finder and choose Get Info from the File menu. The date and time of the last modification appears in the Get Info window, as shown in Figure 5–2. (See Chapter 2 for more complete information on the Get Info command.)

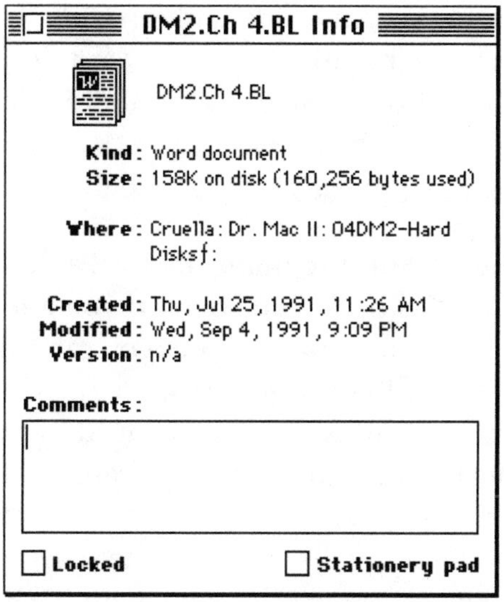

```
DM2.Ch 4.BL Info

        DM2.Ch 4.BL

   Kind: Word document
   Size: 158K on disk (160,256 bytes used)

  Where: Cruella: Dr. Mac II: 04DM2-Hard
         Disksƒ:

 Created: Thu, Jul 25, 1991, 11:26 AM
Modified: Wed, Sep 4, 1991, 9:09 PM
 Version: n/a

Comments:
┌─────────────────────────────────┐
│                                 │
│                                 │
│                                 │
└─────────────────────────────────┘
☐ Locked              ☐ Stationery pad
```

Figure 5–2.   Remember that Get Info shows you the date and time of a file's last modification

A few features are common to every backup program. All of them easily perform the following:

- Complete backup
- Incremental backup
- Backup of selected files
- Complete restore
- Restore of selected files

Other than that, backup utilities differ only in their ease of use, flexibility, and philosophy about how your backup files are stored and catalogued. (Backup programs use an internal technique, called cataloguing, to keep track of where files are stored across a set of backup disks.)

Even if your hard disk came with a utility, you might want to purchase a different one that is better suited to the way you want to protect your work. Although most of the products discussed here are bundled with one hard drive or another, all are also available from dealers and mail-order houses.

Retrospect and Redux

Many fine backup programs are available—Retrospect, Redux, DiskFit Pro, FastBack, and so on. If you already own one and it seems to be working OK for you, you can skip this section.

As for me, I've used Retrospect and Redux successfully for several years. Neither has ever let me down, and both have been continuously updated with new features. In addition, both of their publishers provide excellent technical support. For this reason, I'll limit my discussion to these two programs, which are the only two I can recommend with a clear conscience. This doesn't mean that DiskFit and FastBack (or other programs) are not good, it merely means that I haven't had the opportunity to test them as thoroughly.

Retrospect is a pure archiving program. It always keeps old versions of changed files in the backup set. With Retrospect, when you perform an incremental backup, no files are deleted from the backup disks; instead, your backup set contains multiple versions of all modified files.

Redux can back up or archive. You can decide, on a file-by-file basis, what is to be backed up and what is to be archived. For files that are to be backed up, Redux asks you to insert the specific disk from your backup set on which the changed file resides, then replaces the old version with the new. So rather than keeping a backup set that's an archive of every version and revision, as Retrospect does, Redux keeps a backup set that's a mirror image of your hard disk as of the last incremental backup. Unless you say otherwise.

If you use Redux backup-style (no archiving), a 20Mb drive will never use more than about twenty-six 800K floppies to back up. With Retrospect, you have to keep adding disks to your backup set.

Both programs allow you to back up to floppies, other hard disks, or removable media such as SyQuest or Bernoulli cartridges. Only Retrospect can back up to tape drives. (I'll talk about backup hardware devices in a minute.)

Both are easy to use. Just launch the program, then click a few buttons. If you want a complete backup, there's almost nothing else to do; if you want to choose specific files to back up, that's also easy (see Figures 5–3 and 5–4).

If you don't already own a backup program, you'd be well served to consider Redux or Retrospect. Retrospect has somewhat more sophisticated searching features, especially when you

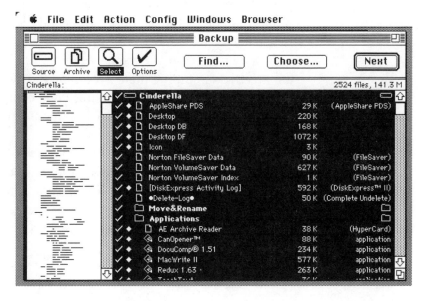

Figure 5–3.   Retrospect is easy to use and provides a complete set of options

🍎 File   Edit   Preferences   Windows   Backup   File List

	Backup: Cinderella			
	2,861 items checked	142 MB to back up		2 disks
Begin Backup	✓ 📁 **Name**	**Size**	**Modified**	**Kind**
Cancel	☑ ▷ 📁 Move&Rename	zero K		folder
	☑ 📄 AppleShare PDS	29K	9/4/91	System f
View by folder ▼	☑ ▷ 📁 Applications	29,892K		folder
	☑ ▷ 📁 Betas	13,194K		folder
Show all items ▼	☑ ▷ 📁 Desktop Folder	11K		folder
	☑ ▷ 📁 Dumbo	21,856K		folder
	☑ ▷ 📁 Fonts	2,944K		folder
----- LEGEND -----	☑ ▷ 📁 Graphics Apps	18,494K		folder
+ New	☑ 📄 Icon	3K	5/9/91	document
≠ Changed	☑ 📄 Norton FileSaver Data	89K	9/5/91	FileSaver
− Deleted	☑ 📄 Norton VolumeSaver Data	626K	9/5/91	FileSaver
( ) Postponed	☑ 📄 Norton VolumeSaver Index	1K	9/5/91	FileSaver
📋 Kept	☑ ▷ 📁 Sounds	2,990K		folder
🗑 Trashed	☑ ▷ 📁 System Folder	13,708K		folder
	☑ ▷ 📁 Telcom	5,679K		folder
	☑ ▷ 📁 Toys	19,899K		folder
	☑ ▷ 📁 Trash	zero K		folder
	☑ ▷ 📁 Utilities	12,434K		folder
🗑	☑ 📄 [DiskExpress Activity Log]	592K	7/20/91	DiskExpr
	☑ 📄 ●Delete-Log●	50K	9/5/91	System f

Figure 5-4.   Redux is also easy to use

need to restore a single file from a huge backup set. Redux is somewhat easier to use, and significantly less expensive. Retrospect works with most tape drives; Redux doesn't. Retrospect can launch itself at a designated time, and perform a backup unattended (assuming there's room on the media you're backing up to). If you don't mind leaving your computer on all night, and you have room on your backup media, this may be the best reason of all to choose Retrospect.

If you're backing up to floppies, you'll probably prefer Redux. If you're backing up to another hard disk or a removable cartridge drive, either one is a fine choice, though only Redux offers your choice of backup-style or archive-style backups. If you're backing up to tape, choose Retrospect.

Using Backup Software

In general, you take the following steps to perform either a complete or incremental backup, regardless of the program you're using:

1. Launch the program.
2. Choose any available options that you want, such as complete backup, incremental backup, or back up selected files.
3. Choose the appropriate command, or click the appropriate button, to begin the backup process.
4. Insert disks one at a time as the program directs you. If you're performing an incremental backup, the program asks for new disks to be added to the set as needed.

If you're backing up to another hardware device, a hard disk, removable cartridge, or tape, you won't have to perform step 4.

One piece of advice: Whatever program you use, read the documentation carefully. These programs have many options, and if you accidentally choose the wrong one, you could accidentally instruct the software not to back up important files.

Tip

If you're backing up to floppies, be sure to have a stack of blank floppies (or floppies that can be overwritten) available during the backup process. The program will alert you to the number of new backup floppy disks you will need before you start. Keep them at hand, along with a set of blank labels so you can identify the backup disk number as you are backing up. Labeling backup disks with the backup disk number is a timesaver if or when you need to restore files to your working or hard disk.

Backup Hardware

If you own a large hard disk, you're not going to enjoy backing up to floppy disks for long. When your budget allows, you'll probably want to look into a high-capacity (anything larger than a floppy) backup device—tape, Bernoulli, SyQuest, optical disk, or even another hard disk.

With the exception of tape drives, you can use all of these devices as an additional on-line storage device, meaning that you can use them as you would another external hard disk to store files. All you need is at least one extra cartridge.

Tape Drives

One of the most popular backup devices is the tape drive. These devices back up your information by reading it from your hard disk and recording (writing) it to something similar to an audio-cassette tape. Tape drives come in cases of various sizes and shapes and are usually no larger than a hard disk. Most come with backup software of their own, though many are bundled with Retrospect. Some are available as combination units, with hard disk and tape drive combined in one case, but I don't recommend this configuration. It seems cost-effective, but if one component—tape or hard disk—should fail, you're without both until repairs are completed.

Tape drives have backup capacities of anywhere from 40Mb to 5 gigabytes (1 gigabyte = 1,000Mb). One of the most popular models is the 150Mb, which can back up as much as 150Mb to a single tape. If you have an 80Mb hard disk, you can use Retrospect's unattended backup feature to have your hard disk backed up at night. A future version of Redux is rumored to include timed backups as well.

APS makes a good 150Mb tape drive, and bundles a copy of Retrospect with it for under $600. Additional tapes run approximately $20.

The coolest, fastest, highest capacity tape drives are called DAT (Digital Audio Tape) drives. A single tape can hold up to 2.6 gigabytes. This is what I use, and I give it my highest recommendation if you can afford it. APS has several models for under $1,500, and all of them include Retrospect.

With tape drives, as with most mass-storage and backup hardware, the higher the capacity, the more expensive the drive.

The cost of tapes varies, but the most commonly used varieties run about $20 each. So backing up even a large hard disk usually requires no more than a tape swap or two, and shouldn't cost more than $40 (2 @ $20 per 150Mb tape) for media. It sure beats 70 or 80 floppy swaps! If you have a DAT drive, one 1.3-gigabyte tape may last all year (though I recommend you only use a tape for a few months before retiring it).

Prices (like prices for most computer hardware) are dropping, and may be significantly lower by the time you read this. A tape backup system may be the most cost-effective way to protect your data.

The biggest drawback of using tape as a backup medium is that you can't use it for anything but backing up. With any other type of removable media, you can use one set of cartridges/disks for backups and another for everyday storage. Having any of these devices connected to your SCSI chain is like having an extra hard disk. You can boot from them and store applications or documents on them. If you can do it with your hard disk, you can do it with a removable-media drive. And when the drive gets full, you slap in another cartridge/disk. Though removable media are usually more expensive than tape, this additional measure of functionality more than makes up for the difference in price.

Although tape drives are one of the least expensive backup solutions, you may prefer removable media because they can also be used as an additional storage device. Think of removable media as giant, fast floppy disks.

Removable Media

Optical Drives   Two relatively new technologies you might like to explore are 650Mb and 128Mb removable optical disks, sometimes called *REOs*. I have no hands-on experience with either, but I have seen them demonstrated at numerous trade shows. I expect they will become more popular—indeed, even become as common as hard disks are today—when prices decrease and their reliability is proven.

Optical drives use a laser beam to read and write to a disk that looks a lot like a CD (compact disk, like what you listen to music on).

Optical drives are presently quite expensive, over $4,000 for a 650Mb model and over $2,000 for a 128Mb.

The 650Mb drives use large cartridges, about 5 inches across; the 128Mb drives use little cartridges, about the size of a floppy disk but slightly thicker. REO drives perform slower than hard disks when used as a primary storage medium. Still, with their huge capacities, they may be an attractive option for backing up large hard disks, especially if the price comes down a bit.

Again, prices may be significantly lower by the time you read this.

SyQuest Drives   These devices are essentially removable hard disks. They use cartridges that contain a platter almost exactly like the ones used in hard disks. The difference is, these are removable; they are encased in a sealed plastic cartridge.

Removable SyQuest drives have proven themselves to be almost as reliable as hard disks. In addition to using them for backups, you can just insert a different cartridge and use it as you would use a hard disk. They're not only great for backing up quickly; they're every bit as useful as a fixed hard disk when they're *not* backing up.

Many companies have products that use the same guts: a 44- or 88Mb removable mechanism manufactured by SyQuest (hence, the name). So the units available are similar. SyQuest 88s sell for about $1,000; SyQuest 44s around $500. Additional cartridges are around $130 and $70 respectively.

I've been using a Mass Microsystems 44Mb SyQuest drive for several years now and have had few problems with it.

Removable SyQuest drives are great both for backup and for everyday use as a hard disk. In fact, if you purchase two of them, you may not need a hard disk at all. You can back up from one drive to another, and you'll have 90Mb of hard disk storage available when you're not backing up. And it's so fast! Backing up a 20Mb hard disk takes less than six minutes, and a complete backup from one 88Mb cartridge to another only takes about 10 or 15 minutes.

By the way, SyQuest 88s can read, but not write to SyQuest 44 cartridges. So if you have a SyQuest 44, you can upgrade to an 88 and still be able to read your old cartridges.

Bernoulli Drives Bernoulli drives are similar to SyQuests, but they are only manufactured by a company called Iomega. They also use a removable cartridge that looks a bit like a giant floppy disk encased in a hard shell that holds 90Mb of data. These drives use a fluid dynamics principle called the Bernoulli effect, which gives them excellent protection against head crashes.

The 90Mb Bernoulli drive, like the SyQuest drives, is about as fast as a hard disk. I've used one for a few months and it's proven to be trouble-free in my limited testing.

Prices for Bernoulli drives and media are somewhat lower than those of comparable 88Mb removable SyQuest drives. The downside is that they are available only from Iomega, so there's no price competition between vendors as there is for SyQuests.

Tape versus Removable

You'll be well served by any of these products—a tape drive, optical drive, SyQuest 44 or 88, or Bernoulli 90. Removables offer the added convenience of an additional "hard disk" on line when you're not backing up; tape drives are somewhat less expensive than removable media; and tapes are significantly less expensive than removable-media cartridges. Shop around and get the device that best suits your needs and your budget.

Recommendations

Being sure your data is safe can involve both hardware and software. Here are my recommendations:

Backup Software

DiskFit Pro

> Dantz Development
> 1400 Shattuck Avenue, Suite 1
> Berkeley, CA 94709
> 510–849–0293
> Approximately $125

An excellent backup utility—almost as nice as Redux.

FastBack II

> Fifth Generation Systems
> 10049 N. Reiger Road
> Baton Rouge, LA 70809
> 800–776–7283
> 504–291–7221
> Approximately $190

A fast archive-type backup utility that uses a proprietary floppy disk initialization technique. Backups are fast, and backups to uninitialized disks are particularly speedy.

HD Backup

Apple Computer, Inc.
20525 Mariani Avenue
Cupertino, CA 95014
800–776–2333
408–996–1010
Mac models: All (not compatible with System 7)

HD Backup is a no-frills backup utility that is included with some Apple System software releases prior to System 7.

Redux

Microseeds
5801 Benjamin Center Drive #103
Tampa, FL 33634
813–882–8635
Approximately $100

Backup-style or archive-style backups with ease and elegance. If you're backing up to floppies, this is probably your best choice; if you're backing up to removable media, it still may be your best choice. Excellent, intuitive interface, and great technical support.

Retrospect

Dantz Development
1400 Shattuck Avenue, Suite 1
Berkeley, CA 94709
510–849–0293
Approximately $250

Tape Drives

Alliance Peripheral Systems (APS)
>   2900 S. 291 Highway
>   Independence, MO 64057
>   800–223–7550
>   816–478–8300
>   Various sizes and prices

Bernoulli Drives

Iomega Corporation
>   1821 West 4000 South
>   Roy, UT 84067
>   800–777–6649
>   801–778–3000
>   Various configurations and prices

Iomega is the manufacturer and inventor of Bernoulli hardware.

45Mb Removable SyQuest Drives

Alliance Peripheral Systems (APS)
>   2900 S. 291 Highway
>   Independence, MO 64057
>   800–223–7550
>   816–478–8300
>   Various sizes and prices

Mass Microsystems
>   810 W. Maude Avenue
>   Sunnyvale, CA 94086
>   800–522–7979
>   408–522–1200
>   Various sizes and prices

Manufacturer of a wide variety of mass storage and video products.

Laser Drives

Pinnacle Micro
Pinnacle Micro
19 Technology Drive
Irvine, CA 92718
800–553–7070
714–727–3300
REO–650 (650Mb Removable Erasable Optical drive):
Approximately $4,000
Additional 650Mb cartridges: Approximately $230

Summary

Don't underestimate the necessity of backing up. It is something you must get used to doing on a regular basis. The best thing to do is set up a routine that provides you with the degree of protection you need, and stick to it. Think about what might happen if your hard disk crashed and everything on it was destroyed. A few minutes a day, and you'll never worry about it.

If you need more convenience and speed than backing up to floppies provides, consider another backup medium. Tape is relatively inexpensive but can't be used as a hard disk between backups; removable media can, but the cartridges are significantly more expensive than tapes.

Some people buy a second hard disk the same size as the first and back up from one to another. This is fast—about the same transfer rate as from a 4Mb SyQuest to/from a hard disk. Considering how quickly hard disk prices are dropping, this may be a cost-effective solution.

Still, I love my APS DAT drive. I leave my computer on at night, and have Retrospect back up both of my hard disks while I sleep. It's fast, the tapes are inexpensive, it's reliable, and each tape can hold months of backups. It's even better on a network. DAT tape is what you buy when nothing but the best will do.

In the next chapter, you'll learn what to do when your system doesn't work, and what to do when it crashes (besides being thankful you made regular backups).

6

File and Disk Recovery

What to do when disaster strikes.

You may be thinking "I can skip this chapter; all my disks work fine." That would be a big mistake. You should take several simple pre-cautions to make recovering files or disks easier if disaster should strike. Remember what I said in the preceding chapter: There are only two kinds of computer users: those who have lost data in a crash, and those who will lose data in a crash.

File and disk recovery is what you need to know when things go bad. The worst possible nightmare of any computer user is losing data, which is generally what you can expect if your files or disks crash.

Now that you know a little about the Mac, the next thing you should learn is what to do in an emergency, preferably before one strikes. What kind of emergency? Glad you asked. In this chapter, you'll learn what to do in these cases:

- *If you see a flashing question mark when you start your Mac*
- *If a disk that used to be good decides it is no longer a Macintosh disk, and asks if you want to initialize it*
- *If your Mac starts crashing for no apparent reason*
- *If you get the dreaded* An application can't be found for this document *message when you try to launch a MacWrite document, even though you know you have a copy of MacWrite on your hard disk*
- *If your internal Mac clock goes haywire*
- *If your Chooser has memory lapses and can't remember its settings*

This chapter is designed to guide you through any heart-stopping problems you might encounter, and it also includes sage advice for avoiding a catastrophe. So don't skip over it just because you don't need it right this second. I can guarantee that a few minutes spent reading this chapter will save you hours someday.

The best insurance, of course, is having good backup habits. But inevitably, no matter how carefully or often you back up your important files, you'll someday need to recover a file that, for whatever reason, wasn't backed up. There are consultants, and even whole companies that do nothing but attempt to recover data from other people's disks. But even the most skilled file and disk recovery artists don't succeed every time. Some files and disks just can't be recovered. Fire and theft also make recovery impossible. The point is, a recent backup, preferably kept off-site, is the only thing that can bail you out of serious trouble (see Chapter 5).

So now that I've terrified you into keeping a backup off-site, let's talk about file and disk recovery. (Besides, there's a whole chapter on protecting your work.) Someday you'll need to recover a file or disk, no matter how prudent you are about backing up. You're about to learn every trick in the book. You'll be ready.

Making a Disaster Disk

A System error, often called a system crash or bomb, occurs when your Mac freezes up or you see a dialog box containing a bomb icon. When you crash, you are almost always forced to restart your Mac, losing any work you've done since you last saved your document(s).

There's no way of telling what caused a System crash, but they happen with depressing frequency. One frequent cause is an INIT or CDEV conflict; another is a poorly written program.

Tip

If you experience a System error every time you perform a specific action, call the vendor of the software immediately.

Sometimes after a System crash, your hard disk won't come back up properly, or your startup floppy disk won't start up. Don't despair. You can do a couple of things if you experience a crash, and I'll get to them soon.

But first let's talk about the things you can do when you have a problem with a floppy or hard disk that won't boot or asks to be initialized.

With a little bit of advance planning, you can create a floppy disk, which I call a *Disaster Disk*, that will go a long way toward getting damaged disks up and running.

I call it a Disaster Disk because it's the first thing you reach for in case of disaster. Your Disaster Disk is your first line of defense in the event your hard disk or floppy disk crashes. Creating it takes only a few minutes and can save you hours of frustration someday. Essentially, you're creating a startup disk with disk recovery tools on it. Complete instructions for creating your own Disaster Disk follow.

Creating Your Disaster Disk

To begin with, you need a copy of the Apple System software disks, for System 6 or System 7. (Information on obtaining System software disks can be found in Chapter 1.)

System 6 with 800K floppy drive(s)

1. Make a copy of the Macintosh System Tools disk (it came with your Apple System software disks).
2. Name the copy Disaster Disk.
3. Drag everything but the System Folder and Apple HD SC Setup to the Trash.

In most cases, the files you'll trash will be Installer, TeachText, Read Me, and Installer Script.

4. Copy the file Disk First Aid from the Macintosh Utilities Disk 1 to your Disaster Disk.

Disk First Aid is a program supplied by Apple with System software releases. It can automatically repair minor damage to disks.

5. Select Disk First Aid and make Disk First Aid the startup application. To do this: Select Disk First Aid on the Disaster Disk by single-clicking it, and choose Set Startup from the Special menu. A dialog box opens to confirm your choices (see Figure 6–1).

If you have a third-party (non-Apple) hard disk, drag HD SC Setup to the Trash, then copy the initialization software that came with your hard disk to your Disaster Disk. Every hard disk comes with software to initialize the disk and install drivers. Apple's is called HD SC Setup; Alliance Peripheral Systems (another hard disk manufacturer) calls theirs Alliance Power Tools. The initializing software is usually supplied on a floppy disk with its own System and Finder. Copy only the utility itself to your Disaster Disk. (You should already have a System and Finder on your Disaster Disk—you copied them from the System Tools disk a minute ago.)

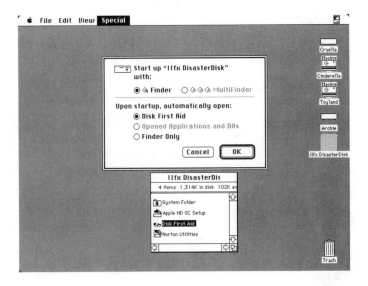

Figure 6–1.   The Set Startup dialog box in System 6, confirming that Disk First Aid is the startup application

System 6 with SuperDrive(s)

1. Initialize a fresh 1.4Mb disk and name it Disaster Disk.
2. Copy the System Folder and Apple HD SC Setup from your Macintosh System Tools disk (it came with your Apple System software disks) to your Disaster Disk.
3. Copy the file Disk First Aid from the Macintosh Utilities Disk 1 to your Disaster Disk.

Disk First Aid is a program supplied by Apple with System software releases. It can repair minor damage to disks automatically.

4. Select Disk First Aid and make Disk First Aid the startup application. To do this: Select Disk First Aid on the Disaster Disk by single-clicking it, and choose Set Startup from the Special menu. A dialog box opens to confirm your choices (see Figure 6–1).

If you have a third-party (non-Apple) hard disk, drag HD SC Setup to the trash, then copy the initialization software that came with your hard disk to your Disaster Disk. Every hard disk comes with software to initialize the disk and install drivers. Apple's is called HD SC Setup; Alliance Peripheral Systems (another hard disk manufacturer) calls theirs Alliance Power Tools. The initializing software is usually supplied on a floppy disk with its own System and Finder. Copy only the utility itself to your Disaster Disk. (You should already have a System and Finder on your Disaster Disk—you copied them from the System Tools disk a minute ago.)

System 7 with 800K floppy drive(s)

1. Make a copy of the Macintosh Disk Tools disk (it came with your Apple System software disks).
2. Name the copy Disaster Disk.
3. Restart your Mac with the Disaster Disk in a floppy drive.
4 Select Disk First Aid and make Disk First Aid the startup application. To do this: Select Disk First Aid on the Disaster Disk by single-clicking it, and choose Set Startup from the Special menu. A dialog box opens to confirm your choices.

If you have a third-party (non-Apple) hard disk, drag HD SC Setup to the trash, then copy the initialization software that came with your hard disk to your Disaster Disk. Every hard disk comes with software to initialize the disk and install drivers. Apple's is called HD SC Setup; Alliance Peripheral

Systems (another hard disk manufacturer) calls theirs Alliance Power Tools. The initializing software is usually supplied on a floppy disk with its own System and Finder. Copy only the utility itself to your Disaster Disk. (You should already have a System and Finder on your Disaster Disk—you copied them from the Disk Tools disk a minute ago.)

Note: The Disk Tools disk (and now, your Disaster Disk) boot under System 6.0.x. System 7 is too big to use from floppy disks.

 System 7 with SuperDrive(s)

1. Initialize a fresh 1.4Mb disk and name it Disaster Disk.
2. Copy the System Folder, Apple HD SC Setup, and Disk First Aid from your Macintosh Disk Tools disk (it came with your Apple System software disks) to your Disaster Disk.

Disk First Aid is a program supplied by Apple with System software releases. It can repair minor damage to disks automatically.

3. Select Disk First Aid and make Disk First Aid the startup application. To do this: Select Disk First Aid on the Disaster Disk by single-clicking it, and choose Set Startup from the Special menu. A dialog box opens to confirm your choices.

If you have a third-party (non-Apple) hard disk, drag HD SC Setup to the trash, then copy the initialization software that came with your hard disk to your Disaster Disk. Every hard disk comes with software to initialize the disk and install drivers. Apple's is called HD SC Setup; Alliance Peripheral Systems (another hard disk manufacturer) calls theirs Alliance Power Tools. The initializing software is usually supplied on a floppy disk with its own System and Finder. Copy only the utility itself to your Disaster Disk. (You should already have a System and Finder on your Disaster Disk—you copied them from the Disk Tools disk a minute ago.)

Note: The Disk Tools disk (and now, your Disaster Disk) boot under System 6.0.x. System 7 is too big to use from floppy disks.

Using Disk First Aid

Now, the next time you start your Mac using the Disaster Disk, it will open automatically to Disk First Aid instead of opening to the Finder as it normally would.

That's all there is to it. If you used a 1.4Mb floppy, use any remaining space on your Disaster Disk for Disk Clinic from SUM II (Symantec Utilities for Macintosh), Norton Utilities for Macintosh, or Microcom 911 Utilities—all are excellent file and disk recovery programs, described later in this chapter. If you have a Mac with a SuperDrive, try using a 1.44Mb disk, as I did in Figure 6-1—everything I need fits with room to spare. The 1.4Mb floppy I used to create the IIfx Disaster Disk was big enough to hold my System, Finder, and Disk First Aid, plus the formatter for my internal hard disk (Apple HD SC Setup) and Norton Utilities—a 600K file and disk recovery program.

Now test your Disaster Disk to make sure it works:

1. Choose Shut Down from the Finder's Special menu.
2. Insert your Disaster Disk in the internal floppy drive.
3. Turn on your Mac.

If you get a happy Mac face, and Disk First Aid launches itself, your Disaster Disk works. If not, repeat the steps above using a fresh floppy disk.

Once you've established that your Disaster Disk works, lock it, put it in a safe place, and hope you never need it. (To lock a floppy disk, just slide the little plastic tab upward until you can see through the little hole, as shown in Figure 6-2.)

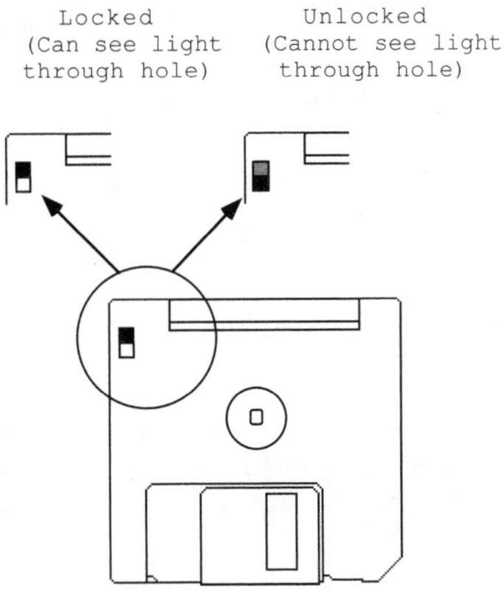

Locked
(Can see light
through hole)

Unlocked
(Cannot see light
through hole)

Figure 6–2.   Locked floppy disk

Disk Recovery

You should know a few things before you get down to the nitty-gritty of recovering programs and data.

First, this chapter discusses several techniques for recovering crashed disks. Although I assume you're working with a hard disk, all of these methods can be used successfully to recover a floppy disk.

Second, these aren't just recovery tools. This chapter is worth reading even if you've never crashed a disk. Sometimes you can detect trouble brewing through warning signals your Mac gives you. For example, you know you're heading for trouble if your Mac bombs more often than usual, or if everything seems to be slow (saving, quitting, opening, and so on). Or if the menus don't seem to work quite right, or programs and/or DAs quit unexpectedly. Or if you get the old *An application can't be found for this document* dialog box, and you're trying to open a MacWrite document when you know darn well you have MacWrite on the hard disk. (This dialog box often appears when your disk or invisible Desktop or directory files are damaged. You'll find out more in a minute.) If you experience any of these warning signs, the first thing you should do is copy any important and unbacked-up files to another disk. Then restart your Mac.

Definition

> *Bomb* is named for the icon in the dialog box you see when your System crashes. Also used to refer to the crash itself: "I was working on my resumé when my Mac bombed."

That's so important I'm going to say it again: *If you experience any of these warning signs—your Mac bombs more often than usual, everything seems to be slow, the menus don't seem to work quite right, programs and/or DAs quit unexpectedly, or you get the old An application can't be found for this document message—the first thing you should do is copy any important and unbacked-up files to another disk. Then restart your Mac.*

Restarting your Mac closes all open files, including invisible files such as the Desktop, properly. It also clears out the RAM in your Mac, allowing it to start up fresh, with no garbage in it.

Tip

> Here's a bit of power-user voodoo for you: A lot of strange behavior can be fixed by nothing more complicated than a simple restart of the Mac. When a friend calls you over to show you that his Mac is doing something strange, save any open documents, then choose Restart from the Special menu. Half the time, it'll come back up and be fine. He'll think you're a genius.

What to Do When Your Hard Disk Doesn't Boot

In the old days, starting up a computer required you to toggle several switches on the front panel, which began an internal process that loaded the operating system. The process became known as *bootstrapping* (later shortened to *booting*), as a reference to "pulling yourself up by the bootstraps," which is what the computer would do when the right switches were toggled.

Today, *boot* refers to the process of starting up your computer. (Some people also use it to indicate starting up an application: "So I booted up Excel and….")

The first thing to remember if your hard disk won't boot is not to panic. I've had problems with dozens of hard disks in my day, and only once was all the data on the disk lost. In every other case either I or somebody else was able to recover everything or almost everything on the disk. So no matter what the symptoms, and even if your backup is old or nonexistent, don't panic.

You've probably done it already, but take a moment to double-check all the cables and power cords. Shut down all of your equipment and unplug and replug all the cables. Remember, stay calm. If it can be fixed, we'll fix it.

Power up the Mac with your Disaster Disk in the internal floppy disk drive (see the earlier section on Disaster Disks). (Don't forget to turn on the hard disk first if it's an external model.) Remember, you've set Disk First Aid to be the startup application on the Disaster Disk, so instead of starting in the Finder, you'll start in Disk First Aid. At this point, one of four things will happen:

- *Situation 1*—Nothing happens.
- *Situation 2*—The Mac boots, but asks if you want to initialize your hard disk (for heaven's sake, say no!).
- *Situation 3*—The Mac boots and, using the Drive button in Disk First Aid, you can see the Disaster Disk but not the hard disk. Because the Disaster Disk is the only disk available, the Drive button is grayed out (see Figure 6–3).

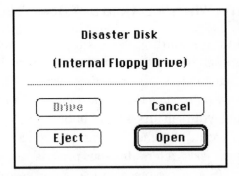

Figure 6–3.   Disk First Aid with only the Disaster Disk available (Note: Drive Button *is* dimmed)

- *Situation 4*— The Mac boots and, using the Drive button in Disk First Aid, you can see the Disaster Disk and the hard disk. In Figure 6–4, clicking the Drive button would allow you to select either the Disaster Disk (left) or the hard disk (right).

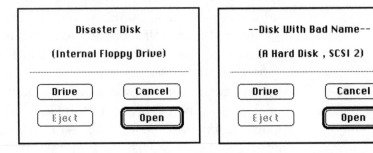

Figure 6–4.   Disk First Aid with two disks available (Note: Drive Button *is not* dimmed)

What to Do in Situation 1 If you power up or restart your Mac with the Disaster Disk in the internal drive and nothing happens, you may have a serious hardware problem. Before you panic, try another startup disk—it's possible your Disaster Disk had a disaster of its own. If, after turning everything off and disconnecting the hard disk, you're still seeing a blank screen, a sad Mac icon, or a flashing question mark, and/or if you hear a series of tones when you try to boot with several different startup disks, your Mac itself needs repairs. Take your Mac to an Apple dealer.

There are a variety of reasons for this situation, including dead disk drives, a chip or board gone bad, or a failed power supply. If you can't get your Mac to do anything at all, there's no way you can troubleshoot any further; it needs to be taken in for service.

What to Do in Situation 2 If you power up or restart your Mac with the Disaster Disk in the internal drive and the Mac boots, but asks you if you want to initialize your hard disk, for heaven's sake, say no! Initializing the disk would make recovery much more difficult, if not impossible. There are still a few tricks you can try. If you can, try each of the fixes listed on the next few pages in turn. Whatever you do, don't initialize your hard disk yet!

In most cases, the hard drive is fine, but its directory, Desktop, hard disk driver, or boot blocks may be damaged. All of these problems can be fixed, usually with little or no loss of data.

Before I go any further, a few definitions are in order.

Definition

Directory usually refers to one or both invisible directory files on every disk: the Volume directory, which contains information about the disk itself, and the File directory, which contains information about the files stored on the disk. The message *This disk is damaged* usually indicates a damaged directory.

The *Desktop* is an invisible file (meaning you can't see or modify it without special tools) on every Mac disk that contains important information for the Finder about the files on that disk.

Definition

> A *driver* is a little piece of software required for communication with a peripheral device. In this case, it refers to the driver that is installed with the initialization application that came with the hard disk. This driver tells the disk how to interact with the Mac. If the driver becomes damaged, as it can from a crash or power interruption, it can cause your hard disk to crash or refuse to mount or boot.
>
> *Boot blocks* are pieces of information written to your hard disk that help the computer pull itself by its bootstraps, by providing information that your Mac's internal read-only memory (ROM) uses to start your computer. Among other information, the boot blocks identify the filing system used on the disk, the names of important system files, the maximum number of files that can be open at once, and so on.

What to Do in Situation 3 or 4   In these situations, when you power up or restart your Mac with the Disaster Disk in the internal drive, the Mac boots and, using the Drive button in Disk First Aid, you can see the Disaster Disk only (situation 3) or both the Disaster Disk and the hard disk (situation 4). Go through the steps outlined in the next section, Recovery Magic. Take these steps one at a time, trying to reboot from your hard disk between each step.

Again, the hard drive is probably fine, but its directory, Desktop, hard disk driver, or boot blocks may be damaged. All of these problems can be fixed, usually with no loss of data.

Recovery Magic

When you need to recover programs and/or data on a hard disk, try the steps below, in the order given. After each step, try rebooting from your hard disk. If rebooting works, you're finished. If it doesn't work, move on to the next step. In general, the steps are as listed below. Complete details for each procedure follow.

1. Repair the disk with Disk First Aid.

2. Install new hard disk drivers.

Drivers are small bits of information your hard disk's initialization software places on the hard disk. These drivers tell it how to interact with your Mac.

3. Rebuild your Desktop.

The Macintosh stores invisible files called the Desktop on every disk it manages. Under System 7 it stores two Desktops—Desktop DF and Desktop DB. These invisible files keep track of what's stored where, and which applications are available for opening documents. Rebuilding the Desktop purges it of unneeded information and often fixes disk problems.

4. Replace your hard disk's System and Finder.

The System and Finder are particularly susceptible to corruption since they are always running when you crash. If your hard disk mounts but you can't boot from it (that is, if you can see its icon in the Finder when you boot from another startup disk, but your Mac won't start up from it), a damaged System or Finder may be the problem.

5. Zap your PRAM/check your batteries.

PRAM stands for Parameter RAM—a small amount of internal RAM, maintained by battery, that keeps your Mac's clock running and stores things such as serial (modem and printer) port configurations. Some of the more obvious signs of PRAM problems are when your Mac clock doesn't work correctly and when the Chooser forgets settings.

6. Resolve INIT/CDEV conflicts.

As INITs and CDEVs are loaded into memory at boot time, they may conflict with one another.

7. If you have more than one SCSI device, check your terminators, and resolve any SCSI ID conflicts.

The SCSI bus allows up to six devices to be daisy-chained to your Mac, communicating at speeds far faster than the modem, printer, or ADB ports allow. Each must have a unique ID number.

Terminators are little devices that help prevent noise and strange behavior on the SCSI bus. You almost always need to plug a terminator into the last unoccupied cable connector in the SCSI chain. External terminators should be available from your local dealer.

8. If your hard disk still won't mount: Use SUM II (Symantec Utilities for Macintosh), Norton Utilities for Macintosh, or Microcom 911 Utilities.

Attempt to Repair the Disk with Disk First Aid Your Disaster Disk is set to start up to Disk First Aid. Power up your hard disk (if it's an external one), then restart your Mac with the Disaster Disk in the internal drive. After the booting procedure is complete, Disk First Aid will launch. Click on the Drive button. If you see your hard disk's name, or a disk called Disk With Bad Name, as shown in Figure 6-5, it's your hard disk. Click the Open button.

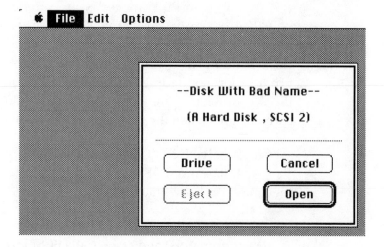

Figure 6-5.   Disk First Aid showing a damaged hard disk

This should bring up the screen shown in Figure 6–6. Choose Repair Automatically from the Options menu. In the dialog box, click Start.

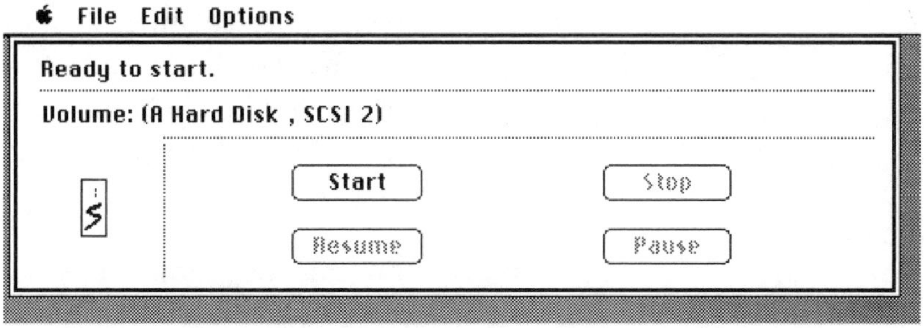

& **File   Edit   Options**

```
Ready to start.
..................................................
Volume: (A Hard Disk , SCSI 2)
..................................................
                 ┌──────────────┐        ┌──────────────┐
  ┌──┐           │    Start     │        │    Stop      │
  │ ⁝│           └──────────────┘        └──────────────┘
  │S │           ┌──────────────┐        ┌──────────────┐
  └──┘           │   Resume     │        │   Pause      │
                 └──────────────┘        └──────────────┘
```

Figure 6–6.   Disk First Aid ready to begin repairs

You'll probably get some kind of message like *Repair Successful, No Repair Needed,* or *Unable to Repair Disk.* In any case, quit Disk First Aid and reboot.

If that didn't fix whatever was wrong, or if you couldn't locate your hard disk by clicking the Drive button, don't worry. Try installing new drivers next.

Install New Drivers Drivers are small bits of information your hard disk's initialization software places on the hard disk. These drivers tell it how to interact with your Mac. If they become damaged, as they can from a crash or power interruption, they can cause your hard disk to crash or refuse to mount. That's why you're going to try to replace them now. This procedure is nondestructive; it won't harm the data on your drive.

Most hard disks come with software used to both initialize and install new drivers. Be careful that you only write new drivers. *Do not initialize the hard disk!*

Don't get confused. The application that comes with most hard disks is capable of many functions. Two of those functions are installing new drivers and initializing. You're only interested in installing new drivers and should be careful *not* to initialize your hard disk accidentally.

Here's how to install new hard disk drivers:

1. If you haven't done so already, quit Disk First Aid and launch your hard disk's initialization program. The Disaster Disk should still be the startup disk.
2. Determine whether the initialization software can "see" your hard disk.

How you do this depends on which hard disk you're using. In Figure 6–7, you can tell that the software *sees* Cruella, my internal hard disk (SCSI ID 0).

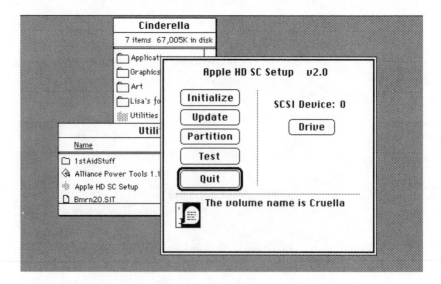

Figure 6–7.   Updating the drivers on an Apple internal hard disk

3. Take one of these two steps:

• If the software *can* see your hard disk, follow the instructions in your hard disk manual for installing drivers (sometimes called *writing* or *updating* drivers). It's usually a simple procedure—one or two mouse clicks. In Figure 6–7, you would simply click the Update button. But be careful: If you don't have a manual and are not absolutely certain what to do, call your hard disk manufacturer for technical support. And once again, do not initialize the disk.

- If the software *can't* see your hard disk, or you can't select its icon using Disk First Aid or your hard disk initialization software, see the section later in this chapter entitled "If Your Hard Disk Still Won't Mount."

4. Quit the hard disk software and try rebooting from your hard disk by ejecting your Disaster Disk from the internal drive and choosing Restart from the Special menu.

If writing new drivers didn't fix it, try rebuilding your Desktop.

Rebuild Your Desktop The Macintosh stores invisible files, called the Desktop, on every disk. It keeps track of what's stored where, and which applications are available for opening documents. As you might guess, the Desktop file for a hard disk with thousands of files can be huge. A large Desktop file slows down a lot of things, such as quitting to the Finder. The Desktop isn't a very good housekeeper either—it sometimes retains information about files that have long since been deleted. This excess information makes the invisible Desktop file grow even bigger. Large Desktop files also have a tendency to become corrupted or damaged over time, which can lead to System crashes or disks that won't mount (that is, whose icons won't appear in the Finder).

If you want to get an idea of how much space your invisible Desktop file is taking up, you can use any utility (for example, DiskTop, miniDOS, FileStar, or ResEdit) that allows you to view invisible files. Figure 6-8 shows DiskTop displaying my Desktop. The insert, which shows the smaller size of 127K, is after I rebuilt the Desktop.

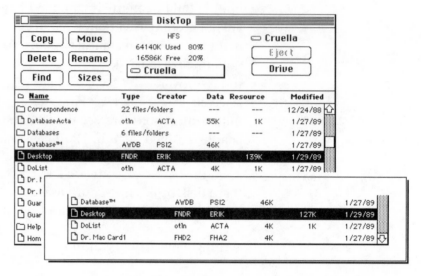

Figure 6–8.   Invisible Desktop file before and after rebuilding

By the way, there's a chance here for confusion. The gray area in the Finder (or the patterned area if you've used the Control Panel to change it) is commonly referred to as the *desktop*. The invisible files created by the Finder to keep track of where things are are also called the *Desktop*. Throughout the book I've used the capitalized version to refer to the invisible files stored on your disks and the lowercase version to refer to the gray desktop area on your screen.

If you can get your hard disk to mount, and you can see its icon on the Finder's desktop, you should try to rebuild your invisible Desktop file. You should also rebuild your Desktop any time things start acting weird—when quitting to the Finder takes *way* too long or when it takes too long to see your hard disk icon at startup time. I consider rebuilding the Desktop preventive maintenance. If my Mac crashes twice in the same day, the first thing I do is rebuild my Desktop.

The only ill effect of rebuilding your Desktop is that you'll lose the comments in the Get Info windows of everything on the disk (see Figure 6–9). I find it a small price to pay. If you're really in love with the idea of commenting icons, DiskTop has a feature called CE Comments that allows you to store comments that will survive a Desktop rebuilding. Personally, I don't use this feature, but I know people who do. You can find out more about DiskTop in Chapter 10.

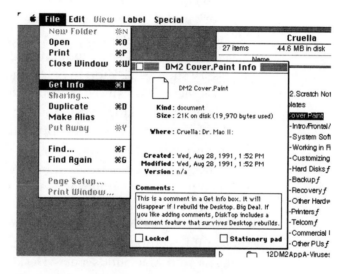

Figure 6–9.   A Get Info window with text typed in the Comments area

If you can get a disk to mount (that is, if its icon does appear in the Finder), you can rebuild its Desktop. Here's how:

- Start your Mac while holding down the Command and Option keys. For every disk that mounts, you'll get a dialog box that asks, *Are you sure you want the Desktop rebuilt on the disk 'Your Hard Disk'? This may take a few minutes.* (You'll see whatever you've named the disk instead of Your Hard Disk.) Click OK. That's all there is to it. Your Mac will whir and spin for a few minutes, then you'll have a brand-new, slimmed-down Desktop. This technique works with System 6 and System 7.

If you use System 6 and don't use MultiFinder, there are two other ways you can rebuild your desktop:

- *Rebuild Desktop 2*—Quit any application while holding down the Command and Option keys. You'll get the same dialog box as described above. This technique does *not* work under System 7, or if you are running under MultiFinder in System 6.
- *Rebuild Desktop 3*—Use a Finder replacement desk accessory such as DiskTop to delete the Desktop. Because these DAs can see invisible files, you can select and delete the Desktop easily. You can't do this while in the Finder; you must be in an application or you'll get a *File is Busy* message. In System 6, you'll also get a *File is Busy* message if you're running MultiFinder. So you must be running an application, and you must be in the Finder, not the MultiFinder, mode.

    When you use DiskTop to delete the Desktop file and then quit DiskTop and the application, there will be a delay as your Mac builds a new Desktop file. The length of the delay depends on the number of files, but the watch cursor will tell you that your Mac is still working. This technique does *not* work under System 7, or if you are running under MultiFinder in System 6.

Now restart your Mac and let it try to boot from the hard disk (remove your Disaster Disk from the internal drive). If you're still unable to boot from the hard disk, try replacing your System and Finder.

Replace Your Hard Disk's System and Finder Crashes (and gremlins) can cause your System or Finder to become damaged or corrupted.

Definition

Corrupted is the term given to a file that has been damaged or scrambled in some way and is no longer capable of functioning properly. Corruption is usually the result of a crash (System error) or power interruption. Any file can become corrupted—documents, applications, System files, desk accessories, fonts, and so on; but the System and Finder are particularly susceptible to corruption, since they are always running when you crash. If your hard disk mounts but you can't boot from it (that is, if you can see its icon in the Finder when you boot from another startup disk, but your Mac won't start up from it), a damaged System or Finder may be the problem. Fortunately, it's easy to install a fresh, uncorrupted copy of your System and Finder.

If you haven't already done so, quit Disk First Aid and return to the Finder. Remember, every time you boot from your Disaster Disk you'll be in Disk First Aid and will have to quit it to get back to the Finder.

Next, open the System Folder on your hard disk and select the System and Finder files. Drag them to the Trash.

Tip

You must trash your System and Finder. If your System or Finder is damaged and you don't trash them before performing the next step—installing new System software—there's a good chance this procedure won't work.

Restart your Mac with the System software disk that contains the Apple Installer (System Tools for System 6.0.*x*; Install 1 for System 7) in your internal floppy disk drive. Go through the procedure for installing System software on your hard disk.

Now restart your Mac and let it try to boot from the hard disk (remove the System Tools or Install 1 disk from the internal drive). Don't forget, if you've installed fonts, sounds, or (System 6 only) desk accessories in your old System file, you'll have to replace them now from a backup copy of your System.

If you're still unable to boot from the hard disk, try zapping the PRAM or resolving INIT conflicts. And, if you have more than one SCSI device, you may need to resolve ID conflicts or add or remove an external terminator. These techniques are described in the next sections.

Zap Your PRAM/Check Your Batteries Your Mac has a small amount of internal RAM, known as Parameter RAM (PRAM), that keeps your Mac's clock running and stores things such as serial port configurations and printers you've selected with the Chooser.

Definition

> *Serial ports* provide serial communications used for connecting peripherals to your Mac. The printer and modem ports are serial ports. A serial port is slower than the SCSI port.

Some of the more obvious signs of PRAM problems are when your Mac clock doesn't work right and the Chooser forgets its settings. If either of these things happens to you, try zapping the PRAM, as follows:

- *PRAM zap for Mac 512 and Plus*—Turn off your Mac and disconnect the power cord. Now remove the battery; it's in a little door on the back of your Mac. After about 10 minutes, replace the battery. This works because the battery provides power to the PRAM when the Mac isn't powered up.

  That's it. It's been zapped! If the trouble continues, try a new battery.
- *PRAM zap for Mac SE, SE/30, II, IIx, and IIcx running System 6*—Because your battery is soldered into place, you'll use a different but no less physically taxing technique. Hold down the Option, Shift, and Command keys while you choose Control Panel from the Apple

menu. That finger contortion will result in a dialog box asking if you really want to zap the PRAM. Say yes.

- *PRAM zap when running System 7*—Restart your Mac with any startup disk—your hard disk, your Disaster Disk, System Tools disk (System 6), or Install 1 (System 7)—and hold down the Command, Option, P, and R keys. You must be pressing this key combination before you get to the Welcome to Macintosh screen. There's no confirming dialog; the PRAM is just zapped.

With the exception of Date and Time, all system-wide preferences are reset by zapping parameter RAM (PRAM). If you've changed the settings of any of the following, you'll probably have to reset them manually:

- 32-bit addressing
- Brightness
- Highlight color
- Cursor blink rate
- Menu blink count
- Keyboard repeat rate and repeat delay
- Disk cache size
- Monitor settings and location of extra monitors
- Mouse tracking and double-click speeds
- Beep sound
- Startup disk choice

The Date and Time settings are read out of PRAM before it is zapped, then written back in afterwards.

If that doesn't fix it, you may need to replace your Mac battery. (All Macs newer than the Macintosh SE have their batteries soldered to the logic board, so if you suspect battery failure and have tried zapping your PRAM several times, see your dealer.)

Zapping your PRAM may help even if your hard disk doesn't mount. Now restart your Mac and let it try to boot from the hard disk (remove your Disaster Disk from the internal drive).

Resolve INIT/CDEV Conflicts   At this point, you've replaced your System and Finder, rebuilt the Desktop, and zapped the PRAM, but you still can't boot from the hard disk. The next thing to consider is an INIT or CDEV conflict. As these startup items are loaded into memory at boot time, they may conflict with one another.

In most cases, you can use quite a few INITs, CDEVs, and other startup items simultaneously. At present, I have about 30 all running together in perfect harmony. However, occasionally a conflict occurs that prevents your hard disk from booting.

When you have such a conflict, every time you start up your Mac with the offending items in your System Folder, you crash or hang at exactly the same point in the startup process. Because most startup items draw their icons on your screen at startup, you can sometimes identify the culprit by looking for the icon that appears immediately before the crash or hang.

Under System 7, you can quickly figure out if an INIT or CDEV is to blame for your problem by turning all extensions off. To do this, restart your Mac and hold down the Shift key until you see the message *Extensions Off*. (If you use a custom startup screen, you won't see this message. Hold the Shift key down until the gray desktop appears.)

Even if you can't identify the culprit by its icon at startup, you can resolve startup item conflict by following these steps:

1. Boot from your Disaster Disk.
2. Quit Disk First Aid and return to the Finder.
3. Create a new folder on your hard disk, name it My Startup Items, and place it somewhere convenient, yet out of the System Folder.

The idea is to remove all of the startup items, INITs, and CDEVs from your System Folder. If you use System 7, you'll have to remove them from the Control Panels and Extensions folders as well. If they're in *any* folder but the System Folder (or the Control Panels or Extensions folders under System 7) at startup, they won't be activated.

 4. Open the System Folder on the hard disk.

If you suspect that the trouble is being caused by a specific startup item (remember what I said about watching the icons at boot time), drag that item out of the System Folder and into the My Startup Items folder. If you're not sure which item is causing the problem, drag every one of them out of your hard disk's System Folder and into the My Startup Items folder.

System 7 stores most startup items in special folders—INITs are usually found in the Extensions Folder; CDEVs are usually in the Control Panels folder. Some INITs or CDEVs may also be loose in the System Folder itself.

If you're using System 6, which does not organize INITs and CDEVs in separate folders, you may find it helpful to view the contents of the System Folder By Kind for this operation. This groups your INITs and CDEVs. (Remember, INITs are called Startup documents; CDEVs are called Control Panel documents.) You'll probably have to scroll down to see the Startup documents. I've got more than 100 files in my System 6 System Folder, so I have to scroll down quite a way to get at mine, as you can see in Figure 6–10.

 5. Eject your Disaster Disk and restart your Mac, allowing
    it to boot from the hard disk.

If that procedure worked, you had a conflict. To find out which item was causing the problem, drag them back into the System Folder one at a time, restarting each time you add one. At some point, the hard disk won't boot. Just remember the last startup item you added, and put it anywhere but your System Folder. It's the culprit. It conflicts with something else, probably another INIT or CDEV, on your hard disk. You will either have to live without it, or keep experimenting until you figure which item it conflicts with so that you can remove that one instead.

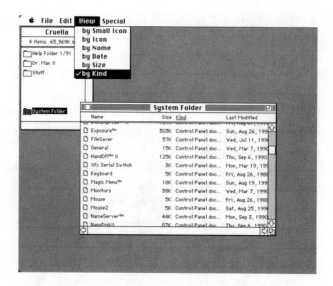

Figure 6–10. In System 6, CDEVs appear as Control Panel documents when you view By Kind

Another thing you can try is to rename the conflicting INIT or CDEV. Try names that begin with *a* or *z*. (QuicKeys 2 would become either aQuicKeys 2 or zQuicKeys 2.) This works because INITs and CDEVs are loaded in alphabetical order. Often, two items that conflict with their original names can be tamed by changing the order in which they are loaded.

Under System 7, the loading order is as follows:

- Items in the Extensions folder (in alphabetical order)
- Items in the Control Panels folder (in alphabetical order)
- Items loose in the System Folder (in alphabetical order)

Finally, a couple of utilities are useful in just this situation. One is called INITPicker, from Microseeds; another is called Startup Manager, and is part of the Now Utilities package. Both let you turn on or off any of your startup items, and set up groups of items you can select on the fly at startup time. You still have to reboot for the changes to take effect, but it sure beats dragging INITs and CDEVs in and out of the System Folder one at a time.

If You Have More Than One SCSI Device: Check Your Terminators A SCSI device is one that connects to the Mac via the SCSI port. The SCSI port is a parallel communications port that provides high-speed data access for hard disks, tape backup systems, printers, and other SCSI devices.

A couple of things can go wrong when more than one SCSI device is connected. First, there's the terminator issue. Terminators are little devices that help prevent noise and strange behavior on the SCSI bus. They look like the 25- or 50-pin plug you find on a SCSI cable, but they have no cable attached. Because almost all SCSI devices have two cable connectors to allow daisy-chaining (linking several peripherals sequentially), you plug the terminator into the last unoccupied cable connector in the SCSI chain. External terminators should be available from your local dealer. (Refer to the *Owner's Guide* that came with your Macintosh model for more information on SCSI devices, ports, and terminators.)

Definition

In this case, *bus* refers to the hardware used to connect peripherals or other computers—the cables and connectors. *Bus* can also be used to refer to hardware that transfers information between different components inside the computer, such as NuBus, 030 Direct, 020 Direct, PDS, or Apple Desktop Bus.

Some devices, such as most internal hard disks, have their own internal terminator. Others require an external terminator. Here are the rules for terminators:

- If you have more than one SCSI device connected, there must be a terminator at each end of the SCSI chain.
- There should be no more than two terminators on the SCSI chain—one at the beginning (usually an internally terminated hard disk) and one at the end of the chain.

- If you have only one device connected, it should be terminated.

Check the owner's manual of your SCSI device to find out if it is internally terminated.

Once you've verified proper termination on your SCSI bus, remove your Disaster Disk from the internal drive, and restart your Mac, allowing it to boot from the hard disk.

Another thing to try if you suspect a problem in your SCSI chain is to use a different cable. Some experts believe that using longer or shorter SCSI cables reduces the likelihood of failure on the SCSI chain. (The camps are evenly divided between longer and shorter.) If you can't think of any other reason you're having a problem, you might try a longer or shorter cable. I've been surprised by how often it helps.

Even if you decide to use one or two longer SCSI cables, it's best to keep the total length of your SCSI chain as short as possible. If the farthest device is more than 20 feet from your Mac, you may have problems.

If You Have More Than One SCSI Device: Check for SCSI ID Conflicts Another problem you may encounter with multiple SCSI devices is the dreaded SCSI ID conflict. This occurs when two devices are assigned the same SCSI ID number.

The Macintosh allows you to connect up to six external or internal SCSI devices. Each can be assigned an ID number (don't use 7 or 0; they're reserved for the Mac itself and for an internal hard disk, respectively). Some devices (SuperMac hard drives, for example) allow you to select the SCSI ID number using software; others require you to set DIP switches, thumb wheels (a small wheel with numbers on it that you use by turning it with your thumb to select SCSI ID numbers for some SCSI devices), or push buttons. Again, consult your owner's manual for details.

The Doctor's
Opinion

DIP switches are an archaic torture device, dreamed up by cheap hard disk (and scanner) manufacturers to save a few cents. Usually they are six or eight little, tiny, up/down switches that you have to set in a particular pattern—1 up, 2 up, 3 down, 4 up, and so on—to change the SCSI ID, for instance. Of course, the switches are minuscule—just try to manipulate them with something bigger than that ultimate in Mac hardware utilities: a straightened paper clip. DIP switches are almost as hateful as internal termination.

In Figure 6–11, which shows my SCSI bus using a shareware CDEV called SCSI Probe, you'll see that my SCSI chain consists of the following:

SCSI ID	Drive
0	Apple 80 internal hard disk (manufactured by Quantum)
4	Protegé 100 hard disk (manufactured by Quantum)
5	Mass◊Microsystems 45Mb removable (manufactured by SyQuest)
6	Alliance Peripheral Systems (APS) 170 hard disk (manufactured by Quantum)
7	The Macintosh itself

The Doctor's
Opinion

Note that SCSI Probe lets you see who manufactures the disk itself—it's rarely the company whose name is silkscreened onto the front of the drive. Quantum disks are popular, and with good reason—they're fast and reasonably priced. I've used many Quantum drives over the past few years, and have had little trouble with any of them.

Had both the Protegé and APS devices been assigned the same ID—say, SCSI ID 4—there would be a conflict on the SCSI chain. The Mac would refuse to boot until I disconnected the SCSI devices or changed the ID number of one or both. The key point is that no two SCSI devices can be assigned the same ID number.

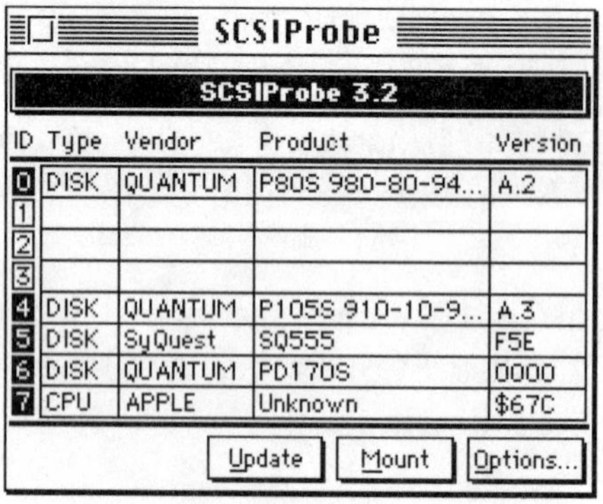
SCSIProbe
SCSIProbe 3.2
ID Type Vendor Product Version
0 DISK QUANTUM P80S 980-80-94... A.2
1
2
3
4 DISK QUANTUM P105S 910-10-9... A.3
5 DISK SyQuest SQ555 F5E
6 DISK QUANTUM PD170S 0000
7 CPU APPLE Unknown $67C
Update
Mount
Options...

Figure 6–11. The SCSI Probe CDEV showing that I have three external SCSI devices at addresses 4, 5, and 6

Once you've verified that every device on your SCSI bus has a different ID number, remove your Disaster Disk from the internal drive, and restart your Mac, letting it try to boot from the hard disk.

Your Mac will attempt to boot from the startup device with ID 0 first (Apple internal drives are shipped set to ID 0), unless there's a startup floppy in one of the drives. Of course, if there's a startup disk in a floppy disk drive, the floppy drive automatically becomes the startup device.

The Mac ROM looks for a startup disk in the following places, in this order:

- Internal floppy disk drive
- Second internal floppy disk drive
- External floppy disk drive
- Internal SCSI hard disk (Mac waits 15 seconds for the internal drive to warm up)
- External SCSI hard disk (if more than one, in descending order by SCSI ID number)

- Internal hard disk (Mac returns to this drive and waits another 15 seconds)

Definition

> *ROM* stands for read-only memory, the nonvolatile memory that resides on a chip inside your Mac. The ROM contains important parts of the Macintosh operating system, and it cannot be erased or changed.

If, after looking in all those places, the Mac doesn't find a startup disk, you will see a flashing question mark on your screen while your Mac waits for a startup disk to be inserted into a floppy drive.

My Mac boots from the Apple internal drive because it is numbered 0. If I wanted to start up from the APS, I would open the Startup Device control panel (it's called Startup Disk under System 7) and select that disk. Of course, the APS drive would need to be a startup disk, with a System Folder, or the Mac would continue looking in the SCSI chain until it found a valid startup disk.

If you don't use the Startup Device control panel to select another device, your Mac will boot from the startup device (a device with a System Folder) that has the highest ID number.

If Your Hard Disk Still Won't Mount If none of the steps so far has gotten your hard disk to mount, there are still things you can try. Norton Utilities for Macintosh, Symantec Utilities for Macintosh (SUM II), or Microcom 911 Utilities can sometimes recover the contents of a disk even when it won't mount. They may even be able to repair it under certain circumstances.

Another option, assuming you have a complete backup and your hard disk's initialization software recognizes the hard disk, is to try to initialize the disk and restore it from your backup.

Otherwise, more drastic measures are called for. At this point, decide whether it's more important to get the disk running again, or more important to recover the data on the disk. Before doing anything further, check around with consultants, dealers, user groups, and data recovery specialists like DriveSavers. It's usually less expensive to fix the drive without attempting to recover the data (another plug for good backup habits), so ask around.

File and Disk Recovery Software

Several programs—Symantec Utilities for Macintosh, Norton Utilities, and Microcom 911 Utilities—can be invaluable in recovering disks and files that can't be recovered using the techniques in this chapter. They're relatively inexpensive, and they provide an additional level of insurance against downtime due to a crashed disk or damaged file. Don't wait until disaster strikes to get a copy of one of these products. They all contain special software you can install now that makes it easier to recover files in case of a crash later.

SUM II (Symantec Utilities for Macintosh) An excellent product, SUM II makes it easy to recover deleted or trashed files from hard or floppy disks. You can often recover an accidentally initialized hard disk. The SUM II package includes three different file-recovery programs, a hard disk optimizer, a fast floppy copier, a partitioning utility, a backup program, and a disk and file editor. (Figure 6-12 shows the Disk Clinic recovery program in action.)

Definitions

An *optimizer* rearranges files and defragments sectors on a disk for maximum speed. A *partition* is a division of hard or floppy disk space into multiple, separate virtual disks, allowing you to use each partition as if it were a separate disk.

This is a first-class collection of utilities, and one you shouldn't wait to buy. It's so useful in emergencies, Apple should probably include it with every Mac! (Several hard disk manufacturers do bundle it with every hard disk they sell.) About the only thing SUM II can't do is recover an initialized floppy (that is, one that has been completely erased or has had its contents replaced with the contents of another disk, as happens when you drag the icon of one floppy onto the icon of another in the Finder).

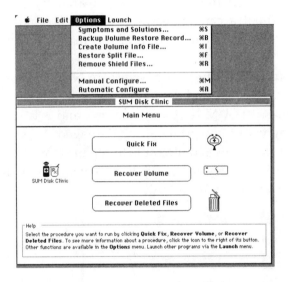

Figure 6–12.   SUM II's Disk Clinic guides you through the recovery process

SUM II requires a small bit of advance planning on your part, though. For maximum effectiveness, you need to drag SUM II's Shield INIT into your System Folder. Next, reboot and follow the simple instructions in the manual, which creates two invisible files that assist SUM II in recovering damaged disks and files. It's painless and takes only a couple of minutes. The manual's instructions are excellent, and the few minutes you spend preparing your hard disk with SUM II will be time well spent.

Shield INIT is a startup document that is active every time you start your computer (as long as it's in the System Folder). It updates the invisible files you created when you first installed it, making it easier for SUM II to recover files and disks after a crash. Since I installed Shield INIT, I've had occasion to use SUM II to recover files. In every case it's been the easiest, fastest, and most painless method I've ever used. Don't wait until it's too late—installing the INIT today could allow you to recover your disk more easily tomorrow.

Even though SUM II is extremely easy to use, give the manual a careful reading. It's possible to damage files when attempting their recovery if you're not sure what you're doing.

Norton Utilities for Macintosh Norton Utilities is another outstanding file and disk recovery program with features similar to those of SUM II. It's easy to use, and it is successful at recovering your files and repairing damaged disks more often than not. It diagnoses and attempts to repair damaged disks with a single click (see Figure 6-13). It also includes a disk optimizer and several other useful utilities.

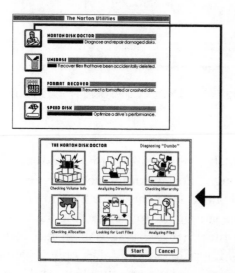

Figure 6-13.   Norton Utilities is easy to use—just click on the Disk Doctor icon, then click Start and your hard disk will be analyzed and repaired automatically

Symantec purchased Peter Norton Computing, and it is presently marketing both SUM II and Norton Utilities for Macintosh. I suspect the two products will someday be merged into one. Don't worry. Either one is an excellent choice; a merged package will be even better.

The Microcom 911 Utilities The Microcom 911 Utilities used to be called 1st Aid Kit (not the same as Disk First Aid which comes with Apple System software). It is another excellent recovery program.

An added bonus is that 911 seems to be better than SUM II or Norton Utilities at extracting text from damaged word processor or page layout files. This can be a lifesaver. Even though you lose the formatting, you won't have to retype the words. And 911 requires no advance preparation. It works fine even if you don't unwrap it until you have a need for it. You'd be missing out if you didn't at least glance through the 300-page manual, which is so detailed it could serve as a textbook for file and disk structure and recovery.

Furthermore, 911 even comes with precrashed sample disks for the tutorial. Though SUM II may provide more features, 911 does a better job of explaining what you're doing and why.

Microcom 911 has several exclusive features. Complete Undelete is a CDEV that, once installed, lets you undelete files quickly and easily through its control panel settings. Also, 911 is the only disk utility that includes virus protection—it comes with the popular Virex program. (See Appendix A for more information about viruses and virus protection programs.)

The Doctor's Opinion

If you're sitting out there with a crashed disk, you'll probably have the most success with Microcom 911 Utilities. If your disks are running perfectly, but you'd feel safer if you had additional protection, I recommend Norton Utilities. It's the easiest to use, and seems to be successful more often than not.

On the other hand, all three products work well, and you'll be in good shape no matter which you choose.

Something to Try When You Crash

Here's a little trick you can try when your Mac crashes (that is, when you get a System error).

Most Macs come with a little piece of plastic called the *programmer's switch* (among those that don't—the Classic, LC, IIsi, and PowerBook). Although the Macintosh *Owner's Guide* warns that it's for use only by programmers, that's not necessarily true. It can be a timesaver for anyone. It came in the box with your Mac; install it according to the directions in documentation that came with your Macintosh. If you can't find it, an Apple dealer may sell you one.

On compact Macs (Plus, SE, SE/30) and full-size Mac IIs (II, IIx, IIfx), the front switch is the reset switch; the rear switch is the interrupt switch.

On the Mac IIcx and IIci, these switches are installed on the lower left side of the front panel, under the Apple logo. The left switch is the reset switch; the right switch is the interrupt.

The reset switch works the same as turning your Mac off and back on with the power switch. If you need to restart your Mac after a crash or freeze, you can push the reset button instead of turning the power off and on.

The interrupt switch can sometimes return you to the Finder after a crash, if you follow the steps listed below. (By the way, the interrupt switch really *is* a programmer's switch. They use it to escape from crashes, too.)

Technically, you're invoking the Mac's built-in debugger when you press the interrupt switch. Typing the suggested sequence into the debugger window (as shown in Figure 6–14) can sometimes allow you to recover from an otherwise hopeless System crash.

I find it's occasionally worth the effort to try this trick, especially if you're running System 6 under MultiFinder or System 7. Even though you will usually lose any unsaved work in the application you were working in when the crash occurred, you may be able to save work in other applications you have open. For example: Let's say you're running Multi-Finder, have documents open in MacWrite and MacPaint, and crash while working in MacWrite. Press the interrupt switch and type the sequences in the next section. If it works, and you're returned to the desktop, you will probably be able to go back into MacPaint and save your work. You'll lose any unsaved work in MacWrite, but at least you will have saved something.

The method given in the next section works only with certain kinds of System errors. There's no way to tell beforehand whether it's going to work; but if you've crashed, you might want to give it a try.

Crash Recovery

In the event of a crash or freeze, press the interrupt switch. It sometimes brings up an empty box with a caret (>) prompt. If it does, try typing the following:

SM 0 A9F4 <Carriage Return>

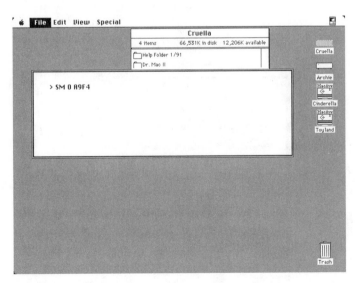

Figure 6–14.   Recovering from a System error (crash) after pressing the interrupt switch

The zeros in this line and the next one you'll type are all numeric 0 (zero). Type the characters exactly the way you see them, spaces and all (see Figure 6–14).

After the carriage return, the box fills with characters, but the first line and prompt remain blank. Type:

G 0 <Carriage return>

That's all there is to it. If it works, you'll be returned to the Finder. If it doesn't work, you'll either get another bomb dialog box, or the box will fill with characters. In either case, press the reset switch to reboot.

Using this trick leaves your Mac in an unstable state—it will probably crash again if you don't restart it soon. If the trick did work, do whatever housekeeping you need to do (that is, save any unsaved documents), then restart your Mac using the Finder's Restart command. The Finder's Restart sequence is infinitely better for your Mac than a crash. Using it minimizes the chance of damage to your Desktop file or disk directories.

I've got one of those little yellow sticky notes posted to my monitor to remind me. You might want to do the same. Mine looks sort of like Figure 6-15.

```
SM 0 A9F4 <CR>
G 0 <CR>
```

Figure 6–15.   A little yellow sticky note reminder on my monitor

Recommendations

Disk First Aid
HD SC Setup

Part of Apple System software. (See the Recommendations section in Chapter 1 for details on where to get it.)

Programmer's Switch

Packed in the box with all Macintosh computers or available from your local authorized Apple dealer.

DiskTop
    CE Software
    1801 Industrial Circle
    West Des Moines, IA 50265
    800–523–7638
    515–224–1995
    Approximately $100

I'll only say it a few more times in the book, I promise. But DiskTop really is one of the greatest utilities ever invented.

DriveSavers
    30-D Pamaron Way
    Novato, CA 94949
    415-883-4232

DriveSavers uses proprietary hardware and software to recover data from disks others can't touch. They can also recover SyQuest and magneto-optical cartridges.

INIT Picker
> MicroSeeds Publishing, Inc.
> 5801 Benjamin Center Drive #103
> Tampa, FL 33634
> 813–882–8635
> Approximately $70

INIT Picker lets you select the INITs you want turned on and off. INIT Picker also allows you to change the loading order of INITs without renaming them. A slick utility if you use a lot of INITs.

Microcom 911 Utilities
> Microcom, Inc.
> 500 River Ridge Road
> Norwood, MA 02062
> 800–822–8224
> 617–551–1000
> Approximately $150

Norton Utilities for Macintosh
> Symantec Corporation
> 10201 Torre Avenue
> Cupertino, CA 95014
> 800–343–4714
> 408–252–3570
> Approximately $130

SUM II (Symantec Utilities for Macintosh)
> Symantec Corporation
> 10201 Torre Avenue
> Cupertino, CA 95014
> 800–343–4714
> 408–252–3570
> Approximately $150
> Mac models: Plus and up

Summary

A lot of the information in this chapter should be standard operating procedure to keep your hard disk running smoothly. It'll work on floppies, too. Here's the regimen I follow:

I replace my System and Finder every few months, whether they need it or not. I also rebuild the Desktop and optimize (defragment) my hard disks every month or two. I rarely have problems with them, and they seem to run faster after this treatment. Try it. You'll like it.

If you're the least bit concerned about recovering files from a crashed disk, hard or floppy, get a copy of SUM II, Norton Utilities, or 911 as soon as possible. After a disk crash, these programs can mean the difference between recovery and failure. They've all saved my hide more than once. (I know, I'm supposed to back up every day.)

Even if you have a recovery program, try the techniques outlined in this chapter first:

1. Repair the disk with Disk First Aid.
2. Install new drivers.
3. Rebuild your Desktop.
4. Replace your hard disk's System and Finder.
5. Zap your PRAM/check your battery.
6. Resolve INIT/CDEV conflicts.
7. If you have more than one SCSI device, check your terminators and resolve SCSI ID conflicts.
8. If your hard disk still won't mount, use SUM II (Symantec Utilities for Macintosh), Norton Utilities, or Microcom 911 Utilities.

Don't forget to reboot between steps. None of these techniques is destructive, so they won't make things any worse. Best of all, they work fairly often. Be sure you've tried everything before you initialize your hard disk or resort to taking it in for service.

Now that you know how to save your hard disk from disaster, the next chapter introduces you to additional hardware you can buy to enhance your productivity.

7

Hardware Upgrades

What and when to buy.

Now that you're up to speed on the basics—the System and Finder, file and disk recovery, and backing up—the next subject I'll discuss is hardware upgrades that can help make you more productive. Adding hardware to your Macintosh system can be expensive, but in many cases, it's worth it. In this chapter, I'll show you why.

Many types of hardware add-ons exist to help you do more work in less time. This chapter covers the three add-ons I consider most productive: RAM upgrades, accelerators, and large-screen monitors.

I'll explain what each category of product is and what it does. I'll give you some guidelines on what kind of user will benefit most, and I'll provide a formula for determining whether the product will be cost-effective for you. Finally, I'll give you my recommendations on what to buy and who to buy it from.

RAM Upgrades

What RAM Is

RAM (random access memory) is the working memory in your Mac. The standard configuration for older Macintoshes (such as the Plus and SE) is 1Mb of RAM (1 megabyte = 1,024 kilobytes), whereas newer models (such as the Classic, IIsi, and LC) come standard with at least 2Mb. You can add RAM to all Macintoshes, up to a total of 4- to 128Mb, depending on which model you own. In a moment, you'll find out why you might want to do so.

Unlike the CPU (central processing unit), RAM has no brains. It's nothing more than very fast memory chips that are used for the temporary storage of information your computer needs to access quickly—more quickly than it could from any disk.

Adding more RAM to your Macintosh is called *upgrading* your RAM. This gives your computer more memory, which lets you run larger applications (that is, applications that require more memory), open larger documents within applications, use more INITs and CDEVs simultaneously, and have more applications open simultaneously. (If you're a System 6 user, you must be in MultiFinder mode to open multiple applications at the same time.)

A technical discussion of RAM could fill this chapter, or even a whole book. In an attempt to prevent confusion, I present in the next section a simplified description of RAM and how it affects you as a Macintosh user.

How RAM Works (Extremely Simplified Version)

Whenever you launch an application program, the program is copied from the disk on which it resides and loaded into RAM. The copy of the program remains in RAM until you quit the application. (The application itself, the one on your disk that's represented by the icon you double-clicked, remains safely on the disk and is unchanged.) Once a program is loaded into RAM, it can execute (run) dozens of times faster than it would if it were running directly from a disk.

That's why your computer has RAM.

Why is RAM so fast? There are no mechanical parts in a RAM chip. When the computer needs to read from RAM, it does it at lightning speed. If it were accessing a disk, there would be a delay as the heads moved and the proper sector was located. RAM is all electronic, so there's no perceptible delay between the time your computer asks for the information and the time it retrieves it from RAM.

More than just programs are loaded into RAM. Parts of the System and Finder are loaded into RAM at boot time, as are INITs and CDEVs. So even if you have 2Mb of RAM in your Mac, there may be significantly less than that available to run applications.

In a nutshell: RAM is the temporary storage area of your computer, where applications, documents, parts of the System and Finder, INITs, and CDEVs are loaded for the fastest possible retrieval.

To find out just how much RAM your System software is using, choose About This Macintosh from the Apple menu in the Finder. (System 6 users choose About the Finder from the Apple menu.) As you can see in Figure 7–1, a Macintosh SE is running System 7 software, which uses over 1,200K. Even so, because it has 4Mb of RAM, it's still got more than 2,800K that can be used to open applications and documents. That's enough to run at least two or three applications at the same time, which is probably the major reason power users prefer to work with a minimum of 4Mb of RAM.

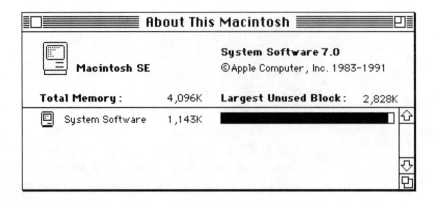

Figure 7-1.   About This Macintosh

To find out how much RAM an application uses, select its icon and choose Get Info from the Finder's File menu. In Figure 7-2, you can see that Word's Suggested Size is 512K. That's approximately how much RAM the program requires to open. The suggested size is determined by the manufacturer and can't be changed.

The number you see below Suggested Size in Figure 7-2, Current Size, is a number you can change to give an application additional RAM within which to run. (If you're running System 6, this number is labeled Application Memory Size, and applies only when you're using MultiFinder.) If you are using System 7, or MultiFinder under System 6, you can allocate more or less RAM to an application. It's almost never a good idea to allocate less RAM than the suggested size. This is because applications require a minimum amount of RAM to run correctly. Allocating less than the suggested amount of RAM can cause your program to freeze or crash. On the other hand, it's often helpful to allocate more RAM to an application by increasing the Current Size number. Allocating more can enable you to load bigger files, and more of them, without running out of memory. As you can see, I've given Word 512K of additional RAM for a total of 1Mb (1,024K). This allows me to open Word and a few large files, such as the chapters in this book, without running out of memory—a handy feature!

Tip

Another way to find out how much RAM a program uses is to choose About the Finder (System 6) or About This Macintosh (System 7) while the program is running in the background. The bar chart reflects the amount of RAM being used by all currently open programs (as shown in Figure 7–9, later in this chapter).

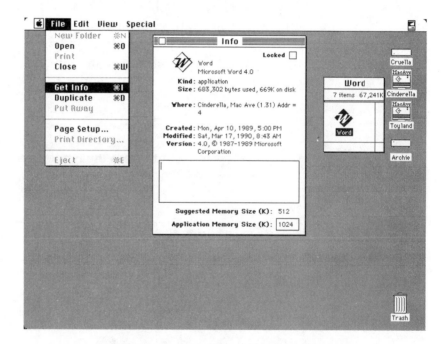

Figure 7–2.   Suggested Memory Size tells you how much RAM an application needs

MultiFinder Under System 6

(If you use System 7, skip ahead to the next section, "RAM Under System 7.") When you have 2Mb or more of RAM, you can use MultiFinder, which has been a part of Apple System software since 1987. When you use MultiFinder, you can open more than one application at a time, and you can switch quickly between them. If you are using System 6, the primary reason for getting more RAM is so that you can use MultiFinder.

If you switch to System 7, there is no Finder mode anymore. The features of MultiFinder are an inherent part of System 7, so you might say it always runs in MultiFinder mode. (This is described more in the next section.)

Although MultiFinder *can* be used on a 1Mb machine, it doesn't do much in that environment. That's because after your System and Finder load into RAM, there's not much RAM left—usually not enough to open more than one application. You might get away with using MultiFinder on a 1Mb Mac and be able to open two applications with very small memory requirements, but the functional minimum for using MultiFinder is 2Mb of RAM.

Tip

If you have a 1- or 2-meg Mac and a particular application won't run for lack of memory, try restarting in the Finder mode. Memory-hungry programs often run better under Finder than MultiFinder.

About the Macintosh® Finder™

| Finder: | 6.1.5 | **Larry, John, Steve, and Bruce** |
| System: | 6.0.5 | **©Apple Computer, Inc. 1983–90** |

Total Memory: 5,120K **Largest Unused Block:** 1,343K

MacPaint 2.0	768K	
Word	512K	
Finder	260K	
System	2,237K	

Figure 7–3.   Although it says "About the Macintosh Finder," it's really telling you about MultiFinder. You can tell it's MultiFinder because multiple applications—Word and MacPaint—are running

To see how MultiFinder works under System 6 (even if you have only 1Mb of RAM):

1. Select your startup disk's icon in the Finder.
2. Choose Set Startup from the Special menu. A dialog box offers you the following choices: Start up "Hard Disk"

with: Finder or MultiFinder (see Figure 7–4), where
Hard Disk is the name of your startup disk.
3. Click MultiFinder in the top part of the box and
MultiFinder Only in the bottom.
4. Restart your Mac. When you get back to the desktop,
you'll be running under MultiFinder.

Another way to start MultiFinder is to open your System
Folder and hold down the Command and Option keys simultaneously as you double-click on the MultiFinder icon.

The most convenient way to occasionally launch Multi-
Finder is the tip in the next section for making MultiFinder a
double-clickable application.

Figure 7–4.   Setting the Mac to start up with MultiFinder on in System 6

Launching MultiFinder from the Finder   If you want to use
MultiFinder but don't want to set your Mac to start up in it,
here's what you do: You trick it into thinking MultiFinder is an
application instead of a System file. Then, when you want to use
MultiFinder, all you need to do is double-click to launch it.

CAUTION: If you do not follow this procedure correctly, MultiFinder will be unusable. So be sure to make a backup copy of MultiFinder in case you make a mistake.

First you need a copy of DiskTop (CE Software), ResEdit, or any other utility program that allows you to change file type and toggle bits on and off. Then, follow these steps:

1. Make a copy of MultiFinder and move it out of the System Folder. Place it at root level (that is, not in any folders) or on the gray desktop.
2. Launch whatever utility you're using to make the modifications (DiskTop, ResEdit, and so on) and change MultiFinder's type, ZSYS,to APPL. (In case you're wondering, ZSYS is a System file type; APPL is an application file type.)
3. Click Bundle to turn on the bundle bit, and click System to turn off the System bit.
4. Click the Change, OK, or any other button appropriate to the program you're using to make the change permanent.

These steps are shown in Figure 7–5, using ResEdit 2.1 to make the modifications.

This procedure safely changes MultiFinder from a System file to an application file. After performing the modification, you'll notice that the altered MultiFinder has a different icon, shaped like an application icon. (Figure 7–6 shows both icons.) From now on, if you want to use MultiFinder, just double-click it on your gray desktop.

By the way, you can't reverse this trick. That is, you cannot quit MultiFinder as you normally quit applications. Once you've launched MultiFinder, the only way to return to the Finder is to reboot your machine.

Using MultiFinder   To witness MultiFinder in action, open one or two folders in the Finder, so you'll see something when

```
┌──────────────────────────────────────────────────────┐
│ ▤□▬▬▬▬▬▬▬▬▬ Info for MultiFinder ▬▬▬▬▬▬▬▬▬ │
│  ┌──────────────────────────────────────────────────┐ │
│  File │ MultiFinder                                  │ │
│  Type │ APPL        │        Creator │ MACS        │  │
│   ☐ System      ☐ Invisible   Color: │ Black    ▼ │  │
│   ☒ On Desk     ☐ Inited      ☒ Bundle              │
│   ☐ Shared      ☐ No Inits                          │
│   ☐ Always switch launch                            │
│  ─────────────────────────────────────────────────── │
│   ☐ Resource map is read only          ☐ File Protect │
│   ☐ Printer driver is MultiFinder compatible ☒ File Busy │
│   Created  │ 3/7/90  12:00:00 PM │      ☐ File Locked │
│   Modified │ 3/7/90  12:00:00 PM │                   │
│      Size   50746 bytes in resource fork            │
│             0 bytes in data fork                     │
└──────────────────────────────────────────────────────┘
```

Figure 7–5.   Using ResEdit to change MultiFinder from a System file to an application

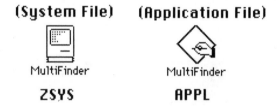

Figure 7–6.   MultiFinder icons—System file and application file

you switch back. Now launch your word processor, type a few lines, and shrink the window enough to see what's behind it. (If you use the word processor FullWrite Professional, from Ashton-Tate, it may use too much RAM for this demonstration to work on a 1Mb Mac. If you're a FullWrite user and you're in a daring mood, go ahead and try it anyway. It could cause a crash, so make sure you've backed up anything you care about, just in case.)

You should be able to see the folders you opened peeking out from behind your word processor window. In Figure 7–7, Microsoft Word is the active application, and you can see the

Finder peeking through behind it. (The *active* application is the one currently being used. Its title bar will have black lines. Dm2.Ch 7–Other Hardware, a Microsoft Word document, is active in Figure 7–7.)

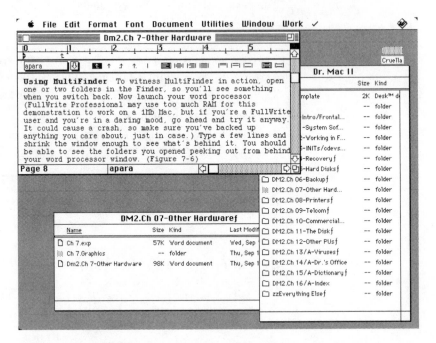

Figure 7–7.   Using MultiFinder when Microsoft Word is active; the Finder can be seen behind it

There are four ways you can switch between open applications and the Finder when you're running MultiFinder. These are illustrated in Figure 7–8.

- Choose the application from the Apple menu.
- Click the icon in the upper right corner of the menu bar to cycle from one open application to the next.
- Click anywhere in a window of the application you want to activate. (Or click any icon in the Finder.)
- Double-click the grayed-out application or document icon. (This option is available only if the Finder is the active application.)

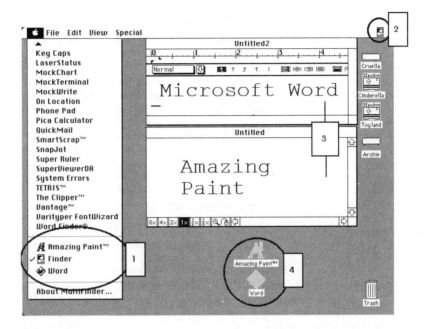

Figure 7–8.   Four ways to switch applications under MultiFinder in System 6

To turn MultiFinder off and return to using the Finder, simply reverse the procedure you used to turn it on. If you've forgotten how you did it, here's what to do:

1. Select your startup disk's icon in the Finder.
2. Choose Set Startup from the Special menu. You'll see the message *Start up "Hard disks" with: Finder or Multi-Finder.* This time, click Finder in the top part of the box and Finder Only in the bottom.

When I wrote the first edition of this book, I had 5Mb in my Mac running System 6, and I used MultiFinder every day. I can't imagine having to do without it; it's perfect for the way I work. For example, I always keep copies of both Microsoft Word and Amazing Paint open. (Amazing Paint is a graphics program from CE Software. It's similar to MacPaint, but has more features and costs less.) That way, I can switch quickly between writing and modifying graphics and screen shots. I don't have to quit Word to touch up a screen shot in Amazing Paint. I just switch from one program to another, using any of the four methods illustrated in Figure 7–8.

My usual technique is to open Word (top window) and Amazing Paint (bottom window). You can also see the Finder peeking through on the right. That's another convenient feature of MultiFinder—you can use the Finder at any time.

In Figure 7–8, the Finder is active. You can tell by the little icon in the right corner of the menu bar. It changes to the icon of whatever application is active at the time—right now, it's the Finder icon. Also notice that the menu bar belongs to the Finder, and that there is a check mark next to the Finder's name in the Apple menu.

RAM Under System 7

System 7 requires you to have at least 2Mb of RAM. This is because, unlike System 6, where you have the option of using either Finder or MultiFinder, System 7 is always running in MultiFinder mode; you can't turn it off and on as you can in System 6. As a result, System 7 software uses up quite a bit of RAM. Figure 7-9 shows the About This Macintosh box under System 7, where the Finder, Word 4.0, and SuperPaint 2.0 are running simultaneously.

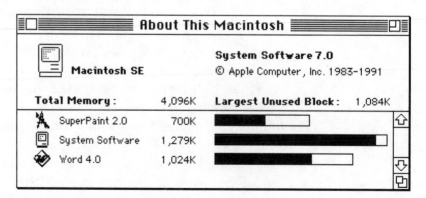

Figure 7–9.   About This Macintosh box shows System 7's multitasking

Similar to using MultiFinder under System 6, when you use System 7, you can open more than one application at a time, and you can switch quickly between them. To witness System 7's multitasking capabilities in action, open one or two folders in the Finder, so you'll see something when you switch back. Now launch your word processor, type a few lines, and shrink the window enough to see what's behind it. You should be able to see the folders you opened peeking out from behind your word processor window. In Figure 7–10, Microsoft Word is the active application, and you can see the Finder peeking through behind it.

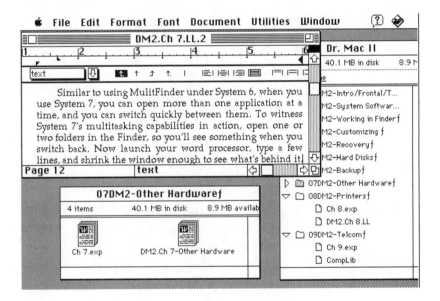

Figure 7–10.   System 7 multitasking—Microsoft Word is active; the Finder can be seen behind it

In addition to having multitasking built into it, System 7 also includes the Hide and Show feature, which is available under the Application menu (see Figure 7–11). By choosing a Hide command, you can hide one or all applications (including the Finder) you have running but aren't using, while leaving the active application window visible on your screen. This way, your desktop looks like the only application running is the current one, and the screen doesn't look cluttered. For example, if I chose Hide Others, the screen in Figure 7–10 would show only the Word window. (Hide and Show are described in greater detail in Chapter 2.)

Figure 7–11.   System 7's Hide/Show feature

There are three ways you can switch between open applications and the Finder when you're running System 7. These are illustrated in Figure 7–12.

- Choose the application from the Application menu.
- Click anywhere in a window of the application you want to activate. (Or click anywhere—on an icon or on the gray desktop—in the Finder.)

Tip

If you hold down the Option key when you click, the current application will be hidden and the application you clicked on will become active.

- Double-click the grayed-out application or document icon. (This option is available only if the Finder is the active application.)

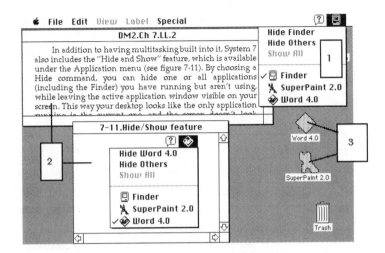

Figure 7–12. Three ways to switch applications under System 7

Another Reason for RAM Upgrades

In addition to being able to use MultiFinder (System 6) or to use System 7 at all, there is another reason to consider additional RAM: Certain programs will run out of memory when you open a large document on a 1Mb machine (or, if you're using System 7, a 2Mb machine), and others (primarily color paint programs and sophisticated page-layout programs) require more than 1Mb to run properly.

For example, Quark XPress, a high-powered page-layout program, and Adobe Photoshop, a color image-processing program, each require 2Mb of RAM. PageMaker, another page-layout program, will run in 1Mb, but recommends at least 2Mb.

Remember, INITs (Startup documents) and some CDEVs (Control Panel documents) also use up RAM. If you're having out-of-memory problems, try moving some of them temporarily out of your System Folder and restarting your Mac. This will leave more RAM to use with applications. If you don't understand, reread the section in Chapter 6 on INIT conflicts.

Even if you disable all of your INITs and CDEVs and are able to open a large file, or one containing complex graphics, you could have problems working with it if you don't have enough RAM. You may begin to get warnings that you are low on memory. Some applications will tell you to close some windows and save your work. The applications I mentioned above are well-behaved on this point and will notify you when RAM is getting full. Others may crash or freeze. The Finder may automatically close the folder's window to free up memory for your work in another open application. Again, the more RAM you have, the less likely you are to have these problems.

If you have scanned images—gray-scale or color—they will usually need 2Mb or more to open successfully, regardless of which program you use to open them.

It seems that the more powerful the application, the more likely it is to be a memory hog. Although some of these programs can run, albeit in a somewhat hindered fashion, on a 1Mb Mac, some programs *absolutely require* more than 1Mb of RAM to operate. The heavily advertised OmniPage optical character-recognition software, which requires 4Mb, is one of the first. Rest assured there will be many more.

One More Thing a RAM Upgrade Will Allow   If you have ever gotten an error message in the Finder when copying files that says *Ran out of Finder memory during copy. Please drag the items in two groups,* you can fix it, as long as you can spare 160K of RAM. You need to increase the Finder's memory size from 160K to 320K. Follow the steps appropriate for the version of System software you are running.

WARNING: Do not attempt the following procedure on a Macintosh with less than 2Mb of RAM.

1. Because the System 7 Finder's Get Info box (see Figure 7-13) does not allow you to change the memory used by the Finder, you need to start up your Macintosh with a System 6 System disk. The System Tools disk that came with the Apple System 6 kit, or any other disk with a System 6 System Folder, will do.

2. Open the System 7 System Folder.
3. Select the System 7 Finder icon.
4. Choose Get Info from the File menu, or press Command-I.
5. In the Get Info window, check the default memory allocation size in the Application Memory Size box.
6. Increase the Finder's memory size in 50K increments, until it is at a size that works best for you (see Figure 7–13).
7. Click the Get Info window's close box to return to the Finder.
8. Restart your Mac using the System 7 System disk you just modified.

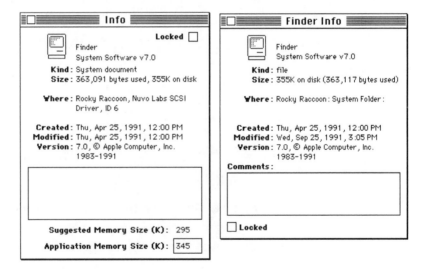

Figure 7–13.   Increasing the System 7 Finder's memory size (left), and the Finder's Get Info window under System 7 (right)

1. Open the System Folder.
2. Select the Finder's icon.
3. With the Finder's icon selected, choose Get Info from the File menu, or press Command-I.

4. In the Get Info window, type **320** in the Application Memory Size box (see Figure 7–14).
5. Click the Get Info window's close box to return to the Finder.
6. Reboot your Mac by choosing Restart from the Special menu.

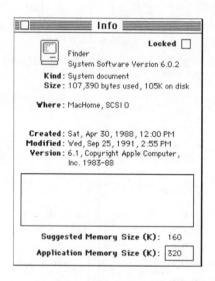

Figure 7–14.   Increasing the System 6 Finder's memory size to 320K

Once you've made this change and rebooted, you should be able to copy several megabytes of files (or more) without having to drag the items in two groups.

A Word about RAM Cache, Virtual Memory, 32-Bit Addressing, and RAM Disks

RAM Cache ("Disk Cache" Under System 7) No matter how much RAM you decide to add, you can coax even better performance out of your Mac by increasing the RAM cache size, as discussed in Chapter 3. The *RAM cache* is a special area of memory (RAM) set aside for frequently accessed data. Because data can be read from RAM far faster than from disk, a cache makes your computer seem to be running faster.

To change the RAM cache to a higher setting:

1. Choose Control Panels from the Apple menu. If you are working in an application, the Mac switches you to the Finder and opens the Control Panels window.
2. In the Control Panels window, double-click the Memory icon to open the Memory control panel.
3. In the Disk Cache area of the control panel, click the up arrow to increase the cache to the desired size (see Figure 7–15). The following discussion offers suggested RAM cache sizes.
4. Click the close box to save your changes. You'll need to restart your Mac for the changes to take effect.

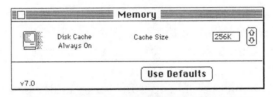

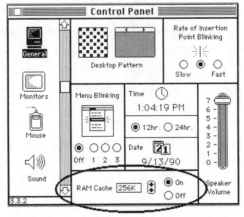

Figure 7–15.   Setting The RAM cache using the Control Panel in System 7 (top) and System 6 (bottom)

1. Choose Control Panel from the Apple menu.
2. In the Control Panel box, click the General icon.
3. In the RAM Cache area of the Control Panel, click the up arrow, or type a number, to increase the cache to the desired size (see Figure 7–15).
4. Click the Control Panel's close box to save your changes.
5. Restart your Mac for your changes to take effect.

I advise against using the RAM cache at all on Macs with only 1Mb of RAM. This is because at settings below 256K, the effect is barely noticeable, and whatever amount of RAM you dedicate to the cache is no longer available for running applications.

On a multimegabyte machine, try setting the cache to at least 128K; you should see some performance improvement, especially when quitting to the Finder from an application. This is because part of the Finder is usually in the cache at any given time. You'll also see an improvement in the speed of the Find and Search functions in many applications with a cache of reasonable size. I keep mine set to 256K, as you can see in Figure 7–15. I arrived at this figure through trial and error—when the cache was smaller, the speed improvement wasn't perceptible; when it was much larger, I didn't notice that much improvement over 256K, and I had less RAM available for running applications. Many power users think that 256K is the optimum setting; others prefer 384K to 512K.

I suggest you try various settings for your cache. (Remember, you'll need to reboot between changes in order for them to take effect.) The speed improvement is subtle, so if you don't feel a difference after a day or two with the setting at 384K or 512K, return to the Control Panel, increase the setting, and reboot. There's no sense wasting perfectly good RAM on the cache if you can't perceive a difference.

I'm pretty sensitive to it. I can tell if it's on or off within minutes of sitting down at my Mac. On the other hand, I know many people who can't. Experiment to find out what's right for you.

Virtual Memory (System 7 only)   If your Mac has a 68030 or 68040 processor, you can take advantage of virtual memory, a scheme by which space on your hard disk is used as if it were RAM. It's recommended that you don't use more virtual memory than you have real RAM, so on a 2Mb machine, you should only use virtual memory to bump it up to 4Mb. (You can, of course, bump it even higher, but performance will suffer.) Although virtual memory is slower than real RAM, it can be handy in a pinch. If your Mac supports it, give it a try, but if you like what it does for you, consider purchasing some more real RAM, which will do the same things, but it will do them a lot faster.

32-Bit Addressing (System 7 only)   Some Macs can use very large amounts of RAM, usually more than 8Mb, by taking advantage of System 7's 32-bit addressing. (Sorry, if you're using System 6, 8Mb is the limit for you!) If you want to keep several memory-hungry programs open simultaneously, or you plan to edit lots of large color documents, you may want to use it. It requires that you have more than 8Mb of RAM installed, and that you turn it on in the Memory control panel. If your Mac doesn't have this capability, it won't appear in the Memory CDEV.

RAM Disks   If you're really into becoming a power user, you might want to use some RAM to create a RAM disk. A RAM disk acts like a hard disk, except that everything you do from it happens much faster. If your System Folder resides on a RAM disk, the Finder is *much* faster; if an application resides on a RAM disk, it launches faster, and possibly runs faster, depending on how often it accesses the disk. Databases almost always run faster from a RAM disk.

Unfortunately, RAM disks have several drawbacks:

- They're volatile. If the power is interrupted, or you have a severe crash, their contents are lost. This is the most severe drawback by far. When you save something to a hard disk, you can pretty much rest assured that it will be there when you need it. Not so with a RAM disk. If power is interrupted, everything on the RAM disk disappears.

- They are expensive. You need at least 4Mb beyond what your System and applications use, and more—much more—if you want to store several applications on it. In most cases, this means upgrading your Mac to at least 16Mb of RAM.
- They require the purchase of additional software or hardware.

Even so, I use a RAM disk on my 32Mb IIci. If you're hungry for the maximum performance, you might want to check it out. The best software RAM disk, and the one I'm currently using, is Maxima, from Connectix. Several companies, including DayStar Digital, make hardware RAM disks. I've never used one, so I can't comment on their suitability.

Who Will Benefit Most from RAM Upgrades?

Unless you use only one application all day, you'll probably benefit from a RAM upgrade and the ability to use System 7 or MultiFinder.

If you find yourself quitting one application, returning to the Finder, then launching another application more than a few times a day, MultiFinder will save you a lot of time.

On most days, my Mac has Microsoft Word, TouchBASE (name and address database), Acta (an outliner, which I use to maintain my to-do list), Canvas, Amazing Paint, or DeskPaint (graphics editing applications) and the Finder running simultaneously. So my telephone numbers, to-do list, plus whatever I'm editing or writing in Word are only a mouse click away. And, because I've got 32Mb to work with, there's enough RAM to open any other program I need, without quitting any of my everyday programs.

If you upgrade to 2Mb (which you have to do in order to run System 7), you'll usually be able to run at least two programs at a time, unless one of them is a memory hog, as discussed previously. If you upgrade to 4Mb or more, you'll be able to open three or four programs at a time.

Is Additional RAM Worth the Cost?

You need to examine your work habits to find out if a RAM upgrade will be cost-effective for you. If you find yourself opening one application, closing it, opening another application, closing it, and so on, you're a logical candidate for more RAM. If you often find yourself copying and pasting between two or more applications, you should think about more RAM and Multi-Finder. If you plan to use System 7 and you have less than 2Mb of RAM, you definitely need to upgrade your RAM. You're also a candidate for more RAM if you intend to use memory-intensive applications such as those mentioned previously, or if you need to create very large documents in almost any application.

If any of the descriptions above matches your habits or needs, try this:

1. Determine how much time you're spending each day, in minutes, moving between applications (or having to disable INITs and CDEVs to free up enough RAM for programs such as Quark XPress or Adobe Photoshop to operate).
2. Determine the cost of the RAM you're considering.
3. Determine what your time is worth per minute.
4. Multiply the amount your time is worth per minute by the number of minutes you'll save each day (that is, the amount of time you figured in step 1).
5. Divide the RAM cost by the result of step 4 to determine how long it would take to pay back the cost of the RAM.

So, if your time is worth $20 an hour ($0.33 a minute), the RAM you're considering costs $700, and you figure you'll save 10 minutes a day, the RAM will have paid for itself in 210 days:

$700 ÷ (0.33 dollars per minute * 10 minutes per day) = 210 days

If you're like me, you'll save a lot more than 10 minutes a day. If so, change the number in the equation to reflect the savings you expect. I'd say I save about 30 minutes a day since upgrading to 32Mb.

This approach works beautifully on your boss.

Which RAM to Buy

RAM is fairly generic. In other words, one vendor's RAM is about the same as another's. You want to purchase your RAM from a reliable vendor: one that offers at least a one-year guarantee. Apple-branded RAM is usually much more expensive than others, so shop around.

There *are* a couple of other things you should know:

- Not all RAM runs at the same speed. RAM is rated in nanoseconds—billionths of a second. Older Macs such as the Plus and SE can use 150ns chips. Mac II, IIx, IIcx, and SE/30 need at least 120ns. Newer machines require 80ns. Make sure you get the right speed for your particular Mac; smaller numbers are faster. The vendor you buy from will be able to help you.

   To make matters more confusing, you can find 100ns, 80ns, or 60ns RAM that can work in most Macs, even if they're capable of using slower RAM. Remember that faster RAM will probably be more expensive, and in most cases, the difference in speed will not be apparent to you. Buy the least expensive speed that works with your Mac.

- RAM (like all the products in this chapter) is available from most computer stores and from a wide assortment of mail-order vendors. Apple-labeled memory is usually more expensive, and, as I said before, there's no difference, other than price, between one company's RAM and another. So you probably want to avoid Apple-labeled memory unless it's competitively priced in your neighborhood.

Every issue of the major Mac magazines is filled with ads for RAM, accelerator upgrades, and large monitors. If you're considering an upgrade, it might be wise to contact a few of the different vendors and get brochures and prices.

I've had good success buying my RAM from Technology Works, here in my home town of Austin, Texas. They offer a lifetime warranty, free installation kits, overnight delivery, toll-free ordering and technical support, and competitive prices.

• 4Mb, 8Mb, and even 16Mb RAM chips have recently become available, which, for all intents and purposes, are useful only if you are running a Mac under System 7. (System 6 can only address 8Mb of RAM altogether.) These chips are more expensive than 1Mb chips, but the cost may be worth it to you. I'm presently using eight 4Mb chips (for a total of 32Mb) in my IIci. I use 12Mb for System memory, and the other 20Mb for my RAM disk. In my opinion, it's expensive but worth it. But before you commit to using a RAM disk, read about their drawbacks in the previous section. This setup is only for the serious power-hungry user.

The best way to find out what will work in your configuration is to talk to a reliable vendor at length before you buy any upgrade. And don't forget to ask about credit card surcharges and taxes, which can affect your total cost.

Most memory upgrades come with complete installation instructions, for those of you who are inclined to install the memory yourselves. I wouldn't recommend doing it yourself if you've got a compact Mac—a Plus, SE, or Classic. There's not much room to maneuver, and it's a pretty delicate procedure. On the other hand, if you have a II series, LC, or Quadra, it's a relatively simple procedure. (I've never opened up a Power-Book or Portable, so I don't know how easy or hard upgrading their RAM is!)

If you don't feel up to doing it yourself, any decent Apple technician should be able to do it for you in less than half an hour.

Accelerators

An accelerator is a circuit board (that is, a card) that is installed inside your Mac and that uses a faster CPU than the one that came with your Mac. With such a board installed, your Mac will run significantly faster.

Accelerator boards come from a wide variety of third-party companies. In addition to third-party accelerators, there are two other ways to make your Mac run faster, and you should consider both carefully before making the decision to speed up your Mac.

- Sell your Mac and buy a faster one.
- Purchase an Apple upgrade, if one is available for your model. Most Macs can be upgraded. (As of this writing, Apple does not have CPU upgrades for the Plus, Portable, SE/30, Quadra, PowerBook, or IIfx.

A faster Mac has tangible benefits: launching programs or documents, quitting from a program, scrolling, screen refreshing, copying files and folders to and from disks, performing calculations and searches in databases or spreadsheets, running the Find command in any program that uses one, and just about everything else happens faster when you use a more powerful CPU.

Accelerator boards are relatively easy to install in SEs, Mac IIs, and Quadras; they usually come with complete installation instructions. If you're timid about poking around inside your Mac, find a dealer or technician to do it for you. It should take less than an hour. If you're going to upgrade a Plus, 512K(e), or Classic, don't do it yourself unless you're comfortable performing ultradelicate surgery on your Mac. The older Macs (for example, Plus or 512K) have little room for upgrades, and the lack of a slot makes installing one even tougher. Let it be someone else's headache—find a qualified technician to do it.

Since I don't use an accelerator (hey, I'm using a 32Mb IIci with a RAM disk—I don't *need* an accelerator. This puppy is faaaast!), I don't really have much of a feel for which one is a good one; however, DayStar Digital and Radius accelerator cards have excellent reputations. DayStar offers a complete line of accelerator cards for Mac SE/30, LC, II, IIx, IIcx, IIsi, and IIci machines and newer machines. Their PowerCache cards offer 25-, 40-, and 50MHz of speed, and are based on the 68030 or 68040 processor. Radius, which also is known for its monitors, has an accelerator card called the Radius Rocket, which was the first 68040 accelerator card, and several other accelerators as well.

A 68040 accelerator will provide performance significantly in excess of the Mac IIfx. Macintosh Quadras use the 68040.

If you're considering buying an accelerator, it would be smart to look at the accelerator comparisons that run in *Macworld* and *MacUser* magazines every year or so. (If you've got a modem, you can get this kind of stuff without leaving your Mac. See Chapter 9 for information on how to search for and read magazine articles on-line.)

The number of variables in accelerator products is great. Some things to think about are discussed in the following sections.

Considerations When Choosing an Accelerator

Clock Speed of the CPU   Clock speed refers to the speed at which the CPU processes information internally. In addition to the different processors used in various Macintoshes, each CPU can run at different clock speeds. Clock speed is measured in megahertz (MHz). Table 7–1 shows the clock speeds of stock Macintoshes.

Table 7–1. Clock Speeds of Different Macintosh Models

Mac	Chip	Clock Speed
128, 512, 512Ke, Plus, SE, Classic	68000	8
Portable	68000	16
II, LC	68020	16
IIx, *IIcx*, SE/30, Classic II	68030	16
IIsi	68030	20
IIci	68030	25
IIfx	68030	40
PowerBook 100	68HC000	16
PowerBook 140	68030	16
PowerBook 170	68030	25
Quadra 700 and 900	68040	25

*Discontinued models in italics

A 68020 is faster than a 68000, a 68030 is faster than a 68020, a 68040 is faster than a 68030, and so on. But here's where it gets tricky: The chip versions used by Apple are not the only versions made by Motorola. Each chip also comes in a variety of other clock speeds.

For example, there are 16MHz, 25MHz, 40MHz, and 50MHz versions of the 68030. By the time you read this, a 25MHz version of the 68040 will be available (it's used in both Quadra model Macs). A 60MHz 68030 chip will probably also be available by the time you read this. At present, Apple isn't using the 50MHz or 60MHz 68030, but I don't think it will be long before they introduce one or both.

Higher is faster. Faster is better. Better is more expensive. Get the picture?

Use of Motherboard RAM   Accelerators access RAM differently than a stock Mac does. Some accelerators come with high-speed RAM (that is, 80ns or even 60ns RAM) installed on them;

others come with none but allow you to install RAM chips of whatever speed you prefer. Still others won't accept any RAM; rather, they use whatever RAM your motherboard has. The fastest accelerators come with fast RAM on board. Of course, they're the most expensive. Shop around.

Definition

> *Motherboard* is the main circuit board in your Mac.

Math Coprocessors   Many accelerator upgrades allow the optional addition of a math coprocessor—an MC68881 or 68882 chip. This is a chip designed to handle math tasks faster than they're presently handled by your CPU. With a math co-processor installed, your CPU doesn't have to work as hard, and the math tasks it used to handle are directed to a custom chip designed especially for math.

I recommend getting the math chip—it speeds up more than just spreadsheets. In fact, it speeds up many programs you don't think of as math-based, such as CAD, drawing, and statistical analysis programs, as well as many other programs that use floating-point math internally.

If a math coprocessor is offered as an option, consider it seriously. It shouldn't add more than 10 or 20 percent to the cost of the board, and it is probably worth it for the additional performance it provides.

Is an Accelerator Worth the Cost?

Let's use the same analysis used earlier for RAM upgrades:

1. Make a rough determination of the time you'll save each day if you install an accelerator. You should save somewhere between 10 and 25 percent of the time you spend at the keyboard to make the investment pay off.

2. Determine the cost of the accelerator that you are considering.
3. Determine what your time is worth per minute.
4. Multiply the amount your time is worth per minute by the number of minutes you'll save each day (see step 1).
5. Divide the accelerator cost by the result of step 4 to determine how long it would take to pay back the cost of the accelerator.

So, if your time is worth $20 an hour ($0.33 a minute), the accelerator you're considering costs $1,400, and you figure you'll save 25 minutes a day, the upgrade will have paid for itself in 169 days:

$1,400 ÷ (0.33 dollars per minute * 25 minutes per day) = 169 days

There is also the intangible benefit: the joy of having a faster, more responsive computer—one that displays the watch cursor for much shorter periods than ever before. How many times have you started something on your Mac, then waited impatiently while the watch cursor spun? The reduction in your frustration level is worth something. You might want to factor that into the equation somehow.

Who Will Benefit Most from an Accelerator?

Almost anyone who wants to be able to do more work in less time can benefit from a faster Mac. You'll be amazed at how much faster menus respond, applications and documents open and close, screens refresh, and files copy. If these things appeal to you, you're a likely candidate for an accelerator, an Apple upgrade, or a new, faster Mac.

Which Accelerator to Buy

This is a tough call. Many Mac models have Apple upgrades available. You can upgrade an SE to an SE/30. You can upgrade a II or IIx to a IIfx, or a IIcx or IIci to a Quadra 700. The truth is, I recommend you take the Apple upgrade path if you can afford it.

But there's the rub. Apple upgrades are usually significantly more expensive than ones available from third parties such as DayStar and Radius. The advantage of the Apple upgrade is that you can rest assured that there will be no major compatibility problems; the disadvantage is that they cost a whole lot more, sometimes as much as two or three times what a third-party accelerator would cost you.

The Doctor's Opinion

For example, when System 7 first came out, some Radius accelerators were not compatible with it. It took several months for Radius to come out with a fix. In the meantime, most Apple machines and Apple upgrades ran System 7 without a hitch.

Another problem is that some applications, INITs, and CDEVs that work fine on Apple-upgraded Macs may conflict with third-party accelerators. The manufacturers of these applications, INITs, and CDEVs are much more likely to make their software work with Apple products than with those from third parties.

A third-party accelerator runs anywhere from $600 to $3,000, with equivalent Apple upgrades running 10 to 50 percent more.

As far as brands go, I've never owned an accelerator. Friends who have, and users on CompuServe, America Online, and other on-line services report good experiences with Radius and DayStar products. Both companies are known for innovative, well-engineered products with strong support. Like many major hardware products, accelerator upgrades are available primarily through dealers who sell and install a complete line of products. If you're comfortable installing the board yourself, or know someone who is, several mail-order vendors advertise in the major Mac magazines. As with any mail-order product, be sure you're comfortable with long-distance service should the board become inoperable. If you aren't, find a good local dealer and buy it there.

The bottom line is that you'll be safer with an Apple upgrade, but you'll get much more for your money with a third-party upgrade. A third-party upgrade may cause you problems, and the problems may take longer to resolve, but then again, it may not. Many users are totally satisfied with their third-party accelerators, but if you can afford it, I recommend you go with the Apple upgrade.

The Doctor's Opinion
☎

Since I don't use them, I'd be interested in hearing about your experiences with third-party accelerators. My electronic mail addresses appear at the end of this book's introduction, or you can send snail mail care of Addison-Wesley.

Monitors

What Monitors Are

One of the biggest and longest-running complaints about the Mac has been the size of the screen. Although it's true that the 9-inch screens used in all older Macs provide a crisper, cleaner image than the screens of most other computers, the fact remains that a 9-inch diagonal screen is too small to see a letter-size page without scrolling.

Fortunately, that complaint has been answered by Apple and third-party developers and is now a thing of the past. Today, you can buy a monitor of almost any size, shape, or color for almost any Mac.

Many kinds of monitors and cards are available today. Some of the terms you should be familiar with include:

Definition

A *video card* is the interface between the monitor and your Mac—it goes inside your Mac.

A *monochrome monitor* displays only black and white.

A *gray-scale monitor* can display eight or more shades of gray. Most gray-scale monitors display 256 shades.

A *full-page display* is a monitor roughly the size of an 8.5-by-11-inch page.

A *dual-page display* is a monitor large enough to show two 8.5-by-11-inch pages side by side. Dual-page displays are usually 19 or 21 inches, measured diagonally.

8-bit color means the monitor can display up to 256 colors at one time.

24-bit color means the monitor can display over 16 million colors at one time.

The number of colors is a function of the video card. Many 8-bit cards can be upgraded to 24 bits; most color monitors can display either 8- or 24-bit color.

Of course, to use any color monitor, you must have a Mac capable of handling color (generally, any Macintosh model that uses a 68020 processor or above). Here's a list of your current monitor options.

If You Own a 128, 512K, 512Ke, Plus, or Classic   These Macs can use only monochrome monitors, either single- or dual-page. You can use only one monitor at a time, and you may or may not be able to use the built-in 9-inch Mac screen when an external monitor is connected.

The availability of monitors for Macs older than the Plus may be spotty.

If You Own an SE   These Macs can use only monochrome monitors, either single- or dual-page. Monitors are easily installed;

the video card goes in the SE slot. You can use only one external monitor at a time, but most external monitors for the SE allow you to use the built-in 9-inch Mac screen even when the external monitor is connected.

If You Own a Mac LC   These Macs come with on-board video support for color or gray-scale capability; you can use mono-chrome, gray-scale, or color monitors. (The LC does not come with a built-in screen.)

If You Own a Mac II Series   These Macs can use monochrome, gray-scale, or color monitors of many sizes and shapes. You can have as many monitors connected at any one time as you have slots. I've got two—a 19-inch monochrome and a 13-inch color. (These machines do not come with a built-in screen.)

If You Own an SE/30   These Macs can use monochrome, gray-scale, or color monitors. (The built-in screen is, of course, black and white.) Many sizes and shapes of monitors are available. You can use only one external monitor at a time, but most external monitors for the SE/30 should allow you to use the built-in 9-inch Mac screen even when the external monitor is connected.

If You Own a Quadra   These Macs come with built-in 24-bit color support for all Apple and most third-party displays. (These machines do not come with a built-in screen.)

If You Own a PowerBook or Portable   Third-party products will allow you to connect a variety of external monitors.

Monitor Components

Macintosh external video systems are almost always made up of two pieces: the monitor itself and the video card that installs inside your Mac. The Apple 8•24 Video Card is considered the industry standard and can be used with monitors from many vendors. Likewise, many third-party video cards can drive an Apple monitor.

Third-party vendors generally produce higher-performance video cards that include capabilities not found in the Apple card, such as panning, zooming, tear-off menus, and custom chips to speed up screen refresh time. On the other hand, Apple's 8•24 GC Card, a graphics accelerator card, provides the highest QuickDraw speed, according to *MacUser* magazine (May 1991).

The newer Macs (the LC, IIci, IIfx, IIsi, and Quadra models) have video support built into them, negating the need for a video card. There is a slight performance penalty if you use the built-in video support on all but the Quadras, which have very fast on-board video. My IIci's color monitor refreshes itself faster when it's connected to an Apple 8•24 Video Card than when I run it from the built-in video. On the other hand, it's not that big a difference, and a separate video card costs hundreds of dollars. Unless you're desperate for the utmost performance, the built-in video should be sufficient for your needs—if your Mac has it, use it. If you must have improved screen performance, check out one of the accelerated video cards.

What Monitors Do

A larger monitor allows you to see one or more pages in their entirety without scrolling. Monitors come in various sizes, from the full- (or single-) page display, which allows you to view a full 8.5-by-11-inch page, to 19-inch and 21-inch models that can easily show two pages side by side.

Even larger monitors are now available—Mitsubishi makes a 50-inch color monitor for the Mac II series and SE/30.

Another thing you might consider if you have one of the Macs that supports 256 colors is a color monitor. However, I don't recommend color unless you really need color capacity. I mean unless you have a *serious* reason—such as preparing color separations with programs such as Adobe Illustrator, Adobe

Photoshop, Quark XPress, or PageMaker; working with gray-scale files using programs such as Photoshop, ImageStudio, or Digital Darkroom; or creating presentations that will end up as color slides.

Still, some people just plain *like* having a color monitor and could care less about the price and performance penalties.

Monochrome monitors and video boards are much less expensive than their color counterparts. And using color slows down a Mac considerably. I've noticed it myself on my Mac IIci, which has an Apple 13-inch color monitor and Apple video card. It runs noticeably faster in the 1-bit (black and white) mode than in the 8-bit (256 colors) or 32-bit (16.8 million colors) color mode.

So, even though my Mac can display glorious colors, most days you'll find me running in the black-and-white (two-color) mode for improved performance. My 19-inch monitor is mono-chrome, and I use it a lot more than the 13-inch color.

Who Will Benefit Most from External Monitors?

The more you scroll around the screen, the more sense a larger monitor will make for you. When I first started out on the Mac, I used PageMaker on my stock Mac Plus and its 9-inch screen. It was annoying seeing only a portion of the page on which I was working. I was constantly changing views or dragging the page around with the grabber hand. It was more than a year before I was able to afford my first large-screen monitor. When I finally upgraded, I looked at everything available and then selected the Radius Full Page Display (black and white) for my Mac Plus. I was amazed at how much time I saved on each project. Scrolling around a complicated page was painfully slow on my Plus, so the fact that I did much less scrolling with my large screen was a real timesaver for me.

Though this is completely subjective, it seems that my projects looked better and more professional after I got a bigger monitor. Another thing I found was that I printed things out less frequently once I was able to view the whole page on the screen. The time I saved not having to print pages to see how they looked at full size was worth the price of the monitor. Being able to view a full page (or more) on the screen is something you can't understand until you've lived with it for a while. Once you have, you'll never want to work on a 9-inch screen again.

If you do any kind of graphics work, design, or layout, a large screen will make a world of difference in the way you work. If you are involved in page-layout work, you'll be surprised at how pleasant working on a full page (or more) is.

If you do a lot of page layout, or manipulate a lot of color or gray-scale images, check out one of the accelerated video products from Apple, Radius, SuperMac, or RasterOps. They make your screen respond much faster, but they are not cheap.

The benefits of a larger monitor aren't limited to people who use Macs for page layout. If you use your Mac for large spreadsheet models, you'll find a big-screen monitor beneficial, as will anyone who regularly works on graphics larger than the built-in Mac screen.

System 7 or MultiFinder users will also benefit greatly from the increased screen size. Because both System 7 and MultiFinder under System 6 allow you to keep several applications open, you'll find a larger screen helps you keep more windows visible. This can be a great timesaver when you're cutting and pasting or switching between programs.

Are External Monitors Worth the Cost?

Once again, let's use the cost-analysis formula:

1. Establish how much time you would save each day, in minutes, if you didn't have to scroll or print as often.
2. Determine the cost of the monitor you're considering.
3. Determine what your time is worth per minute.

4. Multiply the amount your time is worth per minute by the number of minutes you'll save each day (see step 1).
5. Divide the monitor cost by the result of step 4 to determine how long it would take to pay back the cost of the monitor.

So, if your time is worth $20 an hour ($0.33 a minute), the monitor you're considering costs $1,000 (about the least you can pay for a large screen), and you figure you'll save 15 minutes a day, the monitor will have paid for itself in 202 days:

$1,000 ÷ (0.33 dollars per minute * 15 minutes per day) = 202 days

Again, there is an intangible benefit: Your work will probably look better when you're able to compose it on a bigger screen. Like accelerating your Mac, adding a larger monitor will reduce your frustration level. And, you'll find yourself printing fewer documents, making the purchase of a large screen even more attractive.

Which Monitor to Buy

The cost of a larger monitor has dropped dramatically since I bought my first external monitor, a Radius full-page display, in 1987. Whereas I paid about $2,000 for it, single-page displays are available today for around $500, including the video board! I must say, I used the Radius Full Page Display for over eighteen months, and it always performed beautifully. Based on that experience, I recommend Radius video products without hesitation.

I have had good experiences in the past with SuperMac monitors, and I recently used an inexpensive 19-inch display from Mirror Technologies that works well. Ultimately I purchased a Sigma Designs L-View MultiMode 19-inch monochrome monitor. It was somewhat more expensive than the Mirror, but I like it a lot. (See Appendix B for more about this monitor—it's great!) Many of my friends use monitors made by RasterOps. All of them—Radius, SuperMac, Mirror, Sigma, and RasterOps—have reputations for well-made products.

You're going to spend a lot of time staring into your monitor, so be sure you make a selection you can live with. Perhaps more than for any other component, you should arrange to spend some time with the monitor you're planning to buy before you buy it. Hang out at dealers, user groups, and friend's offices and homes—anywhere you might see an external monitor in action. Examine the image near the edges of the screen closely. If there's noticeable distortion, that's probably not a screen you want. Also pay particular attention to whether the image on the screen looks smaller than the same image on the 9-inch Mac screen. Some monitors reduce the image as much as 15 percent, so that 9-point type on the large screen will appear about the same size as 8-point type on a compact Mac's built-in monitor. Pay particular attention to the sharpness of small text characters near the edges and corners of the screen. Another thing to look for is noticeable flickering. There shouldn't be any. If it appears to flicker, look for another monitor.

Tip

> Make sure there are no other monitors or speakers nearby. Both can induce flickering.

Whichever brand of monitor you choose, make sure it's easily serviced. A monitor is about as reliable as a television set—that is, if it works for a few days, it will probably give you years of trouble-free service. Remember, though, that bringing it in for repair to a local dealer is more convenient than shipping it back to a mail-order vendor. And though a local dealer may have a loaner unit in stock, buying a monitor by mail order is usually significantly less expensive. Still, if you need to send a monitor back for repair, be prepared to wait several weeks for its return, and most mail-order vendors don't offer loaners.

It's best if you can find a monitor with a 30-day moneyback guarantee. That way, if it doesn't live up to your expectations, you're not stuck with it. After all, a monitor is a pretty significant purchase—one you'll have to live with for a few years.

One last thing: Don't place the monitor directly on top of the Mac II case unless you use a monitor stand. Two bad things happen when you place the monitor right on the case. First, you can get interference on the screen. Second, you can block the air vents on the top of the II. If you must have your monitor sitting on your Mac II, get a monitor stand made specifically for that. Ergotron and Kensington make a variety of monitor stands for screens of all sizes.

Recommendations

A variety of RAM chips, accelerator boards, and external monitors are available. A complete listing of the products I recommend follows:

RAM

Microtech International, Inc.
158 Commerce Street
East Haven, CT 06512
800–325–1895

Microtech is one of the largest sellers of RAM and also makes a complete line of hard disks and tape drives.

Technology Works
4030 Braker Lane West, Suite 350
Austin, TX 78759
800–688–7466
512–794–8533

Technology Works is the largest direct marketer of RAM and also makes a complete line of Ethernet cards and network management software.

Connectix

2655 Campus Drive
San Mateo, CA 94403–2520
800–950–5880
415–571–5100

Connectix makes Maxima, the RAM disk software I use.

Accelerators

DayStar Digital

5556 Atlanta Highway
Flowery Branch, GA 30542
800–962–2077
404–967–2077

DayStar is a manufacturer of high-performance accelerator products that specializes in cutting-edge technology. It was one of the first to ship a 68030 accelerator.

Radius

1710 Fortune Drive
San Jose, CA 95131
800–227–2795
408–434–1010

Radius is one of the most popular developers of Macintosh accelerators and displays. Started several years ago by a bunch of guys who worked on the design of the original Mac, the company has established an excellent reputation as one of the most reliable suppliers of innovative, well-engineered products.

Monitors

Apple Computer, Inc.
20525 Mariani Avenue
Cupertino, CA 95014
408–996–1010
800–776–2333
Black-and-white, gray-scale, and color video cards and monitors.

Apple monitors are a surprisingly good value. Priced competitively, they perform as well or better than most of the other monitors on the market. You should definitely consider one if you've got any Mac other than a 512K, Plus, Classic, or SE.

Mirror Technologies
2644 Patton Road
Roseville, MN 55113
800–654–5294
612–633–4450
Black-and-white, gray-scale, and color video cards and monitors.

Mirror monitors have a one-year warranty and a 30-day moneyback guarantee, and are only available directly from Mirror.

Radius
1710 Fortune Drive
San Jose, CA 95131
800–227–2795
408–434–1010
Black-and-white, gray-scale, and color video cards and monitors.

Radius has an excellent reputation as one of the most reliable suppliers of innovative, well-engineered products. I have extensive experience with their monitors and recommend them highly.

RasterOps
2500 Walsh Avenue
Santa Clara, CA 95051
800–SAY–COLOR
408–562–4200
Black-and-white, gray-scale, and color video cards and monitors. Systems are priced from approximately $600 to about $2,000.

RasterOps also has an excellent reputation as a reliable supplier of innovative, well-engineered monitors.

SuperMac Technology
485 Potrero Avenue
Sunnyvale, CA 94086
800–624–8999
408–245–2202
Black-and-white, gray-scale, and color video cards and monitors.

SuperMac specializes in display systems for the Mac. This is one of the most popular manufacturers of Macintosh monitors, with a complete selection of display products.

Sigma Designs
47900 Bayside Parkway
Fremont, CA 94538
510–770–0100
800–845–8086
Black-and-white and gray-scale video cards and monitors.

What can I say? When it came time to shell out cash for a 19-inch monochrome monitor, this is the one I chose.

Monitor Stands

Ergotron, Inc.
>   3450 Yankee Drive, Suite 100
>   Eagan, MN 55122
>   612–452–8135
>   800–888–8458

Ergotron makes a wide variety of monitor stands, CPU stands, and security products.

Kensington Microware
>   251 Park Avenue South
>   New York, NY 10010
>   800–535–4242
>   212–475–5200

Kensington is the largest manufacturer of Macintosh accessories, including CPU stands, surge protectors, antiglare filters, and input devices.

Summary

If you typically use many applications in the course of a day, you should consider upgrading your machine's RAM and utilizing System 7 or MultiFinder under System 6.

If you feel your machine is sluggish when opening and closing documents, scrolling, redrawing the screen, or copying files, you should consider an accelerator, an Apple upgrade to a faster Mac, or selling your Mac and buying a faster one.

If you find yourself scrolling around your documents a lot each day, you will probably benefit from a larger monitor.

These hardware solutions are not mutually exclusive. If your budget allows, you might want to consider more than one. A faster Mac, along with a RAM upgrade, will yield a machine that's not only fast, but can run multiple applications simultaneously. That particular combination is possible on any Mac.

A large-screen monitor added to the mix will not only allow you to see an entire page in most applications without scrolling, but will also let you easily see multiple windows in the Finder. If you have a Plus, Classic, or SE, however, you may not be able to have all of these things at the same time. Some manufacturers make products that will allow this configuration on a Plus, Classic, or SE, so if this combination is what you want, check first that it's possible to install everything in your particular Mac.

Now that you have your Macintosh outfitted with more memory, speed, and video display, let's take a look at another important hardware component—printers. The next chapter discusses everything you need to know about printers and printing, and gives tips and hints on how to get the best results possible.

8

About Printers and Printing

Everything you need to know to get the best results, no matter which printer you use.

Using the Macintosh to manipulate images and text on the screen is a breeze. It would seem that getting those images and text to appear on paper exactly as they look on the screen would be simple. After all, we've got WYSIWYG technologies—what you see is what you get, isn't it?

The answer is "sometimes." Depending on the printer and the software, what you see on the screen is not always what you get on the printed page. This chapter will give you some practical tips, hints, and warnings about getting the best results (that is, improving printing speed and the look of your printed material), no matter which printer you're using. The chapter also covers fonts, the difference between screen and printer fonts, and a discussion of PostScript and TrueType fonts.

The chapter begins with some observations on printing in general. Next, specific sections deal with the four most popular printer types— dot-matrix (ImageWriter), inkjet (StyleWriter), laser (LaserWriter), and imagesetter (Linotronic)—plus some tips on printing envelopes and labels, and the familiar "Recommendations" and "Summary" sections.

Printing Basics

Printing documents is as easy as following these basic steps under both System 6 and System 7:

- Make sure your Macintosh is connected to a printer— either directly through the printer port in back of the computer, or indirectly through network cabling connecting either the modem or the printer port of the computer to a printer connected over a network.
- Turn on your printer.
- Make sure your System Folder contains the appropriate printer drivers needed for your Mac to communicate with the printer.
- Use the Chooser desk accessory to choose a printer to use.
- Set page options using your software's Page Setup command.
- Set printing options using your software's Print command.
- Print the document.

It may seem obvious, but bears reminding, that before you can print from your Mac, you need a printer connected to your Mac and the printer needs to be turned on.

Additionally, your System Folder must have a printer driver for each type of printer you want to use. If you're using an Apple printer, such as an ImageWriter, StyleWriter, or LaserWriter, their associated printer drivers come with the System software. When you use the Installer to install Macintosh System software, the Installer copies all the printer drivers and the PrintMonitor program to the System Folder. The PrintMonitor and the printer drivers must be in the Extensions folder in the System Folder in System 7. (In System 6, they are just in the System Folder.)

Definition

> A *printer driver* is software that allows the Mac to communicate with a particular type of printer. Under both Systems, you select a printer driver using the Chooser desk accessory. Printer drivers are usually named for the printer they drive—the LaserWriter driver is called LaserWriter, the ImageWriter driver is called ImageWriter, and so on.

Tip

> You can trash any printer drivers you don't expect to use. For example, most people will never use an LQ ImageWriter or LQ AppleTalk ImageWriter, so if they're in your System Folder (Extensions folder under System 7), you can trash them and gain a bit of space on your hard disk, about 75K for each one you delete.
>   If you someday discover that you need them, they're easily reinstalled from your System software disks.

Choosing a Printer

Once you've verified that a printer is connected and turned on and the printer drivers are in the System Folder, the next step is to choose a printer. Your configuration may have just one printer, or it may have several output devices, connected to your Mac either directly or over a network. In any case, use the Chooser to select a printer (see Figure 8–1).

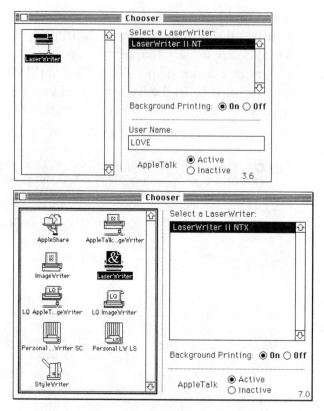

Figure 8–1.   The Chooser window under System 6 (top)
and under System 7 (bottom)

The left area of the Chooser shows the icons of available
output devices. If you are on a network that has been seg-
mented into AppleTalk zones, the bottom left area of the
Chooser shows the zones currently connected to the network.
After you click on an icon, the top right part of the Chooser lists
the names of all printers or other devices connected to your
Mac, either directly or over a network. Below this list are the
options for turning on or off the Background Printing feature.

Background printing, which is available only under System
7 and under System 6 with MultiFinder, lets you perform other
tasks on your computer while documents print *in the background*.
In other words, your computer is not tied up while you print.

Tip

Background printing works only with laser printers and StyleWriters at present.

Below the Background Printing options are the options for making AppleTalk active or inactive. To use network printers or to print to a LaserWriter connected through the printer port, AppleTalk must be set to Active.

Here are the steps for choosing a printer under both System 6 and System 7:

1. Select the type of printer by clicking its icon in the top left area of the Chooser.
2. If you're on a network that has zones, select your printer's zone.
3. Select the specific printer you want by clicking its name in the top right area of the Chooser. (This is necessary only if you have one or more printers of the same type—for example, if you are connected to two LaserWriters.)
4. If you are using System 7 or System 6 with MultiFinder, click On to turn on Background Printing. (Background Printing does take up extra RAM; so if you are low on memory, you may opt to leave this off.)
5. If you are using a LaserWriter or an AppleTalk ImageWriter, click Active to turn on AppleTalk.
6. Click the Chooser's close box to have your settings take effect.

If you always use the same printer, never changing it using the Chooser, you need to do this only once. If you switch between two or more printers, you should begin each work session by choosing the printer you'll be using.

Tip

If you switch between two or more printers, it's important that the first thing you do after switching printers is choose Page Setup in the File menu (of whatever application you're using) and click OK. You don't have to change anything in the Page Setup dialog box—just open it and click OK.

Get into the habit of doing this each time you switch printers, and before you start working on your document. It will ensure that your document is formatted properly for the printer you plan to use.

Setting Page Options

Next, after choosing the printer you want to use, you need to set page options in the Page Setup dialog box (which is described in Chapter 2). As a review, whether you are printing from the desktop or from within an application, you follow these basic steps to set printing options under System 6 or System 7:

1. Choose Page Setup from the File menu.
2. In the Page Setup dialog box, select or change the options you want. Page Setup dialog box options include paper size, page reduction/enlargement, horizontal/vertical page orientation, and various printer effects. These options vary by the type of printer you select in the Chooser.
3. Click OK.

Printing a Document

So, you've selected your printer, set page options, and now you are ready to print:

1. Select the document you want to print in the Finder, or open the document in the appropriate application.
2. Choose Print from the File menu, or press Command-P.
3. In the Print dialog box, specify or change any printing

options you want. Print dialog box options include number of printed copies, range of pages to print, cover page options, paper-feed method, printed color, and destination of printed output. These options vary by the type of printer you select in the Chooser.

4. Click Print to begin printing.

If you have set Background Printing On in the Chooser, a printing status box and the watch cursor appear on the screen for a second or two. When they disappear, you are free to resume other work while your printing job is in progress. You can check the printing status at any time by opening the PrintMonitor. To do this, choose PrintMonitor from the Appli-cation menu (System 7) or from the Apple menu (System 6). The PrintMonitor window opens, displaying the current status of your printing job (see Figure 8–2).

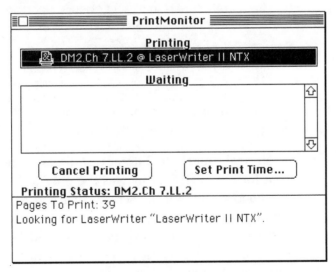

Figure 8–2.   The PrintMonitor window

With the PrintMonitor window open, you can cancel print-ing, set the time you want documents to print, and generally monitor the printing process.

You can also cancel most printing jobs by typing Command-. (Command-period).

Introduction to Fonts

Three font formats are in use today: bitmapped, PostScript, and TrueType. In the ImageWriter section of this chapter, you'll learn how to use bitmapped fonts to get decent results. I recommend you do this only if Adobe Type Manager or TrueType isn't available.

Working with bitmapped fonts is archaic in today's Macintosh environment. If you're using System 6, I heartily recommend you use PostScript fonts with Adobe Type Manager; if you're using System 7, either PostScript or TrueType fonts provide better results.

The Doctor's Opinion

> Fonts can be a confusing issue. I have two bits of advice that will almost certainly make your experiences better and more fulfilling:
> 1. Upgrade to System 7 if you haven't already. System 7 is much more intelligent about managing your fonts than previous systems, and requires you know a lot less about what kind of font you're using and where it should be installed.
> 2. If you plan to use more than a handful of fonts, get a copy of either Suitcase or MasterJuggler to manage them, even under System 7. (There's a discussion of these utilities and why they're important in Chapter 10.)

Historical Interlude Bitmapped fonts were the original Mac font format. In 1984, this was the only technology available. To get good results on the screen, you had to install a bitmapped font for each and every size you wanted to use. And to get good results when you printed them, you had to install sizes two or three times as big as the size used in your document. Even then, bitmapped fonts printed with discernible jagginess. But it wasn't a big problem—we only had dot-matrix printers; laser printers had yet to be invented.

To make matters worse, fonts were installed and removed with a totally unintuitive piece of software known as Font/DA Mover.

In 1987 the LaserWriter was introduced. It produced pages using a brand new technology called PostScript, a device-independent page-description language created by Adobe Systems, which provides a way for files created on any computer to be output at the highest resolution the printer allows. It also allowed your printed text to look good no matter what size you chose.

Of course, in order to do this, you needed to use a new kind of font, called a PostScript font. (Postscript fonts are sometimes called Type 1 fonts. There is also such a thing as Type 3 PostScript fonts, which work almost the same as the more common Type 1 format, but they're rarely found these days. Nobody knows if there was ever a PostScript Type 2.)

PostScript fonts built on the old bitmap technology. They came in two pieces: the screen font, which was nothing more than an old fashioned bitmapped font, and the printer font, which was automatically sent to the printer whenever you used the screen font of the same name in a document.

Things were a little rocky for a while. Users often tried to print bitmapped fonts on LaserWriters, with predictably bad results. Early software sometimes had trouble automatically sending the proper font to the printer.

And even though PostScript fonts always (all right, not always, but usually) printed just fine regardless of the size you used, they would look good on the screen only if you had the proper sizes installed.

And PostScript fonts had their drawbacks, the most significant of which was that they worked only if you used them with an expensive PostScript laser printer such as the Apple LaserWriter.

That all changed in 1988, when Adobe began shipping a product called Adobe Type Manager (ATM). ATM is a wonderful Control Panel device that makes your fonts look great on the screen and on the printer, regardless of the size you choose or the printer you use!

ATM became extremely popular among users of non-PostScript printers such as the ImageWriter, StyleWriter, LaserWriter IIsc, and DeskWriter, because it improves the resolution of their output dramatically, and it doesn't require that you have the correct size of screen font installed. If ATM is running, any PostScript Type 1 font will look excellent on the screen or on the printed page, regardless of which sizes of screen fonts you have installed.

Tip

This last statement isn't entirely true. Small type sizes—below 14 points—look better on the screen if you install the appropriate screen font as well. That's because the screen (bitmapped) fonts are hand-tuned to look good on a 72dpi screen.

With the release of System 7, Apple introduced its TrueType outline font technology, which works a lot like the combination of PostScript fonts and ATM. TrueType is built into System 7 software, and System 7 comes with several TrueType fonts. If you use TrueType fonts, you'll get good results without having to install various-size bitmapped fonts as explained above.

The other big thing System 7 introduced was drag-and-drop font installation. No more Font/DA Mover. (Yea!) With System 7, you install any font by dragging its icon onto the System Folder.

The Difference between TrueType and Type 1 Fonts Technically, Type 1 fonts are PostScript fonts, and TrueType fonts aren't. To you, the end user, there is little difference. If you're using ATM, both look good on the screen in any point size; both print beautifully at any point size, on any printer. Unless you're involved in desktop publishing and working with a service bureau that provides high-resolution output (in which case you should probably stick to PostScript fonts—more on this later in the chapter), you can mix and match them with no ill effect.

Perhaps the only noticeable difference to you, the user, is that a Type 1 font comes in two (sometimes three) pieces—a bitmapped screen font, a separate printer font, and in many cases, a font metrics (AFM) file. TrueType fonts come in one piece—a single file that contains both the screen and printer fonts. Each type of font—screen (bitmap), PostScript Type 1, or TrueType—has a distinctive icon. All screen fonts have a little suitcase icon; all TrueType fonts have an icon with three As on it; printer fonts (and AFM files) from different vendors have different icons. Figure 8–3 shows the icons for each of the different types of font.

 TrueType font icon

Avant Garde

 Screen font icon

Adobe Caslon

 PostScript printer font icon (Adobe)

ACasReg

 PostScript printer font icon (Bitstream)

Latin

Figure 8–3 .   Each kind of font has a distinctive icon

Tip

Recently, Apple and Adobe announced that ATM will be built into a future version of System 7 software. At this writing, the details of this agreement are sketchy. But, in theory, this is what this agreement means to Mac users: ATM will be built into the System 7 software; it probably won't be called ATM anymore. This will give you the ability to drag any font onto your System Folder, whether it's the pieces of a PostScript font or a one-piece TrueType font. It will be installed in the proper place, and look good on the screen and in printed output. This is very good news.

Check with your user group, on-line service, or dealer for details.

Where to Get Fonts

You can go forever without obtaining any fonts beyond what are supplied with your System software—there is no law saying you must get more fonts. Still, chances are someday you'll become bored with the standard Apple fonts and will want to add to your collection.

When you do, you can either buy commercial fonts, or look for shareware or public-domain fonts. Literally thousands of commercial fonts are available from dozens of different vendors such as Adobe, Bitstream, DUBL-CLiCK, and Casady & Greene. Or, you can get hundreds of shareware and public-domain fonts from user groups and on-line services. Many excellent fonts are available as public-domain software or shareware.

Tip

If you don't own a laser printer, but you want to have your document(s) printed on one, laser printer or Linotronic service bureaus are all over the country. Most will provide you with screen fonts for use with their printers for no cost or at a low price (usually no more than the price of the blank disks). Just use their screen fonts in your document, then bring the document on disk to the service bureau for printing. There's more on service bureaus later in the chapter.

About Printers in General

The way your printouts look will vary depending on the printer or other output device you use. The chief distinction between printers is resolution. Resolution is measured in dots per inch (dpi). The higher the resolution (that is, the more dots per inch), the sharper and clearer characters and graphics will appear on the printed page.

In general, there are four types of printers, listed here from low to high resolution:

- Dot-matrix printers
- Inkjet printers
- Laser printers
- Imagesetters or typesetting machines

Dot-matrix printers work by imprinting a pattern of dots for each character on the page. If you examine dot-matrix printed output closely, you can actually see the dots that comprise each character. An ImageWriter II is one of the more popular dot-matrix printers for the Macintosh.

Inkjet printers operate by first heating up an element in the inkjet cartridge. As the ink in front of the heating element begins to vaporize and expand, pressure is increased, forcing the ink to shoot onto the paper through a nozzle. Most inkjet printers, such as the Apple StyleWriter and the Hewlett-Packard DeskWriter, can produce output at 300 or 360dpi.

Laser printers, such as Apple's LaserWriter series of printers, are better-than-letter-quality, sometimes called near-typeset-quality. LaserWriters produce printed output at 300dpi. The latest LaserWriters, the IIg and IIf, use sophisticated built-in technology to enhance their resolution and make your pages appear to have been printed at 400 to 600dpi. They're also capable of printing more levels of gray than earlier LaserWriters.

Don't be fooled by the terminology. If you want a document to have the professional look obtained by typesetting, you'll have to use an imagesetter such as the Linotronic 300, which produces true-typeset-quality pages at 1,270 to 2,540dpi on paper or negative film.

The Linotronic and other very high resolution image-setters are not really printers at all; rather, they are sophisticated typesetting machines capable of printing documents created on the Macintosh. It's unlikely you or your company will own one—they start at more than $30,000. Fortunately, there are organizations, called service bureaus, all over the country where you can bring your disk and have it output at very high resolution for less than $10 a page. Look in the

Yellow Pages under Typesetting to locate one near you. (Again, the section on Linotronic imagesetters later in the chapter has a complete discussion of using the Mac for typesetting.)

Select the Proper Printer for the Job

Casual correspondence or invoices may look fine printed on a dot-matrix printer, but a newsletter printed on an ImageWriter will always have a sloppy, amateurish look. If you can afford one, a LaserWriter should be used. If not, inkjet printers can offer acceptable and affordable output. If you don't own a laser printer, there's probably a service bureau in your city that will let you print documents on a laser printer for a small charge per page. Many quick print shops now have this capability; AlphaGraphics is one of the largest chains to offer it.

If your budget allows, output from the Linotronic is even more professional looking than from the LaserWriter. Almost anything you plan to have printed professionally is probably worth typesetting on a Lino.

ImageWriters and Tips for Using Them

ImageWriters are dot-matrix printers. That means the image is placed on the page by an array of wires (pins) that strike a ribbon, producing dots. The ImageWriter II, with a 9-pin print head, has a range of resolution from 72dpi in its lowest-resolution mode (called draft mode) to 144dpi in its highest-resolution (called near-letter-quality or NLQ mode). By contrast, the discontinued ImageWriter LQ, which has 27 pins, provides letter-quality, its best mode, at 216dpi.

ImageWriter printers are most often used for printing correspondence and business forms. The ImageWriter LQ was particularly flexible in handling forms and envelopes but was plagued by mechanical problems and made a *lot* of noise, so much that it was referred to by many owners as the "printer from hell." Avoid the ImageWriter LQ at all costs.

Now, let's move on to specific tips for using these printers.

Getting the Best Results

The first part of this section applies to both System 6 and System 7, but a couple of improvements—TrueType and ATM—are built into System 7. Though the following technique will work fine with System 7, you'll get the best results, and it will be a lot easier for you, if you use TrueType or Type 1 fonts. Complete explanations appear later in this section.

Assuming you don't have System 7 or ATM, the first thing you need to know in order to get the best results from your ImageWriter is how to get good-quality text to print using only bitmapped fonts. To begin with, when you choose Print from the File menu, the Print dialog box presents options for printing to an ImageWriter, if this is the printer you chose in the Chooser. Be sure to specify Best as the printing mode. When you specify Best in the Print dialog box, the Mac searches through your installed fonts, looking for either:

- A font two times the size of each font used in the document (ImageWriter, ImageWriter II)
  or
- A font three times the size of each font used in the document (ImageWriter LQ)

The Mac looks for these sizes because it can scale them better than other sizes. (A more complete discussion of scaling bitmaps appears later in the chapter under the heading "Magic Laser Printer Scaling Percentages.")

Screen fonts are bitmaps, just like graphics created with MacPaint. That means they are a collection of dots on the screen, 72 to the inch, arranged to look like letters and numbers.

If the size you selected isn't installed, your Mac will attempt to scale another size of that font. The results will be unappealing unless it finds an installed size it can accurately scale (that is, a font two or three times the size of the one used in your document, depending on your printer).

For your convenience, installed screen font sizes always appear in outlined letters in the menu, as shown in Figure 8–4.

Figure 8–4.   Installed font sizes always appear in outlined letters

So, in this illustration, you can see that I've got Geneva 9- and 12-point fonts installed. If I wanted to print a document in Geneva 12 at the highest resolution possible on an ImageWriter, I would have to install Geneva 24.

Here's another example:

If your document uses Helvetica 12 point and Times 10 point, for Best quality printing, you need to have:

- Helvetica 12 and 24 and Times 10 and 20 screen fonts installed (ImageWriter, ImageWriter II) or
- Helvetica 12 and 36 and Times 10 and 30 screen fonts installed (ImageWriter LQ)

If you don't have those sizes installed, get them and install them (you can use Suitcase II or MasterJuggler). It will make a big difference in the way your Best quality printing comes out. Or, use only fonts you already have in the proper sizes.

If you insist on using System 6, get a copy of ATM and use it with PostScript fonts, or upgrade to System 7. Both will allow you to avoid all this two-times-the-size nonsense.

Fast, Legible Draft Printing

The ImageWriter can print quite quickly, up to 250 characters per second, in the draft mode. Unfortunately, if you just select Draft in the Print dialog of your word processor, you're likely to end up with something that looks like Figure 8–5. Note the unpredictable spacing.

```
The ImageWriter is    capable of    printing
quite fast, up  to  250  characters    per
second, in the draft mode.   Unfortunately,
if you just try printing   in the    draft
mode, you're likely to  end up         with
something that looks like   this.
```

Figure 8-5.   Badly spaced draft printing on an ImageWriter

You can do a couple of things to ensure better-quality draft printing. The first is to change your entire document to the Monaco font, 9-point size. This is because Monaco is the high-speed draft font built into ImageWriters.

To change the font:

1. Just before you print a draft, select all the text in your document. (In many applications, you can press Command-A to select all text.)
2. Change the font type to Monaco by choosing Monaco from the Font menu.
3. Change the font size to 9 by choosing 9 from the Font or Size menu.

It's also a good idea to make sure your text is left-aligned, not justified. You'll get better word spacing if you don't print justified text. If you align your text ragged right, and change the text font to Monaco 9, your draft printouts should look like Figure 8–6.

```
The ImageWriter is capable of printing quite
fast, up to 250 characters per second, in
the draft mode. If the text is Monaco 9, and
not fully justified, you'll get much better
results. The ImageWriter is capable of
printing quite fast, up to 250 characters
per second, in the draft mode. If the text
is Monaco 9, and not fully justified, you'll
get much better results.
```

Figure 8–6.   ImageWriter draft printing with optimized spacing

To ensure that your draft prints at the highest speed possible, you must press the button on the ImageWriter marked Print Quality to select Draft; in addition, you must specify Draft in the Print dialog box. This will speed up printing of draft-quality documents. As far as I can tell, the Print Quality button doesn't have any effect on documents printed at settings other than Draft—printing documents using the Faster or Best setting in the Print dialog box seems to ignore the Print Quality button setting on your printer. Nobody I've asked knows why.

What about Ribbons?

ImageWriter ribbons can be replaced with NEC 8023, C.Itoh 8510, or DEC LA50 ribbons. These should be available at any good office or computer supply store. They may be considerably less expensive than Apple-branded ribbons.

If you use your ImageWriter a lot, a re-inker may be a good investment for you. A re-inker is an electromechanical device that uses a small motor to run the entire ribbon over a felt-covered inkwell. The one I use came from Computer Friends, a company that carries re-inkers for many types of ribbons, including color. They average about $60.

I've had good success with re-inked ribbons, and I think they produce a superior image—blacker blacks and less splatter—once they get worked in. I rotate four ribbons, re-inking them when they begin to print lightly and storing them in a sealed plastic bag until they're used.

Another way to extend the life of a ribbon is to open the case of a used ribbon carefully and spray the ribbon with WD-40 spray lubricant. Reassemble the case and let the ribbon dry for a while before you use it. This can often coax a few more days of life out of an almost-dead ribbon.

Whichever method you choose, don't let your ribbons get old and frayed. Throw your ribbons away at the first sign of tearing or shredding. A frayed ribbon can damage your print head by clogging it with microscopic pieces of ribbon.

Color ribbons are available for all ImageWriters. They have four colors, and they can be used with many programs to create low-resolution (but still attractive) color output. Look in the application's manual to find out if the program supports color output on the ImageWriter. If there's no information in the manual, call the manufacturer and ask.

ImageWriter Warnings

Large Black Areas   If you plan to print documents with large areas that print black or a dark gray or pattern, be careful not to overheat your print head. There's no real way to tell until it's too late. You'll know it's too late if you smell a strange burning odor coming from your printer. If you can smell something, stop the print job immediately. You're probably very close to damaging your print head, or you have already damaged it.

The solution is to print only one page at a time and wait a few minutes between pages to let your printer's head cool off. Replacing a burnt-out print head can be expensive. It's avoidable. Just give your printer a rest after printing pages with lots of dark areas.

Gummy Labels If you use any kind of sticky label in your ImageWriter, beware: You should *never* roll the page backward while labels are loaded in your printer. In other words, when you use the knob to move the paper through the printer, don't ever move it backward when you have labels loaded. If you do so, labels may become jammed between the platen and the print head, which can result in an expensive trip to the dealer.

Definition

> The *platen* is the rubber roller that serves as a backing for the paper during printing and paper loading.

Instead of bothering with trying to print labels on the ImageWriter, you may want to consider CoStar's LabelWriter printers, which are designed specifically for printing labels from any Macintosh. The two models, LabelWriter II and LabelWriter II Plus, use linear thermal print heads, which are similar to the technology used by inkjet printers, and sell for about $250 and $400, respectively. The LabelWriter II uses a 1-inch-wide print head to print on 1⅛-inch by 3½-inch labels, and the LabelWriter II Plus uses a 2¼-inch print head to print on a wider variety of label sizes (including a floppy disk label). If you print a lot of labels, the LabelWriter printer would be a good investment for you.

Inkjet Printers and Tips for Using Them

Inkjet printers use a thermal inkjet technology to eject ink onto a page. The Apple StyleWriter and HP DeskWriter printers are two of the more popular inkjet printers for the Mac.

Inkjet printers offer excellent resolution at an affordable price. For example, the Apple StyleWriter printer provides a resolution of 360dpi at a retail price of $599, and the HP DeskWriter prints at 300dpi and retails for $729. An additional benefit of inkjet printers is that they are quiet; you hardly know they are working. Inkjet printers are ideal if you want superior resolution but don't want to pay a premium price.

The Apple StyleWriter works great with bitmapped screen fonts (you need to follow the same rules as for the ImageWriter to get good results), TrueType fonts, or PostScript Type 1 fonts (you'll need to use ATM if you're running under System 6; by the time you read this, ATM should be built into System 7). The Hewlett-Packard DeskWriter also works with all three font types.

Unfortunately, inkjet printers do have drawbacks. First, be aware that the print may smudge. The ink tends to smear if you get it wet. Secondly, and more importantly, inkjet printers, especially the Apple StyleWriter, are slow. Because inkjet printers do not come with any RAM or internal processor, the work of imaging a page is done by the Mac's CPU. So the slower your Mac, the slower your printer will be at producing a printed page. For example, the StyleWriter coupled with the Classic prints at about the same speed as an ImageWriter printer.

Another thing to consider is that, if you are using a printer in a workgroup environment, the StyleWriter cannot be networked. Unlike the ImageWriter or LaserWriter printers, the StyleWriter cannot be connected over an AppleTalk network. This printer is best used by an individual Mac user.

Laser Printers and Tips for Using Them

Laser printers are a different breed of printer from dot-matrix printers. They work using a principle similar to your office copier—using electrostatic charges, toner cartridges and powder, and lasers to create crystal clear images on the page.

Definition

A *toner cartridge* contains toner powder, which serves as the laser printer's "ink," used in the printing process.

As mentioned previously, laser printers offer greater resolution than dot-matrix printers—usually 300dpi, although this may vary by brand. (The LaserWriter IIf and IIg models, by the way, print at 300dpi, but the resolution is enhanced by a technology called FinePrint. FinePrint does to laser-printed output what ATM does to dot-matrix-printed output.) The increase in resolution does cost you in terms of speed; laser printers do not print as quickly as dot-matrix printers set to draft mode. For example, the LaserWriter IINTX is rated at eight pages per minute, but in most cases it prints slower. Depending on what kind of data your document contains, a single page may take a minute or more to print.

Unlike dot-matrix or inkjet printers, laser printers have their own RAM and a CPU. A laser printer uses this RAM to store fonts that come with the printer and the CPU to quickly process the image your Mac sends. You can also add additional fonts to your printer's RAM, a process known as downloading fonts. (More about downloadable fonts in the next section.) Finally, with some laser printers, you have the option of daisy-chaining one or more hard disks (or other SCSI device, such as a CD-ROM drive) to the printer for better font management.

Laser printers generally fall into two categories: PostScript printers and non-PostScript printers.

LaserWriters and Other PostScript Printers

Most Apple LaserWriter printers (as well as the Linotronic imagesetter, discussed later in the chapter) create pages using PostScript, a page-description language created by Adobe.

Here's how PostScript works, in a nutshell: The LaserWriter driver and Laser Prep file in your System Folder convert the image created by your application (Word, Canvas, Excel, or any other application) into PostScript code, which is sent to the printer. A few applications—most notably PageMaker, which uses its own Aldus Prep file instead of Laser Prep—create their own PostScript, bypassing the Apple printer drivers.

Because PostScript is an accurate page-description language, you can create and preview complex images on the screen and then print a page that is, with few exceptions, the same as what you see on the screen. (This capability is known as WYSIWYG, or What You See Is What You Get.) The resolution will be the highest the printer allows, because PostScript is what's called a device-independent page-description language. That means PostScript files automatically print at the highest resolution the printer allows. PostScript is what makes alphanumeric characters print so nicely on a laser printer or a high-resolution imagesetter such as the Linotronic.

Using PostScript Fonts   Under System 6, fonts designed for use with PostScript printers consist of two (or three) parts: the screen font, which you install with the Font/DA Mover (or a utility such as Suitcase II or MasterJuggler); the printer (or downloadable) font; and (in some cases) a font metrics file, which you place in your System Folder.

Under System 7, you simply drag all of the parts—the screen font, printer font, and AFM file if there is one—onto your System Folder, and they're placed in the proper places automatically. The screen font is installed in your System file; the printer font is placed in the Extensions folder inside your System Folder; the AFM file, if there is one, remains loose in the System Folder.

The printer font is downloaded (that is, loaded into the printer's memory) automatically when you use the corresponding screen font. You don't have to do anything more than have the proper screen and printer fonts to make this happen.

To make things even more confusing, some fonts are built into your laser printer. When you're using one of these fonts, you need only have the screen font installed to produce high-resolution printouts; no separate printer font is required.

Fonts that are built into most laser printers include:

- Times
- Helvetica
- Courier
- Symbol

In addition to the plain style, bold, italic, and bold-italic styles are included with all of these except Symbol.

Also built into the LaserWriter Plus, the LaserWriter IINT, IINTX, IIf, IIg, and many third-party PostScript and PostScript-compatible printers are the following fonts:

- Palatino
- Avant Garde
- Bookman
- Helvetica Narrow
- New Century Schoolbook
- Zapf Chancery
- Zapf Dingbats

In addition to the plain style, bold, italic, and bold-italic styles are included with all of these except Zapf Chancery and Zapf Dingbats.

So for any typeface included with your printer, you don't need a printer (downloadable) font if you have the screen font available. As long as you have the proper screen font, the printer will supply the high-resolution font from its internal memory.

If you would like to use fonts other than those permanently installed in your printer, you'll have to purchase them from a third-party vendor such as Bitstream or Adobe. (In addition to inventing PostScript, Adobe also sells an extensive line of downloadable fonts.)

You should know which fonts are permanently installed in the printer you plan to use. The manual should list them, or you can find out using LaserStatus (part of the DiskTop package from CE Software). Once you know which fonts are permanently installed in the printer, you need to get the screen fonts for those you want to use. Most printers come with a disk containing a complete set of screen fonts that match the built-in fonts. (See the section earlier in this chapter for where to get screen fonts.)

Remember this: If it's not built into your printer, and you don't have the downloadable font in your System Folder (or Extensions folder if you use System 7), don't use it. It will look lousy.

Many good PostScript and PostScript-compatible printers are made by third-party manufacturers.

The Doctor's
Opinion
☎

PostScript-compatible printers use a clone, a PostScript work-alike, instead of true Adobe PostScript. Compatibility of PostScript-compatible printers has been, for the most part, very good. Clone printers are significantly less expensive, and usually print any page that can be printed on a true PostScript printer. Many clone printers are faster than their true Adobe PostScript counterparts.

Special Considerations Under System 7 The inclusion of Apple's TrueType and Adobe's ATM font technologies into System 7 software eliminates much of the confusion about fonts and laser printers. TrueType uses a single font outline file to create smooth-looking characters at any point size; and ATM's technology accomplishes basically the same result using two-part fonts—screen fonts coupled with printer fonts. No matter which fonts you have installed—TrueType, Adobe Type 1, or other third-party Type 1 fonts—System 7 seamlessly outputs fonts at the best resolution your printer (or monitor) is capable of producing.

To install a font under System 7, just drag its icons onto the System Folder's icon, and it will install and configure itself automatically. If it's a PostScript font, there will be more than one piece to drag onto the System Folder's icon for the font to work properly.

Initially, you'll receive a handful of TrueType fonts with your System software. But almost every third-party font vendor has pledged to provide their libraries in TrueType format. And don't worry about your old fonts—System 7 still supports all your old bitmapped and PostScript fonts; TrueType merely provides a third option.

One Final Basic Tip   If your laser printer seems stalled out and/or your Mac has frozen, restart both of them. This happens occasionally when you send a page that's too complicated for the printer to understand. First restart the Mac, then restart the printer by turning it off, waiting a few seconds, and turning it back on. (Remember, restarting clears your RAM, so you can start out fresh.) Now that both machines have been restarted, try again. If the page still refuses to print, try using a different Mac and laser printer, preferably ones with more memory (both Mac and printer) than the ones you first tried it on.

About Non-PostScript Laser and Inkjet Printers

Some laser and inkjet printers don't use PostScript. The Apple LaserWriter IISC, the Apple StyleWriter, the GCC Personal Laser Printer, and the HP DeskWriter are the most popular. Instead of PostScript, they use QuickDraw, the descriptive language built into every Macintosh (it's in the ROM). Though they're significantly less expensive than their PostScript counterparts, they also have some drawbacks.

First, they are significantly slower than PostScript laser printers.

Second, they may have problems printing large or complex documents. Unlike PostScript printers, which process your file at the printer, a QuickDraw printer uses your Mac to do the processing, then sends the processed information to the printer. Because your Mac is doing more work, QuickDraw printers may require more than 1Mb of RAM on the Mac to print certain documents.

Third, some applications (FreeHand, Illustrator '88) are almost useless without PostScript. This is becoming less of a problem as non-PostScript laser printers become more popular, but it is something to check into before you buy. If you plan to purchase a QuickDraw (that is, non-PostScript) printer, you should first test it extensively with the applications you use most frequently.

Finally, QuickDraw printers don't work as well as a PostScript printer for proofing before output on a Linotronic. That's because the Linotronic is also a PostScript device, so the page it prints will be an exact match of the page you printed on a PostScript printer, except that the Linotronic will print it at the highest resolution it can. All spacing will be exactly the same, whether you use a PostScript laser printer or a Linotronic. The only difference is that the laser printer output will be at 300dpi, and the Linotronic will be 1,270 or 2,540dpi, depending upon which model you use.

A non-PostScript laser printer will serve you well if you use it for correspondence, graphics created with compatible programs (such as Canvas 3.0 or SuperPaint 3.0), and reports. If you plan to do serious page-layout work, if you want to use powerful drawing programs such as FreeHand and Illustrator '88, and especially if you plan to use a Linotronic for camera-ready output, you'll want a laser printer with PostScript.

Laser Printer Tips and Hints

Getting Rid of the Startup Page   Most laser printers spit out an annoying startup page (sometimes called the test page) when you turn them on. There are two ways to prevent it:

- Use Widgets. It comes with DiskTop, from CE Software (see Chapter 10). It has a menu item for turning the startup page on or off.
- Pull the paper tray out a little bit before turning your laser printer on. Don't push it back in until your laser printer is warmed up, usually one or two minutes. This fools the printer into thinking it's already printed the startup page.

Blacker Blacks and Less Toner Flaking   If you want your laser-printed pages to be even better looking, go to an artist's supply store and buy a can of spray fixative. It's a protective coating for artwork, used primarily by artists. It also happens to be wonderful when used on laser-printed output.

Krylon is the brand I use. It comes in matte and crystal clear finishes; I prefer matte, which doesn't create as shiny a finish, but you should try them both. When your page comes out of the laser printer, give it a misting with this stuff. Black areas will get blacker and the page will stand up better to handling because the fixative binds the toner to the page. It's also helpful if you use laser-printed output as camera-ready art for printing.

Definition

Camera-ready is a printing and publishing term used to mean the output is in its final form, ready to be prepared for the printing press.

Spray fixative on anything you're going to have reproduced, even if it's being copied on the office copier. The blacker blacks and lack of toner flaking will make the results more aesthetically pleasing. For the same reason, it's especially important to use fixative on anything you're taking to the printer to have professionally printed. You'll be surprised at how much better pages look after fixative is applied.

One word of warning: Don't use too much, or you'll end up with a runny mess. A light mist is all that's needed.

The Question of Paper   For everyday use, the cheapest photocopier paper you can get is fine. There's even a school of thought that says it's better than more expensive paper because there is less powder between the sheets (to keep them from sticking together).

For better-quality output, especially for documents that will be printed or photocopied, I find Hammermill Laser Plus to be as good as any paper. You'll find it at any good office supply store or paper distributor; look in your local Yellow Pages. At about 2.5¢ a sheet, it's somewhat more expensive than cheap photocopier paper, which can usually be found for less than 1¢ a sheet. Laser Plus has a finer finish, it is a little sturdier, and it seems to take the toner better than cheap photocopier paper.

Whenever I prepare final, camera-ready documents on a laser printer for reproduction or printing, I use CG Graphic Arts LASEREDGE paper. It's even more expensive than Hammermill Laser Plus (between 7¢ and 12¢ a sheet), but it's whiter, and the dots appear crisper. LASEREDGE papers are treated with a special chemical coating that ensures 100 percent of the toner is applied to the surface of the paper and none is absorbed. Most other papers absorb at least a part of the toner into the sheet. This is why LASEREDGE paper is the best paper I know for final camera-ready work.

With most kinds of paper, a misting with a spray fixative will improve the appearance and durability of your page. It is not necessary if you use LASEREDGE papers, since they are formulated with a special coating that prevents toner flaking. If you're unsure, print two copies of the same page, and mist only one with fixative. Now examine them both closely, preferably with a magnifying glass. Choose the one that has the most perfectly formed characters and/or the richest black tones.

Magic Laser Printer Scaling Percentages   If you're printing a bitmapped graphic (that is, one created with MacPaint, Amazing Paint, or most programs with *Paint* in their names) reduce it by one of these percentages before printing it on a laser printer: 96, 72, 48, or 24 percent. You can reduce a bitmapped graphic in the program you used to create it. (Or, if you are using Microsoft Word or most other word-processing packages, press and hold down the Shift key as you click and drag the bottom left selection handle of the graphic. Word shows the scaled percentage in the bottom of the document window.)

Here's why those percentages are so important:

Your Mac screen displays 72 dots per inch. MacPaint images are stored at 72dpi. In order for dots not to be squashed (that is, distorted and showing a lot of jaggies) when being converted from 72dpi to 300dpi, you need to scale them by the appropriate percentage.

If you don't reduce the paint image, your laser printer must print 4.166 dots (at 300dpi) to represent each dot on the screen (72dpi):

$$300 \div 72 = 4.166$$

Because the printer can't print fractions of a dot, paint images that aren't reduced by one of the magic scaling percentages may show more jagged edges than those that are. In fact, jaggedness in printouts of nonreduced images will be greater than what you see on the screen.

If you *do* reduce the paint image to 96 percent of its original size, your laser printer can print exactly 4 dots (at 300dpi) to represent each dot on the screen (72dpi):

$$300 * .96 = 288$$

$$288 \div 72 = 4.000$$

Because there are no longer any fractions of a dot, paint images will print with less jaggedness.

There is an automatic way to reduce images by the largest magic percentage, 96 percent: Select Precision Bitmap Alignment from the Page Setup dialog before you print. This reduces your entire page to 96 percent of its original size.

If that's undesirable, as it may be if your final output must exactly match the dimensions you used to create it, most page-layout software allows you to scale only the bitmapped graphics. PageMaker even does it for you if you scale an image while holding down the Command key. The Clipper (discussed in Chapter 10) allows you to scale bitmapped images for use in programs that don't support scaling.

Some image distortion occurs at reductions greater than 96 percent. That's because the density of the dots increases as you reduce the graphic more. At 24 percent, many bitmapped graphics, particularly those with large patterned or black areas, squash down into unattractive blobs. Still, at percentages other than the magic ones, the distortion is almost always worse.

Toner Cartridges

Toner cartridges contain the powder, or ink, that gets printed on a laser-printed page. Most laser printer manufacturers recommend that you replace the toner cartridge once a year, or after printing every 4,000 pages. You will know when it's time to replace the cartridge when the Low Toner Level light stays constantly lit on your printer. Also, if your pages start to look too light, or if you see thin vertical white lines in dark images, it's time to replace the cartridge.

When you decide to replace the cartridge, you have the option of recharging your old cartridge rather than purchasing a new one. There is a great deal of controversy over whether it is safe to use recharged toner cartridges. Most printer manufacturers don't recommend it. That's to be expected—they make lots of money selling you new toner cartridges!

A new toner cartridge costs around $100. A recharge from a reputable supplier is about half of that. My experience is that you can usually recharge a cartridge at least two or three times before discarding it.

Many recharging companies advertise in the major Mac magazines. If you're not interested in having your cartridges recharged, some places pay about $10 for used ones. These companies also advertise in the Mac magazines.

I've had good luck with LaserCharge here in Austin, Texas. Their address and phone number appear in the "Recommendations" section at the end of the chapter.

If you want to have your laser cartridges recharged, be sure to ask the following questions:

- Do they drill a hole in your cartridge?
  If the answer is yes, find another recharging company.

The better ones completely disassemble your cartridge, clean it, replace worn components, and fill it with toner.
- Do they "pool" their cartridges?
In other words: Do you get back the same cartridge you sent in, or do they send a recharged cartridge out of inventory? You don't want to use a company that pools cartridges. You could send in a cartridge that's never been recharged, and get back one that's been recharged seven or eight times. Definitely not what you want.

I couldn't swear to it, but the recharged cartridges seem to print blacker blacks than a new cartridge. According to the rechargers, that's because the toner they use for refilling is more active (that is, the particles have a stronger charge) than the toner used in new cartridges. This makes sense.

Another thing I've noticed is that recharged cartridges seem to last longer, perhaps 10 to 20 percent longer than new ones. Again, the rechargers claim this is because they use more toner when they refill a cartridge than it came with originally.

I've never had a problem with any of the cartridges I've had recharged. If you ask the questions listed above before letting anyone refill yours, you shouldn't have problems either.

Envelope Advice for All Printer Types

How to print envelopes easily is an issue, no matter which printer you use. Envelopes are the biggest hassle on the ImageWriter. If you want to print a return address, it takes an interminable amount of adjusting to get one right. Sometimes the envelopes jam. And occasionally, no matter what you do, they smear.

Envelope Printing with the ImageWriter

If you haven't already done so, adjust the paper thickness lever to 3 or 4. The paper thickness lever is located in different places on various models. If you're not sure where yours is, refer to the manual. Also, be sure to adjust it back to single thickness when you're done printing envelopes.

This helps clear up jamming and smearing problems. Here are two easy ways to minimize the pain of envelope printing:

- Use window envelopes
- Get pin-feed envelopes

If you use window envelopes, then you can just type the name and address in the proper place on the letter or form, and you're in business. Window envelopes imprinted with your logo or return address aren't expensive, and this solution means never dealing with envelopes through the ImageWriter again.

Pin-feed envelopes are attached with a temporary glue to pin-feed paper. Believe it or not, you can get pin-feed envelopes at any good office supply store. They're especially convenient if you need to address a bunch of envelopes at a time.

Tip

Recyclable window envelopes reduce waste.

The LaserWriter II series printers (discussed in a later section) work extremely well for printing envelopes, especially if you purchase the sold-separately envelope paper cassette (which lists for about $90).

Envelope Printing with the Original LaserWriter

Unless you have purchased an envelope tray (available separately from your Apple dealer), envelope printing on one of the original LaserWriters—the LaserWriter and the LaserWriter Plus—can be tricky. You need to feed envelopes into the manual feed slot very carefully, at just the right time, or they'll jam. (If you have any of the LaserWriter IIs, or an inkjet printer, envelopes shouldn't be much of a problem. They have better envelope-handling capabilities than the LaserWriter and LaserWriter Plus.)

Here's how to print a perfect envelope every time on an original LaserWriter or LaserWriter Plus:

Make sure the address will print where you want it to. You do this by following steps 1 to 3 (below), which prints a sample of your envelope on whatever paper is loaded in your laser printer.

1. Choose Page Setup from the File menu, and click the icon on the right under Orientation. (This icon corresponds to what is called Landscape, or horizontal, page orientation.)
2. Choose Print from the File menu in your application.
3. In the Print dialog box, click Automatic Feed to select it. This prints a mock-up of your envelope on whatever paper is loaded in your laser printer. Make sure the placement of all elements is correct.
4. Now, repeat steps 1 and 2. In the Print dialog box, click Manual Feed to select it.
5. (Now for the tricky part…) Run quickly to the laser printer and place the envelope in the feed tray. Put a bit of gentle pressure on the back (trailing) edge of the envelope (see Figure 8–7).

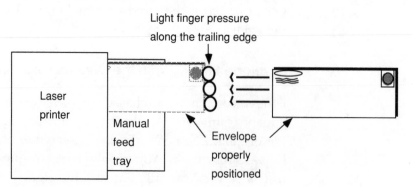

Figure 8–7.   Envelope printing on a LaserWriter printer

The Ultimate Easy Envelope Printing Software

Another problem you may have with printing addresses on envelopes is getting them to print in just the right spot. The trial-and-error method in step 1 above is a pain. One sure way is to purchase a copy of Kiwi Envelopes. Kiwi Envelopes automatically prints the address and return address in the proper places on the envelope no matter what printer you use, even an ImageWriter I or II.

With Kiwi Envelopes (see Figure 8–8), you simply type or paste the address and/or return address into the proper window, select the envelope size you are using, then click the Print button and feed an envelope to your printer (use the trailing-edge trick above if you're using a LaserWriter or LaserWriter Plus).

Kiwi Envelopes automatically pastes whatever is on the Clipboard into the mailing address field. If you copy the mailing address you need from a letter or database before invoking Kiwi Envelopes, it will appear automatically on your envelope.

The return address field comes up blank. This is good for preprinted envelopes. You also have the option of typing in a return address or even pasting in a picture.

Figure 8–8.   Kiwi Envelopes makes printing an envelope easy on any printer

The Doctor's
Opinion

Several personal database programs—Address Book Plus, DynoDex, and TouchBASE—also make printing labels and envelopes easier. If you print a lot of envelopes or labels, and/or manage a substantial list of names, addresses, and phone numbers, programs such as these bear investigation.

Third-Party Envelope and Label Printers

Another option to consider if you plan to print out numerous envelopes is the AddressWriter from CoStar Corporation. The AddressWriter is a printer specifically designed for printing envelopes. Besides doing a great job of eliminating the envelope-printing hassles, the AddressWriter is also useful for printing postcards and labels.

The AddressWriter, which carries a retail price of $595, is a small impact dot-matrix printer measuring 8.7 inches in height by 8.5 inches in width and weighing nine pounds. Its standard configuration holds up to 100 envelopes or 250 postcards. The device plugs into the printer or modem port of the Mac, and comes with its own printer driver. The AddressWriter is compatible with System 6 and System 7, and with both TrueType and Adobe Type 1 fonts.

Linotronic: Typesetting Driven by a Mac

The Linotronic imagesetters are very high resolution output devices capable of printing pages at resolutions as high as 2,540dpi. Technically, these aren't printers; they're typesetting machines. They are used when the 300dpi output of a laser printer isn't good enough. The pages in this book, for example, were output on a Compugraphic 9400 at 2400dpi before being sent to the printer for printing and binding. Color separations and high-resolution black-and-white halftones are possible using the 2,540dpi output of the Linotronic 300 or similar device. An imagesetter works on a principle similar to that used by a laser printer, except that instead of fusing toner to the page, the laser in a Linotronic device is used to print the images to high-resolution film. Of course, as in other PostScript printing devices, the image is described in PostScript, but unlike those from other printers, the pages that come out of a Linotronic need to be processed using a procedure similar to developing film from a camera.

The Doctor's
Opinion

Throughout this chapter I've referred to all high-resolution imagesetters as Linotronics. That's not really the case. Several other manufacturers (Agfa-Compugraphic and Monotype) make high-resolution imagesetters. Linotronic was the first, and it is still the most popular, so I refer to high-resolution imagesetters collectively as Linotronic because it's the brand you're most likely to encounter.

In fact, the word *Lino* has become synonymous with high-resolution output, even if it's printed on an Agfa or Monotype imagesetter. Users often say "I'm sending this job out to the Lino," or "I'm going to get this Linoed," regardless of which brand of imagesetter will actually be used.

Most people don't own a Linotronic. Rather, when they need pages printed on one, they go to a service bureau, where they can have them output for a price per page, usually not more than $10, sometimes substantially less. If you decide to use a service bureau, here are some tips you should take with you.

Tips for Working with Service Bureaus

The results you get from work done by a service bureau can range from breathtaking to hair-raising. You can do a few things to ensure that your service bureau job runs smoothly:

- Talk to your service bureau before you begin work. Your service bureau representatives can help you and your typesetting job a great deal. Tell them what software and fonts you plan to use, and tell them what type(s) of graphics (Paint, PICT, EPS, TIFF, and so on) are used.

They may want you to supply files containing the fonts you used in your document, or they may want you to supply the System Folder you used to create the document. They may even want you to provide a copy of the program used to create the document. In any case, start your jobs right by talking to your service bureau *before* you begin.

- Get and use the right fonts. Most service bureaus will give or sell you the screen versions of their PostScript fonts. Use them. Plain, italic, bold, and bold-italic screen fonts are available for most popular PostScript fonts. If your service bureau can't provide them, most are available in the Adobe forum on CompuServe.

- Proof your work on a LaserWriter or other PostScript or PostScript-compatible laser printer. If you proof your work on a dot-matrix or even a non-PostScript laser printer, you may be in for a surprise when you print your document on a Linotronic. Line and character spacing, as well as object placement, may change.

  A PostScript printer will give you a page proof that shows you almost exactly what your page will look like when printed on a Linotronic.

  Line weights and gray shading print differently on a laser printer than they do on a Linotronic. For example, the LaserWriter prints gray shades darker than the Linotronic does. So the LaserWriter's 20 percent gray is somewhat darker than the same 20 percent gray output on a Linotronic. Quarter and half-point lines are printed as one point on a LaserWriter; they print accurately on a Linotronic.

- Unless you're confident in your telecommunication skills, don't try using a modem to send your files when you're on deadline. One of the ways you can work with a service bureau is by way of modem. If sending files to a service bureau via modem is an option you'll find useful, try a dry run when you aren't facing a deadline.

Call and talk to a service representative before you try your upload. Get instructions, pricing, and delivery information. Then, after uploading your file, follow up on your transmission. Call and make sure the file was received and will be processed and sent to you as agreed.

More Tips from a Service Bureau Owner

M & L Typesetting Services, here in Austin, Texas, was responsible for typesetting *MACazine* on their Linotronic 100 every month. They also typeset the first edition of this book. I send them PageMaker files (they're generally too big to send over modem—I usually just give them disks); they send back typeset, camera-ready pages. I interviewed the owner, Wayne Matthews, who had these tips:

- Protect your disk. Don't put disks in plastic bags. The static electricity can scramble them. Protect them in some way, and keep the shutter from bending. There's nothing more disappointing than getting to the service bureau and finding that your disk is damaged. A cardboard disk mailer or almost any kind of disk holder will help. If you transport a lot of disks, you should give this subject some thought.

  You might even consider taking two copies of your work, on separate disks. Also, never take your only copy of a disk or document to a service bureau—always have at least one backup copy in another location.

- Bring in a list of fonts used in the document. Quark XPress has a command that displays a list of all the fonts used in a document. If you use PageMaker or other page-layout software, however, no such list is available through the software, and a list of the fonts you used will help your service bureau print your pages better.

- If you haven't bought a page-layout program yet, we prefer to work in PageMaker. Quark XPress has presented problems for us in the past, with pages printing slowly or not at all. Version 3.0 is much better, but we've found Aldus' technical support for PageMaker to be vastly superior, especially for the Linotronic operator. They almost always have an answer when we have a question on using PageMaker with our Linotronic.
- Don't make your pages too complex. There is a breaking point for the Linotronic. Pages with complex PostScript, TIFF, or bitmapped graphics—or, God forbid, a combination of these—may cause the Linotronic to run out of memory. A single page with six or eight complex charts plus text in a couple of fonts may refuse to print.

  Some examples of complex graphics are large bit-mapped graphics, large TIFF files containing gray-scale information, and encapsulated PostScript files with large numbers of objects or sophisticated PostScript special effects, such as rotated text, text along a path, and graduated fills.

  If you can, avoid having more than one complex graphic on any page.
- Don't use fonts with city names, such as New York or Chicago. Almost none of the fonts called by city names are laser fonts. If you aren't familiar with PostScript fonts, talk to your Linotronic operator about it. You need to use the Adobe screen fonts. M&L Typesetting Services is glad to copy them onto a disk for you when you come in. Your service bureau should too.

Recommendations

A wide variety of printers are available. The products I recommend follow:

Printers

Apple Computer, Inc.
20525 Mariani Avenue
Cupertino, CA 95014
408–996–1010
800–776–2333

Apple's printers are excellent performers, but they may be significantly more expensive than other brands. The advantage of Apple's dot-matrix printers (ImageWriter II, LQ) is that they're designed to work with your Mac right out of the box. Other brands of dot-matrix printers may not be as compatible (that is, they may require some tinkering with dip switches or special printer drivers to work properly). For that reason, I recommend Apple products if you're considering a dot-matrix printer.

That's not the case for laser printers, particularly PostScript models. Most other PostScript and PostScript-compatible printers, such as those offered by QMS, are just about as easy to configure as the Apple products, and cost significantly less.

One significant advantage to buying a laser printer from Apple is that your printer can be upgraded to a more powerful model later. For example, if you purchase an Apple LaserWriter IISC, a non-PostScript printer, you can later upgrade it to a PostScript IINT (about $1,000) or NTX (about $3,000) by having your Apple dealer install the appropriate upgrade. No other manufacturer presently offers this kind of upgrade capability.

CoStar Corporation
22 Bridge Street
Greenwich, CT 06830
800–4–COSTAR
203–661–9700

AddressWriter (dot-matrix), LabelWriter II (inkjet), and LabelWriter II Plus (inkjet).

GCC Technologies
580 Winter Street
Waltham, MA 02154
617–890–0880
800–422–7777

GCC makes a wide variety of dot-matrix and laser printers.

Hewlett-Packard
19310 Pruneridge Avenue
Cupertino, CA 95014
408–865–6200
800–752–0900

DeskWriter (inkjet), DeskWriter C (color inkjet), and LaserJet.

Linotype Company, Inc.
425 Oser Avenue
Hauppauge, NY 11788
516–434–2016
800–633–1900

Linotronic imagesetters are available starting at about $30,000.

QMS/Laser Connection
P.O. Box 81250
Mobile, AL 36689
205–633–4300

Two divisions of the same company; both manufacture a wide variety of PostScript and non-PostScript laser printers.

Fonts

Adobe Systems, Inc.
1585 Charleston Road
Mountain View, CA 94039
800–833–6687
415–961–4400

Adobe offers one of the widest selections of PostScript fonts, which is not surprising, since they invented PostScript.

Bitstream
Athenæum House
215 First Street
Cambridge, MA 02142
800–522–3668
617–497–6222

Bitstream offers a variety of PostScript and TrueType fonts.

DUBL–CLiCK Software, Inc.
9316 Deering Avenue
Chatsworth, CA 91311
818–700–9525

DUBL–CLiCK offers a variety of PostScript and TrueType fonts.

Casady & Greene
22734 Portola Drive
Salinas, CA 93908
800–359–4920
408–484–9228

Casady & Greene offers a variety of PostScript and TrueType fonts.

Paper

CG Graphic Arts Supply, Inc.
481 Washington Street
New York, NY 10013
800–342–5858
212–925–5332
LASEREDGE paper

A sampler with fifteen sheets of five papers plus eight sheets of clear and tinted transparencies is available for approximately $20.

Hammermill Paper Co.
1540 East Lake Road
Erie, PA 16533
800–242–2148
814–870–5000

Hammermill paper is not available direct from Hammermill; it can be obtained through paper distributors and some office supply stores. Check your local Yellow Pages.

Miscellaneous

Computer Friends
14250 NW Science Park Drive
Portland, OR 97229
800–547–3303
503–626–2291

Ribbon re-inkers starting at approximately $40.

DiskTop (includes Widgets and LaserStatus)
CE Software
P.O. Box 65580
West Des Moines, IA 50265
515–224–1995

Kiwi Envelopes
> Kiwi Software, Inc.
> 6546 Pardall Road
> Santa Barbara, CA 93117
> 805–685–4031

LaserCharge
> 1130 Metric Boulevard
> Austin, TX 78758
> 800–299–8134
> 512–832–0079

Recharges toner cartridges for laser printers. LaserCharge will give you instructions for sending your cartridge to the main office in Austin, or they will provide the name of a local approved LaserCharge dealer—call for details.

Summary

Probably the best advice I can give you is to allow more time for printing than you think you'll need. You'll almost always find something you want to change in your first printout. Don't cross your fingers as you hit the Print button at 9:59 to print the reports for that ten o'clock meeting. Allow extra time to scrutinize your print job.

Another thing: You don't have to buy an Apple laser printer. QMS makes excellent PostScript laser printers, as do several other vendors. You may save hundreds or even thousands of dollars buying a third-party PostScript printer.

Finally, when you need professional-looking results, try using a Linotronic service bureau. You'll be surprised how little effort it takes to create beautiful, typeset pages on your Mac. This book, for example, was typeset using QuarkXpress 3.0, a LaserWriter IINT (for proofing), and a Compugraphic image-setter (for final camera-ready output).

Now let's take a look at telecommunications and the different places your Mac and a modem can take you.

9

Telecommunication

Using a modem to connect with the world.

I think my modem is the one peripheral I'd have the hardest time doing without. I could probably exist without my hard disk or my large-screen monitor. But take away my modem and you've cut me off from the rest of the world.

I use my modem a dozen times a day. As a contributing editor for MacUser, I need timely feedback on Macintosh hardware and software from people who actually use the stuff. My modem makes it possible for me to collect it without leaving my desk.

I talk to friends and check my electronic mail on CompuServe, GEnie, and America Online every day. I post questions asking how people like products they've purchased. I look for messages about bugs and problems. If a product shipped yesterday, tomorrow I'll be reading users' experiences with it on CompuServe, GEnie, or America Online.

A modem is more than just a way to get information about the Mac. It is a magic carpet; it can take you anywhere. Not only can you communicate with hundreds of thousands of computer users, with a modem you can even investigate or order goods and services without leaving your keyboard. My wife and I recently used the Consumer Reports forum on CompuServe for much of our research when we were shopping for a new car.

A modem allows you to do so many things, such as:

- *Transfer text or files between Macintoshes in different locations*
- *Chat with other computer users in real time*
- *Send messages asking for help with your hardware or software*
- *Read messages about hardware or software that interests you*
- *Send electronic mail faster and cheaper than by Federal Express*
- *Download thousands of public-domain and shareware programs, DAs, and fonts*
- *Order merchandise—books, software, televisions, and so on*
- *Buy stocks and securities, or check their prices*
- *Search for magazine articles on specific topics*
- *Reserve airline tickets*

A modem opens up the world to your computer. This chapter will help you select hardware and software for connecting your Mac to the world as well as give you an idea of what to do once you're hooked up.

Telecommunication Basics

To use your Macintosh to telecommunicate with other computer users, with your friends, with commercial on-line services, or with a bulletin board service, you need to have the following equipment:

- A Macintosh
- A modem

- Telecommunication software
- A phone line and telephone cables
- An on-line service account or subscription (if you plan to use an on-line service)
- A bulletin board's phone number (if you plan to access a bulletin board)

Definition

A *modem* is a device that allows your computer to communicate with other computers via telephone lines. Modem is an acronym for modulate/demodulate.

Telecommunication software is the software you use to control your modem.

On-line services and *bulletin boards* are other computers you can connect your computer with, using a modem and telecommunication software.

These terms will be explained in greater detail later in this chapter.

Once you have your Macintosh configured for telecommunications, it's easy to go on-line for information or just for fun. In fact, it can become addictive!

A typical telecommunication session involves these steps:

1. Specify connection settings and session options.
2. Initiate a connection.
3. Exchange data, files, or messages with another computer, computer user, or on-line service.
4. Save any data you want to keep.
5. Disconnect.

This chapter covers how to select a modem, what telecommunication software is available for use with your modem, where you can go with your modem, and an important piece of utility software that will save you time and money when you telecommunicate.

Selecting a Modem

A modem is a device that allows your computer to communicate with computers of almost any type, via telephone lines. Unlike modems for the PC and other computers, the vast majority of Mac modems are external.

Technically speaking, a modem converts digital information (bits and bytes) from your Mac into analog information (noise) that can be sent over standard phone lines; at the same time, it converts incoming analog information into digital information your Mac can understand.

A modem is a little box that plugs into the printer or modem port on the back of your Mac. It also needs to be connected, using standard modular phone jacks, to a telephone line. Finally, it requires AC power, so it needs to be plugged into a power outlet. Figure 9–1 shows a typical modem configuration on a Mac.

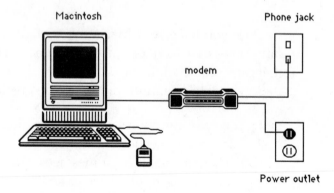

Figure 9–1.   Typical modem configuration

If you expect to use your modem a lot, you should consider having a separate phone line installed for it. That way, you can have uninterrupted service for both voice and data. I use my modem so much I couldn't possibly do without a separate line for my modem.

Tip

> If you have call-waiting on your phone line, you should contact your phone company and find out if it can be temporarily disabled. Many phone companies allow you to turn call-waiting on or off using the # or * key on your phone. If you're in the middle of a modem session and call-waiting clicks in, your modem connection will be be broken, wasting time and money.

Modem Terminology

You should understand a few terms before you purchase a modem:

Baud Rate Technically, *baud rate* describes the number of discrete signal events per second occurring on a communications channel. Though it is technically incorrect to do so, *baud rate* is often used to refer to bits per second (bps).

Baud rate measures how fast your modem works. Higher rates mean faster sending and receiving, but although doubling the baud rate does improve throughput quite a bit, it doesn't quite double it.

The speed of transmission between any pair of modems cannot be faster than the slower modem of the pair. For example, if you have a 19,200-baud modem and your friend has a 2,400-baud modem, you'll communicate at 2,400 baud. This makes sense: a 2,400-baud modem isn't capable of running at 19,200 baud. If it were, why would anybody buy a more expensive, higher-baud modem?

Baud rate is tricky: Slower modems are cheaper, but they cost you more in the long run. This is because you pay for both telephone time and most telecommunication services by the minute. Although some services charge more for faster baud connections (though most now have the same rate for 300, 1,200, and 2,400), the difference in cost is more than offset by the higher throughput a faster modem provides. A slow modem (300- or 1,200-baud) takes longer to send or receive. Also, you pay for phone time. Slower modems will cause you to stay connected longer, increasing your phone bill as well as your on-line charges.

The most common modems run at 2,400 baud and can be found for between $100 and $300 (street price). Modems that run at 9,600 baud are becoming more popular because of their great speed, with prices becoming more attainable: starting at about $500. Modems at 19,200 baud, the highest speed available, are quite expensive, with prices starting at just over $1,000. If you need to telecommunicate data at very high speeds between two locations, 19,200-baud modems might be just the thing. But if you're buying a modem to telecommunicate with friends, business associates, on-line services, or bulletin boards, bear in mind that few services support baud rates above 9,600, and many only go as high as 2,400.

A word about standards: Standard protocols exist for modems running at 2,400 baud and lower—at these speeds, almost every brand can be used with almost any other without concern that your modem won't be able to communicate with your friend's modem. The accepted standard for sending and receiving data across 9,600-baud modems is the V.32 protocol. Most 9,600-baud modems support V.32. This means that if you buy a 9,600-baud modem from Company X, be sure it supports the V.32 standard. Otherwise, you run the risk of your modem being incompatible with the modem to which you are connecting.

Tip

Before buying any ultra high-speed equipment (9,600 baud or faster), make sure it will be compatible with any modems you plan to communicate with.

Hayes-Compatible Modems *Hayes-compatible modems* are modems that comply with the command set created by modem manufacturer Hayes Microcomputer Products, which has become the *de facto* standard for telecommunication. The Hayes command set is sometimes called the *AT command set.* This is because

Hayes-compatible modems generally precede commands you issue to the modem with the letters *AT*.

In theory, any modem that is 100 percent Hayes-compatible should work properly with any software or other modem. That's because the vast majority of hardware that runs at 2,400 baud or less, as well as every software package I know of, assume Hayes compatibility. Although it is possible to configure a modem that's not 100 percent Hayes-compatible to work with other modems that *are* Hayes-compatible, it's a hassle and not for the faint of heart or inexperienced.

If you select a modem other than a Hayes, make sure you can obtain a refund if it doesn't prove to be 100 percent compatible. Some off-brand discount modems are only partially Hayes-compatible, and they may cause you headaches when you try to use them with modems that are completely Hayes-compatible.

File-Transfer Protocols   When you shop for telecommunication software, you'll run into terms such as *XMODEM, YMODEM, Kermit* (which may or may not, depending on who you ask, have something to do with a frog), and *MacBinary*. These are protocols that allow your Mac to send data back and forth to other computers; these protocols also automatically check for errors and correct them if possible. Most programs support all four of these protocols, and some may support others.

Definition

> A *file-transfer protocol* is a set of rules governing the exchange of information between computers and other computers or peripheral devices. SCSI, XMODEM, YMODEM, MacBinary, AppleTalk, Ethernet, and Kermit are examples of such protocols.

XMODEM is by far the most common protocol. It can be used by any two computers, no matter what the brands, as long as both are equipped with software that supports XMODEM.

MacBinary is a standard used to transfer Macintosh documents and applications over phone lines. It ensures that all the information necessary to reproduce the file, with all of its Macintosh attributes, comes through at the receiving end.

All of the software discussed in this chapter supports XMODEM and MacBinary transfer, which is probably all you need. If you know you'll be communicating with a specific computer, find out what file-transfer protocols that computer's software supports, and select a program for your Mac that also supports it. For example, many academic institutions have mainframes that use the Kermit protocol.

Shopping for a Modem

When you shop for a modem, get the fastest (in terms of baud rate) Hayes-compatible modem you can afford. The 9,600-baud modems are rapidly becoming the standard (remember to get one that supports V.32). CompuServe already allows you to log on at 9,600 baud from many U. S. cities; I suspect it won't be long before America Online and GEnie offer 9,600-baud service as well.

Dozens of modem brands are available. I've had good experiences with Hayes and U. S. Robotics, both of which are widely available. Whichever brand you select, make sure you can obtain a refund if it proves not to work properly with the software and on-line services you choose. If you can't get the modem to function after reading the manual, give the manufacturer a call for technical support.

Once you've shopped for and selected your modem, you will need to purchase telecommunication software before you can actually use the modem to telecommunicate.

Telecommunication Software

Telecommunication software tells your modem what to do. Even the most basic software allows you to send one application or document at a time or to converse with a person at a remote computer by typing messages that appear on the screen at the remote location as you type. It seems a little spooky at first, but trust me, it's lots of fun. More sophisticated software allows you to perform many of your telecommunication chores without intervention.

After you purchase your telecommunication software, you need to install it on your Mac and specify communication settings. In general, here are the steps for setting up your telecommunication software:

1. Launch the telecom program.
2. Using the appropriate commands and dialog boxes, specify your connection settings. Connection settings are typically such things as specifying modem settings (baud rate, parity, and so on), port settings (printer or modem port), file-transfer protocols, and the telephone number to dial. The modem settings you use must correspond to the type of modem connected to your Mac.
3. If you will be using your telecommunication software to connect to an on-line service, you may also need to specify your user identification, which includes a user name or ID number and a password.
4. You are ready to initiate a connection.

Most commercial telecommunication applications include features that allow you to automate most of your telecommunication chores: logging on, typing in your account number and password, and downloading your electronic mail.

If you have more than 1Mb of RAM and your telecommunication program supports it (most do), you can conduct a telecommunication session in the background under System 7 (or under System 6 with MultiFinder). This means you can use your computer for something else, such as word processing, spreadsheet manipulation, or database functions, even when a telecommunication session is in progress. You may notice a slight slowing of all tasks when a telecommunication session is running in the background, but the slow-down is usually quite tolerable (10 to 20 percent decrease in performance) on a Plus or SE and hardly noticeable on 68030 or 68040 Macs.

MicroPhone II (Software Ventures), White Knight (FreeSoft), and Smartcom II (Hayes) are the three leading telecommunication software packages for the Mac.

Now I'll briefly describe the strengths and weaknesses of these packages.

MicroPhone II

MicroPhone II is probably the most powerful of the currently available telecommunication programs. It is the most expensive as well.

MicroPhone II's biggest strength is its flexibility. It's probably the easiest program to use to create scripts or automate repetitive tasks. Figure 9–2 shows the interface of MicroPhone II's script editor. In the illustration, I'm working on a script to log onto CompuServe, one of the most popular commercial on-line services. The script, which I've named CompLogon, dials the CompuServe phone number, sends two carriage returns, and waits for the appropriate response from CompuServe. It then initiates the connection by sending the text string CIS and, when CompuServe asks for my user ID, it types my Compu-Serve ID number.

MicroPhone II also lets you create scripts using the Watch Me feature. This feature records your keystrokes as a macro, which can then be automatically played back whenever you like. Here's how it works:

1. Choose Watch Me from the Scripts menu.
2. Perform the sequence of actions you want to have recorded as a script.
3. When you're done, choose End Watch Me from the Scripts menu.

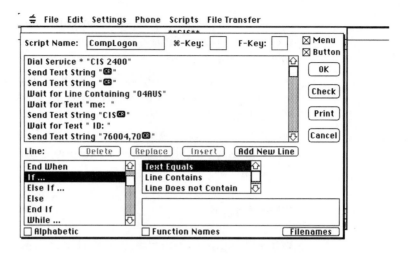

Figure 9–2.   MicroPhone II's Script Editor (version 3.0)

4. If you want to modify or change anything about the script you've just recorded, choose Modify Script from the Scripts menu, and change whatever you like using MicroPhone's script editor.

After that, you'll have a macro that can be played back with a single keystroke. If it sounds suspiciously like QuicKeys2, that's because it is. Most telecommunication programs have a built-in macrolike ability. (There's more information about QuicKeys2 in the next chapter.)

As we went to press, Software Ventures had announced version 4.0 of MicroPhone II. This version adds more user interface tools and increased support for System 7. One of the most innovative System 7–savvy features of version 4.0 is that you can integrate a communications session directly into another application. For example, by taking advantage of System 7's interapplication communication (IAC) capability, a spreadsheet can launch MicroPhone II, request it to call Dow Jones and download the latest stock quotes, and plug that data back into the spreadsheet for graphing and further processing. MicroPhone II 4.0 also includes an interface builder, called Dialoger Professional, which allows you to create dialog boxes, floating palettes, and pop-up menus for your scripts.

Other useful and possibly invaluable features (depending on your needs) include support for nonstandard modems (those that are not 100 percent Hayes-compatible), for all major file transfer protocols (XMODEM, YMODEM, and Kermit), and for terminal emulation (TTY, VT52, VT100, VT102, VT220, and VT320), which allows your Mac to function as a dumb terminal when connected to a larger computer via a modem. The well-written, easy-to-follow documentation is another of MicroPhone II's strengths.

White Knight

White Knight (formerly Red Ryder) is one of the oldest programs available for the Mac. It's also the least expensive telecommunication program. Programmer Scott Watson considers this program his first-born child. It has undergone almost continual upgrades, including a total rewrite in a more powerful programming language, which resulted in the powerful new version 11.

White Knight version 11 is a world-class program. It supports modems running at 300 to 57,600 baud. Scripting is as powerful, or perhaps even more powerful, than that offered by MicroPhone. Using White Knight's Procedure Language to write *procedures*, which are essentially the same as scripts, you can create automatic log-on and system-navigation sequences. Then you can run your procedure through White Knight's two-pass compiler to speed up playback of the procedure. (Most other script languages found in other telecommunications software are interpreted, not compiled.) White Knight also includes a point-and-click Procedure Editor for modifying your procedures.

Watson says White Knight will never be finished. As he has released something like twenty versions over the past four years, I suspect he means it. He listens to his users, and new versions are likely to incorporate features suggested by owners of the program. Not only that, if you call for technical support, there's a good chance Scott will take the call. You can also get technical support on-line; Watson has a special section set aside on GEnie, one of the major on-line services. (There's more about GEnie later in this chapter.)

Other features include a full range of terminal emulation settings, support for almost any file-transfer protocol you're likely to need, and a built-in phone book.

On the down side, the documentation is occasionally unclear or confusing, although Watson's wit and humor shine through on almost every page. In addition, the user interface is ugly and somewhat bewildering at times. In Figure 9–3, you can see that many of White Knight's preferences are accessed from submenus from the Customize menu. Also notice the two-key Command-key equivalents, which are typical keyboard short-cuts in White Knight. Although keyboard shortcuts are useful, you may find the two-key equivalents unintuitive.

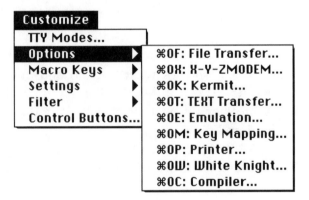

Figure 9–3.   White Knight's interface isn't as slick as MicroPhone II's

Most of these choices bring up large, ugly dialog boxes with a plethora of choices, as shown in Figure 9–4. (Large ugly dialog boxes are a hallmark of Watson's work.)

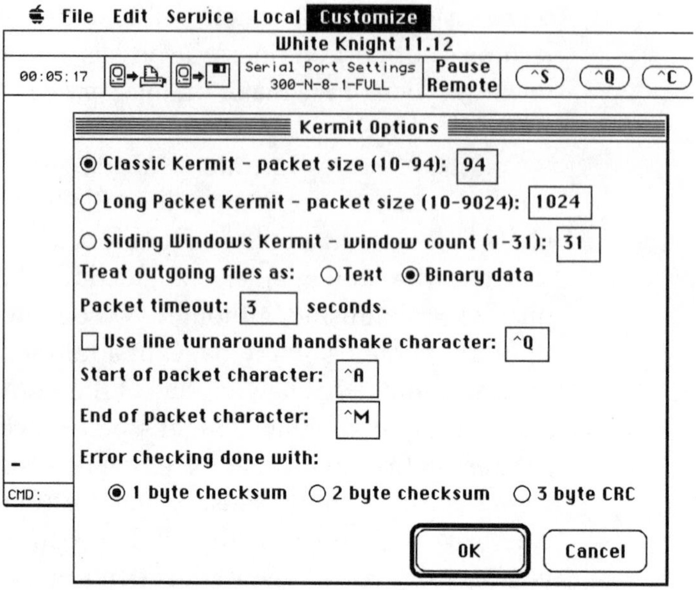

Figure 9–4.   One of White Knight's unwieldy dialog boxes

White Knight has a feature called Write A Procedure For Me, which watches what you do and automatically writes a procedure. This feature is similar to the Watch Me feature found in MicroPhone II. You can then modify the procedure using the Procedure Editor.

All things considered, you get a lot of telecommunications power for a low price with Watson's White Knight.

Tip
✔

Watson also makes a product called Okyto, which is the easiest, most trouble-free software I know of for transferring files from one Mac to another. If you're not interested in bauds and bits and protocols, this is the software you want.

Though it lists for $39.95, unless Watson has changed his policy, it will be included with your copy of White Knight at no extra charge. If you're looking for a fast, easy way to send and receive files between Macs, Okyto is it.

Smartcom II

Smartcom II is the software product of Hayes Microcomputer, the same folks who make Hayes modems and who invented the now-famous Hayes command set. Smartcom II is the easiest to learn and use of the three programs discussed here.

Smartcom II has a simple icon-driven interface, which is one of the reasons why it is popular among those who want a fairly powerful telecommunication program that's easy to learn as well as easy to use. Once you specify your modem and connection settings, you click on the phone icon at the bottom of the screen to initiate a session. During a communications session, you can use any of the other icons along the bottom to print the current screen, save it to disk, send or receive a file, or even draw. Version 3.3, which is System 7–compatible, features a status box with icons showing you the progress of your communications session (see Figure 9–5).

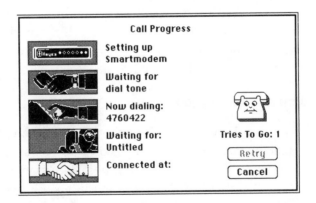

Figure 9–5.   Smartcom II's Call Progress display features icons to show how your connection is progressing

Smartcom II is the only telecommunication package with on-line help, as shown in Figure 9–6. The help is excellent. To invoke the help, click the ? icon along the bottom of the screen. A small Help window comes up, listing topics on which you can get help. You can resize and move the Help window any way you like. If you like the convenience of having on-line help

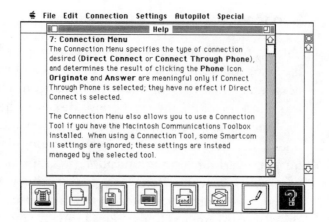

Figure 9–6.   Smartcom II offers excellent on-line help

available, you should definitely consider Smartcom II. In addition to Smartcom II's own context-sensitive help, version 3.3 fully supports System 7's Balloon Help.

Smartcom II is priced between White Knight and MicroPhone II. Though its scripting capabilities are not as powerful as those of either MicroPhone II or White Knight, its ease of use and learning make it an excellent choice for your first telecommunication software package.

Which Package to Buy

I use MicroPhone and recommend it if you can afford it. If price is a factor in your decision, but you don't want to give up power, consider White Knight. It is almost as capable as MicroPhone, although it's harder to learn and master and its documentation leaves something to be desired. Its low price may more than make up for these shortcomings if you're on a budget. Plus, it's a pleasure doing business with Scott Watson. Finally, Smartcom II is an excellent compromise if you're looking for something that's extremely easy to use and you don't mind giving up some of the more advanced scripting features of White Knight and MicroPhone.

The bottom line is that any of these three programs will do exactly what they're supposed to; which to use is purely a matter of choice.

One other thing—some integrated software packages, most notably Microsoft Works, ClarisWorks, and Symantec GreatWorks, include telecommunications modules. These modules are perfectly serviceable bare-bones telecom programs, and may, depending on your needs, be all the telecom software you need. If you own one of these programs, I urge you to use its telecom module for a while. Then, if you find you need more power, and additional features, by all means invest in more powerful telecommunication software.

Places Your Modem Can Take You

Now that you've got a modem and telecommunication software, the next thing to do is find a reason to use them. You can go many places with your modem. It can connect you to:

- Other Macintoshes equipped with modems and telecommunication software
- Non-Macintosh computers, including minis, micros, and mainframes, as long as they're equipped with modems and some sort of telecommunication software
- Commercial on-line services, such as CompuServe, GEnie, and America Online
- Noncommercial bulletin boards

Now let's take a look at communicating with other computers (Mac and non-Mac), and connecting to and using on-line services and bulletin boards.

Using a modem and telecommunication software, your Mac can communicate with almost any computer equipped with the same. A modem can connect you to another Mac, a minicomputer, microcomputer, or even a mainframe.

If your company has a large computer, it may be possible for you to log on from a remote location and download information from the big computer to your Mac; however, if you're connected to a computer other than a Mac, you will be limited to sending and receiving text only.

If you're connected to another Mac or one of the commercial online services, you can send or receive almost anything—text, formatted word-processor files, graphics, fonts, sounds, or even an application.

CompuServe

CompuServe is the granddaddy of on-line services. You can buy a starter kit (at most software stores or from a mail-order house, such as MacConnection) that includes an account number, password, user's manual, and list of local phone numbers you can use to log on.

In operation almost twenty years, CompuServe is the largest and most complete service in the world. Hundreds of thousands of users access it with a local phone call from more than 300 cities in North America and 79 foreign countries. The hourly charge for connecting to CompuServe is the same, no matter when you use it. Other services, such as GEnie, have significantly higher charges for daytime usage.

CompuServe was designed for instantaneous communication and information retrieval in the home or office. Subscribers can choose from a selection of more than 1,000 subject areas, including information resources, communications, and transactional services.

Among the services offered are electronic mail, special-interest forums, real-time conferences, news, stock quotes and financial market information, weather, sports, travel, and electronic shopping.

The best reason for joining CompuServe, in my opinion, is to access the Macintosh forums—probably the finest collection of Macintosh minds ever gathered in one (virtual) place.

Thirteen different Macintosh forums are on CompuServe (complete descriptions of each are given later in this chapter). In each forum, the message areas and data libraries are subdivided into logical sections, making it easier to find what you're looking for.

Definition

A *forum* is the electronic equivalent of a gathering place. There are message areas, where you can ask a question or share information with others, and data libraries that are filled with public-domain and shareware programs.

One of the nicest features of the forums is that if you leave a message asking a question, you're notified automatically if you received any responses the next time you visit that forum. It's a great way to get answers. Leaving a message is often called *posting a message,* because a message in a forum is a lot like a message physically posted on the bulletin board at your school or office.

The only cost to you is your connect charge. (Of course, if you use any of the shareware you download for more than a few days of trial, you should send the author the shareware fee. It's usually small—rarely more than $20.)

I heartily recommend the Mac forums on CompuServe. I log onto CompuServe and visit the Mac forums at least twice a day to find out what's going on in the Macintosh community, share ideas, ask questions, scan the data libraries, and say hello to my friends.

It's easy to use CompuServe, despite its old-fashioned command-line interface. It's menu-driven, and fairly easy to operate once you get the hang of it. Once you've dialed your local phone number and typed in your user ID and password, a series of menus and prompts make CompuServe's incredible array of goods and services almost manageable. Although it takes some getting used to after the point-and-click simplicity of the Mac, it isn't all that complicated.

Tip

Two special software packages sold by CompuServe—CompuServe Navigator and CompuServe Information Manager—make using the service a lot easier. Though you can use any telecom software to log on, these two programs make using CompuServe a lot more Mac-like. There's more about both of them later in this section.

The first menu lists general areas of information. You can access any of these areas by typing a number corresponding to the given area at the ! prompt. After you've used CompuServe a few times and you know where you want to go, at any ! prompt just type **GO**, followed by the command associated with a particular forum or other area of CompuServe. When you decide to log off CompuServe, just type **OFF** at the ! prompt.

In Figure 9–7, the words that appear after the "!" prompts are those that I typed after accessing CompuServe. I first typed **Go Macintosh** at the first ! prompt to get to the Macintosh section, then typed **1** to enter the Applications Forum.

```
 1 Use FundWatch Online Surcharge-free
 2 Download SNIPER Scope for Color Play
 3 Lotus 1-2-3 for Windows Demo in Forum
 4 ZD BookNet Makes Debut on ZiffNet
 5 Search Multiple Libraries in Forums
 6 Win $500 Software Package at The Mall
 7 New Video Founder in Multimedia Forum
 8 Join CB Club and Receive Usage Credit
   (Above Articles Are Free)
 9 Online Today
10 Specials/Contests Menu (Free)

Enter choice !go macintosh

Macintosh/Apple        MACINTOSH

 1 Applications Forum
 2 Communications Forum
 3 Community Clubhouse Forum
 4 Developers Forum
 5 Entertainment Forum
 6 Hypertext Forum
 7 New Users and Help Forum
 8 Systems Forum
 9 File Finder
10 Mac Vendor Forums
11 Apple News Clips
12 Zmac: MacUser/MacWEEK On-line
13 Macintosh System 7 Forum

Enter choice !!
```

Figure 9–7.   CompuServe's Main Menu and the Macintosh section's Main Menu

Macintosh Forums (MAUG—Micronetworked Apple Users Group) The best part of CompuServe, at least for Macintosh users, is MAUG—the Micronetworked Apple Users Group on CompuServe. To get there, type **Go Macintosh** at any prompt.

Within MAUG, there are thirteen forums dedicated to the Macintosh. Each Macintosh forum is made up of two sections: messages and data libraries. Each of these sections is subdivided into ten to fifteen categories. Figure 9–8 shows the names of the subsections in the Applications message section (top) and the Applications data libraries (bottom).

```
Mac Applications Forum Sections Menu

Section names (#subjs/# msgs)
 0 New Uploads  (10/22)
 1 Forum Business  (20/56)
 2 Word Processing  (26/179)
 3 Databases  (45/164)
 4 Spreadsheets/Models  (10/23)
 5 Accounting/Finance  (25/80)
 6 General Business  (47/199)
 7 Desktop Publishing  (19/61)
 8 Multimedia  (15/66)
 9 Art Hints/Tips  (2/8)
10 Paint Programs  (5/19)
11 Draw Programs  (5/9)
12 Color Art  (1/3)
13 Using RLE/GIF  (1/2)
14 Engineering/CAD  (14/58)


Mac Applications Forum Libraries Menu

 0 New Uploads
 1 Forum Business
 2 Word Processing
 3 Databases
 4 Spreadsheets/Models
 5 Accounting/Finance
 6 General Business
 7 DTP Templates
 8 Multimedia
 9 Graphics Tools
10 MacPaintings (B&W)
11 Illustrations (B&W)
12 Color Artwork
13 RLE/GIF Images
14 Engineering/CAD
15 Misc. Applications
```

Figure 9–8.   Message and Data Library subsections in the Applications Forum

In addition to forums, you can also join any on-line conferences that may be in progress. Frequently, conferences feature such industry notables as John Sculley of Apple. At these conferences, you log on and can ask questions of these people in real time, just by typing. Conferences are publicized by an announcement message you see before you enter the forum.

Now, let's take a quick look at the thirteen different Macintosh forums. (The words in parentheses after the name of each forum are what you type at any CompuServe prompt to get to that forum. A complete set of Go words, as well as other information on using CompuServe effectively, can be found in the user's guide you receive when you join.)

Macintosh Applications Forum (Go MACAP)   For all Macintosh users. This forum is filled with messages about using and mastering all kinds of application software and has a data library packed with excellent public-domain and shareware programs. Here's the place to talk with other users about general-interest application programs and how to get the most from them. Sections cover a wide range of interests including word processing, databases, spreadsheets/models, accounting/finance, desktop publishing, general business, multimedia, using Paint and Draw programs, engineering, and more. This is one of MAUG's two general-interest forums for people interested in the Macintosh. The other one is the Macintosh Systems Forum.

Macintosh Systems Forum (Go MACSYS)   In this forum, discussions and programs are associated with both System software and System hardware. Whether you have a question on using the System or Finder files, on installing desk accessories, or what INITs or CDEVs might be, this is the place to look and learn. Likewise, if you wish to discuss what hardware to add to your System, from hard disks through monitors to printers, check out the expert opinions offered here. This is one of the two MAUG general-interest forums (the other one is MACAP), and it is also one of the busiest.

Macintosh Communications Forum (Go MACCOM)   In this forum, you can find sections and data libraries devoted to such things as the CompuServe Navigator program (described later in this chapter), other terminal programs, and general information about using modems and telecommunications products.

Macintosh Community Clubhouse Forum (Go MACCLUB) This forum is one of the busiest Macintosh forums, and it is an excellent place for beginners to hang out and learn more about the Mac. Users exchange opinions on new software and hardware products, and share with others their latest insights on using the Mac.

Macintosh Developers Forum (Go MACDEV)   This one is for developers and programmers. In the MAUG community, you can find both programming novices as well as some of the world's foremost Macintosh developers. The famous, the not-so-famous—hey, even the infamous—all get together here to trade tips and techniques, to learn, and to teach. Here you can communicate with other developers and compare notes on programming languages, debuggers, editors, and linkers. Sections cover such things as BASIC, assembly language, C and Pascal, object-oriented programming, using *Inside Macintosh*, tools/debuggers, and learning to program. The data library contains programming tools, utilities, source code examples, and much more. Here you will also find the System software that Apple licenses for electronic distribution, always including the latest versions of such things as the System, Finder, MacsBug, ResEdit, and more.

Macintosh Entertainment Forum (Go MACFUN) This forum is just the thing for anyone hoping to discover new and creative ways to use the Macintosh. There are messages about games, graphics, music, art, design, education, and more. Sections here cover such interests as music with and without MIDI, arcade and action games, adventure and role-playing games, board games, card games, and even game design. There are also data libraries filled with music and images in MacPaint, PICT, EPS, and color formats, not to mention hundreds of shareware games. You can also find challenging templates for commercial games, as well as musical programs, musical scores, and scads of funny sounds to make your Mac talk, beep, sing, and carouse. Oh, and don't miss the popular R-rated databases wherein Rubens and Vargas would both feel at home.

Macintosh HyperText Forum (Go MACHYPER)   This is the forum for HyperCard users. When Apple Computer released the HyperCard program, it was making more than history; it generated a revolution in how people use computers to do whatever they personally need accomplished. StackHeads can find sections on things such as HyperTalk, stack ideas, XCMDs, and other such hypertopics. Now that other manufacturers have brought out programs such as SuperCard (Silicon Beach) and

Plus + (Spinnaker), this forum also includes support areas for those programs. The data library has thousands of stacks for downloading.

Macintosh New Users and Help Forum (Go MACNEW or MACHELP)   This forum is the place to come for users new to the Macintosh and to the MAUG community. You'll find information on how to use MAUG. It's also the place for both new and old members to get emergency help with problems involving disk storage, viruses, and system conflicts.

Macintosh File Finder (Go MACFF)   File Finder is an on-line comprehensive keyword-searchable database of file descriptions from Mac-related forums. It was designed to provide quick and easy reference to some of the best programs and files available in the forums, including these forums:

Adobe	Mac Developers Forum
Mac Art and Design Forum	Mac Entertainment Forum
Aldus	Borland Applications
Borland Programming A	HyperText Forum
Ashton-Tate	Mac Productivity
Mac A Vendor Forum	Mac B Vendor Forum
Microsoft Applications	WordPerfect Support Group B
Communications Forum	Mac Community/
Symantec	New Users Forum
Lotus Spreadsheets Forum	Microsoft Systems Forum

Macintosh Vendor Forums (Go MACAVEN, MACBVEN, and MACCVEN)   These three forums are where vendors of Mac software and hardware answer questions about their products and provide on-line technical support. Vendors here include Acius, CE Software, Claris, Microseeds, Deneba, and many more. The data libraries contain updates and hints on using each vendor's products as well as templates and samples.

Apple News Clips (Go APPLENEWS)   This forum is designed to keep you informed of news stories related to Apple Computer and its products. Stories are clipped from various news sources including AP, UPI, and the Washington Post. You can select articles to read by choosing the appropriate number(s) from the News Clips menu. Discussion related to issues in the news can be found in the various message sections of the Apple and Macintosh Forums.

Macintosh System 7 Forum (Go MACSEVEN)   In this forum, you can find information on the new System 7.0 software for the Macintosh. Discussions include everything from installing System 7.0 to tricks such as pasting icons, as well as discussions of compatibility and much, much more. Also on this forum you have access to many of Apple Computer's own System 7.0 team. This is a special-event forum and is not permanent, but if you want to get the latest news, information, tips, tricks, and hints on using System 7, this is the forum for you.

Zmac: MacUser/MacWEEK On-line (Go ZMAC)   This is a forum of Ziff-Davis Publishing Company, the publishers of *MacUser* and *MacWEEK* magazines. Here's a brief rundown on the services available on Zmac.

- **MacWEEK News Beat:** Read the top stories in the next week's issue of *MacWEEK*. Important stories that appear in Monday's paper edition are posted on Zmac the Friday beforehand.
- **MacUser Power Tools:** Download all of the scripts, templates, programming code, and utilities mentioned and developed by the editors of *MacUser*.
- **Editorial Forums:** Interact with the editors, writers, and columnists of *MacUser* and *MacWEEK*. I spend a lot of time in the *MacUser* Editorial Forum.
- **Download & Support:** The Download & Support Forum is where *MacUser* and *MacWEEK* join forces to offer you

the best in shareware and freeware plus an open area to help solve your technical problems. Read the General Announcement in each of these forums for details on their purpose and charter.

- **Reference Databases:** Four important reference tools are available to help users locate, buy, and use products. These four databases include Buyer's Guide, Expert Database, Computer Library, and the *MacUser/ MacWEEK* index. Although there is a surcharge for using some of them, they are often the fastest and easiest way to locate information on a specific product. I use them all the time, and I find them a lot more useful than a trip to the local library.
- **Surveys:** Participate in an important marketing survey and help shape the way vendors view the marketplace.

Threads   The message sections in each forum use a concept called *threads*. You can read a single message, or you can read a message and all its associated replies—a *thread*. You can also leave a reply and become part of the thread.

The people who use the Macintosh forums are among the best-informed Mac users I've ever known. They are happy to answer questions and help first-time users learn the ropes.

Let's look at how threads work. The following example shows a typical set of questions, responses, and replies to the responses. My comments appear in the same typeface as the text of this book.

In the example, you will see *Person 1* or *Person 2* in the From or To field; ordinarily, you'll see a person's real name. (The symbol <CR> always means type a carriage return.)

To get to the point where this example starts, I logged on, typed my account number and password at the appropriate prompts, then typed **GO Macintosh** at the main menu. After arriving in MAUG, I selected the Applications forum, typed **2** to get to the messages section, and selected the option to search for messages by keyword. In this case, the keyword was Applecare.

You can also search for messages by date or get a summary of all new messages since the last time you logged on. In this example, I'm reading a thread about AppleCare, which has six participants (only a few of them are included in this example).

The header, the first five lines of each message, tells you which subtopic you're reading (S1/Forum Business), the date, subject, and who the message is from and to. Every message contains these items.

```
#: 105161 S1/Forum Business
    10-Nov-88 02:46:22
Sb: #Applecare
Fm: Person #1
To: Person #2


I've always looked at insurance (and things
like AppleCare) as hedges or safety nets. It isn't
so much how many people fall off the high wire,
it's what happens to those who do without a net.
After all, the loss ratio is 100% to those people
who have the loss. Remember the CPA who drowned in
a stream that was, on the average, 2 ft. deep?

There is 1 Reply.
Press <CR> for next or type CHOICES !rr
```

I typed **rr** because I'm interested in reading the reply. If I wanted to read a different thread, I would have typed a carriage return (<CR>). Typing **CHOICES** would have allowed me to reread the message, reply to it, go on to another message, or return to this forum's main menu.

```
#: 105240 S1/Forum Business
    10-Nov-88 11:14:16
Sb: #105161-#Applecare
Fm: Person #3
To: Person #1
```

```
     An  absurd  statistic  I  like  even  better  is
that  the  great  majority  of  people  have  more  than
the  average  number  of  legs.

There  are  2  Replies.
Press  <CR>  for  next  or  type  CHOICES  !rr
```

Courtesy of CompuServe, Incorporated

This is a reply from a new person, #3, to the originator of the first message, #1. Again, I typed **rr** so I could follow the responses.

As you can clearly see, the thread concept allows you to hold conversations, even though the other participants may be thousands of miles away.

Data Libraries   In addition to the message sections, the forums also offer data libraries, which allow you to search for files using keywords. You can also see a list of all files if you like by selecting the Directory of Files option.

Here's another example, which shows how you find a file or files in a data library. To get to the point where this example starts, I logged on and typed **GO MACAP** to go directly to MAUG's Applications forum. From the Forum menu, I typed **3** to get to the Library (Files) section, and selected library 9, Graphics Tools, from the MACAP Libraries menu (see the bottom of Figure 9–8, shown earlier):

```
Mac Applications Forum Library 9

Graphics Tools

1 BROWSE Files
2 DIRECTORY of Files
3 UPLOAD a File (FREE)
4 DOWNLOAD a File to your Computer
5 LIBRARIES

Enter choice !1
```

I typed **1** because I want to browse by keyword. Had I typed **2**, I would have been asked how old was the oldest file I was interested in. After typing a number of days, I would have gotten a list of every file uploaded in that time period. Typing **3** or **4** would prompt me through the procedure to upload or download a file, and typing **5** would take me back to the library menu (shown earlier in Figure 9–8).

```
Enter keywords (e.g. modem)
or <CR> for all: paint
```

I typed **paint**. CompuServe now searches for files that have *paint* as their keyword.

```
Oldest files in days
or <CR> for all:
```

I typed a carriage return, because I want to search all of the files. Had I only wanted to search files uploaded in the last 90 days, I would have typed **90** instead of <CR>.

Here is the result of my search for files with the keyword *paint*, no matter how old they are:

```
[70566,1474]
BEZIER.SIT/binary  03-Jun-88 23296
Accesses: 443

    Title : Desk accessory for drawing bezier
curves
        Keywords: BEZIER  CURVE  PAINT  DA  DESK
ACCESSORY BITMAP PICT GRAPHIC GRAFIC
        FREE

    This DA drawing program allows easy creation
of Bezier curves. It shares PICTs and bitmaps with
the Clipboard. Copyrighted, but free.
    Press <CR> for next or type CHOICES !
```

I typed a carriage return, so that I could see the next file that met my search criteria. Had I typed **CHOICES**, I would have been presented with a menu with options for downloading this file or returning to the forum's main menu.

```
[70701,1420]
COLORS.SIT/binary  11-Aug-89 12546
Accesses: 222

    Title : A range of colors with SuperPaint 2.0
        Keywords:  SUPER  PAINT  SUPERPAINT  2.0
COLOR COLORS TEST

    SuperPaint 2.0 document(s) showing the range
of colors (you might be surprised) it is possible
to simulate using only the six colors plus black
and white available with the ImageWriter II and
color ribbon, using gradient fills. Explanation of
how it is done included.

    Press <CR> for next or type CHOICES !
```

I'm still looking, so I again typed a carriage return.

```
[71041,144]
CITDEM.SIT/binary 07-Sep-91 510848
Accesses: 10

    Title : Demo version of Color It! 32-bit
paint program
        Keywords: COLOR IT MICROFRONTIER 32 BIT
PAINT PHOTO IMAGE DEMO

    This is a demo version of the amazing new
32-bit color paint program called Color It! from
MicroFrontier, Inc. This demo is fully functional
for Save, Print, and exporting the Clipboard.
Example images are contained in the file
CITIMG.SIT and a text file description is
contained in CITDES.TXT.
    Press <CR> for next or type CHOICES !
```

I'm still browsing, so I once again typed a carriage return.

```
[71041,144]
CITDES.TXT/binary 07-Sep-91 8064  Accesses: 8

Title : Description of Color It! Demo
     Keywords: COLOR IT MICROFRONTIER 32 BIT
PAINT PHOTO IMAGE DEMO

This is a text file describing the demo
version of the new 32-bit color paint program
called Color It! from MicroFrontier, Inc.

Press <CR> for next or type CHOICES ! choices
```

Courtesy of CompuServe, Incorporated

If I had wanted to, I could have continued typing carriage returns until I had seen all the files. Instead, I typed **choices** and returned to the forum's main menu.

All things considered, joining CompuServe and frequenting the Macintosh forums may be the best way to become a power user. Sure, reading this book is a good start, but what if you need help with something I haven't covered? The people who use CompuServe are nice, knowledgeable, and helpful. But more than that, more power users are hanging out on CompuServe than anyplace else I know. They'll be happy to answer your questions, and so will I. (All of my electronic addresses appear in the introduction to this book, if you care to drop me a note.)

Tip

The Macintosh forums were undergoing a facelift as this book went to press. New software was being installed on the CompuServe host computer, which could cause things not to work exactly as shown in my examples. If you have a problem, refer to the CompuServe documentation .

The Rest of CompuServe   CompuServe offers more than just Macintosh information. In addition to the Apple forums, there are dozens of other computer forums, including Microsoft (publisher of Word, Excel, and Works—GO MSAPP), Aldus (publisher of PageMaker—GO ALDUS), and Adobe Systems (lots of screen fonts, and technical support for Adobe products—GO ADOBE).

In addition to computer-related services, CompuServe offers an abundance of information on just about anything you need to know. Goods, services, information, and much more, are just a local phone call away.

For example, you can arrange travel reservations—including airlines, hotels, and rental cars—and charge them to a major credit card, without leaving your home or office. The travel section on CompuServe includes the Official Airline Guide (GO OAG), American Airlines EasySabre travel reservation system (GO EAASY), the ABC Worldwide Hotel Guide, which features listings of over 28,000 hotels (GO ABC), as well as dozens of other travel-related sections.

Thousands of items, including cars, televisions, and computer hardware and software, can be investigated on-line and ordered with a major credit card by shopping in CompuServe's Electronic Mall (GO MALL).

So far, you've seen that you can get many kinds of information as a CompuServe subscriber. But wait—there's more: You can send electronic mail to almost anyone in the world, using CompuServe's powerful electronic mail network, Easy-Plex. For a small additional charge, you can have it sent through MCI Mail instead of EasyPlex (if the person doesn't have a CompuServe account) or sent to a fax machine (GO EASY).

One of CompuServe's most powerful features is that you can query large databases for information on a wide variety of subjects. For example, there's a full-text encyclopedia (GO ENCYCLOPEDIA) that can be searched by keyword, a business demographics database (GO BUSDEM), census bureau data (GO CENDATA), and IQuest, CompuServe's information retrieval service. IQuest provides access to more than 800 databases, including Dialog, BRS, NewsNet, and full-text databases of hundreds of publications (GO IQUEST).

There is an additional charge for some services. You will see a $ on each menu choice that has a surcharge. The charges range from a few pennies to several dollars per inquiry.

One of the surcharged areas is the stock-market quote database (GO QQUOTE). It's relatively inexpensive (1.5¢ each, at this writing).

How to Check Stock Prices   The following example shows the procedure for checking three stocks—Apple Computer, ACM Government Spectrum Fund, and Spinnaker Software. At any CompuServe prompt, you type **GO QQUOTE** to enter the Quick Quote forum.

```
!GO QQUOTE

One moment please. . .

Quick Quote QQUOTE

Quotes are delayed over 15 minutes. Compu-
Serve does not edit this data and is not respon-
sible or liable for its content, completeness,
or timeliness.

DOW 30 is up 10.73 at 5:02 EDT

Quotes are surcharged 1.5 cents each.

Enter ticker symbols (i.e. HRB,SP 500), an
asterisk followed by the beginning of a company
name (i.e. *BLOCK), /H for HELP or /EXIT.

Issue: AAPL,SI,SPKR
```

Here I entered the ticker symbols from the daily newspaper for the three stocks I'm interested in: Apple Computer (AAPL), ACM Government Spectrum Fund (SI), and Spinnaker (SPKR). If I didn't know the symbol for one of them, I could type an asterisk before the company name (for example, *Apple) instead of the ticker symbol.

What follows is the result of the above query, for two different days—January 4 and February 25:

```
•— Quotes, 1/4/91, 12:14:50 PM —•
AAPL,SI,SPKR


Name                    Volume Hi/Ask Low/Bid Last  Change Update
--------------------    ----   ----    ----   ----  ----   ----

APPLE COMPUTER INC COM  11152  44.250  43.000 43.500 0.500  2:52

ACM GOVT SPECTRUM FD INC  301   8.750   8.625  8.625 -0.125 2:39

SPINNAKER SOFTWARE CORP C 149   2.250   2.000  2.125 0.063  2:41




•— Quotes, 2/25/91, 4:10:41 PM —•
AAPL,SI,SPKR


Name                    Volume Hi/Ask Low/Bid Last  Change Update
--------------------    ----   ----    ----   ----  ----   ----

APPLE COMPUTER INC COM  31923  60.500  57.500 58.000 -1.750 2/25*

ACM GOVT SPECTRUM FD INC  724   9.000   8.875  9.000 0.500  2/25

SPINNAKER SOFTWARE CORP C  59   2.875   2.625  2.625 -0.125 2/25

* To access current news on these companies, enter /CONEWS ($15/hr surcharge).


Issue: /Exit
```

Courtesy of CompuServe, Incorporated

The asterisk at the end of the Apple Computer stock quote line for February 25 indicates that there is news of interest to Apple investors. If I wanted to read this news, I would type **/CONEWS** (for company news) at the Issue: prompt. Because this takes you to the Dow Jones News/Retrieval network, it costs extra (a $15 per hour surcharge, at this writing).

CompuServe offers many other services for investors and speculators. The user guide you receive with your subscription has complete details on them.

Although you can log onto CompuServe using any terminal program, CompuServe also offers a pair of excellent software packages, called CompuServe Navigator and CompuServe Information Manager.

If you decide to subscribe to CompuServe (and I recommend it highly), be sure to drop me a note and say "hi." My address is 76004,2076.

Tip

At this writing, there is a surcharge for 9,600-baud access to CompuServe, and I expect that the other services will have a surcharge as well when they initiate 9,600-baud support.

I believe that if you're downloading files at 9,600 baud, you'll save some money and time, even with a whopping surcharge; if you're typing or reading messages, log on at a lower, less expensive baud rate.

My advice is to monitor your usage and bills to discover if 9,600 baud is economical for you; it may or may not be, depending upon what tasks you perform when you're connected.

CompuServe Navigator   Navigator provides Macintosh owners with almost total automation, and it is designed to save you time and money. It does this by letting you decide what information you want before you log on (that is, before the meter starts running), then it logs on and grabs what you asked for at the fastest speed possible.

Navigator lets you log on, get lists of new messages and files from almost any forum, then log off and decide what you want to read or download. You simply double-click your choices, then log back on. Navigator does all the work. In all of the following illustrations I was off-line. That means I was deciding what interested me without having to pay the hourly charge. Without Navigator, you'll spend a lot more time and money getting around CompuServe.

Figure 9–9 shows the setup box for the Macintosh Applications Forum (MACAP). I've used the pull-down Message menu to instruct Navigator to enter this forum, get all my new messages, get text summaries of messages in subtopics 1 to 13, and automatically search for new files in library 0. After making my selections, I instruct Navigator to run the session with a menu selection called Run.

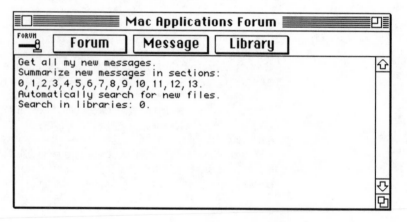

Figure 9–9.   Telling Navigator what forum subtopics interest you

Figure 9–10 shows the result of the run I set up in Figure 9–9. It's a summary of messages from all of the subtopics in MACAP that I selected in Figure 9–9. I've double-clicked the message with the bullets and T in front of it: Acta 7 bug. Since I'm an Acta user, I'm interested in reading about this alleged bug. The complete text of the Acta 7 message will be captured the next time I log on.

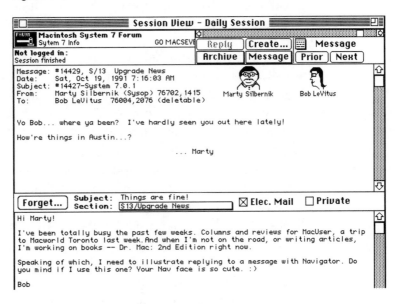

▤□▨ ═════════ **Session View** – **Daily Session** ═════════ ▨⯐▨
```
╔══════════════════════════════╦═══════════════════════════════╗
║ [FORUM] Mac Applications Forum ║◆▨▨▨▨▨▨▨▨▨▨▨▨▨▨▨▨▨▨▨▨◆║
║      Applications and Productivity  GO MACAP ║ Reply │ Create...│▨ Message   ║
╟──────────────────────────────╫───────────────────────────────╢
║ Not logged in:               ║ Archive │Summary │ Prior │ Next ║
║ Session finished             ║                               ║
╚══════════════════════════════╩═══════════════════════════════╝
```

```
[Navigator: Listing new messages]                               ⇧

Message   Tasks Subject                    Originator        New  All
~~~~~~~~  ~~~~~ ~~~~~~~                     ~~~~~~~~~~        ~~~  ~~~
          Section 2: Word Processing
 21918    ●-T--- Acta 7 bug                 Terry Harpold      1    7
 21927    ----- Best Word Processor?        John Kendrick      2    6
 21932    ----- Frnch/Spnsh sp checker?     Jeff Estes         1    2

          Section 3: Databases
 21930    ----- Touchbase                   Walt Campbell      1   11
 21921    ----- DB for texts                Lawrence Lessig    1    6

          Section 4: Spreadsheets/Models
 21926    ----- Claris Blunders            John Kendrick      1   27

          Section 5: Accounting/Finance
 21922    ----- Thanks!                     Bill Taylor        1    1

          Section 6: General Business
 21928    ----- SoftPC 2.5 bad              Iris B. Sitkin     1   36
 21929    ----- SL Spool and FGS            Ron Carter         1    1

          Section 7: Desktop Publishing
 21919    ----- Type-setting                Randy Borst        1    2


[Navigator: Setting last message read to 21932]

[Navigator: Library 0 had a previous automatic search today]
```

Figure 9–10.   The summary resulting from the requests made in
Figure 9–9

▤□▨ ═════════ **Session View** – **Daily Session** ═════════ ▨⯐▨
```
╔══════════════════════════════╦═══════════════════════════════╗
║ [FORUM] Macintosh System 7 Forum║◆▨▨▨▨▨▨▨▨▨▨▨▨▨▨▨▨▨▨▨◆║
║      Sytem 7 Info         GO MACSEVE║ Reply │ Create...│▨ Message  ║
╟──────────────────────────────╫───────────────────────────────╢
║ Not logged in:               ║ Archive │Message │ Prior │ Next  ║
║ Session finished             ║                               ║
╚══════════════════════════════╩═══════════════════════════════╝
```

```
Message: #14429, S/13  Upgrade News                             ⇧
Date:    Sat, Oct 19, 1991 7:16:03 AM
Subject: #14427-System 7.0.1          [face]         [face]
From:    Marty Silbernik (Sysop) 76702,1415  Marty Silbernik  Bob LeVitus
To:      Bob LeVitus 76004,2076 (deletable)


Yo Bob... where ya been?  I've hardly seen you out here lately!

How're things in Austin...?

                    ... Marty

                                                               ⇩
```

```
┌─────────┐  Subject:  Things are fine!
│ Forget... │  Section:  S13/Upgrade News        ☒ Elec. Mail  ☐ Private
└─────────┘  ──────────────────────────────
Hi Marty!                                                      ⇧

I've been totally busy the past few weeks. Columns and reviews for MacUser, a trip
to Macworld Toronto last week.And when I'm not on the road, or writing articles,
I'm working on books -- Dr. Mac: 2nd Edition right now.

Speaking of which, I need to illustrate replying to a message with Navigator. Do
you mind if I use this one? Your Nav face is so cute.  :)

Bob
```

Figure 9–11.   Replying to a message using Navigator

After I log on again, Navigator retrieves the messages I double-clicked, and any messages sent to my CompuServe address. It then makes it simple to send a reply. When I ran this session, I received a message from Marty Silbernik when Navigator visited the System 7 forum. Since it was addressed to me, Navigator automatically picked it up. I've clicked on the reply button and typed in my text as shown in Figure 9–11. The next time I log on, my reply will be sent back to Marty automatically.

You can use Navigator to search the data libraries just as easily as I've searched for messages in the examples above.

Navigator makes using CompuServe even easier and will save you a lot of money if you use CompuServe frequently. I've found it's cut my on-line time in half—I now spend at least 50 percent less time on CompuServe than I did before Navigator. Incredibly, I'm getting twice as much use out of it. It's gotten to the point where I refuse to use MicroPhone to log on anymore.

Navigator is available directly from CompuServe. You can call them to order a copy or download it and be billed on your credit card. Just type **Go Order** at any prompt.

CompuServe Information Manager (CIM)   Another program, called CompuServe Information Manager (CIM), works similarly to Navigator, using a point-and-click interface to tame Compu-Serve's text-based interface. The major difference is that with Navigator, you tell it what you want it to do, then run the session; with CIM, you log on and perform your tasks in real time.

CIM, also from CompuServe, is an interactive front-end for Macintosh users of CompuServe. Unlike Navigator, which is considered a batch tool because it automates a CompuServe session, CIM replaces CompuServe's command-line interface with a Mac-like interface. CIM gives you real-time on-line interaction with CompuServe. Navigator, on the other hand, is designed to help do as much as possible off-line.

The first time you use CIM, you are prompted for your name, user ID, password, and the local telephone number to be used to dial and connect to CompuServe. You have to do this only once. Having done that, CIM presents you with three windows on the initial desktop: General Services, Favorite Places to Go, and a stopwatch.

The General Services window (see Figure 9–12), which is labeled Browse, shows several icons that represent logical groupings of CompuServe services, such as Computers, Investments, Shopping, Travel, and so on. You use the icons in this window to explore CompuServe through a series of tree-structure menus. If you are not already connected, double-click any one of these icons to connect to CompuServe and get a list of related service areas. For example, if you double-click the Computers icon, you connect to CompuServe, and CIM presents a list of browsing services—including hardware forums, software forums, connectivity services, and so on—from which you choose to narrow down your desired place of interest.

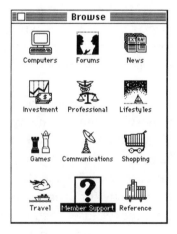

Figure 9–12.   CIM's General Services window, used for browsing through CompuServe

Also on the initial CIM desktop is the Favorite Places to Go window. This window lists forums and other areas of Compu-Serve that are most popular and most pertinent to Mac users. Figure 9–13 shows the Favorite Places to Go window with pre-set services listed.

Figure 9–13.   The Favorite Places to Go window in CIM

You can use the icons along the top of the window to add, edit, or delete a service listed in the window. To connect to CompuServe and go directly to a listed service, simply click on the desired service to select it, and click the Go icon.

If you want to access a particular area of CompuServe, but don't want to add it to the Favorite Places window, you can choose Go from the Services menu, and type **GO** in the box. Once you click OK, CIM connects you and transfers you directly to the desired service or forum.

Another good feature of CIM is the stopwatch window (see Figure 9–14). A constant issue for users of any on-line service is the fact that you can quickly lose track of your connect time. Once you're on-line, it's easy to get addicted to it and spend lots of time (and money) during the connection without even realizing it. CIM's stopwatch window is always displayed on your screen, so you can keep track of how much time you've spent on-line during a particular CompuServe session. (If this feature doesn't appeal to you, you can set CIM to hide the stopwatch window through the Preferences dialog box.)

Figure 9–14.   CIM stopwatch

CIM requires a hard disk and at least 800K of memory for the application to run. If you use MultiFinder under System 6, CompuServe recommends you increase the Application Memory Size (Get Info window) to 1024K. This gives you greater performance under this configuration.

If you've never used CompuServe, and you aren't sure what areas will interest you, CIM is a great way to explore. If, on the other hand, you know exactly what you want from CompuServe, choose Navigator.

Other On-Line Services

GEnie   GEnie is another large on-line information system, with thousands of subscribers, though not nearly as many as CompuServe. Its chief attraction is that it is significantly cheaper than CompuServe for non–prime time use (that is, use between 6 PM and 8 AM). But you'll have to log on in the evening to take advantage of the lower rate—if you log on in the daytime, the rates are substantially higher.

GEnie uses a command-line interface similar to CompuServe's and has much of the same stuff as CompuServe— electronic mail, computer forums, encyclopedia, business news, and so on—only less of it.

Unfortunately, the message sections aren't arranged in threads. Instead, GEnie organizes messages into Categories and Topics. I think threads make it easier to follow an on-line conversation—you have to pick and choose what to read on GEnie, then read it in the order it was posted. You can't really tell who's replied to which message, which makes it less intuitive than CompuServe's threads. Also, message traffic on GEnie is lighter than on CompuServe.

Finally, GEnie doesn't offer a Macintosh software package like Navigator. A package called MacGEnie is rumored to be coming soon, and it may make using GEnie easier. Personally, I find the combination of CompuServe and Navigator much easier to use than GEnie. Still, if all you want to do is download public-domain and shareware programs in the evening, GEnie is an inexpensive way to go.

The crowd on GEnie is friendly and knowledgeable. They have a well-stocked library of shareware and public-domain software and are eager to help first-time users.

If you do decide to join GEnie, be sure to drop me a note. My address there is R.LeVitus.

America Online   America Online is the newest on-line service, with tens of thousands of subscribers. It was designed specifically for use with the Macintosh, so it requires special software to log on. The software is free, and it comes with your subscription in a small, neat package with just the right amount of documentation to get you up and running, and to familiarize you with the America Online services.

The first time you use America Online, you are prompted through a one-time registration process, where you supply the name you want to use on-line, a password, and billing information. After you register, America Online automatically connects you to the service. The first time in, it's a good idea to visit the What's New & Online Support area, where you'll find a schedule of events, contests, and conferences, and a Members' Online Guide.

America Online has an easy-to-use interface, with windows, icons, and pull-down menus that make it easy for you to quickly go to the areas that interest you most. The first window you see after connecting lets you know if you have mail and gives you the headline of the top news story of the day. Click the button called Departments at the bottom of this window to open the main window, called America Online Departments (see Figure 9–15).

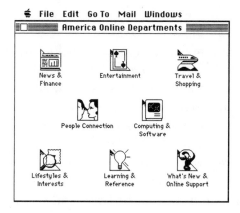

Figure 9–15.   America Online's main window

The different areas within America Online are called departments. To get into any one of them, click once on the appropriate icon. Here is a brief description of the eight main America Online departments.

- **News & Finance**—This department gives you all the latest news stories of the day. You can also go into this area to get stock quotes on your favorite companies. Stock information is presented in an easy-to-understand format, and you can add a particular issue to your own portfolio. (Yes, you can get updates for only stocks you specify!)

- **Entertainment**—Here you will find the latest gossip from Hollywood, news from the world of sports, your horoscope, and a variety of clubs, such as the Comedy and Trivia clubs.
- **Travel & Shopping**—Use this department to purchase airline tickets and make flight reservations, or shop for just about anything you want.
- **People Connection**—This department is a place where you can go to chat with other America Online users by typing "live."
- **Computing & Software**—Here you'll find all kinds of computer-related forums, including developer forums, where you can ask technical questions of software developers about their products. Microsoft and Claris are two of the many software developers accessible through America Online's software forums. There are also dozens of software libraries, featuring thousands of programs you can download to your computer. Figure 9-16 shows the Computing & Software department window. The directory on the left lists the computing forums, and the icons on the right correspond to other computer-related areas of America Online.

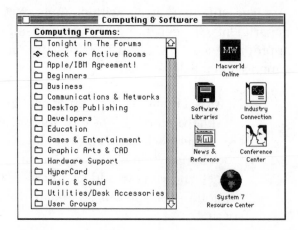

Figure 9–16.   America Online's Computing & Software department

- **Lifestyles & Interest**—This department is where you can telecommunicate with other America Online users about a variety of interests and hobbies, such as cooking, genealogy, electronics, or model airplanes.
- **Learning & Reference**—This department features an on-line encyclopedia and a variety of other databases and learning tools you or your kids can use for research.
- **What's New & Online Support**—This is the first place you should go if you are using America Online for the first time. You can get answers to your questions about using America Online. You'll also find the Members' Online Guide, up-to-date information on your bill, the Customer Relations hotline, and a schedule of on-line events.

I must say the Macintosh software supplied by America Online is extremely easy to use. America Online, like CompuServe and GEnie, features electronic mail, information forums, product support, and stock information. Its prices are lower than those of CompuServe and about the same as GEnie for non–prime time access. Prime-time access is somewhat less expensive than either CompuServe or GEnie.

Unfortunately, like GEnie, the lack of threads makes using the message sections awkward, at least for conversations. You can post public messages, and other America Online subscribers can easily reply to them. The problem arises when you want to follow all of the responses to a message; America Online doesn't currently offer an automatic way of reading through them. That shortcoming is almost made up by America Online's ease of use, which is due to its Mac-like point-and-click interface. America Online is probably the least expensive on-line service. Another bonus: You don't need any software but the America Online software you get when you sign up.

The people who hang out on America Online are a nice, helpful bunch. They are friendly and glad to help if you're just learning.

I spend a lot of time hanging out in the Mac Utilities and Mac Business forums. If you do decide to join America Online, be sure to drop me a note. My address there is LeVitus.

Bulletin Board Systems (BBSs)

A BBS (bulletin board system) is a smaller version of the on-line services discussed earlier. They are called *bulletin boards* because they operate like an electronic version of the traditional bulletin board. Many bulletin boards cost nothing beyond the cost of the phone call; others have a small annual charge for access—you pay it and receive a password for that BBS.

Most BBSs are run by *sysops* (system operators) who, for the most part, are doing it for fun, not money. Better systems offer electronic mail, messaging, and downloading of shareware and public-domain programs. There are literally thousands of bulletin boards in the U. S. The best lists of BBSs, surprisingly, can be found on CompuServe, GEnie, or America Online. Try a keyword search for *BBS* or *bulletin* in one of the telecommunication data libraries. Another good way to find a BBS is to ask your local user group—many of them even operate a BBS of their own. Also, the classified section of most local weekly newspapers often lists BBS numbers in your area.

Try to find a good bulletin board near you and check it out. You'll know it's good if the messages are interesting and the download libraries are large. The quality of BBSs ranges from exceptional to not-worth-the-phone-call. Most larger cities have at least one great Mac-oriented BBS.

Utility Software for Telecommunication

StuffIt Classic

If you're going to get involved in telecommunications, you need to know about a shareware program called StuffIt Classic.

StuffIt Classic is a file archive utility, written by Raymond Lau, that is commonly used to reduce the size of uploaded files. An *archive*, in this sense, is a single file created by StuffIt that contains one or more Macintosh files. StuffIt Classic also allows you to optionally compress archived files, generate a report of the entries in an archive, segment large files, and create self-unstuffing archives. Of course, StuffIt Classic also allows you to "unstuff" files that have previously been archived (or "stuffed") by you or another user.

Gathering many files into an archive allows you to transmit many files as one over a modem or network. Compression of the files saves disk space and/or on-line time when transmitting or receiving files by disk or modem. Compression of rarely used files will allow you to better utilize available disk space.

The big advantages of StuffIt are that it reduces the time needed to download or upload files by compressing all of the files in the archive and that it allows a group of related files to be combined in a single archive.

To use StuffIt, you first must create an archive, following these simple steps:

1. Choose New Archive from the File menu.
2. In the dialog box, type a name for the archive and place it in the appropriate folder.
3. Click New.

Figure 9–17 shows an archive called Dr Mac Archive.SIT, which includes two folders: Introduction *f*, containing three files, and 9.1 Glossary *f*, containing four files.

The suffix .SIT is automatically added to the archive name. Notice that, after stuffing the seven files in these two folders, the archive's size is only 320K, whereas the combined size of them before archiving was 789K. So to download all seven files in two folders, I actually download one archive, 320K in size, then use StuffIt to extract the three files.

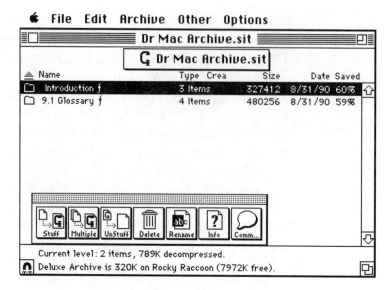

Figure 9–17.   A StuffIt Classic archive

You can also send StuffIt Classic files to people who don't have the application by creating them as self-unstuffing files. To do this, first create the archive file as you normally would. Then choose Self-Unstuffer from the Other menu (see Figure 9–18). StuffIt attaches a self-unstuffer to the archive file. You have the option of attaching the standard self-unstuffer or customizing your own. The archive file and the self-unstuffer attachment together become a double-clickable file the other person can then access without having a copy of StuffIt.

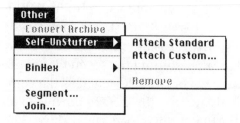

Figure 9–18.   Creating self-unstuffing archive files

StuffIt Classic also provides a general-purpose facility for segmenting large files into parts (segments). This feature is useful for fitting large files onto floppies, or for sending a large file in segments over a modem.

StuffIt Classic, the original, is a shareware program available from all of the usual places—user groups, on-line services, BBSs, friends, or colleagues. StuffIt Classic is the newest version of the long available StuffIt software.

StuffIt Deluxe

Early in 1990, Aladdin Systems introduced StuffIt Deluxe, which offers more functionality than StuffIt Classic, and is sold commercially through dealers, mail-order houses, or direct from Aladdin. StuffIt Deluxe comes with a well-written manual, which includes a comprehensive reference section and scores of hand-holding tutorials. StuffIt Deluxe provides an easy-to-use interface, designed specifically for novices, including a simplified menu structure and PICT and text viewers.

Version 3.0 of StuffIt Deluxe offers many System 7 capabilities, such as Apple Events (where other applications can talk to StuffIt Deluxe without user interaction), TrueType support, Balloon Help, and support for virtual memory.

Recommendations

A modem is your magic carpet to the world. Many brands are available, too many to mention here. The software I recommend is listed below.

Telecommunication Software

MicroPhone II
Software Ventures
2907 Claremont Avenue, Suite 220
Berkeley, CA 94705
800–336–6477
510–644–3232

Strengths:
- *Good balance between ease of use and powerful features*
- *Support for many nonstandard (that is, not 100 percent Hayes-compatible) modems*
- *Easy-to-use script/automation editor*
- *VT-100 and TTY emulation for communication with mainframes and minicomputers*
- *Excellent documentation*

Weaknesses:
- *Most expensive*

MicroPhone II is the program I use most frequently for telecommunications with services other than CompuServe and America Online (for which I use Navigator and the America Online software, respectively). It's excellent, but it's also quite expensive. If your budget permits, MicroPhone II is a choice you won't regret.

Smartcom II

Hayes Microcomputer Products
P.O. Box 105203
Atlanta, GA 30348
404–840–9200

Strengths:
- *Easiest to learn*
- *Slick icon-driven interface*
- *Excellent on-line help*
- *Good documentation and technical support*
- *Reasonable price*

Weaknesses:
- *Significantly less powerful than MicroPhone II or White Knight*

White Knight & Okyto

The FreeSoft Company
105 McKinley Road
Beaver Falls, PA 15010
412–846–2700

Strengths:
- *Low price*
- *Support for many protocols*
- *Powerful automation features and procedural language*
- *Phone book*
- *Excellent technical support on GEnie and by phone, often by program author Scott Watson*

Weaknesses:
- *Documentation that is occasionally vague and confusing (though almost always witty)*
- *Ugly and unwieldy interface*
- *Complicated procedure automation, especially for beginners*

On-Line Services

America Online

8619 Westwood Center Drive
Vienna, VA 22181–9806
800–827–6364

CompuServe

5000 Arlington Centre Boulevard
P.O. Box 20212
Columbus, OH 43220
800–848–8990
614–457–8600

GEnie
401 North Washington Street
Rockville, MD 20850
800–638–9636
301–251–6475

Utility Software

StuffIt Classic/StuffIt Deluxe
Written by Raymond Lau
Published by Aladdin Systems, Inc.
165 Westridge Drive
Watsonville, CA 95076
408–761–6200

StuffIt Classic is shareware and should be available from any on-line service or user group. If you are unable to find it elsewhere, it is also available directly from the author for about $25.

StuffIt Deluxe 3.0 is faster, and offers new choices in compression methods, along with optimizers for text and MacPaint files. Version 3.0 is System 7–compatible.

Summary

By all means, get yourself a modem and communications software. A Mac without a modem is an island. A modem makes you a part of a network of power users and gives you access to a treasure trove of public-domain and shareware programs.

CompuServe is the greatest communications service. After three years of frequent telecommunication, I've come to realize that CompuServe offers me more of what I telecommunicate for—more members, more messages each day, and more files in its libraries. GEnie is OK, and America Online is both inexpensive and easier to use, but I truly believe that you get the most for your money on CompuServe.

One of the best things you'll be able to do with your modem is ask for help with software you own, or to get a recommendation about software you're planning to buy from someone who's already made the purchase.

Whenever I need an answer to a computer-related question, I post it in a public forum on CompuServe or America Online. The next day (sometimes within hours), there are always one or two helpful responses.

The next chapter will introduce you to some of my favorite software—the stuff I refer to as "the Macintosh user's best friend"—utility software.

10

Utility Software

The power user's best friend.

Now we come to the real meat of this book, the utilities.

Utility software owes its usefulness to the computer—a utility would be meaningless without a computer to run it on. A word processor is not a utility, because its functionality can be duplicated by pencil and paper or a typewriter. A spreadsheet isn't a utility either; its functions mimic the calculator, adding machine, or accountant's worksheet. Graphics programs are also not utilities; they replicate artists' tools.

Utilities separate the serious computer user from the amateur— they're the software that makes using a computer better and more fulfilling. Utilities aren't designed to emulate something that can be done without the computer; they are programs designed solely to make your computing experience more productive.

The backup programs discussed in Chapter 5, the file- and disk-recovery programs in Chapter 6, and programs such as Suitcase and QuicKeys are utilities. Without a computer, there would be no need for them. Each of the products in this chapter fits this bill: From Finder replacements to macro generators, they make sense only if you own and use a Mac.

Over the past few years, I've discovered that utilities are the best way to be more productive at your Mac, because they save you tons of time and effort. I've assembled quite an arsenal of utility software, and I assure you, my collection of utilities makes using my Mac easier and faster. I'd hate to be without them.

This chapter is organized in two sections, followed by my "Recommendations" and "Summary" sections. The first section, "The Essential Utilities," covers the programs I wouldn't dream of being without. The second section, "The Best of the Rest," deals with other utilities that are useful, but more a matter of personal preference.

I really do love my utilities—the ones described in this chapter are the tools I use every day to make the time I spend at my Mac more productive. In this chapter, I'll tell you everything you need to know about the ones I recommend.

The Essential Utilities

The utilities that I consider essential include DiskTop, macro-generation programs such as QuicKeys 2, and extension utilities such as MasterJuggler and Suitcase II. These are essential utilities because they offer features that almost everyone will benefit from.

DiskTop

I consider DiskTop, a multifunction desk accessory from CE Software, the most indispensable of utilities. It has most of the functions of the Finder and much, much more. Once you install DiskTop, you'll find it does everything the Finder can do, and much more. DiskTop is one utility I recommend for almost everybody.

It's an incredible timesaver. With DiskTop, you can:

- Move, copy, rename, or delete files or folders
- Launch programs or documents from a handy pop-up menu
- Get information on the size and number of files or folders
- Erase, eject, or unmount disks
- Create new folders
- Search for files using many more options than Apple's Find file

Figure 10–1 shows DiskTop's main window. You can copy, move, delete, rename, find, and get information on sizes with the click of a button. Best of all, each of the buttons has a Command-key equivalent, so you don't have to use the mouse if you don't care to.

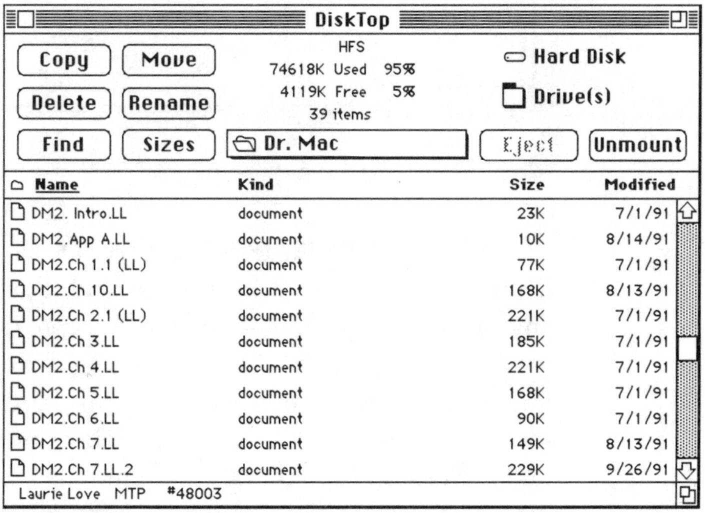

Name	Kind	Size	Modified
DM2. Intro.LL	document	23K	7/1/91
DM2.App A.LL	document	10K	8/14/91
DM2.Ch 1.1 (LL)	document	77K	7/1/91
DM2.Ch 10.LL	document	168K	8/13/91
DM2.Ch 2.1 (LL)	document	221K	7/1/91
DM2.Ch 3.LL	document	185K	7/1/91
DM2.Ch 4.LL	document	221K	7/1/91
DM2.Ch 5.LL	document	168K	7/1/91
DM2.Ch 6.LL	document	90K	7/1/91
DM2.Ch 7.LL	document	149K	8/13/91
DM2.Ch 7.LL.2	document	229K	9/26/91

DiskTop window: Copy, Move, Delete, Rename, Find, Sizes, Eject, Unmount. HFS 74618K Used 95%, 4119K Free 5%, 39 items. Hard Disk, Drive(s), Dr. Mac. Laurie Love MTP #48003

Figure 10–1.   The DiskTop main window

In addition, you can configure DiskTop to launch your favorite applications, associated documents, or utilities. Once you've done so, you can launch the application (or document) three ways—from the DiskTop menu, from the DT Launch window, or from a pop-up menu that appears anywhere on the screen when you click while holding down a modifier key— Command, Option, Control, and/or Shift, or any combination of these keys. Figure 10–2 shows the DT Launch window open, listing launchable applications on the left and associated documents on the right.

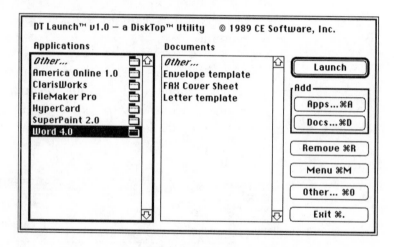

Figure 10–2.   DiskTop's DT Launch window

Figure 10–3 illustrates one of DiskTop's most powerful features, an incredibly flexible file-finding function. You can use any or all of the criteria—file name, type, creator, creation date, modification date, or size—whenever you search for a file or files. Once the files are found, they all appear together in a list, so you can act on them—move, delete, or whatever—one at a time, or as a group. Though System 7 has a better Find function than previous versions of the System software, DiskTop's is far superior.

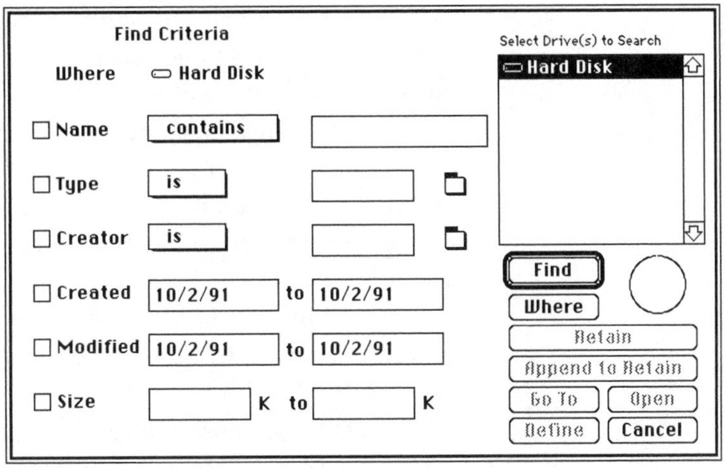

```
┌──────────────────────────────────────────────────────────────────┐
│    Find Criteria                         Select Drive(s) to Search │
│                                         ┌─────────────────────┐    │
│   Where      ⊂⊃ Hard Disk               │⊂⊃ Hard Disk       ⇧│    │
│                                         │                     │    │
│  ☐ Name      │ contains │    │        │ │                     │    │
│                                         │                     │    │
│  ☐ Type      │  is  │       │        │ │                     │    │
│                                         │                     │    │
│  ☐ Creator   │  is  │       │        │ │                   ⇩│    │
│                                         └─────────────────────┘    │
│                                         ┌──────────┐               │
│  ☐ Created │10/2/91│ to │10/2/91│       │   Find   │    ◯          │
│                                         │  Where   │               │
│  ☐ Modified│10/2/91│ to │10/2/91│       │   Retain   │             │
│                                         │ Append to Retain │       │
│  ☐ Size    │       │ K to │      │ K    │ Go To │ │ Open  │        │
│                                         │ Define │ │ Cancel │      │
└──────────────────────────────────────────────────────────────────┘
```

Figure 10–3. DiskTop's Find dialog box

Even System 7 or MultiFinder users, who can use the
Finder at any time without quitting an application, will find
DiskTop a timesaver because, unlike the Finder, DiskTop has
many keyboard shortcuts for selecting and acting on files,
folders, and disks. And, it seems to copy files much faster than
the Finder.

It's those keyboard shortcuts that make DiskTop so convenient for me. I hate to say it, because the mouse is part of what
makes using a Macintosh special, but reaching for the mouse is
one of the biggest bottlenecks to faster computing. One of the
Finder's biggest drawbacks is the fact that most actions can be
performed only with the mouse. And although System 7 adds a
lot of keyboard control to the Finder, it doesn't go far enough—
you can't copy or move files without reaching for the mouse.
Fortunately, every function in DiskTop is accessible from the
keyboard: Applications, files, and folders can be opened,
moved, copied, or deleted without your having to touch the
mouse. Even files that are nested six folders deep become easy
to find and open using DiskTop.

The DiskTop package includes two bonus programs—
Widgets and LaserStatus. Widgets is another multifunction program that lets you:

- Create startup screens, allowing you choose a picture to replace that boring Welcome to Macintosh dialog box you see on startup.
- Change PICT files into paint files, so files created in MacDraw or another program capable of saving files in the PICT format can be modified using MacPaint or other programs capable of reading files saved in the paint format.
- Print thumbnails, which are small minidrawings that represent finished full-size drawings. This feature lets you print up to sixteen miniature MacPaint documents on a single page (laser printers only).
- Customize paper sizes for the ImageWriter. If you have a need for custom paper (such as invoices, note-size paper, or the like), Widgets can create a custom paper size for your ImageWriter, allowing you to select that size from Page Setup thereafter.

LaserStatus, the other bonus program included with DiskTop, provides tools for keeping track of what the laser printer is doing. You can:

- Monitor printer use from your Mac. LaserStatus tells you if the printer is busy, and if so, who's using it. This is great on networks that share a laser printer.
- Reset the printer, which is like restarting your Mac; it clears out RAM and lets the printer start out fresh (your laser printer has RAM too, as described in Chapter 8). LaserStatus can also tell you how much printer memory is being used and how much is available.
- Examine the fonts installed in your laser printer. You can find out which fonts are built into the printer as well as what downloadable fonts are presently in the printer's memory (RAM).
- Disable the annoying startup page. Most laser printers, when started, print a startup page telling you some basic

information about your printer. This practice wastes both time and paper. Fortunately, LaserStatus allows you to turn the startup page on or off at will.

All three products—DiskTop, Widgets, and LaserStatus—have even more features than I've described here. At less than $100, DiskTop may well be the best utility value around. Version 4.01, which is System 7–compatible, also includes GOfer 2.0, a utility to find words and phrases *within* any document, which then lets you copy and paste them wherever you'd like—a powerful utility in its own right. (GOfer is also available separately from Microlytics.)

Although System 7 offers many of the features found in DiskTop, DiskTop offers a more flexible interface with improved keyboard control. Also, DiskTop's ability to search for files by multiple criteria in one pass is much slicker than that of System 7. If you're a System 7 user, you will no doubt find yourself using DiskTop regularly for file management and searching for files.

CE Software is an excellent company that is known for maintaining its products well, and it usually offers reasonably priced or free upgrades. It also has terrific technical support—some of the best in the business—by phone or on CompuServe or America Online.

Macro Utility Programs

Macro programs, sometimes known as *keystroke recorders*, allow you to record the keystrokes involved in repetitive tasks, enabling you to recall them later with a single keystroke. Even mouse movements and clicks can be recorded for later playback with a single keystroke. This can be an *incredible* timesaver.

Each of the macro utilities discussed is either a System extension (INIT) or a Control Panel document (CDEV), so they're a breeze to install. Just place the file in your System Folder and reboot. (Remember, System 7 places extensions and CDEVs in their respective folders within the System Folder.)

Macros are great for tasks you perform frequently. I have macros set up for just about everything. With just one keystroke, I can do the following:

- Open frequently used applications, documents, desk accessories, Control Panel documents, and utilities.
- Automatically type several lines of text, such as an address:
  > Bob LeVitus
  > c/o Addison-Wesley
  > Route 128
  > Reading, MA 01867

  or my name and title:
  > Robert A. LeVitus
  > Freelance writer and all-around interesting guy.
- Insert today's date in any program.
- Use the scroll bars without touching the mouse.
- Add Command-key equivalents to menu options in programs that don't provide them, or change existing Command-key equivalents to a combination you prefer. (Don't you hate programs that don't print when you press Command-P?)

With a macro program such as QuicKeys (more about that later), even if the developer has used a different Command-key shortcut, you can override it with any key combination you like. Now, every application I use will print when I type Command-P, quit when I type Command-Q, and so on, regardless of whether the developer followed Apple's recommendations.

A macro program can automate almost anything you do on your Mac. Have a custom size for your newsletter? Create a macro to select Page Setup from the menu and fill in each of the custom dimensions. You'll never do it manually again.

When I want to compose a letter, I use a macro (created with QuicKeys) that, with a single keystroke, performs these steps:

- Changes the font from Geneva, the default font (that is, the font the program uses when it first opens if you don't select a specific font), to Courier. I prefer Geneva for composing articles and books, and Courier for correspondence.
- Changes the line spacing from the default of 2, which I prefer for books and articles, to 1.5, which I prefer for letters.
- Types seven carriage returns, types the date, types two more carriage returns, then types the word *Dear* and places the cursor one space after the *r* so I can begin my letter.

The Doctor's Opinion

Apple Human Interface Guidelines: The Apple Desktop Interface, which is the "bible" software developers are supposed to adhere to, says the following Command-key combinations "should be used only for the operations listed below and should never be used for any other purpose":

Apple menu:

    Command-?   Help

File menu:

    Command-N   New

    Command-O   Open

    Command-S   Save

    Command-Q   Quit

Edit menu:

    Command-Z   Undo

    Command-X   Cut

    Command-C   Copy

    Command-V   Paste

Interrupting an operation:

    Command-period (Command-.) is used to stop the current operation before it completes.

    Interestingly, the book suggests that Command-P be used for plain text, not print (though it does allow Command-P for other uses if there is no Plain Text menu selection). In the real world, though, almost all developers have adopted Command-P as the command for printing.

    If all developers followed these rules, every application would use the combinations listed above. Unfortunately, more than a few software developers appear not to have heard of them.

Power users love macros. Macros make repetitive tasks into no-brainers. You don't have to worry about your typing; macros play back perfectly every time, provided you've created them properly. You don't have to remember the date. You don't have to remember custom page sizes. Macros let you customize your Mac in ways you never realized were possible.

Tip

> If you like macros as much as I do, you might want to consider an extended keyboard—one with additional function keys numbered 1 through 15. Using various combinations of the Command, Option, Control, and Shift keys as modifiers, the numbered function keys can control more than 100 macros.
>
> Another reason to consider an extended keyboard is that most have an additional key, called the Control key, which is a modifier key, like the Command and Option keys. The Control key can be used in combination with any other key to play back macros. For example, Microsoft Word uses almost every Command- and Option-key combination for something. Using the Control key for my macros in Word ensures that I don't use a Command- or Option-key combination that is already in use by Word.
>
> The advantage of the Control key is that, because it's not on every keyboard, few programs use it. Thus, you rarely run the risk of assigning a macro to a key that does something in a program.

There's no reason not to use a macro utility. They're inexpensive (all are under $150), they don't affect your Mac's performance in any way (at least in any way that might be perceived as negative), they use only a small amount of RAM (typically under 100K), and they save a lot of time.

QuicKeys 2 CE Software, which also makes the highly recommended DiskTop, is the publisher of QuicKeys 2, the finest macro product around. As far as I'm concerned, it's the easiest to use, and the easiest to get into the habit of using. It's another utility I'd never want to be without.

Using QuicKeys 2, with one keystroke I can:

- Insert text—up to 255 characters.
- Launch frequently used applications, desk accessories, Control Panel documents, or even documents.
- Select any menu item in any application.
- Click and drag in predetermined sequences. Under System 6, I had a macro that clicked on a floppy disk icon in the Finder and dragged it to the Trash, which ejects the disk and also dismounts it. I prefer this to using Command-E (eject) or Command-Shift-1 or -2, because neither of those methods dismount the disk. All they do is eject it, leaving its grayed-out icon on the desktop. Under System 7, the Put Away command in the File menu does the same thing. So my System 7 macro clicks in the spot where the floppy disk's icon is, then chooses Put Away from the File menu.
- Click buttons in dialog boxes. I have QuicKeys commands for many often-used buttons such as Cancel, No, Yes, Don't Save, and so on.
- Use the scroll bars without touching the mouse.
- Restart or shut down the Mac.
- Create sequences that may include any or all of the above.

QuicKeys has an easy-to-use interface (see Figure 10–4) that you call up with a single user-defined keystroke, or you can open the QuicKeys Control Panel document. In either case, you use the interface only to create and assign a key to a macro. After that, the macro plays when you press the appropriate keystroke, without your having to bring up the QuicKeys interface.

In Figure 10–5, you can see that I'm about to set up a QuicKey macro that will have the same effect as clicking the mouse in the right arrow in a vertical scroll box—known in QuicKeys as a Column Right. I assign the keystroke

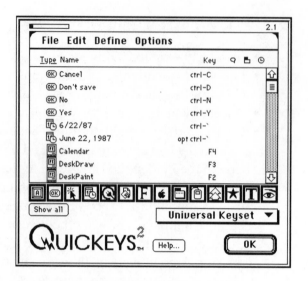

Figure 10–4.   QuicKeys 2 interface

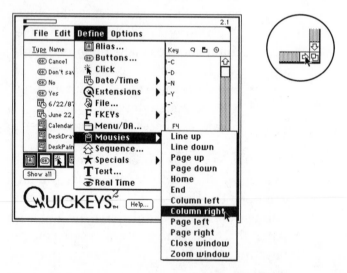

Figure 10-5.   Defining a Column Right macro, which clicks the right
scroll arrow as shown in the circle at the upper right

Command–Right Arrow to this macro. From then on, when I
press those keys, it has the same effect as clicking the mouse in
the right arrow of a vertical scroll box.

Once you've opened QuicKeys 2, you simply select the
kind of action you want to record, perform it, then assign it a

keystroke combination for playback. You can have universal macros, which play back in any application as well as in the Finder, or you can have application- or Finder-specific macros, which take effect only when you're using a particular application or when you're at the Finder's desktop.

For example, I have set up application-specific QuicKeys in all of my telecommunications programs so that Control-G logs me on. (Control-G for Go—I always think of telecommunications programs as going out on the telephone lines and getting stuff. So the mnemonic device of using Control-G makes sense to me. Use whatever makes sense to you.) No matter which program I use, if I type Control-G, it dials the proper phone number and types out my account number. Without fail. All I have to remember is to type Control-G once I've opened my telecommunications program.

I have a lot of telecommunications programs—on any given day, I may use CompuServe Navigator, AppleLink, America Online, and MicroPhone II for GEnie or MCI Mail. Each connects automatically when I type Control-G. To make things even easier, the programs are launched with combinations of the Control key and numerical keypad numbers. I prefer using the keypad numbers for this set of related macros because QuicKeys considers the numbers on the keypad to be different than the numbers at the top of your keyboard. By using the keypad numbers for telecommunications-related macros, I save the numbers 1–9 and 0 on the regular keyboard for other macros:

> Control-Keypad 1: CompuServe Navigator (CompuServe)
> Control-Keypad 2: AppleLink software (AppleLink)
> Control-Keypad 3: MicroPhone II (MCI Mail)
> Control-Keypad 4: America Online software (America Online)
> Control-Keypad 5: MicroPhone II (GEnie)

So two simple keystroke combinations—Control-Keypad #, followed by Control-G—launch the appropriate program and log me on. Believe me, it's a lot easier than finding and launching the appropriate programs, and it's faster, too.

The newest version at the time of this writing, QuicKeys 2 version 2.1, does an excellent job of supporting System 7's IAC facility by offering the ability to "drive" applications that support Apple Events through QuicKeys' Apple Events Extensions.

QuicKeys 2 is a utility I'd hate to do without. I've trained it to do so many useful things that I'd be lost without it.

Tempo II Plus   Tempo II Plus, from Affinity Microsystems, is the most ambitious, powerful, and expensive macro program. It is worth mentioning because it's the only macro program that offers conditional branching, where a macro can branch to another macro based on a specified condition. This feature allows you to build macros that include custom dialog boxes for the user to respond to (yes, no, cancel, and so forth). The program executes the appropriate macro depending on the user's choice.

Tempo II Plus is also the only macro program that can compare a value to the Clipboard. This function is extremely helpful in a spreadsheet or database. You can create a macro to select a cell or field, copy it (to place it on the Clipboard), then compare it to another value using six different comparisons: less than, greater than, equal to, not equal to, less than or equal to, or greater than or equal to. You can then branch to a different macro depending on the result of the comparison.

The new Tempo II Plus includes over forty Tempo Externals. These are small programs that perform special functions, such as finding a window name, determining available disk space, or playing sound files. By the time you read this, Affinity will have shipped version 2.10 of Tempo II Plus, which is fully System 7–compatible and includes support for Apple Events.

The price for this power, aside from the higher list price, is that Tempo II Plus is more complicated than the other programs. Still, Tempo has many satisfied users, and it is the only choice for certain macro tasks.

MacroMaker   Worth mentioning because it's free from Apple, MacroMaker is included with System 6. (It is not included with System 7.) It's the least powerful of the three other macro programs mentioned here, and it's saddled with a clumsy interface that tries to mimic a tape recorder. MacroMaker lacks many of the advanced features, such as conditional branching and special commands (date, column left, user-definable dialog boxes, and so on), that make QuicKeys 2 and Tempo II Plus so powerful. If you're running System 6, go ahead and check it out, but when you get serious about macros, get a copy of QuicKeys 2.

Tip

MacroMaker is known to conflict with Microsoft Works and may also conflict with other programs. It is not recommended for use with System 7.

Font/DA Extending Utilities

Until System 7 came out in the summer of 1991, the System software had a limit of fifteen desk accessories and fifty-two fonts on the System. Even worse, the Apple-imposed System forced you to use Font/DA Mover to install any font or DA *before* you wanted to use it. This meant, if you played by their rules, you could have only fifty-two fonts and fifteen DAs installed, and you needed to know which fonts or DAs you planned to use before you started working in an application.

Fortunately, System 7 removed these restrictions on fonts and DAs, and even got rid of the Font/DA Mover. In System 7, you just drag fonts into or out of the System file to install or remove them, respectively. (Chapter 3 describes Font/DA Mover in detail, including the difference between adding and removing fonts and DAs under System 6 and System 7.)

The System 6 limitation on fonts and DAs, and the requirement of using the Font/DA Mover in System 6, led to the

invention of font and DA extending utilities such as Suitcase II
and MasterJuggler. With either of these programs running under
System 6 or System 7, you can use as many fonts as you like
without installing them in your System in advance. Under
System 6, you are also free to install as many DAs as you like.
Both Suitcase II and MasterJuggler are INITs (also called Startup
documents under System 6 and Extensions under System 7).

If a mounted disk contains the fonts and/or DAs you want
to use, you can open and use them on the fly—without quitting
what you're doing, without planning ahead, without waiting
for them to be installed in the System file, or, under System 6,
without using Font/DA Mover.

Both MasterJuggler and Suitcase II offer these features:

- They give you access to hundreds of fonts and DAs, as
  well as FKEYs and sounds. (And if you use System 6,
  you don't have to use Font/DA Mover or ResEdit to
  install them in your System.)
- They compress screen fonts so that they take up less disk
  space.
- They provide utilities for resolving font-numbering
  conflicts.
- They allow you to view fonts in their actual faces. Figure
  10–6 shows MasterJuggler's implementation; Suitcase II
  has a similar feature.

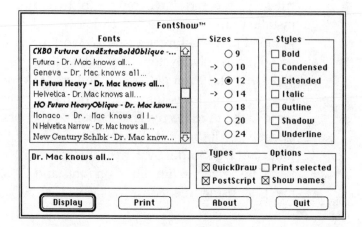

Figure 10–6.   MasterJuggler's FontShow

You can't believe how useful these utilities are. Avoiding the use of Font/DA Mover in System 6 and being able to use any font or DA at any time is reason enough to buy one of these utilities. However, the other functions (compressing fonts to save disk space, resolving font conflicts, viewing fonts in their actual faces) are equally useful.

If you use more than a few fonts (System 6 or 7) or DAs (System 6 only), you have a definite need for one of these utilities.

MasterJuggler   MasterJuggler, from ALSoft, is known as the Swiss Army knife of utility software. In addition to the functions it shares with Suitcase II (see the previous section), MasterJuggler provides several useful features *not* found in Suitcase II.

MasterJuggler's sound manager allows you to assign different sounds to specific System events such as Startup, Shut Down, Insert Disk, and Launch Application. Each event can have a distinctive sound.

MasterJuggler also includes a pop-up file launcher, which allows you to launch programs or documents. In Figure 10–7, you can see that I've configured MasterJuggler to include all of my frequently used applications and documents. To pop up the list, I hold down the Command, Option, and Control keys and click anywhere on the screen. One of the best features here is control of System 7's Show and Hide function—I use it all the time. You can also use this pop-up list to switch between applications.

The choice of keys, known as *hot keys* is user selectable; I could have used any combination of the Command, Shift, Option, and Control keys, as shown in Figure 10–8. I selected Command-Option-Control-click because I know I'm not using that particular combination with any other software.

Almost every MasterJuggler option can be configured by the user. Figure 10–8 shows my selections of hot keys for MasterJuggler. On my Mac, Command-Shift-K brings up a list

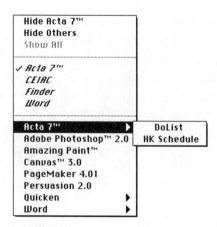

Figure 10–7.   MasterJuggler's pop-up application and document launcher

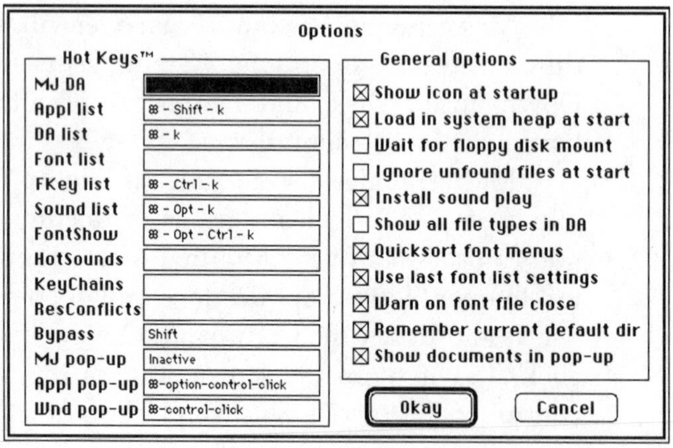

Figure 10–8.   MasterJuggler allows the user to select the hot keys used

of applications; Command-Option-Control-click pops up a similar list wherever I click, as shown in Figure 10–8. Both lists contain the same applications, which I installed previously; installing applications is a simple procedure.

Other pop-up lists include FKEYs, fonts, DAs, and sounds. You select the hot keys to call up each list, and forever after your lists are available with a single keystroke.

Suitcase II Suitcase II lets you install unlimited fonts and show up to 255 items in any given application's font menu. (Under System 6, you can also have up to 255 DAs in the Apple menu.) Once Suitcase II is running, you can install and use any font, DA, or FKEY just by using Suitcase II to bring it in. Versions 1.2.11 and later of Suitcase II are completely System 7–compatible.

Although Suitcase II, from Fifth Generation Systems, is a solid performer, it has fewer features than MasterJuggler. As you can see in Figure 10–9, Suitcase II, like MasterJuggler, allows access to unlimited fonts, DAs, FKEYs, and sounds. Both provide utilities for resolving font conflicts and presenting your fonts as they'll appear on the screen (see Figure 10–10). Only MasterJuggler, however, offers the convenient pop-up lists and sound-managing features. Although Suitcase II is slightly less expensive (about $60 compared to about $90 for MasterJuggler), I think you get more for your money with MasterJuggler.

Some people prefer Suitcase II; others prefer MasterJuggler. I prefer MasterJuggler—a collection of utilities that saves me time and effort dozens of times a day.

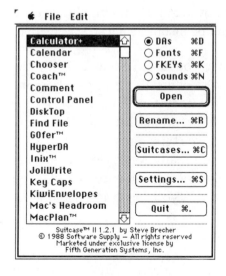

Figure 10–9.   Suitcase II allows you access to unlimited fonts, DAs, FKEYs, and sounds

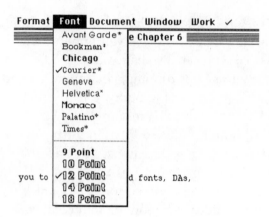

Figure 10-10.   Suitcase II also displays fonts in menus as they look on the screen

Even under System 7, there are clear advantages to using one of them:

• The fonts you need can be loaded in seconds.
• The fonts you need can be in any folder on any mounted volume, even a file server.
• Your System file remains slim and trim, because you won't be installing a ton of fonts in it.

Whether you use System 6 or System 7, you avoid the manual process of installing fonts—dragging them into or out of the System file in System 7, or using Font/DA Mover in System 6. And both programs are equally useful whether you use PostScript or TrueType fonts.

If you use many fonts, you want one of these utilities. If you'd also like the convenience of a file launcher, and the fun of a sound manager, you need MasterJuggler.

Now Utilities

If MasterJuggler is a Swiss Army knife, then Now Utilities from Now Software is a Swiss Army arsenal. It provides useful utilities that help make you more productive and enhance your Macintosh environment. The latest version, 3.0, fully supports System 7, and it is the best value in System 7 utilities currently on the market.

The majority of the programs that come with Now Utilities are Control Panel documents. If you're running System 7, the Now Utilities Installer automatically places the files in your Control Panels folder in your System Folder. (If you're running System 6, the Installer places them in your System Folder.) The Installer lets you choose which of the ten Now Utilities you want to install. Under System 7, the Installer supports Balloon Help, so you can get information about anything appearing in the Installer window, including a brief description of each of the Now Utilities.

Three of the slickest utilities in this collection are Multi-Master, NowMenus, and Super Boomerang.

MultiMaster   MultiMaster is a file-launching utility that, like the file launchers that come with DiskTop or MasterJuggler, eliminates the need to search through endless folders when you want to launch an application or document.

MultiMaster is somewhat more sophisticated than the file launchers included with either DiskTop or MasterJuggler—in addition to launching files, it can change monitor configurations and sound levels for any application you launch. So, for example, if you have a game that only plays in the black and white mode (assuming you're using a color Mac), Multi-Master can automatically switch your monitor to black and white when you launch that game, without requiring you to open the Monitors control panel.

Using the MultiMaster configuration window (see Figure 10–11), you configure MultiMaster to include frequently used applications and related documents on the MultiMaster file-launching menu.

In Figure 10–11, you navigate through folders on the left side of the window to locate the applications you want included, and click Open to move them into the Application List on the

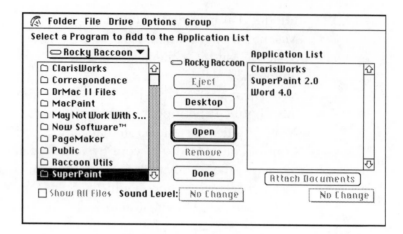

Figure 10–11.   Now Utilities' MultiMaster configuration window

right side of the window. To attach documents to an application, select the application from the list, click Attach Documents, and choose the documents you want included.

Once configured, these applications and files are available instantly through a pull-down menu that appears to the left of the Apple menu on the menu bar, as shown in Figure 10–12. (The same menu also appears to the far right side of the menu bar.) Like the DiskTop and MasterJuggler launchers, you can set a hot-key combination that, when pressed, brings up the MultiMaster menu in a pop-up window anywhere on the desktop.

NowMenus   NowMenus makes it easier to use your Apple menu, whether you're using System 6 or System 7. Under System 6, it creates a submenu containing each of your Control Panel documents and Chooser devices. Under System 7, though, it really shines—in addition to Control Panel and Chooser submenus, it creates submenus (up to five levels deep) for folders and aliases of folders.

One of the nicest things about NowMenus under System 6 or System 7 is that it makes it much easier to get at Control

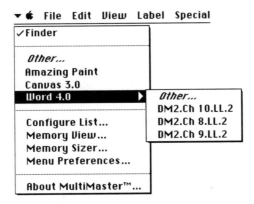

Figure 10–12.   The MultiMaster menu

Panel documents. For example, Figure 10–13 shows all of my installed control panels in a submenu to the right of the Apple menu.

NowMenus also provides shortcut access to the entire menu bar. By pressing a series of keys and clicking the mouse, NowMenus pops up the menu bar of the current application (including the Finder) wherever you clicked on the desktop. If you have a large monitor, or more than one monitor, this is a nice feature, and one you'll use often.

The best feature of NowMenus, in my opinion, is the way it can add submenus for folders under System 7. As you can see in Figure 10–13, I've got aliases of all of my frequently accessed folders in the Apple menu, so I can open any file, document, application, CDEV, and so on, right from the Apple menu.

You may be thinking that this is similar to a file launcher, and it is, but unlike a file launcher, NowMenus requires no advance planning. Everything in any of the folders in my Apple menu is instantly available, without any configuring.

Super Boomerang   Perhaps the best reason to buy Now Utilities is Super Boomerang, which is by far the finest enhancement to Open and Save dialog boxes ever invented. Super Boomerang helps you quickly navigate your hard disk's maze of folders by listing your most frequently used files and folders in all Open and Save dialog boxes, as well as in the Apple menu. Figure

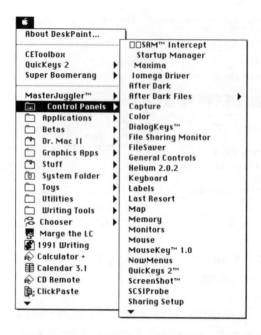

Figure 10–13.   NowMenus adds hierarchical support to the Apple menu

Tip

I like the folders to appear at the top of the Apple menu, and Control Panels to appear as the first folder. So I begin their names with spaces—three spaces before the Control Panels folder, two spaces before the names of all the other folders, and one space before the Chooser. Spaces sort first alphabetically, and the Apple menu displays its contents in alphabetical order. Thus, by putting spaces before these file and folder names, items in my Apple menu appear in the order I like.

Under System 6, you can't begin a file or folder name with a space, but it won't matter in this case, because under System 6 you can't have folders in your Apple menu anyway! (Actually, you can begin a file or folder name with a space under System 6; you just have to trick the operating system a little. Here's how. Let's say you want to name a folder <sp> Folder, with the <sp> standing for a single-space character and x standing for any character you can type. Simply type an **x**, then a space, then **Folder**. So your folder name would now look like this:

x <sp> Folder

Now place the cursor just to the right of the x and backspace. Voilà! The file name is now <sp> Folder.)

10–14 shows how Super Boomerang enhances Open and Save dialog boxes. A menu bar along the top of the dialog box lets you quickly navigate to a particular folder, open a particular file, switch disk drives, change to another group of files, or set other options. And it's smart about it—the files you see in the File menu are files that can be opened by the current application; all other files are grayed out and unavailable. Better still, there's an option called DirectOpen; if you turn it on, a submenu gets attached to the Open command and displays your most recently opened files. (See Figure 10–15.)

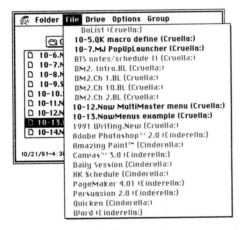

Figure 10–14.   Using Super Boomerang in Amazing Paint's Open dialog box

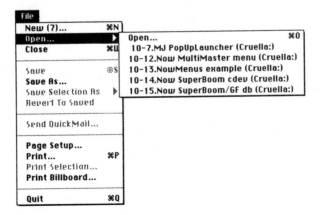

Figure 10–15.   Using Super Boomerang's Direct Open feature from Amazing Paint's File menu

Using the Super Boomerang control panel (see Figure 10–16), you can customize Super Boomerang by determining how many files or folders should appear in the menus on a temporary or permanent basis. You can also change hot-key settings for all Super Boomerang features, as well as set and change groups of files to display by application.

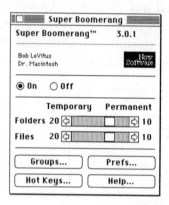

Figure 10–16.   The Super Boomerang control panel

Once you've configured Super Boomerang, you don't have to go up and down through disks and folders to find the file you want buried ten folders deep. Once you've told it how many folders and files to remember, it stores them for you. So, if you've set it to remember twenty files and folders, it remembers the last twenty files and the last twenty folders you opened!

Super Boomerang also has a powerful Find Files command that can search your disks and find a file or folder by its name or even by a word inside the document. Powerful stuff, and one of my all-time favorite timesavers!

The Rest of Now Utilities In addition to these three outstanding utilities, Now Utilities includes the following:

- **DeskPicture**—Lets you customize the standard desktop pattern with your own color or black-and-white picture.
- **AlarmsClock**—Displays a configurable alarm clock on the menu bar. You define multiple alarm clocks for

different events, times, days, and so on. Figure 10–17 shows a customized alarm set to sound at 5:30 PM to remind me to stop working.

- **NowSave**—Automatically saves your documents after a specified length of time, number of keystrokes, or number of mouse clicks.
- **Screen Locker**—Lets you password-protect access to your Macintosh.
- **StartUp Manager**—Manages which INITs and CDEVs are loaded into memory at startup, and in what order. If you've ever had an INIT or CDEV conflict (see Chapter 6), you'll appreciate how handy this is.
- **Profiler**—Analyzes your System and its configurations by tracking software and System conflicts.
- **WYSIWYG Menus**—Similar to MasterJuggler's FontShow, shows fonts in their actual faces in the Font menu. This utility also groups font families together, displaying them in submenus.

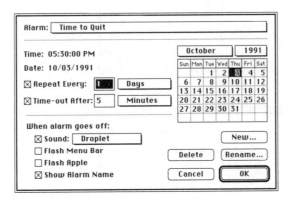

Figure 10–17.   Now Utilities' AlarmsClock is customizable

Those are the essential utilities: DiskTop, QuicKeys 2 (or another macro program), MasterJuggler (or Suitcase II), and Now Utilities. These are utilities almost everyone will benefit from—a Mac without them is underpowered. But you might find dozens of other utilities useful. The next section takes a look at the best of the rest.

The Best of the Rest (Other Utilities)

HandOff II

HandOff II, from Connectix, is a set of Finder enhancements that simplify and automate the process of launching applications and opening documents. One of the things that differentiates Hand-Off II from other file launchers is Automatic Application Substitution, which lets you open documents if you don't have the creator application. This includes the ability to open DOS files into compatible Macintosh applications. If you try to open a document by double-clicking it, and you don't have the original application, HandOff II automatically opens a window where you can choose a substitute application. In Figure 10–18, I tried to open a MacDraw document; but I don't have MacDraw, so I am substituting SuperPaint 2.0. From now on, when I double-click a MacDraw document, SuperPaint will launch.

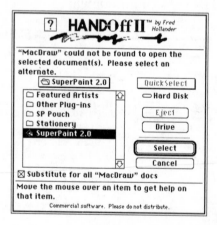

Figure 10–18.   HandOff II's Automatic Application Substitution feature

HandOff II also includes two features specifically designed for System 7 users: AutoHide Others and SuperMenu. AutoHide Others takes System 7's Hide/Show feature in the Application menu one step further. With this feature, you can always keep your desktop tidy by automatically hiding all inactive windows from view. SuperMenu works like Now Utilities' NowMenus by adding hierarchical support to the Apple menu.

Also unique to HandOff II are briefcases, which allow you to launch frequently used applications or documents, either separately or simultaneously, by choosing them from the pop-up menu. You create briefcases that contain related files and applications. This feature allows you to simultaneously launch a given application and its files with a single mouse click. Or, you can launch two applications, and a document into each of them. It's really flexible and easy as pie to use. Just add applications and documents to the HandOff II Launch menu much like you do in Now Utilities' MultiMaster. Figure 10–19 shows the HandOff II Launch menu editor, where you can assign hot keys to applications and files, and set other options.

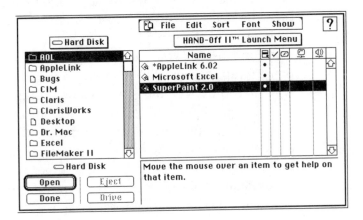

Figure 10–19.   HandOff II's Launch menu editor

Like Now's MultiMaster, HandOff II can change monitor configurations and sound levels for any application you launch.

You can also see from Figure 10-19 that HandOff II includes context-sensitive help right in this window. Aside from that, HandOff II offers an excellent on-line help facility covering all of its features.

If you're buying one of the other products that includes a file launcher, such as DiskTop, MasterJuggler, or Now Utilities,

HandOff II is somewhat redundant. But if you're looking for the most powerful and configurable file launcher around, this is it. And don't forget that it includes SuperMenu, which works like NowMenus.

SmartScrap/The Clipper

If you use graphics, these are a pair of Scrapbook and Clipboard enhancement utilities you're going to love. SmartScrap and The Clipper, from Solutions, Inc., are packaged together, so you get two incredible desk accessories at once.

SmartScrap is a Scrapbook replacement that reads and writes standard Scrapbook files but has some significant advantages. It can read your old Scrapbook files without any modification and is one of the most trouble-free desk accessories I own. Because it works almost exactly like the Scrapbook DA that comes with Apple System software, it's incredibly easy to learn and use. If you currently use the Apple Scrapbook DA, SmartScrap is going to knock you out. Here are a few of the ways it improves on the Apple Scrapbook.

SmartScrap has a pictorial table of contents (see Figure 10–20); the Apple Scrapbook DA doesn't. This makes it simple to find images when you use SmartScrap. The Apple Scrapbook forces you to look at one page at a time, and it can only move pages sequentially. SmartScrap allows you to jump directly to any image by simply double-clicking it.

SmartScrap has horizontal and vertical scroll bars (see Figure 10–21); the Apple Scrapbook has none. Without scroll bars, you can view only part of the image. Additionally, Smart-Scrap has a selection rectangle (see Figure 10–21); the Apple Scrapbook doesn't. This selection rectangle lets you easily select any part of an image, whereas the Apple Scrapbook allows you to copy only an entire page.

SmartScrap lets you create and rename multiple Scrapbook files, and they can be stored in any folder on any volume; the Apple Scrapbook lets you create only one, and it must be named Scrapbook File and stored in your System Folder.

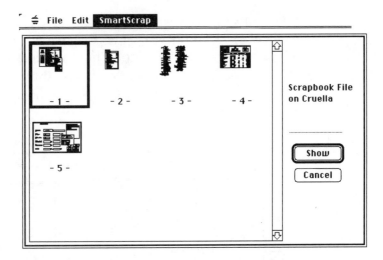

Figure 10–20.   SmartScrap's table of contents

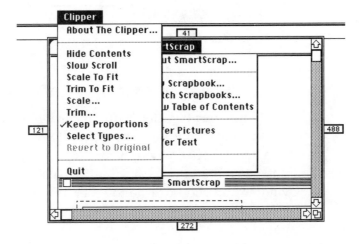

Figure 10–21.   SmartScrap has scroll bars and a selection rectangle

The Clipper, which is the other half of this dynamic duo of desk accessories, is just what the doctor ordered if you've ever needed to scale or crop an image, particularly in a program that doesn't have this feature.

The Clipper is a tool for cropping and scaling images. It's easy to use: You simply copy any image to the Clipboard, open The Clipper, and paste. Once you've pasted your graphic into

The Clipper, you can show or hide its contents. If you hide the contents, The Clipper becomes transparent. That means you can see through it to your application, which allows you to resize The Clipper's window while looking through it at your application. In Figure 10–22, The Clipper's contents are showing (that is, not hidden).

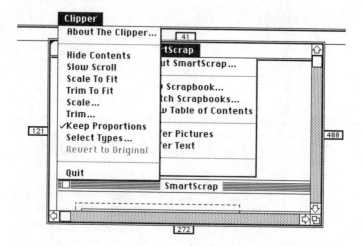

Figure 10–22.   The Clipper lets you scale or trim graphic images

Once you've pasted a graphic image into The Clipper, you can scale or trim it in many ways. If you choose Scale or Trim from the Clipper menu, you can specify scale or trim percentages numerically via a dialog box. Or, you can resize the window and choose Scale to Fit or Trim to Fit from the Clipper menu, which scales or trims your image to the exact size of the window.

Using the Scale or Trim to Fit command in conjunction with the Hide Contents feature allows you to resize the window the usual way, by dragging the little box in the lower right corner of The Clipper's window, while looking through the transparent Clipper window. Because the contents are hidden, you can see right through The Clipper to your document, which makes it easy to adjust the window to just the right size. Fiddle with the window until it's exactly the size you want your graphic to be. Then, choose Scale or Trim to Fit. Once you're satisfied with the resized image, just copy it and close The Clipper. Now you're ready to paste the image into any application you choose.

The Clipper is an ideal tool for resizing bitmapped images using the magic laser printer scaling percentages discussed in Chapter 8.

Desktop publishers will love The Clipper's ability to scale a graphic to the precise dimensions of open space in the publication. If you ever copy and paste graphic images, The Clipper will be a helpful addition to your bag of tricks.

DiskExpress II

DiskExpress II, from ALSoft (the same people who make MasterJuggler), is a utility for defragmenting disks, particularly hard disks. Defragmenting, also called optimizing, is a procedure that rewrites files on your disk so they occupy contiguous sectors. Fragmented files take longer to access, so if you're serious about performance, you'll want to use DiskExpress regularly. I run it about once a month.

You can use the DiskExpress control panel (as shown in Figure 10–23) to set a variety of options. You can have Disk-Express monitor and optimize your hard disk automatically. If you don't want DiskExpress to continuously be defragmenting your hard disk, you can turn it off in the control panel.

Figure 10–23.   The DiskExpress II control panel

DiskExpress II monitors your file activity while you work to determine the best way to optimize your disk. It even works with TOPS and maintains AppleShare settings.

Version 2.07 is fully System 7–compatible, supporting all of System 7's features including aliases and Balloon Help. Disk-Express II also gives special treatment to virtual memory files and startup System extensions, enhancing virtual memory performance and improving your Mac's startup speeds.

Depending on the degree of fragmentation on your disk, DiskExpress II can speed disk access enough for you to notice. It is also discussed in Chapter 4.

Screen Flipper

Screen Flipper is an INIT that allows color Mac users to toggle between monitor configurations—black and white, or 4, 16, 256, or millions of colors—from a pop-up menu (see Figure 10–24). If you have a Mac II, you'll love not having to make a trip to the control panel every time a program wants to be run in black and white (some programs are not designed to work in color and refuse to run in the color mode). Screen Flipper does not affect the color setting you choose in the control panel. After you have used Screen Flipper to select a different mode, when you reboot your Mac will start up in whichever color mode you selected in the control panel.

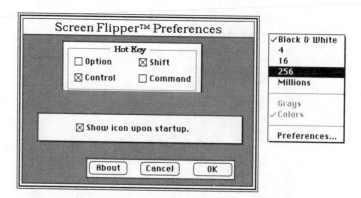

Figure 10–24.   Screen Flipper's Preference dialog box and pop-up menu

Screen Flipper is shareware, so you can pick up a copy from most of the on-line services, on-line bulletin boards, or user groups.

Recommendations

As I said, I love utility software. The products I recommend are listed below for your convenience.

The Essential Utilities

DiskTop

CE Software, Inc.
1801 Industrial Circle
West Des Moines, IA 50265
800–523–7638
515–224–1995
Approximately $100

MasterJuggler

ALSoft
P.O. Box 927
Spring, TX 77383
713–353–4090
800–257–6381
Approximately $90

Now Utilities

Now Software
520 SW Harrison, Suite 435
Portland, OR 97201
800–237–3611
503–274–2800
Approximately $129

QuicKeys 2
>CE Software, Inc.
>1801 Industrial Circle
>West Des Moines, IA 50265
>800–523–7638
>515–224–1995
>Approximately $150

Suitcase II
>Fifth Generation Systems
>10049 N. Reiger Road
>Baton Rouge, LA 70809
>800–873–4384
>504–291–7221
>Approximately $55

Tempo II Plus
>Affinity Microsystems
>1050 Walnut Street, Suite 425
>Boulder, CO 80302
>800–367–6771
>303–442–4840
>Approximately $170

The Best of the Rest

DiskExpress II
>ALSoft
>P.O. Box 927
>Spring, TX 77383
>800–257–6381
>713–353–4090
>Approximately $90

HandOff II

Connectix
2655 Campus Drive
San Mateo, CA 94403
415–571–5100
800–950–5880
Approximately $100

SmartScrap & The Clipper 2.1

Solutions, Inc.
30 Commerce Street
Williston, VT 05495
802–658–5506
Approximately $90

Screen Flipper

Shareware by Michael Whittingham
Available from user groups or on-line services.

Summary

By all means, get yourself copies of QuicKeys 2, DiskTop, and Now Utilities. They are three of the most effective productivity-enhancing utilities on the market. I just can't recommend them highly enough. If you use more than a few fonts or DAs, or you want the ability to easily choose between available sets of them, get MasterJuggler or Suitcase II.

If you work with a lot of graphics, SmartScrap and The Clipper are useful.

New utilities are always coming out—better backup utilities, better Finder replacements, better everything. Keep your eye on the Mac magazines for reviews or cruise the on-line services for power-user recommendations. (Chapter 9 contains further information on telecommunications and on-line services.)

Oh, and one last thing: Be careful when you begin using a utility for the first time, especially if it's an INIT or CDEV like most of the utilities in this chapter. Make sure you've got a reliable backup of any startup disk on which you plan to install a new utility. In some cases, your new INIT or CDEV may not get along with other programs (usually other INITs or CDEVs) on your hard disk. If you add an INIT and have trouble rebooting, see the section on resolving INIT conflicts in Chapter 6.

Armed with your utility software, you're ready to find out what other power users think you should know.

11

What Other Power Users Think You Should Know

Tips, hints, and advice from power users all over the world.

When I began to work on this book, I knew there was little chance of my remembering everything I've learned about the Mac over the past few years. So I enlisted the help of friends, acquaintances, and just about anybody with a Mac and a modem who would listen.

As I told you in Chapter 9, using a modem to get information is the greatest thing since sliced bread. So, because the folks who hang out on CompuServe, GEnie, and America Online are so nice and know so much, I enlisted their help.

I logged onto each of the services and left the following message in the public message area:

Fellow telecommunicator:

Thank you for reading this message. For those of you who don't know me, allow me to introduce myself: my name is Bob LeVitus. I'm the former Editor-in-Chief of MACazine, and currently a contributing editor for MacUser and the author of a book entitled Dr. Macintosh: Tips, Techniques, and Advice for Mastering Your Macintosh (Addison-Wesley, 1989). Which is what this message is about.

I'm working on the second edition of the book—the System 7-Studly version—and I am planning to include a section called "What Other Power Users Think You Should Know." That's where the part about being famous comes in.... If you're reading this, you are probably a pretty advanced Macintosh user. You know how to use a modem to get help with your Macintosh. That makes you just the kind of person this book's reader wants to hear from.

I don't know everything. And most of what I know, I learned here. Which is why I'm asking for your help.

Here's the deal: I need some great power-user hints. Especially hints on getting the most out of System 7. This book is aimed at the beginning-to-intermediate Macintosh user. If that described your best friend, what would you teach him or her? Anything that helps someone do something better, faster, or more elegantly is eligible. If you have a favorite hint or shortcut, submit it.

What is the most valuable thing you could teach another Macintosh owner?

Submit your best power-user tip (or tips). In return, if I use it in the book, you'll get to be famous for 15 minutes (give or take, depending how long it takes to read your submission...). I'll also mention which electronic service you used to communicate it, so readers will get a feel for the kind of people who hang out here. And, I'll send you an autographed copy, inscribed any way you like.

I'd appreciate it if you would post your tip here, in the public forum, so everyone can share it for now. I'll also need your mailing address and a daytime phone number. Feel free to send those by private mail if you like.

Thanks for your help.

Bob LeVitus

I expected to get some good hints and tips, but I never expected the response I got: More than 200 tips and hints were submitted in the two months after I posted the original message. For the second edition, I collected almost 200 more! And the quality of the tips was outstanding! Even after removing duplicates, there are over 200 tips in this chapter. Reading through them for the first time was fascinating. There was so much I didn't know, and so much that I'd forgotten.

By the way, when I wrote the first edition of this book, an on-line service called MacNet was popular. You'll find some of the tips in the following sections are from MacNet users. Since that time, MacNet has changed its name to Connect, and shifted its focus away from individual users and to corporate users. I no longer use it, nor does anyone I know. At the same time, a new service, America Online, has become extremely popular, and you'll find some tips from America Online users (none of which appeared in the first edition, as America Online didn't exist at that time) sprinkled through the chapter. See Chapter 9 for more information about on-line services.

This chapter is structured a little differently from the others. There are a lot of hints and tips, organized into several categories. Each hint is credited to its author. The name of the telecommunication service they used to send the tip appears in parentheses. I've added graphics anywhere I felt they were appropriate, and my comments appear in italic type to set them off from the words of others. I've also added, in italics, procedures that are specific to a particular version of the operating system (for example, System 6 only, or System 7 only).

There are so many gems and so few clunkers, I suggest you read the whole thing—even the parts that don't interest you today. You never know when that obscure bit of Mac information will come in handy. Tuck it away for future reference.

It was hard to categorize all of this information, but I did manage to instill some sense of order. The material is broken down into nine categories:

- *Shortcuts*
- *Backing up*
- *System software*
- *Shopping*
- *Hardware*
- *Software*
- *Printing/typesetting*
- *Potpourri*
- *The last resort of power users everywhere: RTM*

You'll find "Potpourri" is the longest section; I used it as a repository for anything that didn't exactly fit elsewhere. You may notice a little bit of repetition, especially in the Potpourri category. Make note of these—if more than one of these power users recommends something, it's probably worth remembering.

This is by far the most useful part of the book, and it's because of all the nice folks out there who used their modems to contribute to this chapter. So before we begin, I want to take a moment to again thank the members of the on-line community who helped out. Thanks! Your autographed copy is on the way!

Now, on to the best advice you can get—what other power users think you should know.

Shortcuts

Using Finder/MultiFinder

Here are a couple of shortcuts I can think of for using the Finder:

Hold the Command key in Finder when dragging an icon to "grid" the drag. How about holding the Option key when you quit an application so that the Finder closes all of the open windows to avoid clutter?

One of the best tips I can think of is one a lot of people don't use: In the Finder, you use the DA Find File to locate a file that you want to browse or print. Select the Move to Desktop option, then double-click the document to open it or select Print from the File menu to print it from the Finder. When you're done, just select the document icon on the Finder and choose Put Away from the File menu. The document will be put back wherever it was. This is a great timesaver when a document is five or ten levels deep in your hard disk, as is often the case with a large disk or a system with many users. (*System 7's Find command is even more convenient, as you don't have to use Move to Desktop or Put Away.*)

Craig Blackstone (GEnie)

P.S. You can reset the interleave on a hard disk (dangerous!) in HD SC Setup (*the hard disk initializer that comes with Apple System software*) by pressing Command-I at the menu before you choose Initialize.

- ◊ -

If you can get someone to tell you how to line up the icons in a desktop so that they're staggered instead of in a straight line with titles overlapping, I'll *buy* the book—heck, I'll buy two copies! I did it once, but can't remember how for love or money.

Anne Inda (GEnie)

No problem, Anne: To get the icons on the desktop to line up so they're staggered, you can either use ResEdit to change the vertical phase of the large icon, or use Layout 1.9 (freeware) to change the icons' spacing. Layout is much easier and allows you to turn on "grid drags" so that whenever you move an icon, it lines up with the grid. Keeps things neat and tidy. It also allows you to change the default view for new folders, adjust small icon spacing, and much more. It's a wonderful little piece of freeware. Unfortunately, Layout doesn't work with System 7. On the other hand, System 7's Views control panel can do a lot of what Layout used to do.

For example, all you have to do is check the Staggered Grid option in the Views control panel for staggered grids all the time.

- ◊ -

It wasn't until I was looking over someone's shoulder that I realized you could eject a floppy via the keyboard (no need to drag to Trash), *and* have its icon removed from the Finder's desktop. When the floppy in question is selected, just press Command-Option-E. The trick is to hold down the Option key until the disk icon disappears. (*It works a little differently under System 7—instead of Command-Option-E, press Command-Y, which is the keyboard shortcut for the Put Away command in the Finder's File menu.*)

Oh, one more tip just occurred to me. You know what to do when the Finder insists that you insert a disk that you *know* it doesn't really need anymore? Well, try Command-period a few times. Usually that convinces the Finder that it didn't need that disk after all.

Owen W. Linzmayer (CompuServe)

System 7–Specific

Several products can make your Apple menu (under System 7) hierarchical—HAM, NowMenus, HandOff II, and I'm sure I'm missing some. Put an alias to your hard disks in your Apple menu. Then, in one menu selection (going through several hierarchical menus, of course), you can go through any folder up to five levels deep, and directly open any file or folder!

Donald Brown (America Online)

Don is absolutely right—these utilities make using System 7 a lot easier. Look at Figure 11–1 to see how easily I can get to any item in my Applications folder. If you use System 7, you are missing something really wonderful if you're not using Now Menus, HandOff II, or HAM. All are excellent products; you'll be well served by whichever you choose.

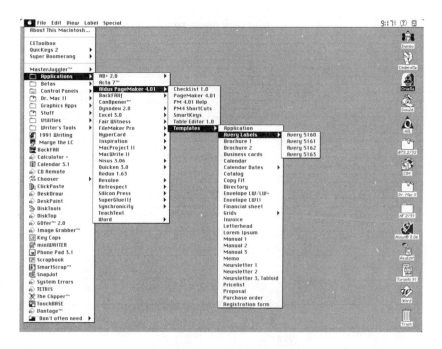

Figure 11–1.   One of the utilities that provides a hierarchical Apple menu is must-have if you use System 7

- ◊ -

Good idea, Don! It is also a timesaver to place an alias for the folders in which you most frequently work right at the top of the heap *(by beginning their name with one or more spaces, as I've done with my folders in Figure 11–1)*. Also, if you are beginning a long-term task on a single document, an alias for that document in the Apple menu would be helpful as well. Another alias that is useful is one for the Apple Menu Items folder itself, so you can make changes quickly and easily.

You might also place one or more of the most frequently used aliases on a row on the right side of your desktop, above the Trash icon. *(I do that, too! See Figure 11-1.)* These might include applications, disk (shared as well!) icons, documents, folders, and so on. You'll have an instant application-launching area as a result.

Gene Steinberg (America Online)

- ◊ -

System 7 tips? Well, most of the blatantly obvious (backup) ones have been (Backup) covered already. (BACKUP!) But when it comes to actually getting down and making System 7 useful in managing your computer environment, I'd have to say that aliases are incredibly useful. Examples:

Of course there's the obvious ones. You have some application, let's say PageMaker. You use it frequently, but it's got all these support files that have to be present in the same folder. You'd much rather have it on the desktop, or in the Apple menu. Make an alias and put it there.

Or you have something that normally hides a few folder levels down (such as ResEdit, which is in Utilities: Programming: ResEdit for me). Once again, make an alias and put it somewhere useful.

When it comes to making applications easier to get at by making aliases of them, it's often handier to put the alias right on the desktop rather than in the Apple menu. Why? Because if it's on the desktop, you can drop and drag a document onto the application alias, and automatically open it with the application. (Handy for those apps that open other formats than their own.) You can't do this in the Apple menu. (Note: An INIT named DroppleMenu will give you drop and drag on the Apple menu. But I'm sticking with a vanilla 7 for this discussion.)

You can use aliases to access your files remotely. With File Sharing enabled, make an alias of your hard disk (or a folder on your hard disk). Copy it to a floppy. Take the floppy to another Mac on your network that has File Sharing, and open the alias. A password later, you're accessing the files on your Mac from the other end of the building.

Aliases are also great for file management. I've got a moderately large collection of TrueType fonts (70+). I only use a few of them regularly; the rest I've put on 1.44Mb floppies labeled TrueType1, 2, 3. . . .

Once I had put them all on floppy disks, I write-locked each disk, inserted them one at a time into my Mac, and made aliases of everything on the disk by opening the disk using Select All from the Edit menu, and then Make Alias from the File menu. (Note: When you make an alias of something on a write-locked disk, it places the alias on your boot drive. Saves the step of copying the alias.)

When I was finished, I had 70+ aliases (about 75K), one for each TrueType font. I stuck all the aliases into a folder called TrueType Fonts on my hard disk. Now, when I need one of the fonts I've archived on disk, I simply find its alias icon and double-click. My Mac prompts me for the disk it resides on, and opens it up. No need to keep long library lists or exotic coded archival schemes—the alias knows where the original is. This is a great way for organizing file archives you might have (be they fonts, letters, games, whatever).

Jim Gaynor (CompuServe)

- ◊ -

System 7 only: Using QuicKeys 2.1, select Menu/DA from the Define menu. Then select an opened application (say Microsoft Word) from the upper right-hand corner of the screen. Assign a *Universal* key (such as Command-M) to that application.

Now from the QuicKey pop-up above the OK button, choose the name of the application, Microsoft Word, so that you can assign an *application-specific* QuicKey.

Select Menu/DA again, and this time choose Hide Microsoft Word. It will say this because you just selected it and
brought it forward when you assigned the Universal key.

Now assign the *same* QuicKey you just used, Command-M.
A dialog will warn you that you're using the same QuicKey in
the Universal keyset. Click OK.

This will let you hit a command key to bring forward an
opened application, and use the same key command to hide it.

It's great. That's what I use all my function keys for. On
startup, I load about eleven apps and desk accessories. I have a
QuicKey that hides them all (you can use MultiMaster for this
as well). Then when I want my calculator, for example, I hit F9.
It instantly appears. When I'm done, I hit F9 again. . . it hides. I
don't have to remember two separate commands—one for
bringing forward, one for hiding. The same key does both.
Labeling the function keys makes it super slick.

Hope this helps someone.

Rob Hahn (CompuServe)

- ◊ -

If you've messed with System 7's Finder much, you've
noticed it takes forever to get an insertion point (the flashing
vertical bar) when you are trying to change the name of a file.

To speed up the process, move the mouse slightly to one
side right after clicking on the file's name. Works like a charm.

Kerry Clendinning (CompuServe)

*Kerry is the author of HeapTool, a dynamite utility for expand
ing your System heap. You won't need HeapTool if you're running
System 7, as it manages the size of your System heap much better than
System 6 did.*

- ◊ -

System 7 remembers where you put the Trash can and whether it's open, so let that make things a bit easier for you: Open the Trash and make the window as wide as your screen. (Or perhaps leave enough room for the Trash icon itself, if you like.) Now drag the open Trash window down to the bottom of your screen, so that only the title Trash and the area that says *0 items* or *3 items* or whatever, are visible. Now you can drag disks, or folders, or digitized photos of your boss, down to the bottom of the screen without having to slow down and carefully get the arrow *right* onto the Trash can. There's something really satisfying about slamming icons carelessly into the bottom of the screen and having the right thing happen. After all, why do you think they call it "trashing"?

The Finder has always had a cool command called Put Away. In System 7, it's even cooler in that it has a keyboard equivalent (Command-Y) and it knows where to put floppies and their icons. So, when inserting floppies to browse their contents or available space, you can simply type Command-Y and the floppy is dismounted. Much easier than fooling with the mouse, even if you make use of my first tip.

System 7 automatically installs an extension that System 6 didn't. It's called Easy Access, and it's wonderful for many people who don't use the keyboard and/or mouse in the way that the designers originally had in mind, but potentially non-wonderful for people who do. Easy Access can become activated without your wanting it to, and it can cause everything from curious sounds and icons in your menu bar to an apparently broken keyboard. Take a quick look at Appendix D in the System 7 reference manual. Think about how cool it is that Apple pays attention to a lot of people who are usually ignored, and if you don't need the special features of Easy Access, drag it right out of your Extensions folder.

Peter Shank (CompuServe)

Before you drag it out of the Extensions folder, take a look at the tip from Neil K. Guy, in the "Other Shortcuts and Secrets" section.

Standard GetFile Dialog Boxes

I've been a power user from the beginning, and I didn't know until recently that, whenever you have to choose a file to open from the standard GetFile *(the dialog box you see when you choose Open from the File menu of most programs)*, you can use the letter keys to pick the file.

For example, to choose *MACazine letter*, you can type an **m** and the list will scroll to the first M file. If you have more than one M file, type the second and third letter until you get to the one you want. If you wait too long, you will start the selection over. You can use the Up-Arrow and Down-Arrow keys to move the selection bar one file at a time. Also, Command–Up Arrow and Command–Down Arrow move up and down through the folders. You can also move down into a folder by hitting Return with the selector bar on the folder name.

Michael Shulman (CompuServe)

- ◊ -

In Open dialogs, the little box above the scrolling window of files is a pop-up menu. Hold down the mouse over it, and you'll see a menu of all the folders between the folder you're currently looking at and the hard disk itself. Pressing Tab is the same as clicking the Drive button. Typing the first letter of the file you want will automatically highlight (but not open) the first file starting with that letter. If you can type fast enough, you can type the first few characters of the file name to select it, instead of the first file with the initial letter you typed. As soon as you have typed enough to distinguish your file's name from the rest of the files in the current folder, it will be highlighted. (This also works for folder names.) Pressing Return is the same as clicking the Open button. Clicking on the name of the disk *(as shown in Figure 11–2)* will show you the files in the folder that is one step closer to the hard disk (root) than where you currently are. (I wish you could do this with the keyboard.) *(You can! Just press Command–Up Arrow. It works the same as clicking on the name of the disk—it takes you one level closer to the root directory.)* Typing Command-period is the same as clicking Cancel.

Ken Hadford (MacNet)

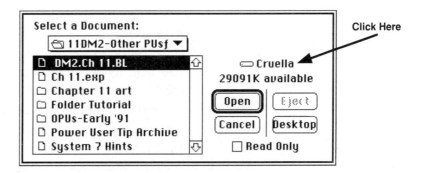

Figure 11–2.   Clicking where indicated moves you up one folder— closer to the Desktop

Other Shortcuts and Secrets

Provide shortcuts past your menus via the Option, Control, and Command keys (particularly in HyperCard, but in other applications, too). Shortcuts are especially useful when you can bypass several menu selections with them. This will make you more productive and happier with the application, and it will give you a generally more pleasant outlook on life.

Bruce A. Carter (CompuServe)

- ◊ -

If you play with buggy software a lot, you'll invariably encounter a frozen mouse at some point. When this happens, everything seems normal except you can't move the mouse. Well, be prepared! Keep a copy of Apple's Easy Access INIT in your System Folder, and use its keyboard equivalents for the mouse when necessary. Press the Shift key five times to turn on Easy Access, then type Command-Shift-Clear to turn the numeric keypad on your Macintosh into a mouse controller. This doesn't always work, but it works often enough for me to keep Easy Access on my Dangerous Software disk.

Neil K. Guy (MacNet)

- ◊ -

Command-W is a semistandard key to close the foremost window. Finder supports it, America Online supports it, CE Software's DAs support it, and so on. Try to use Command-W. It may save you time, on-line costs, and possibly medical costs derived from wrist troubles.

Kaz Matsuk (America Online)

- ◊ -

I can't imagine trying to compute without QuicKeys. Being a Microsoft Word user, I never use Command or Command-Shift with QuicKeys—anywhere. It makes the combinations too hard to remember. I organize my keys as follows:

- Control-key combinations call up DAs (Control-W = Word Finder, Control-F = Find File); function as buttons (Control-Y = Yes, Control-N = No, Control-C = Cancel); and select menu items that don't already have Command keys (such as Control-S = Save As).

- Control-Shift combinations call applications by name from under the MultiFinder menu—no mousing around (Control-Shift-W = *Word*, Control-Shift-R = *Red Ryder*, Control-Shift-H = *HyperCard*, and so on). I also use Control-Shift for text strings: Control-Shift-7 types 73270, 302, my CompuServe address.
- Option-Control-Shift combinations launch applications. This beats double-clicking your way through folders in the Finder. The combination is not as hard as it sounds— three fingers kind of fall on the keys once you try it a few times.
- I lay down a fist (that is, use the Option-Command-Shift-Control combination) for keys that will be defined as part of a sequence. *(A sequence is a series of linked QuicKeys, executed in a predefined order by a single keystroke. Each of the steps that makes up the sequence must be assigned a separate key combination; for these, it makes sense to use an obscure key combination.)*

I also use QuicKeys extensively in Word. Word wants the numeric keypad for its own nefarious designs, which bugged me at first. Now I celebrate the decision, especially because some keys are left over and because QuicKeys treats keypad characters as separate from their main keyboard counterparts. Here's what I've built:

- The * does a save, / italicizes, and – boldfaces—the commands I tend to use most in Word. Heavy formatters could use them for style sheets. A presidential aide could use them for hidden text.
- The Enter key does a single-click on the document; great for deselecting.
- Esc toggles windows (this macro functions as an alias for Word's built-in finger-contorting combo to toggle windows—Command-Option-W).
- Control-Clear zooms windows.

(I've also got lots of sequences that are too painful to try to explain, such as auto word count, selection, and button poke.)

By the way, how many ADB keyboard owners know that the Control key is sitting there, ready for QuicKeys to use? You'd be surprised. You should have seen the look on the face of this self-styled techno-weenie I know when I pointed this out. He was building QuicKeys for Quark XPress for a local newspaper, using Shift-Option-Command combinations galore.

Try using Control-key combinations instead of Shift-Option-Command if you have a keyboard with a Control key.

David Swift (CompuServe)

I agree. QuicKeys is superb for customizing any application with Command-, Option-, and Control-key shortcuts. It's one of the few utilities I would never want to do without.

- ◊ -

System 6 only: How about holding Command-Option-Shift-Delete at startup to prevent the mounting of an internal hard disk? This can be really handy if you need to do something flaky, or you want to run "suspicious" software without putting your hard disk at risk.

J. L. Doherty (GEnie)

- ◊ -

If you commute with either your Mac or your hard drive, get power cords and SCSI cables for both home *and* work. Not only is the Mac or hard drive easier to carry without cables, but having already plugged-in cables waiting on your desk (and not having to get on your hands and knees or reach behind the CPU to plug something in) is one of those things that makes every-day life a little bit easier.

Jason Taylor (CompuServe)

- ◊ -

One thing nobody mentioned is that the Finder shortcuts in the Balloon Help menu (System 7 only) are dynamite! If you use System 7 and haven't memorized them, do so right now. They'll save you a ton of time, as well as wear and tear on your mouse hand!

Backing Up

(This should appear in) large red letters on the first page of the book: THOU SHALT BACK UP.

David Ramsey (CompuServe)

- ◊ -

If you back up regularly, you will never have a disk crash. If you don't, you will have a total crash and burn the day before that important work is due. This is an immutable Law of Nature. You are not lucky. Anyone who tells you otherwise is a Minion of The Devil.

Richard Reich (CompuServe)

- ◊ -

One of the most basic of tips:
As soon as you take the master disk or disks out of the package, lock the lock tab on the disk. Make a backup copy of it,

put the master away out of sight, and do not use it; instead, use the backup copy. The master is only to make backup copies with.

Ross W. Smith (CompuServe)

- ◊ -

It is a little-known fact that hard drives are conscious, at least to the extent that they know when you haven't made a backup recently. As soon as they have determined that this is the case, they will crash. And incidentally, if you are contemplating the purchase of a large (80Mb or larger) hard drive, look into backup options at the same time. Backing up that much data onto 800K floppies can be a drag.

Jeanne DeVoto (CompuServe)

- ◊ -

Backups on the fly: Hard disk users are naive if they don't zap a floppy copy as often a paranoia dictates. The Save As command is not as convenient as it could be, however; you'll realize how spoiled you've been by your hard disks when you start waiting on floppy writes. (HyperCard's Save a Copy command should be adopted far and wide.)

Instead of copying from within the application, use Disk-Top. Set it to view files by their time of modification. The last files modified will be at the top of the window for quick grabbing or copying.

Figure 11–3 shows me using DiskTop to do just that—the only file changed today is ResEdit DA Handler. To complete my backup on the fly, I'll copy that file to another disk or volume at the end of my session.

(The Finder's View by Date command works just as well, but DiskTop allows you to select and copy the files in one step. Another way to accomplish the same thing under System 7 is to use the Finder's Find command, as shown in Figure 11–3.)

Another way to keep a backup copy handy: Copying a 100K file from one part of a hard disk to another is ridiculously fast—three seconds in my case. Hence, I use SUM's HD Partition (one of the benefits of buying a Jasmine hard disk) to build a 500K "second hard disk" in which I dump backups of modified files during the session. At the end of the day, when I'm ready to shut down, a Select All (Command-A) of this partition lets me instantly copy final backups onto a floppy.

David Swift (CompuServe)

System 7's Find command (in the Finder) can also find by modification date.

If your typical work day causes you to work on so many files that this strategy becomes impractical, you should investigate disk backup utilities. There's a complete discussion of them in Chapter 5.

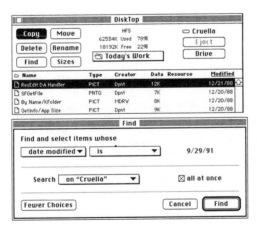

Figure 11–3.   DiskTop (top) or System 7's Find command (bottom) make it easy to find recently modified files

- ◊ -

Back up often, and then experiment. You'll learn a lot, and you won't lose anything important.

Lofty Becker (CompuServe)

System Software

Always use the Installer to upgrade your System software. It's important to use the Installer because a System upgrade consists of more than just a couple of new files. Many people have had problems upgrading to Systems 5.0 and 6.0 because they just dragged files, often neglecting to include such things as the MultiFinder file and the Print Monitor file. Then (surprise!) they're perplexed when MultiFinder and background printing don't seem to work. Future System releases may have other files and resources that aren't immediately obvious. Also, just dragging files clobbers any customized resources (fonts, desk accessories, FKEYs, and so on) that you may have had in your System. Although early versions of the Installer were buggy, the current versions are very solid and are the best way to upgrade and maintain System software.

Don't keep more than one System file on a volume.

David Ramsey (CompuServe)

David Ramsey has worked for Apple, was responsible for much of MacPaint 2.0, is a Sysop for CompuServe, and is a columnist for MacWEEK. *He also wrote numerous articles for* MACazine *and is REALLY a power user. He should know: Always use the Installer!*

- ◊ -

Don't use an INIT or CDEV unless you know exactly what it does and you *really* need it. Eventually you will pay for violating this rule. The more INITs you have in your System Folder, the more unmanageable will be the combinatorics of finding the badly interacting ones.

Richard Reich (CompuServe)

- ◊ -

Obvious advice: Unless you've got lots of memory, lots of hard disk space, and lots of patience, don't load your system down with trillions of fonts, INITs, DAs, FKEYs, sounds, and CDEVs. A staggering number of System errors I've seen have been caused by INIT conflicts, lack of memory owing to too many fonts, and the like. If you *must* have a lot of fonts, DAs, and FKEYs, use commercial products such as Suitcase II or Font/DA Juggler (a less powerful version of MasterJuggler). These products make life much easier.

Neil K. Guy (MacNet)

- ◊ -

When you keep running out of memory and discover that the System is taking up enormous amounts of space, check the Disk Cache first. (It's in the Control Panel DA; select the General icon.) That may save you from hours of trying to figure out what kind of virus made the system grow so huge. . . . Yes, I've had a nasty day working on this one.

Nick Arnett (CompuServe)

(Under System 7, the cache is in the Memory control panel, not General. It's a good tip regardless of which version of System software you use.)

- ◊ -

After you've been working in several programs, you may experience a *Finder out of memory, please quit programs or close windows* error. This seems to occur most often when no programs are running. A suggestion to give you a little more room is to boot off a System 6 startup disk, do a Get Info (Command-I) on the System 7 Finder, and add 10 or 15K to the figure you see in the Application Memory Size box.

Sue Clark (America Online)

Heck, if you've got 5Mb or more of RAM, use this technique to add 100 to 150K to the Finder. You'll find it eliminates the error message Sue mentions as well as the one that tells you that there's not enough Finder memory to copy all those items, and suggests that you try copying them in smaller groups.

By the way, you have to boot under System 6 to make this work because under System 7 you're not allowed to change the application memory size of the Finder.

If you're working under System 6 and see one of the above messages, just select the Finder, choose Get Info from the File menu (or Command-I), and increase the application memory size.

Shopping

My first and foremost rule for any novice Macintosh or other computer purchaser is really simple: Don't listen to the salesperson (sorry, guys). Go to a place where they're not paid on commission, and find the owner or manager of the store. If he or she will let you sit down at the computer and take as much time as you want to evaluate it in the store, then that's the place where you should do business—from both a hardware and a software standpoint. This technique gives you a better understanding of whether the dealership is being represented by a bunch of bozos who don't know anything other than the price of the software or hardware, and what the outside of the box says it does, or whether you really have found that gem in the computer world—the dealer who really knows his or her stuff.

Marty Silbernik (CompuServe)

- ◊ -

Don't buy all your software at once. If you are buying a Mac to do five things, start with just the software for one or two of them. As you learn them, you'll be in a better position to pick out the best choices for your other applications.

Scott Harris (CompuServe)

- ◊ -

Find the best dealer you can and cultivate him or her. Buy most things through mail order; it'll save you money. But if you take up a dealer's time getting information about a particular program, buy it from that dealer or not at all.

Lofty Becker (CompuServe)

- ◊ -

1. Find a good dealer. In spite of the fact that most of the press is fixated on dealer bashing, the truth of the matter is that a good dealer is the shortest distance between you and a useful, functional Mac. You may rightly point out that 90 percent of the dealers out there are crap, but I would then remind you that 90 percent of *everything* is crap. Hang in there until you find the right dealer, then stick with them.
2. Pay a lot of attention to your choices in software. Don't be misled by popularity or by magazine articles. Try it before you buy it on a configuration and under working conditions that are as similar as possible to those under which you will be working.
3. Don't be afraid to experiment. In life, this is a sure-fire formula for accelerating your learning curve. This is especially true on the Mac. If you think it would be neat if a program worked in a certain way, you will be surprised at how often the author has already thought of that!

4. Buy more than you need. You will *never* regret buying too much computer. You will *always* regret buying too little. This piece of advice applies to memory, hard disk capacity, computing horsepower, printer quality, the whole shooting match. Trust me on this one. Buy as much as you can reasonably afford. (For myself, I have always bought *more* than I could reasonably afford, and I have never regretted it!)

John Galt (America Online)

- ◊ -

Authorized Apple dealers, if they're worthy of the designation, are an excellent source of information. They often have public-domain software, which they will give to you if you bring your own disks. If you hear that a new version of the System is out, bring some blank disks to the authorized dealer and you'll get it free (without any documentation, though).

Ken Hadford (MacNet)

Some Apple dealers won't allow you to copy the System software; they insist you buy the shrink-wrapped package with documentation. When a dealer tries this with me, I leave the store and never return.

- ◊ -

When you're shopping for new stuff, magazine reviews are useful, but they should be just one factor in the selection process. Don't assume the author's priorities are the same as your own. Too often I see someone who wants one product over another because of its "5 mice" (MacUser's *highest rating*) or another, glowing review. Although it is undoubtedly a good product, it is entirely possible that another program—even one given a poorer rating—may better suit that user's needs. Try to see the program and/or its manual first. By the way, as a dealer, I have to agree with Lofty *(see three notes earlier)*: If a dealer is helpful, gives suggestions, and lets you read the manuals or try out the software, don't buy it elsewhere just to save money! Someone else here said not to trust dealers. Naturally I disagree (and, I hope, so would my customers). But the point of trying to distinguish a knowledgeable dealer from the proverbial used-car salesman is certainly valid. The fact that buyers will probably pay more at a knowledgeable dealership, and should expect to, might also be worth a mention.

Scott Harris (CompuServe)

- ◊ -

More about reviewers and magazines: The only good review for a business program is from someone who makes their living using that particular program. And the best recommendations are from those who have made the product—page-layout programs, financial programs, spreadsheets, graphics programs, and so on—work for them in the trenches, day to day. Even the best magazine reviews are based on first impressions, even if they are well-researched and conscientious first impressions.

Also don't be fooled by feature comparisons. Some programs do everything but tie your shoes. But they may not come through day after day as the workhorse that some plainer, less feature-filled program does. I have no problem with features; we all want them. But the more features are imposed on a program and not part of the basic design, the more chance for bugs.

Steve Hannaford (CompuServe)

- ◊ -

Don't be hardware wise and software foolish. People will spend many thousands of dollars on a high-end system, but will balk at buying a program for a couple of hundred if they perceive that it duplicates many functions of some program they have. There *will* be overlap between programs, but it still pays to have the right tool for the job when you need it. One of the nice things about the Mac is that learning, for instance, one graphics program means that it's rather easy to learn a second. Having a variety of graphics programs, desktop publishing programs, or whatever, can save you many hours when you have a project that one program can do easily, but another does only with difficulty.

Scott Harris (CompuServe)

- ◊ -

Buy older versions of software at highly discounted prices, and take advantage of publishers' upgrade offers. Many software publishers offer extremely liberal upgrades for little or no cost.

Don Mayer (CompuServe)

- ◊ -

When you're designing a project, take a brief look at what is out there already. Not only will this prevent you from wasting time if the perfect application for your needs already exists, but it may also show up some weak points in your design, new options, and other brain tweakers.

In relation to that, when researching a project, don't become obsessed with collecting every single example of any application even remotely connected to your project idea. You'll spend a lifetime (yours and the project's) reviewing the material, and you'll never actually get around to any development. Actually, this goes for users, too—you can research a purchase to death and never get around to making the buy.

Bruce A. Carter (CompuServe)

- ◊ -

Wet-suit companies have been making a ton of money by selling pieces of wet suits to Mac owners to use as mouse pads. Folks, that is not the way to go. Wet-suit material actually impedes the movement of your mouse. If you are like most people, your next mouse pad is free. And it will be the best one you ever used.

Find an old vinyl three-ring notebook. You do have one lying around, don't you? Tear off the covers and throw away the spine and rings. You now have two of the best power mouse pads ever made. Your mouse will skate across the surface.

Be sure you use a smooth, hard notebook cover, not the padded variety.

Phil Russell (U.S. SnailMail)

Hardware

Disk drives: If you somehow manage to get a disk stuck in your disk drive, straighten a paper clip and push it straight back through the hole to the right of the disk drive slot. This will force the drive to eject the disk.

Ken Hadford (MacNet)

Be gentle, though; you can damage the drive if you use too much force.

- ◊ -

In purchasing the IIcx, I wanted to utilize the sound chip but didn't want to pay the exorbitant prices for the (admittedly high quality) Bose speaker system with its built-in amps. So I ran on down to the local Radio Shack and picked up a simple, no-frills stereo amplifier on sale for $19.95 and two of their bookshelf speakers. Works great, and the speakers are an off-white color that blends right in with the CPU, monitor, and other components.

Don Peaslee (GEnie)

- ◊ -

When plugging and unplugging cables, always turn the Mac off. You might get away with it sometimes, but eventually, when you least expect it and most need your Mac, you'll possibly fry or slightly injure a component.

RTideas (America Online)

- ◊ -

When all else fails, try the following sovereign sequence (known to power users everywhere):

1. Rebuild Desktop
2. Replace System
3. Zap PRAM
4. Curse Microsoft

Jeanne DeVoto (CompuServe)

See the "Recovery Magic" section of Chapter 6 for details.

- ◊ -

Always use Shut Down to turn off a Mac II or Portable, and use it prior to turning off a Plus, SE, Classic, or LC.

David Ramsey (CompuServe)

Software

Don't use copy-protected software. It's not worth the fuss and bother. If you must use a copy-protected package, don't install it on your hard drive—some copy-protection schemes provide a way to do this, but these techniques may alter formatting or do other things to the hard drive that can cause major problems, up to and including loss of all your data.

Jeanne DeVoto (CompuServe)

- ◊ -

Using a spreadsheet: When you have several "areas" that you are putting on a spreadsheet, don't put them side by side or on top of each other; rather, put them in a diagonal line starting in the upper left-hand corner and going to the lower right-hand corner. *Reason:* If you have the sections side by side or on top of each other and insert or delete a column or a row, your action affects all the sections. If you have the sections in a diagonal row, inserting or deleting a column or a row will have no effect on the other sections because none of them fall into the same rows or columns at any point in the spreadsheet. *Hint:* To find your way from section to section using this technique, just name each section with its own name, and make a macro that goes to that section.

Dave Duty (MacNet)

- ◊ -

Charts created in Microsoft Excel and Microsoft Chart can be copied to the Clipboard and then pasted into a MacDraw or MacDraft document. Some shading may be lost, but each piece of the chart (each bar or line segment and each text item) turns into a separate MacDraw object. This allows you to dress up the chart to your heart's content. For example, this is handy for putting more than one chart on a single piece of paper.

Phil Reed (CompuServe)

- ◊ -

Something I've found useful: Save all your original program disks, even when a newer version comes out. Sometimes (especially with utilities), the manufacturer will change the mix of programs included. For example, CE used to include Widgets with DiskTop but does not now. Also, software companies often offer cheap upgrades if you send in a competitor's original disk. The old versions work just as well for this as the current version, and you still have your current version's original disk.

Hank Gillette (CompuServe)

- ◊ -

Microsoft Word has its own Page Setup and Print dialogs. To get the usual ones, simply hold down the Shift key while selecting the item with the mouse.

Ken Hadford (MacNet)

- ◊ -

Though this is mentioned in most Word manuals, I find few people know the advantages of Word's outliner.

As an outliner, it's kind of klunky, but I use it every day to move paragraphs and items in lists around—without cutting or pasting!

Hit Command-U, and you are in outline mode. Each paragraph (or item in a list) has a little symbol at the beginning of it. Click and drag, and you can quickly shuffle around paragraphs and items. Promote or demote items to higher or lower outline levels, and you can get even fancier!

Unless you fool around with the styles for the different levels, when you hit Command-U and go back to regular mode, your document formatting has not been affected.

Steve Born (America Online)

I'm a big fan of outliners. I tend to use Acta more than Word's built-in outliner, but no matter which you choose, I think you'll find the outlining metaphor excellent for organizing your thoughts. By the way, in Word 5.0 the keyboard shortcut is Command-Option-O, not Command-U as it was in earlier versions.

- ◊ -

In all versions of Aldus PageMaker for the Mac, the program doesn't really delete anything, because it operates as a database does (it just flags the records as deleted). Therefore, to conserve disk space or to make a file as compact as possible before sending by modem, you should use the Save As command, rather than Save. You don't have to give it a new name.

Save As compresses the file by actually deleting anything you've removed from your document. This is documented in the manual's description of the Save As command, but we experienced Mac users figure we know what Save As does, so we don't read that section of the manual. I suggested to Aldus that in future versions they include a Compress command. The product manager replied, "Great idea. Nobody here thought of that."

Nick Arnett (CompuServe)

This is particularly true of PageMaker files, but sometimes works on files created by other programs. You may be able to save hundreds of K on a large document by selecting Save As after making final changes. So remember: If you're trying to conserve disk space, use Save As when you're finished with each document. You'll be surprised how much disk space you can save.

If you have a more severe need to save disk space, you should check out StuffIt Classic, the shareware file archive utility. It can compress files as much as 40 percent. There's also a convenient DA version called UnStuffIt that can be used to extract files from an archive even when you're working in another application.

Or, choose DiskDoubler or StuffIt Deluxe, commercial applications that can shrink your files transparently as you work.

- ◊ -

When computerizing (is that a word?) one's financial system, continue on a parallel manual system until the auto-mated one has proven itself—a matter of months or even a year. My biggest heartache in England was having people's accounting systems crash on their Apple IIs, simply because the software couldn't handle the quantity of data. We would then discover their manual system to be hopelessly out of date. This probably holds true of most operations, not just financing.

Richard Scorer (CompuServe)

- ◊ -

Try to put aside enough time to learn about the software you use; don't just use it.

Richard Scorer (CompuServe)

- ◊ -

Most new users learn enough of the basic operations of a given program to "just get by" and then don't want to go through the effort of learning additional features. I don't know how many times I've heard: "I don't have the time. I just want to do it the way I've always done it." This cop-out attitude guarantees that you will never be a power user. Don't settle for the status quo. Even under a deadline, be adventurous. The best way to learn software is to use it on a real project and refer to the manual when you get stuck on a specific feature. Yes, this will slow you down in the short term. However, the time you seem to be wasting now with the learning process will be made up in the long run, because you will be able to select the best and fastest way to get future projects done based on your early efforts. I call this "reaching for critical mass." Each program mastered in this way makes the next one easier to learn.

John A. Noel (CompuServe)

- ◊ -

Send in your warranty/registration cards! You'll get notified about upgrades (most of the time), and you'll be helping the publisher compile some seriously unwieldy databases.

Robin Lane/Microseeds (CompuServe)

Microseeds publishes the highly recommended backup utility Redux, HAM (Hierarchical Apple Menu), and INITPicker, for turning INITs and CDEVs on and off at startup time.

Printing/Typesetting

Get a copy of the LaserWriter printer driver and put it in the System Folder. Before starting *any* job that will ultimately be printed on the LaserWriter, select the Chooser DA, and select the LaserWriter printer. This will work even if you are not currently hooked to a network with a LaserWriter. Then choose Page Setup in whatever application you will be using to make sure the page size is correct. In many applications, the page width for the ImageWriter is 8.0 inches, and the width for the LaserWriter is 7.5 inches. Failure to select the LaserWriter before starting may result in the rightmost one-half inch of the document being chopped off, or possibly placed on a second page.

Bruce Giles (CompuServe)

- ◊ -

Get copies of the screen fonts for the LaserWriter fonts and use them. Understand the difference between bitmapped fonts for the ImageWriter and PostScript fonts for the LaserWriter. Know when to use each type of font (and when *not* to use them as well). Understand the effect of the Font Substitution and Smoothing check boxes in the Page Setup dialog box.

Bruce Giles (CompuServe)

- ◊ -

If this is your first time working with a LaserWriter, start with a simple one-page document and make sure it works correctly before trying something more complex.

It's easy to spot the people who haven't learned these rules. They're the ones who spend all night (not to mention many dollars) trying to figure out why their 20-page MacDraw document in Toronto and Chicago fonts, which printed just fine at home on the ImageWriter, has turned into a 30+-page monstrosity with page breaks in the wrong places, and why it still looks like it was printed on an ImageWriter.

Bruce Giles (CompuServe)

- ◊ -

Many Mac II programs won't print in color on the ImageWriter or ImageWriter LQ, because the drivers of these printers use old QuickDraw (8 colors) rather than color QuickDraw. However, if you can get these files into GIF format (using GIFFER or one of several programs that understand GIF), you can use the GIFConverter program over in the PICS forum *(GO PICS on CompuServe)* to bring the 256-color GIF file into old QuickDraw format. You can then print in color on an ImageWriter. Looks pretty good, too (although it takes forever).

Jeanne DeVoto (CompuServe)

GIF is a special CompuServe graphics format.

- ◊ -

After installing a system update, it's fairly common for someone printing or using ATM to find that their fonts (usually Times, Helvetica, and Courier) aren't appearing correctly. Usually this happens to users of Suitcase or MasterJuggler. The solution is to remove the problem fonts from the System file, since they are installed by the Installer program even if they are not present, and, often, users of those Font/DA managers keep their fonts in suitcase files. The System chokes when one font family (that is, Times, Helvetica, Courier) appears in two places—a suitcase file being accessed by Suitcase or MasterJuggler, and in the System file too.

Brad Pettit (CompuServe)

- ◊ -

Previewing laser files: If you're using somebody else's LaserWriter printer, you'll have a lot of trouble previewing the documents properly on an ImageWriter printer. This is partly because the LaserWriter can't print as close to the paper edges

as the ImageWriter can and partly because the printers use
different printing software (QuickDraw versus PostScript).
However, you can trick a Mac into using the LaserWriter Page
Setup dialog box by installing the LaserWriter drivers in your
System Folder, and selecting them from the Chooser. Because
AppleTalk must be turned on, be sure not to have an Image-
Writer or something plugged into the printer port; otherwise,
you'll be greeted by a large pile of spurious characters. Do a
normal page setup, and you'll then be able to preview the
document on the screen. Be sure to turn off AppleTalk before
reselecting a printer other than the LaserWriter.

Neil K. Guy (MacNet)

- ◊ -

Quotation marks: One of the sure giveaways that something
was printed on the Macintosh rather than being professionally
typeset is the lack of true quotation marks. Real quotation marks,
known as curly quotes, curved quotes, true quotation marks,
printers' quotation marks, or smart quotes, curve around the text
(" and "), as do real apostrophes (' and '). Generally, type-
writers and ordinary computers can only do neutral quotation
marks and apostrophes (" and ') that don't curve and thus look
rather ugly. The Macintosh is, of course, quite capable of doing
true quotation marks, but it's not completely obvious how. If you
pull down the Key Caps DA from the Apple menu, you'll see
that proper quotation marks are typed in with Option-[and
Shift-Option-[, whereas apostrophes are created with Option-]
and Shift-Option-]. Once you get the hang of it, this isn't too
difficult, but it is a bit of a nuisance. Fortunately, you can generate proper quotation marks automatically. One method is to
purchase a commercial program, such as LaserAuthor or Full-
Write Professional, that has so-called smart quotes built in.
Alternatively, you could pick up shareware utilities that do the
same thing for whatever you type. The Smart Quotes desk

accessory is one such utility, as is the terrific INIT Quote INIT. The latter is probably the best, as it's a self-installing INIT file that takes up a minuscule 1K on disk and that can be turned on or off. The last feature is very useful, as some programming languages (4th Dimension's procedural language, for instance) need neutral quotation marks, ugly as they may be.

Neil K. Guy (MacNet)

- ◊ -

Italicizing: Before the advent of the typewriter, all text that was to be emphasized was *italicized*, but most typewriters can't do this. As a result, underlining came into practice, as it is something that primitive typewriters can handle. With the Macintosh, however, it is no longer necessary to underline anything, as very nice italic features are built into the machine. Underlining is also stunningly ugly, whereas italics are much more elegant, so give italics a try next time—especially on the LaserWriter.

Neil K. Guy (MacNet)

- ◊ -

Ligatures: In many typefaces, particularly those with serifs (the small horizontal and vertical lines at the end of a letter), the letters *f* and *i,* when written in lowercase, look rather silly side by side. This is because the upper loop of the *f* and the dot of the *i* tend to overlap. Fortunately, most Macintosh laser fonts have built into them nice *fi* ligatures in which the *i* has no dot and the *f* has a more prominent loop. Type Option-Shift-5 to get this. There is also the *fl* ligature, available (in most fonts) as Option-Shift-6. It's often easiest to type normally, and then do a case-sensitive search-and-replace operation (you don't want to replace *FI* and *Fi*). Those aren't the only ligatures in the laser fonts. If you're typing in French or other languages, the *œ* ligature (as in *œuf*) is produced by typing Option-q. The *æ* ligature, suitable for English spellings of words such as *æsthetic,* is made by typing Option-apostrophe. These two ligatures also have uppercase equivalents, brought about by holding down the Shift key.

Neil K. Guy (MacNet)

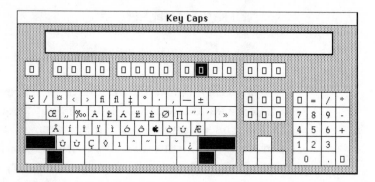

Figure 11–4.   Special characters in the Key Caps DA

If you forget where all these characters are hidden, hold down the Option or Option and Shift keys in the Key Caps DA (see Figure 11–4).

- ◊ -

Hyphens: Another artifact left over from the days of type-writers is the practice of using two hyphens (- -) to represent a long dash (em dash). The Mac can help you excise this horrible custom from your work, as well. Typing Shift-Option-hyphen gives you an em dash, which is the same width as the letter M in the font you're using. These longer dashes are best used to separate an additional idea from a sentence—as shown here. The Mac also has en dashes, hyphens the width of the letter N in the font you're using; these are created by typing Option-hyphen. En dashes are used to separate numbers (pp. 25–32, or 512–258–1127, for example).

Neil K. Guy (MacNet)

- ◊ -

Fonts in general: These last few tips have focused on specific features available in most fonts. You shouldn't forget, however, that any North American Macintosh can type in English, French, German, Spanish, Italian, Swedish, Norwegian, Danish, Portuguese, and other languages without any modification! You can also produce a myriad of special characters, from currency symbols such as the British pound sterling (£) and the Japanese yen (¥) to embellishments such as bullets (•) and diamonds (◊). Experiment with the Key Caps desk accessory and your user manual for more details.

Neil K. Guy (MacNet)

If you've been blissfully oblivious to the kind of stuff Neil is talking about, I urge you to pick up a fantastic little book called The Mac Is Not a Typewriter *by Robin Williams (Peachpit Press, 1990). I guarantee it will teach you how to create great-looking documents. Robin is an wonderful instructor, an excellent designer, and a darn good writer, too. Her gentle tone and sage advice make this one of my favorite Mac books, and the second one (Dr. Macintosh, Second Edition is the first!) I buy for my friends when they get a Mac.*

Potpourri

"What is the single most valuable thing you could teach another Macintosh owner?"

If something unexpected happens, mentally (if not physically) back away from the keyboard and mouse and think about it for a moment.

Some people, after doing something that produces unexpected results, will hastily try to fix it, perhaps "before someone notices" or "before it gets worse." (For example, accidentally hitting the Delete key while having a very large selection—suddenly the screen looks nothing like it did before.)

With few exceptions, it's better to pause, examine the screen, and try to figure out what you just did.

This is especially true on the Mac because we usually have Undo, and usually only one level of it. Undo will often fix the original problem, but once you enter a hasty command, Undo can only undo the hasty command.

Randy Waki (CompuServe)

- ◊ -

Everyone knows that you can cut and paste within an application, and most people should know that you can cut and paste between standard applications as well. However, many people forget that you can also cut and paste between desk accessories and applications. So, if you need the current time in your text document and the program you're using doesn't have the ability to do this, just pull down the Alarm Clock DA and copy the time from there. If you want to calculate a complex equation, type it first into a text document (or the Notepad DA), and then paste it into the Calculator DA. The buttons will flash merrily away and you'll have your answer, which can then be pasted back into whatever you were working on.

Neil K. Guy (MacNet)

- ◊ -

Remember the Clipboard! In these days of programs that import and export zillions of file formats, it's easy to forget that there is a simple way to transfer graphics and text between applications. I can't count the number of people who have called trying to transfer graphics between, say, ImageStudio and PixelPaint, distraught because they were unable to find a common file format. I ask them, "Have you tried copying and pasting?" It works.

Jeanne DeVoto (CompuServe)

- ◊ -

The Clipboard and the Scrapbook really do work! Yes, you can copy a graphic or text item from program A onto the Clipboard, quit program A, run program B, and paste the contents of the Clipboard into program B. It drives me up the wall to see a Mac user at the photocopier with rubber cement and scissors doing graphics and text integration the old-fashioned way. No matter how hard I push this at work, there are always users who cannot make the leap in faith it takes to try it out or who think it is too much trouble. Make yourself use this feature. It is at the crux of what the Macintosh user interface is all about, and it works.

John A. Noel (CompuServe)

- ◊ -

If you do a lot of work with ordinary text files and you find yourself messing around translating documents into different formats using large applications such as MacWrite, WriteNow, Microsoft Word, and so on, then take another look at Apple's TeachText utility. It's a small and handy, if simple, text editor. And while you're using it, try pulling down About TeachText from the Apple menu with the Option key held down.

Neil K. Guy (MacNet)

I save a lot of things in text format; text files take up a great deal less disk space than their counterparts stored in a formatted word processor file. For example, after I've printed a letter and it's been sent, I save the letter as text only.

- ◊ -

The most important power hint I can recommend for users is to be organized. In my company, we have several new Mac users, and their hard disks are a mess. They don't know how to organize their files and their information in a logical manner. I recommend organizing all of the files on a hard disk in this way. Name the folders: System Folder, Applications, Private (or Personal) files, and Utilities. Keep only System files and related INITs and CDEVs in the System Folder. Break down the Applications folders with individual folders for programs such as MacWrite, Microsoft Word, PageMaker, MacTerminal, and so forth. Break down the Utilities folder into folders for Fonts and DAs, copy applications (for programs such as Copy II Mac), INITs, and CDEVs (in which you can store extra INITs and CDEVs that are useful but not always needed).

This is just an example. The main point I am trying to make is that without some form of organization, users will end up with multiple copies of files and not know where to find things. Without this benefit, all other power hints are useless. I hope this helps.

Jeffrey Dumm (MacNet)

- ◊ -

1. You can get System 7 to work with AppleTalk Phase I. (I will probably be burned at the stake for this one, but I had to find a way around.) Just install Phase II with the Installer, and also copy the Phase I driver into the Extensions folder manually. This seems to work fine with Shiva's Etherport. This is most definitely frowned on in polite society, but sometimes it is the only way to get there from here.

2. SCSI drivers. You cannot point to them; most don't even know what they are. But third-party drive owners could have one that is not compatible with System 7 and not even know it. Apple's Installer just looks at their Apple's driver. I have had plenty of strange crashes that appeared to be one thing, but were really the fault of a SCSI driver. In my case, the driver was supposed to be compatible, but I suspect it was not quite stable. Get the Hard Disk Toolkit from Hammer, or SilverLining, and reformat all the SCSI drives with them.

3. Backup. Reverse. Retrograde. Fire retros. Hire the play-mate of the month to call you up and remind you if you must, but BACK UP EVERYTHING, or pay the penalty. (Imagine your internal hardliners taking control of your machine out from under you and being held under machine arrest until you re-create all of your work.)

4. See #3.

5. Consider buying a UPS (uninterruptable power supply) system to protect the hardware investment.

6. Don't answer any questions like this in public, just write your own book. Judging from the number of books about System 7, I'd say some publishers must think that there is a wide open market. [Just kidding :)]

7. Keep an emergency boot floppy disk around at all times. In case of a crash, you may be able to at least reboot from it, and copy or print that very important file you were working on.

8. A macro program is worth its weight in gold. Especially if your time is, too.

9. If you are into serious telecommunications, 9600-baud modems will save more than their cost in a few months in connect time and phone charges.

10. System 7 will change the world of computing forever (or until the next system release, whichever comes first). Seriously, AppleEvents and IAC are going to make a real difference—it's not just marketing hype.

Oh yeah, and Thunder 7 types my name and address faster than I ever could, so get that, too.

Robert DeLaurentis (CompuServe)

See Chapter 3 for more on Thunder 7.

- ◊ -

1. If you *must* switch between System 6 and System 7, always run Disk First Aid (version 7.0) as the last thing you do under System 6, or the first thing you do under System 7. There's a bug in the System 6 file system that can (though it usually won't) destroy the disk if you switch to System 7 and write files without fixing the problem.
   (Note: This is very rare. I switched back and forth for months without it ever happening, and I know many others who switched back and forth without any problems. Even so, Lofty knows his stuff, and it wouldn't hurt to follow this advice if you're switching between System 6 and 7.)

2. Get one of the hierarchical Apple menu INITs, and spend a few minutes putting aliases of your commonly used folders in the Apple Menu Items folder. Put an alias of the Apple Menu Items folder in the Apple Menu Items folder to make adding and subtracting things easy.

3. If you're getting a lot of -97 errors trying to run System 7– type DAs (that is, DAs that have been dragged out of a suitcase), it's probably one of two things:
   a. (This from Billy Steinberg, who figured it out.) A few INITs—SUM Partition is one—will impolitely grab a driver slot (12) reserved for DAs. Since most DAs are stored to go in slot 12, they won't open and you'll get a -97 error. Billy has a patch for SUM Partition, and he may have patches for others.
   b. If you've been running DAs from a large suitcase file, with Suitcase or MasterJuggler, some of the DAs

may have been renumbered by Font/DA Mover to an ID that conflicts with something else, and you'll get an ID -97 error. It's generally best always to make System 7 DAs from the original DA file, not from a suitcase into which you've copied the DA with Font/DA Mover.

4. Some older DAs make the assumption that they're running in the System file, and they will crash if run as System 7 DAs. Solution: Either move them into the System file, or use Suitcase II and run them from a suitcase.

5. Don't empty the Trash too often.

6. Get Last Resort. If you don't, sooner or later you'll be sorry.

7. Spend some time customizing your icons. Your desktop will look prettier, and the visual clues will help you work faster. Put a row of aliases of your five or ten most-used applications and documents at the bottom of your screen.

8. You can paste nearly any kind of PICT resource into the icon box of a file's Get Info window, but often the mask isn't quite right. If the resulting icon looks wrong, open the file with ResEdit and make more of the mask black; the icon will look better.

Lofty Becker (CompuServe)

- ◊ -

I violate this advice all the time, but maybe you'll be smarter: Never be the FIRST. Wait two weeks before installing anything new, zippy, and red hot. Let someone else find the killer bugs.

Richard Reich (CompuServe)

- ◊ -

System 7 only: You can have your most frequently used Apple menu items appear at the top of the Apple menu by adding a space before their name. Two spaces will place an item even higher on the list than one space, and so on.

Randall Flagg (CompuServe)

This is incredibly useful in organizing your Apple menu. In Figure 11–5, you can see that I put two spaces before the names of the folder aliases (Applications, Betas, Control Panels, and so on), and one space in front of the names of important files (1991 Writing, Marge the LC). I also do it inside other folders so files I need frequently (DM2.Scratch Notes, Templates, DM2 Cover.Paint) appear first. An added advantage is that files with spaces in front of their names appear first in GetFile and PutFile (Open and Save) dialog boxes.

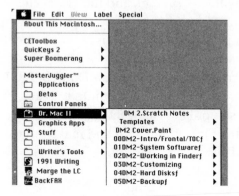

Figure 11–5.   Using spaces at the beginning of file names to make items appear closer to the top of the Apple menu

- ◊ -

If you want to get work done, don't buy version 1.0 of anything.

Lofty Becker (CompuServe)

- ◊ -

Someone asked me the other day how to print a list of all of the files in a folder. All I could think of was to open the window, do a screen dump, scroll the window, do another screen dump, and so on. Then she asked me: "What does this Print Directory option in the file menu of the Finder do?" *(It does exactly what she wanted.)* So my advice is: Be sure to read all of the choices on the menus before accepting that it can't be done.

Michael Shulman (CompuServe)

- ◊ -

Better to learn four programs well than forty badly.

Lofty Becker (CompuServe)

- ◊ -

Tips to new people, huh? Well, as it happens, a friend who never owned a computer before purchased a Macintosh IIci last week, and here a few of the things I told him in no particular order:

1. Buy at least an 80Mb hard disk. The days of 40Mb seeming like forever are over. More and more applications are being delivered on three or more 800K floppy disks—sometimes even compressed. Price points now are reasonable enough that the savings does not justify limiting yourself to 40Mb.
2. Make sure that the machine has the latest System and Finder on it. My friend's was delivered with a System from about 12 B.C.
3. One meg of RAM is never enough. Don't think you will not like MultiFinder; you will, and you will regret it later if you don't give MultiFinder room to play in.

4. Get color. Otherwise, it's pretty hard to design multi-level circuit boards. All the stuff about how the lovely resolution of the Mac's B&W display makes up for the lack of color was invented by George Orwell (a little known Partner-level developer).
5. Don't be afraid of it. It senses fear.
6. Join MAUG<—paid political announcement.
7. For God's sake, don't just do with it what you think it is that you bought it for! Buy some games, buy some art programs, buy some business programs, buy stuff you think will never appeal to you or that will be totally useless. Hey, ten years ago did you think you wanted a computer?
8. You are now entitled to sneer at IBM users and to say "Big Blue" in *that* tone. Go ahead, it's fun and doesn't hurt anyone but IBM owners, and who cares about them anyway?
9. Never unplug the keyboard or mouse while the computer is running. It will work fine forever until it doesn't, and THEN you'll be sorry.
10. Never use it in the shower.

Neil Shapiro (CompuServe)

Neil is the chief Sysop and grand poobah of MAUG, the Macintosh user forum on CompuServe.

- ◊ -

If you try to rename your hard disk and can't, here are two tips that will work: (1) Restart your Mac with a System 6.*x* floppy, then rename the disk; or (2) Turn off File Sharing, which will also allow you to rename your disk.

Larry Beck (America Online)

- ◊ -

My tip and the thing that helped me most was simply reading.

Buy every magazine you can and don't throw anything away for the next year. If something is too complex or doesn't seem to apply to you now, it may very well be critical later, so hold onto it. Reread everything six months after buying your Mac, and you'll be amazed how much more sense it all makes. One thing leads to another with all this neat stuff.

When going to a user group meeting or even a Macworld Expo, pick up everything with print on it and put it away in a file. By the time you need much of it, you'll find that you've already built a valuable library of resource information.

David Winograd (CompuServe)

- ◊ -

As soon as you buy the computer, buy a modem and a CompuServe subscription kit. This group (MAUG) is a group that no Apple user should be without. If you have a question or problem, this should be your first and foremost resource for technical support. If you don't get the answer to your question or problem from the author here, you'll get at least two or three responses from people who know that piece of software or hardware intimately. I have learned more about my Mac by following these two rules than anything else.

Marty Silbernik (CompuServe)

- ◊ -

Problem: You open a file that was created on a Mac using a different-size monitor, and the active window's title bar is off of the screen. You can't move the window and you can't see the zoom box.

Solution: Hold down the Option key while opening the window. Most of the time, it will resize the window and center it in the screen of the monitor you are using.

Michael Lilly (CompuServe)

- ◊ -

Electronic bulletin boards and conferences: If you buy a modem, you are instantly connected to an excellent supply of public-domain and shareware software, as well as excellent advice relating to your questions. Most bulletin boards (BBSs) are free, but you can also use a modem to connect to pay services such as MacNet, GEnie, and CompuServe. Even if there are no Macintosh BBSs in your area, there is likely to be one running on an MS-DOS computer with the Opus BBS software. If you are nice enough to the person operating the BBS, you might convince him or her to pick up the EchoMac conference. This instantly links you with other Mac users all over the world. If you live near a respectable university or college, check with the people there; they may be connected to an educational network, such as UseNet or BitNet. If you can arrange an account, this is another way to communicate with Mac users around the world. UseNet has News, a worldwide conferencing system, with a Mac area called comp.sys.mac and subareas called comp.sys.mac.programmer and comp.sys.mac.hypercard. BitNet isn't quite as nice, carrying only INFO-MAC, a digest of discussions from UseNet and other electronic services. There could be a Mac-specific area on BitNet, but if there is, the University of Calgary doesn't receive it.

Ken Hadford (MacNet)

- ◊ -

Here's a specific tip that has saved me a lot of heartache: If you think your Mac has "frozen" (the cursor won't move across the screen when you move the mouse, typing doesn't work, and so on) make sure that your keyboard is still plugged in!

More general advice: After you think you know your Mac pretty well, find someone with lots of experience with the Mac (preferably a power user) and watch him or her use the Mac for a few hours. You'll undoubtedly pick up lots of nuances (that may or may not be in the manual), and you won't be embarrassed to ask stupid questions. Example: The first time I watched an experienced Mac person, I noticed he selected more than one file at a time in the Finder by positioning the cursor, not on a folder, but on the space *between* folders, and then dragging to select a bunch of them. I never knew you could do that!

Anne Lyndon Peck (CompuServe)

Anne is a vice-president at Inline Design, makers of such wonderful games as Mutant Beach, 3 in Three, Tesserae, Darwin's Dilemma, and Swamp Gas. She is also a former "Fab Babe" of MAUG.

- ◊ -

Take the shrink wrap off the manuals. They work much better that way.

Buy a modem, subscribe to a service, and gain access to all known things in the universe. And meet some pretty cool people.

Never put floppy disks back into those plastic sleeves. There's an off chance you could create some static and zap your files.

Join a user group. There are over 1,300. If you don't know of one, call Apple's user group referral number: 1–800–538–9696, Extension 500. This service will gladly give you the name(s) and contact(s) of the user group(s) in your area.

Don't be afraid to experiment . . . just do it on a copy.

Consider getting a safety deposit box, and put one set of backups in it. You never know. It may save your professional life.

Go to a Macworld Expo at least once in your lifetime. Once you get there . . .

- Attend any workshop Danny Goodman participates in.
- See how many exhibitors actually let *you* use the product.
- Crash at least one party.
- Count how many booths you see with Guy Kawasaki selling something.

Finally (if you're married), never, but NEVER, leave loose change on the coffee table.

Tom Petaccia (CompuServe)

In addition to being both witty and wise, Tom is a frequent contributor to MacUser *magazine.*

- ◊ -

The computer doesn't tell you when there isn't room on the disk for a screen dump (Command-Shift-3); it just doesn't do anything. So if your screen dumps don't seem to work, check for room on the startup disk. *(Screen dumps take between several and several hundred K, depending on screen size and number of colors.)* If there's plenty of room on the hard disk, the Mac may be trying to write to a nearly full floppy, so put your application on the hard disk and try again. I can't tell you how many times I've forgotten this and wondered why a screen dump wouldn't work.

Nick Arnett (CompuServe)

- ◊ -

To help new users, I start pointing out things that work in common among various programs, and I show them how some operations (such as selecting areas) work similarly across applications. A really important similarity is the behavior of windows—stacking, shrinking, and so on. Some people are really amazed at the way their use of the Mac changes when, for example, instead of opening and closing the Scrapbook each time they need a picture, they align Scrapbook and application windows so that they can just click to activate the window they need.

Allen Wessels (CompuServe)

- ◊ -

Here are my suggestions.

1. Always buy Macintoshes (Macintoshim?) in pairs so both you and your spouse can have one. This avoids arguments that begin with one spouse saying: (a) "Ever since you got that ******* thing, you never spend any time with me anymore!" or (b) "You spend so much time playing your silly games that I can't get my work done."
2. Three things to do as soon as you get a new application: Open the write-protect tab (if it comes to you on a floppy disk), check it with a antiviral application, and make a copy on a (second) floppy.
3. SCSI precautions: ALWAYS check the SCSI address and reconnect the cables of any SCSI device that you've moved, even if only by a few inches. I have inadvertently reset the SCSI address in rearranging my office—and spent several hours wondering why I couldn't get my computer to boot (until, having exhausted all other alternatives, I finally thought to check the addresses). Never use a T cable to connect SCSI devices—they virtually guarantee that some of your data will be corrupted.

4. SCSI precautions and backing up: Not only should you back up your files on a regular basis, but you should also (a) use an application that allows the backup files to be checked against the originals, and (b) make use of this option (even if backups take longer because of it). If the application reports discrepancies between a file and its copy on the backup medium, this is a good indication that there is a problem somewhere in the SCSI chain. Retrospect is especially sensitive in this regard, and I recommend it highly. There are also other applications that can verify the integrity (or lack of it) of one's SCSI chain: for example: Disk Checker, bundled with DiskDoubler 3.7.

5. A good macro program is more essential than ever if you want to take full advantage of System 7.0's features. I believe QuicKeys is easily the best of the bunch, because it has been written to use those features to the maximum.

6. Get a modem, subscribe to CompuServe, and join MAUG. There is no other source of reliable information so cheap and quickly available. And where else can you spend a month sending questions to John Sculley that he will either evade or ignore?

7. Brush your teeth twice a day and see your dentist twice a year.

Frank Kofsky (CompuServe)

- ◊ -

A few tips:

1. SCSI is a black art, but if you are having problems with your SCSI chain:

   • Make sure your cables are good quality
   • Make sure all connected devices are powered on

- Try putting devices into the chain one at a time to isolate the problem
- If you're using short (18-inch or 3-foot) cables, try replacing them with 3-foot or 6-foot
- Try adding an external terminator at the very end of the chain

2. If you get an *Application has unexpectedly quit* dialog under MultiFinder, save your changes and restart as soon as possible. That dialog is the moral equivalent of a system bomb: It indicates that the application has crashed, and that application may have left an unpleasant little surprise in your System heap, just waiting to cause another crash. Restarting will clear out the System heap and fix any hidden problems.

3. If you're considering a hardware purchase from a company whose service reputation you're not familiar with, use this quick-and-dirty test: Call their support number and ask a technical question about the product. If you cannot get through to tech support, or if promises to return your call go unfulfilled, or if the person on the other end of the line can't answer your question and doesn't volunteer to find out the answer, avoid that company like the plague. You do *not* want to have tech support be unavailable or unhelpful when your hard disk goes down the day before an important presentation.

4. Don't purchase software from a company that charges for basic technical support, unless there is truly no alternative product available. Charging for custom programming work and other extended support is one thing, but any software company should be willing to stand behind its product at least far enough to answer basic questions about operation and bugs from paying customers.

5. Sometimes you will be advised to use the Installer to replace a corrupted System. If you suspect there's

something wrong with your System file, throw it in the Trash before running the Installer. The Installer program replaces only specific resources—not the whole file—so it may not correct problems with other file resources. Throwing the file in the Trash forces the Installer to rebuild the entire file.

6. If you have a color screen, you'll find that the ability to use the Finder's Color menu to set the color of various icons is more than a cute cosmetic feature; it's invaluable in organizing folders. I use color in the System Folder to distinguish between INITs (red), preference files (blue), standard Apple files (brown), and print drivers (green). *(There's less need for this under System 7, as INITs and printer drivers are stored in the Extensions folder, preferences go in the Preferences folder, and so on. And wouldn't you know it, under System 7, the color feature, now called labels, is even more powerful!)*

7. If a floppy disk sticks in the drive, don't EVER try to pull it out by force. If you do this, you WILL tear off the read/write heads and destroy the drive. Instead, try pushing the disk back into the drive and ejecting it again, either with the Finder's Eject command or by poking a straightened paper clip into the small hole next to the drive slot. If you still can't get the disk out, take the Mac to a dealer; it's cheaper to pay a dealer to open the case and get the disk out than to pay for a new floppy drive.

8. Buy a bigger disk than you think you'll need. If you think you need x megabytes now, you will regret it within a year if you buy less than $1.5*x$ or so.

Jeanne DeVoto (CompuServe)

- ◊ -

If you use shareware software (or any of the various variations thereof), SEND IN YOUR SHAREWARE FEES! You might think that your one little holdout won't hurt anything, but when several hundred or even thousand people are thinking the same thing, the result is that the poor (literally and figuratively) shareware author thinks nobody likes the software, gets depressed, goes broke, gives up computers, becomes a hermit, and never writes another program for the rest of his or her pathetic, isolated, thoroughly depressed life. Well, maybe that's overstating it a bit, but you get the idea. . . .

Bruce A. Carter (CompuServe)

I couldn't agree more. There are a lot of useful shareware programs floating around. Authors such as Ray Lau (StuffIt) and Lofty Becker (DateKey, TimeLogger) should be rewarded for their work. If you don't pay for what you use, eventually nobody will bother to write shareware anymore. Shareware works only if we all make it work. If you use it, you really should pay for it. End of sermon.

- ◊ -

Don't use bootleg software. It's unfair both to you (you're not getting the full power of the package because you don't have decent documentation) and to the people involved in the production of the material (they aren't getting the money). And it promotes a generally bad attitude that will probably contribute to the downfall of life as we know it.

Bruce A. Carter (CompuServe)

- ◊ -

People with IBM-compatible computers hack at them with Debug, a utility that comes with their computers. Mac users do it much more elegantly with ResEdit. (Check to see if your authorized Apple dealer can give it to you—it's free. It's also available on CompuServe, MacNet, and GEnie.) You know you're a Mac power user when you harness the power of ResEdit. ResEdit and a copy of *Inside Macintosh* Volume 1 will teach you a great deal about how your Mac works. Feel free to poke around in COPIES of all your Mac software. . .just as long as you have the original locked up somewhere in case something goes wrong.

Ken Hadford (MacNet)

- ◊ -

Don't be afraid to ask more advanced users for help. Generally they don't bite (well, not very hard, anyway), and they are usually flattered and happy to help. I wouldn't recommend calling Danny Goodman at home, but asking on forums like this certainly will provide you with plenty of input (more, no doubt, than you ever expected—or even wanted).

Bruce A. Carter (CompuServe)

- ◊ -

When you have a problem with your machine, hardware, software, or whatever, document the problem completely. This means everything: Version numbers of all of your applications that are having problems, System versions, and so on. Write down names and revisions of *all* of the CDEVs, INITs, and other possibly screwy things.

Write down any ID numbers associated with the bombs, sad Macs, crashes, and so forth. This means *all* the numbers, in the order in which they appear on the screen.

Describe the problem in more detail than "the screens are all messed up." If the screen is a checkerboard, how many "checkers" are on the screen horizontally and vertically? Before you send an E-mail to Dave Ramsey about the line on your color monitor, look at the threads up here on CompuServe.

Are you running under MultiFinder, Switcher, or—God forbid—Servant? Try turning it off and see if that fixes the problem. If you are running any extra hardware such as accelerators or large screens, disable them if possible to see if the problem goes away. If that doesn't work, and you are technically competent, remove them.

Try running from a floppy with a virgin System if possible. By *virgin*, I mean as few generations from Apple as possible without modification. Barring that, try removing CDEVs and INITs one or several at a time until you are as close to virgin as possible. This also means that you should keep an unmodified System disk at all times. *Never* use it except for making copies. Don't even put it in a suspect machine.

Write down how long the machine was running before the crash. Does it crash every five minutes, or once a week? Was it in an exceptionally hot or cold room? If it crashes when you first turn it on, let it warm up a while (as long as there is no smoke or anything like that), and see if it still crashes.

If it crashes on a power up, let it crash and then try the reset switch.

If a hard drive crashes when trying to boot, try booting from a floppy with a copy of the System on it.

Then call for technical support. You can save immense amounts of time and many headaches for yourself and the nice people in technical support by doing this. After you have an RMA *(returned merchandise authorization)* number for something to send in, send a copy of *all* of this documentation with the product, because the people that will repair it won't have gotten anything from technical support except that "It's messed up." And don't forget a return address! It's amazing how many boxes we've gotten over the years with nothing but a board in them.

Doug Gilbert (CompuServe)

Doug should know: He works for Levco, which manufactures a complete line of high-quality performance hardware products for the Mac. If you follow his advice, chances are your experience with technical support will be a positive one.

- ◊ -

Say something nice to hot-line and user-support people once in a while. It brightens their day, and it's no skin off your nose. Besides, they might remember you and buy you a drink at a conference someday (this should give you an indication of how few people follow this tip).

Bruce A. Carter (CompuServe)

The Last Resort of Power Users Everywhere: RTM

Known by the acronym RTM, this tip entails quite a bit more work than any others mentioned above. Maybe that's why it's so radical (and why I saved it for last). It is: *Read the manual!* Doug Clapp has already said it, but it hasn't been heard enough; many of the tips you hear about are actually in the manual that came with the software. A sure-fire way to amaze your friends and pets.

Ken Hadford (MacNet)

While you're reading through the manual, be sure to study the Command-key shortcuts. You'll be surprised how much time you save when you access menu choices from the keyboard. Get into the habit of using keyboard shortcuts.

- ◊ -

RTM before you call technical support. We're glad to help someone who's having a problem (it's our job), but it does get a little wearing to literally read the manual out loud to someone who can't be bothered to look up the installation procedure, or whatever. . . .

Jeanne DeVoto (CompuServe)

- ◊ -

It's a fact that these days, support costs money (either you have to pay for long distance, or you have to pay for some kind of extended support program, or you pay up front in higher program costs), so to get the most for your money, here's a few suggestions: Before you need support, find out what System version you're using, how much memory you have, and what kind of Mac you are using. The easiest way to find out what kind of Mac is to look at the front of your Mac. To find out your System and memory, go up to the Apple menu in the Finder and choose About the Finder (under System 6.0.*x*) or About This Macintosh (under System 7). Under System 7, this will also confirm what model Mac you are using. Write these numbers down, or remember them when you call.

Second, you should find out what Startup Documents (called Extensions under System 7) and Control Panels you are using. If you are using System 6, open the System Folder and choose By Kind from the View menu, then print the contents by choosing Print Directory from the File menu. Keep this handy for when you have a problem. Under System 7, open the System Folder and choose By Kind, then click on the triangle to the left of the Extensions, Control Panels, and Startup Items folders to show their contents. Print the contents, and keep them handy in case you need them.

Now, before you call for tech support, first check your manual and the on-line help in the program, and any Read Me First files on the original program disk. At the place where I work, something like a quarter of all support calls involve telling people what's in the manuals. If those don't help, try the action that caused the problem again to see if it recurs. If it helps you, take notes about what the problem is and what steps you took that caused it. If the problem does happen again, then it's time to call tech support.

When you do call for tech support, it is best if you can be at the machine when it happens. If the support people know what the problem is, then they will probably want to run through the solution with you to make sure that everything is working properly. If they don't recognize the problem, they'll probably want you to try a few possible solutions to the problem and observe the results. If you aren't at your machine, they'll only be able to make suggestions for you to try later, and you may need to call again later.

If the support people are unable to help you with a technical problem, please don't get angry with them. They really do want to help work out your problems, but sometimes they just aren't able to be solved in one phone call. On occasion, we have to examine problems in our offices and figure out just what is going wrong and how to correct it. If they can't solve your problem in one call, give them a chance to find out what the difficulty is and get back to you. If you do have a legitimate complaint about the support or customer support you receive, complain, but do so calmly. Screaming doesn't help, either.

Finally, stay focused on the problem at hand, and try to address only one problem at a time. If the company makes more than one program you own, ask only one question at a time, and make sure the answer is clear before you move on. Also, please remember that one company's support people usually can't answer questions about other companies' products. (I once had a customer ask me for assistance on a "major spreadsheet" that I've never used before in the middle of a call about one of our products. Needless to say, I was not able to help her with her spreadsheet problem satisfactorily.)

Cecil Habermacher (America Online)

Cecil should know. He's the head tech-support honcho for Kent Marsh, Ltd., which makes a variety of Macintosh security products such as MacSafe, NightWatch, and FolderBolt.

- ◊ -

As an absolute last resort, look it up in the manual. Trees died for that document.

Bruce A. Carter (CompuServe)

Appendix A

Viruses

All you need to know to remain safe from computer viruses.

The mainstream media has given a tremendous amount of coverage to the computer virus problem. For most of you, the threat is remote.

A virus, if you haven't already heard, is a nasty little piece of programming that replicates and spreads from disk to disk (or around your network) like a disease. Some viruses are supposedly nondestructive; others can damage files or disks with little or no warning. Nobody knows who creates stuff like this or why, but it *is* happening. Recently, two or three new strains of viruses have been discovered, and several Fortune 500 companies, as well as NASA, have reported viral infections.

With luck, the perpetrators will be caught. Barbara Krause, Apple's public relations manager, says: "We're taking these viruses very seriously. It is a criminal act, and we are working closely with law enforcement authorities." I hope they lock up the jerks who write them and throw away the key.

There's no cause for panic. Few viruses have been discovered, and it appears that only a handful of users have been affected so far. Still, the potential for damage is real, and you should be aware of it. The key to keeping viruses from spreading is awareness, so tell a friend.

Speaking of awareness, it bothers me when I hear people say that the media glorifies these terrorists by giving them coverage. That may be, but it would be irresponsible to ignore the problem. I hate having to devote space to such an ugly topic, but if it keeps someone from getting infected, it's worth it.

Your risk is minimal if you don't have a hard disk, are not part of a network, don't use the on-line services, and use only software you've personally copied from locked master disks. Although a few early Aldus FreeHand demos had a virus (fortunately a relatively harmless one), the chances of getting one from commercial products, especially after that episode, are slim. Some publishers have gone as far as using only "sterile" Macs for development and disk mastering.

Your risk is higher if you use disks someone has used on another Mac, if you are on a network, or if you download software via modem.

If you're at risk, you should probably consider some form of protection. Disinfectant by John Norstad and VirusBlockade by Jeffrey S. Shulman are freeware and shareware, respectively. Both can eradicate viruses they discover, and defend against viruses on an ongoing basis. They are available from on-line services and user groups.

In addition, several commercial software packages for detecting and eradicating viruses are also available (see the "Recommendations" section at the end of this appendix).

Because I've never been infected, I can't tell you how these programs work for eradicating (that is, removing) viruses. All of them should offer a high level of protection from infection in the first place.

If you're in a high-risk group for viral infection, you should consider one of the commercial products. Each of the publishers has stated a commitment to providing reasonably priced updates as new viruses are discovered. If you choose Symantec Anti-Virus for Macintosh (SAM), you can call a special phone number to receive instructions for updating your copy to defend against newly discovered viri without the necessity of upgrading to a new version of the software (as you would with Redux or Virex). The excellent shareware program VirusBlockade is updated the same way. Other virus utilities, such as Rival and Virex, require a new version of the software every time a new virus is discovered, which makes them, at least in my opinion, more of a hassle than SAM or VirusBlockade.

Remember, the problem won't go away until every virus is eliminated from every disk. Until then, a little precaution goes a long way. If you're at risk, please take appropriate action.

Someday, the viruses will die out. But even after they're gone and almost forgotten, a dark cloud will remain over the Macintosh community. The days when you could use any disk without a second thought are gone.

If I ever meet someone who created a virus, I'll ask the question posed by Don Brown in the instructions for Vaccine (the first, and now obsolete, virus prevention program): "Why would we want to take such a gigantic step backward?"

After that, I'll probably have to be restrained.

Recommendations

Disinfectant and VirusDetective are freeware and shareware respectively, and should be available from on-line services and user groups. The three commercial products available for combating viruses are listed below.

Rival

Microseeds
5801 Benjamin Center Drive #103
Tampa, FL 33634
813–882–8635
Approximately $100

Rival is a control panel that protects, detects, and repairs. Its unique method of scanning files avoids the dialog box that appears when you insert a disk and are using any of the other commercial virus detection programs. Unfortunately, if a new virus is discovered (as they are several times a year), you'll need a software upgrade at additional cost.

Symantec Anti-Virus for Mac (SAM)

Symantec Corporation
10201 Torre Avenue
Cupertino, CA 95014
800–343–4714
408–252–3570

SAM is a virus-defense system made up of two components: an application to detect and repair damage, and an INIT to protect you from infection or recontamination. Both can be configured to detect newly discovered viri by typing in a new virus description, avoiding the need for frequent software updates.

Virex
> HJC Software
> P.O. Box 51816
> Durham, NC 27717
> 919–490–1277

Virex is the commercial offering of programmer Robert Woodhead, who is also the author of the shareware program Interferon. Virex can detect and repair damage caused by known viruses, and it includes the Virex INIT for ongoing protection. Unfortunately, if a new virus is discovered (as they are several times a year), you'll need a software upgrade at additional cost.

Appendix B

The Doctor's Office

The hardware and software I know and love
(and use every day).

This isn't really a chapter—it's an afterthought, a bonus of sorts for those of you who have stuck it out this far.

Over the years since the first edition of this book was published, I've found that people I meet are curious about my work setup—the hardware and software I use each day. When I speak at trade shows such as Macworld Expo, the thing people ask me most is "What do you use for Fill-in-the-blank ?" I also realized that, although much of this stuff is mentioned in the text, there is much that is not. This chapter, therefore, is designed to provide a walk through my office: a look at the hardware and software I use every day and have come to depend on enough to feel it deserves mention.

One thing the rest of this book doesn't address is application software —word processors, databases, spreadsheets, and so on. That's not an oversight, it's by design. Application software could easily fill another complete book (which I may write someday), but for now, I've included a section where I briefly describe the application software I use, and why I choose to use it.

The products in this chapter are the things I'm using today, a crisp October day in 1991. By the time you read this, I could well be using something newer and better. Don't worry. Everything in this chapter has been tested under fire—I've put each product through the paces and found it to perform admirably. So even if I do move on to something newer, the products you'll read about here are all first-class and should remain so for years to come.

So, with no further ado, let's explore my office...

On the Desktop

Smack dab in the middle of my desk sits the heart of my system, a Mac IIci with an 80Mb internal Apple hard disk, 32Mb of RAM (8 x 4Mb, from Technology Works), and a Technology Works Cache Card.

I use Connectix Maxima software to create a 20Mb RAM disk, leaving 12Mb of memory for System software and applications. I find this setup perfect for most of the things I do. When it's not, I can easily disable the RAM disk and use all my RAM—32Mb of it—for System software and applications.

Atop the CPU sits a Sigma Designs L-View Multi-Mode 19-inch monochrome monitor. I've used a lot of 19-inch monochrome monitors in my day; this one rates among the best. It's got excellent focus, even near the edges, and I find it easy to look at for extended periods of time.

The Multi-Mode feature lets me change resolutions—120, 92, the standard Macintosh 72, 60, 46, or 36dpi (dots per inch)—with a single keystroke. So, for example, if I set it to 120dpi, everything appears much smaller than on an ordinary 72dpi Mac screen. At normal resolution, 72dpi, I can't view two 8½-x-11-inch pages side by side in PageMaker. But at 92 or 120dpi, I can see all of them with room to spare. Or, if I set the resolution to 36dpi, everything on my screen is twice as big as usual: perfect for demonstrating software to someone seated beside me. One other thing: Sigma Designs L-View monitors are low-emission—they meet the strict guidelines for electromagnetic emissions established by the Swedish National Board for Measurement and Testing. I'm not sure if ELF or other radiation can cause damage to a human, but I feel a little better knowing that at least one of my monitors is a low-emission model. On the other hand, I tested an inexpensive 19-inch monitor from Mirror Technologies last year, and it was pretty darn good (though not as good as Sigma Designs').

Speaking of monitors, my other one is an Apple Color 13-inch, connected to an Apple 8•24 Video Card. Though Apple monitors and video cards are somewhat pricier than third-party products, they are always among the top performers. The Apple Color monitor is three years old, and it's still bright and crisp.

To the right of the CPU and Sigma monitor sit my SCSI devices and modem. The SCSI devices are an APS ARDAT DAT tape drive, an APS 340Mb hard disk, and a Bernoulli Transportable 90. The modem is an Orchid fax modem.

In my closet are my spares: a U.S. Robotics 9,600-baud modem, an APS hard disk (a 210 megger), and a Mass Microsystems SyQuest 44.

My keyboard is an Apple Extended. I've tried others, but I keep coming back to this one.

I switch between a trackball and a mouse with amazing regularity—I get tired of using one, then the other. The trackball is currently a MicroSpeed, but I'm about to plug in a Stingray from CoStar. The mouse is an Apple mouse.

For printing, I've got a LaserWriter IINT on loan from Apple while my Jasmine DirectPrint (same as the Qume CrystalPrint) is in the shop for repairs. The IINT is a nice printer, but a bit overpriced.

I'm a firm believer in creating a comfortable environment for yourself at the computer, which is why I'm a big fan of wrist pads. I have one sitting in front of my keyboard, and half of one (I cut it in half myself) sitting before my mouse/trackball. If you spend a lot of time at the keyboard, a wrist pad can make you more comfortable, and it may help you avoid a repetitive strain injury.

Another thing that helps me spend endless hours at the keyboard is the Balans chair I use. It's a funny-looking stool with an angled pad for my knees. You don't sit on a Balans chair as much as kneel in it. As strange as it looks, and as awkward as it feels at first, it's the best chair I've ever used. I rarely get back or neck pain since I got it.

Last but not least, I have a pair of Monster MacSpeakers—self-amplified stereo speakers—on the windowsill. They make even the cheesy, built-in Mac sounds sound great.

Coming Soon

I'm saving up for one of the speedy Quadras and one of the little PowerBooks as well. In addition, I will probably replace the Bernoulli with a 128Mb read/write optical drive as soon as the prices become more reasonable. Last but not least, I'll soon be replacing the Jasmine printer with one of Apple's models, the IIf or IIg.

I had an Apple CD-ROM player, but it broke. I'll probably get one from somebody else real soon. Truth is, there just aren't that many truly great CDs yet, though I seem to be seeing more and better CDs over the past few months.

Chances are you won't need equipment this expensive or elaborate, but it's my job to stay on top of the latest, greatest Mac technology. I know, it's a tough job, but somebody has to do it. (As we say on-line, <vbg>, which stands for "very big grin.")

Inside My System Folder

I put my System Folder (see Figure B-1) on the RAM disk and use the RAM disk as my Startup disk. (See Chapter 7 for more information about RAM disks.) This makes my Mac run significantly faster. Startup time from the RAM disk is at least twice as fast as when I start up using a hard disk, even my fastest one.

I run System 7 all the time. On the rare occasion when I need to use System 6.0.7 (for example, compatibility testing for an article or book), I have a Bernoulli 90 cartridge that I designate as the Startup disk using the Startup disk control panel.

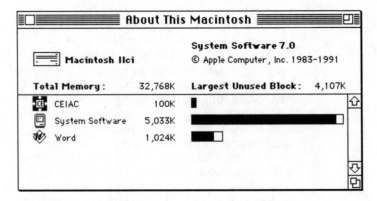

Figure B-1.   My System software, with all my INITs and CDEVs, consumes over 5,000K of RAM!

Control Panels

I have a lot of control panels—more than thirty-five in my Control Panels folder at last count, though some are usually turned off using StartUp Manager (part of Now Utilities).

Each of them is useful in its own way; here is a quick summary:

Maxima
Memory extension utility and RAM disk. If you have 16Mb or more of RAM, you need this. See Chapter 7.

StartUp Manager
Lets you turn INITs and control panels on and off at startup, create groups of INITs and CDEVS, and reorder INITs and CDEVS without changing their name. Part of Now Utilities package (see Chapter 10). Other similar (and also very good) products are INITPicker (Microseeds) and INIT Manager (Baseline).

Iomega Driver
Required for mounting Bernoulli 90 cartridges (see Chapter 5).

L-View
Required for my monitor.

Tip

These four CDEVs—Maxima, Startup Manager, Iomega Driver, and L-View, and the SAM Intercept INIT—have a space or null character as the first character in their names. That's because the manufacturer wants it to be the first INIT or CDEV to load. (When you sort alphabetically, a space comes before any character.) But I've got *five* that want to load first!

It was easy. StartUp Manager let me rearrange their loading order. In a minute or two I came up with an order that seemed to work. Further testing proved it reliable.

Moral of the story: If you have a lot of INITs and CDEVs, an INIT manager is a must-have when experimenting with loading order and isolating conflicts.

After Dark
The best screen saver ever. When computer screens are left on for extended periods of time, screen phosphor is destroyed. This can leave a permanent ghost image on your screen, called *burn-in*. A screen saver prevents burn-in by sensing when your computer has been idle for a while, then generating a pattern on your screen.

After Dark is a modular screen saver that comes with over twenty-five different effects—kaleidoscopes, fireworks, flying toasters, swimming fish, and more. You can choose your favorite, or have After Dark switch between modules at random.

If you have a monitor (you do), and you leave your computer on for any length of time, you want After Dark (Berkeley Systems, 415–540–5535).

Backmatic
Automatic backup utility (see Figure B-2). Backs up selected folders (or entire disks) at user-definable intervals. When I'm working on a serious project, such as a book or article, I tell Backmatic to back up that folder every hour. Once an hour, Backmatic politely asks if I want to back up the files in that folder.

I usually back up to the Bernoulli 90 or a 1.4Mb floppy. Backing up all the files I've changed in the past hour with Backmatic takes about two minutes. Call me paranoid, but I'd rather be safe than sorry. For me, those two minutes an hour are a small price to pay for the sense of security I feel when my important files are backed up that frequently. (Magic Software 402–291–0670)

The Doctor's Opinion

Besides, you're not supposed to be at the keyboard for more than an hour at a stretch—it's bad for your back, neck, wrists, and hands.

If you can't remember to take regular breaks, Visionary Software (503–246–6200) makes a program called LifeGuard that monitors your computer and reminds you to take a break if you work too long.

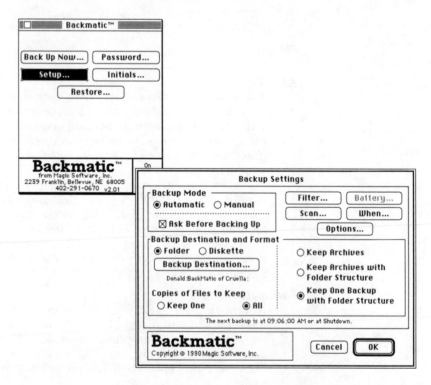

Figure B-2.   Backmatic—perfect for the forgetful (like me) Mac enthusiast

Capture

One of three fine screen capture utilities I use regularly. In my line of work, I do screen dumps almost every day. I switch between three excellent utilities — ScreenShot (Baseline Publishing, Inc.; 901–682–9676), Capture (Mainstay; 818–991–6540), and Image Grabber (Sabastian Software; 207–861–0602). I'd be hard pressed to choose my favorite. All three can capture all or part of a screen and save in a variety of file formats. Only ScreenShot can capture and isolate a single window or menu; only Capture saves in two flavors of TIFF; both Capture and Image Grabber can perform time-delayed screen dumps. Capture and Screen-Shot are control panels (CDEVs), which load into memory at boot time; Image Grabber is a desk accessory and doesn't.

You'd be well served by any of the three.

Color

Apple System software.

Complete Undelete

Part of Microcom 911 Utilities (see Chapter 6) and also sold separately, Complete Undelete lets you quickly resurrect a file, even after you've thrown it in the Trash and emptied it. It doesn't always work; the longer it's been since you deleted the file, the less likely it is to be resurrectable. Even so, I often find I've trashed something, and only after the Trash has been emptied do I discover that I need it back. Complete Undelete gets it back for me more often than not. (Microcom; 800–822–8224, 617–551–1966)

DialogKeys

Part of the QuicKeys 2 package. Allows you to select buttons in dialog boxes using the keyboard instead of the mouse. I use it every single day. See Chapter 10. (CE Software; 515–224–1995)

FileSaver

Part of Norton Utilities (see Chapter 6). Saves information that will make it easier to recover data if my hard disk should become damaged.

File Sharing Monitor

Apple System software.

General Controls

Apple System software.

Helium 2.0.2

An extremely useful utility that allows you to hold down modifier keys to see Balloon Help in the Finder as well as any programs that contain Balloons. My modifier keys are Option–

Control, so when I hold down Option and Control and point at anything on the screen that has one, its Help Balloon appears. If I release the Option and Control keys, the balloon disappears. This handy gadget all but eliminates trips to the Balloon Help menu; you'll wonder why Apple didn't build it into the system! Neat! Shareware by Robert L. Matthews.

Keyboard
Apple System software.

Labels
Apple System software.

Last Resort
"Typing Retrieval System for people who can't afford to lose important text." This ingenious device allows you to retrieve typed text, whether it was saved or not, even in the event of a crash or freeze. It saves every keystroke to a time- and date-stamped text file. It works invisibly; you can't tell it's there. When you crash, though, almost everything you typed since your last save should be recoverable. (Working Software; 408–423–5696)
Maybe I am paranoid…

Map
Apple System software.

Memory
Apple System software.

Monitors
Apple System software.

Mouse
Apple System software.

Mouse2
Mouse Tracking overdrive. Doubles the speed of your mouse tracking. I like it. Shareware by Ryoji Watanabe.

NowMenus
One of the best parts of Now Utilities. See Chapter 10.

QuicKeys 2
See Chapter 10.

ScreenShot
See Capture above.

SCSIProbe
Lets you see what devices are connected to your SCSI chain. It can also mount unmounted disks such as SyQuests and Bernoullis. Freeware by Robert Polic.

Sharing Setup
Apple System software.

Sound
Apple System software.

Startup Disk
Apple System software.

Super Boomerang
Another of the best parts of Now Utilities. See Chapter 10.

Thunder 7
The ultimate spelling checker and thesaurus. Works in every program, can watch "over your shoulder" and beep when you make a mistake, or batch-check anything from a word to an entire document. Thunder can even replace commonly mis-spelled words automatically as you type! So when I type **ot**, Thunder automatically changes it to *to*. Or **recieve** to *receive*. Best of all, it works in almost every program, so you won't need multiple proprietary dictionaries on your hard disk. Thunder is definitely one of my favorite utilities. (Baseline Publishing, Inc.; 901–682–9676)

TW Cache Card
Turns my Technology Works Cache Card on or off.

Users & Groups
Apple System software.

Views
Apple System software.

Wallpaper
Useless but extremely likable, Wallpaper lets you "wallpaper" your desktop with patterns up to 128 x 128 pixels. Great in color, but works in black and white, too. It includes hundreds of patterns, or you can create, edit, and store your own.

~ATM
Adobe Type Manager (see Chapter 8). (Note that it's named ~ATM, with a tilde as the first character. That makes it load last, after all other control panels.)

Extensions

I have a lot of these puppies, too. As you know, you drop Extensions (INITs) into your System Folder and they install themselves when your Mac starts up. See Chapter 6 for more information on INITs and INIT conflicts.

Here's the stuff I use every day:

SAM Intercept
Antivirus software. I use it because you can upgrade it to defend against new viruses by simply typing in a code. Other antivirus software such as Rival and Virex require a software upgrade each time a new virus is discovered. See Appendix A.

Apple CD-ROM
Apple System software.

AppleShare
Apple System software.

CEIAC
Allows QuicKeys to utilize Apple Events.

CEToolbox
Part of QuicKeys 2 package (see Chapter 10).

ClickPaste 2.1 INIT
Very cool pop-up Scrapbook replacement (see Figure B-3). Hold down your modifier keys (mine are Option–Shift), and a pop-up menu of all the pictures and text you've stored in ClickPaste will appear. Click and hold on a graphic's name, and a small preview of that graphic appears in a cute little balloon. Release the mouse and that graphic is pasted into the active document. (Mainstay; 818–991–6540)

DAL
Apple System software.

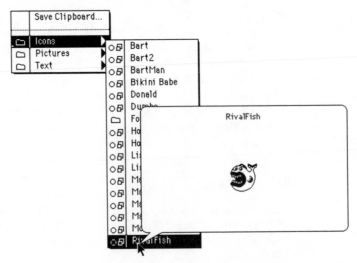

Figure B-3.   ClickPaste, an excellent Scrapbook replacement

FaxInit

> Lets me use my fax modem. Fax modems are OK, but somewhat inconvenient. Plus, you need a scanner if you want to fax hard copy to someone. On the other hand, faxes sent from your fax modem look significantly better than those sent from a sheet-fed fax machine. Also, fax modem software keeps getting cool features such as broadcasting, which lets you easily send a single fax to multiple locations, and delayed sending, which tells the software to wait until a certain time, like 11:00 PM, when phone rates are the lowest, to send your faxes. In addition, documents created on your Mac and sent via a fax modem arrive looking better than documents fed into a sheet-fed fax machine.
>
> For most people a fax modem should be an adjunct to a stand-alone fax machine, not a replacement.

File Sharing Extension

> Apple System software.

First Things First

> Simple menu-bar clock and reminder system (Visionary Software; 503–246–6200). Has a lot of the same features as AlarmClock, which is part of the Now Utilities collection, but is a lot sexier looking (see Figure B-4).

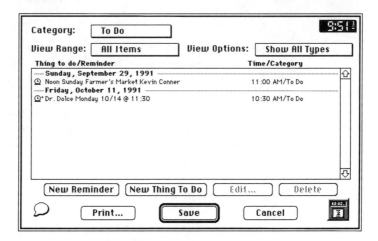

Figure B-4.   First Things First provides a floating calendar clock (top left) or digital menu-bar clock (top right) and lets you store pop-up reminders and things to do (bottom)

Foreign File Access
>   Apple System software.

LaserWriter
>   Apple System software.

MailSaverII
>   Part of my fax modem software (see FaxInit above).

MasterJuggler
>   See Chapter 10.

Network Extension
>   Apple System software.

PrintMonitor
>   Apple System software.

Retro.Startup
>   The INIT that makes Retrospect (see Chapter 5) launch automatically and perform a script. In my case, it launches every morning at 4:00 AM, and backs up all of my hard disks to digital audio tape (DAT).

Suitcase II
>   See Chapter 10.

The Apple Menu Items Folder

To begin with, I have aliases for six or seven of my most frequently used folders in the Apple Menu, as well as aliases for frequently used documents. My desk accessories are listed below.

Calculator +
>   Superb calculator with multiple functions and a printable paper tape option (see Figure B-5). Part of the File Director package. (Fifth Generation Systems; 504–291–7221)

Calendar 3.1
>   A simple calendar DA (see Figure B-6). You can type as much text as you like for each date; dates with text entries are denoted by a check mark. Part of the File Director package. (Fifth Generation Systems; 504–291–7221)

Chooser
>   Apple System software.

ClickPaste
>   The other part of the ClickPaste extension (see above).

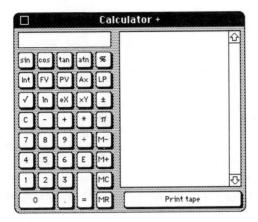

Figure B-5.   Calculator + is like the Apple calculator on steroids

Sat, Sep 28, 1991					2:33 PM		Notes for Sat, Sep 28, 1991
September 1991							This is a note for Saturday, Sept 28th.
Sun	Mon	Tue	Wed	Thu	Fri	Sat	
1	2	3	4	5✓	6	7	
8	9	10	11	12	13	14	
15	16	17	18	19	20	21	
22	23	24	25	26	27	28	
29	30	1	2	3	4	5	
6	7	8	9	10	11	12	
Jan	Feb	Mar	Apr	May	Jun	90	
Jul	Aug	Sep	Oct	Nov	Dec	92	

File Director™ from Fifth Generation Systems

Figure B-6.   Calendar, a handy pop-up calendar desk accessory

DeskDraw

Excellent drawing program in a desk accessory. I use it all the time for quick editing of PICT files.

DeskPaint

Excellent paint program in a desk accessory. I use it all the time for quick editing of paint, PICT, and TIFF files.

DiskTools

Similar to DiskTop—a file organizer in a desk accessory (see Figure B-7). Lets you quickly find (using multiple criteria, if you like), delete, move, copy, rename, or launch files. Part of the File Director package. (Fifth Generation Systems; 504–291–7221)

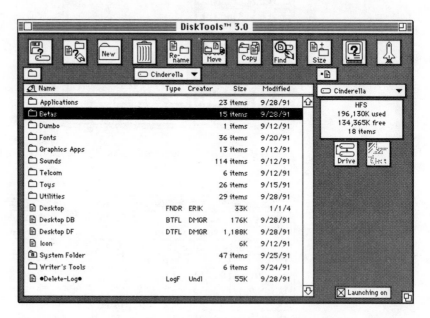

Figure B-7.   DiskTools allows you to quickly find, delete, move, copy, rename, or launch files

DiskTop

See Chapter 10.

GOfer 2.0

GOfer is a desk accessory that can search for text within files created by most applications. So, for example, you could instruct GOfer to search your hard drive for files containing the word *Apple* (see Figure B-8). It's capable of sophisticated searches using operators such as AND, OR, and NEARBY, and you can scroll through found documents and copy text to the Clipboard. It searches almost every kind of file—text, word processor, database, spreadsheet, and so on. If you forget where you put things and can't find them by file name alone, GOfer is just the ticket. (Microlytics; 716–248–9150)

Another product that searches within files is On Location. It's similar to GOfer, but much faster. Its only drawback is that it requires advance preparation—you have to go through a procedure called *indexing*, which creates a special file to help On Location find the text you're looking for. This index must be updated periodically, though the program can be configured to do it for you automatically. The trade-off is, On Location is ten or twenty times faster than GOfer. It searches the average hard disk in well under a minute, and it can be used successfully on slower media such as optical disks and CD-ROMs. It's not presently installed on my hard disk because version 2, which provides complete System 7–friendliness and several new features, is expected to ship any day now. I haven't seen version 2 yet, but I am waiting for it with bated breath. If version 2 is as elegant as version 1, I'll use it often. (On Technology; 617–876–0900)

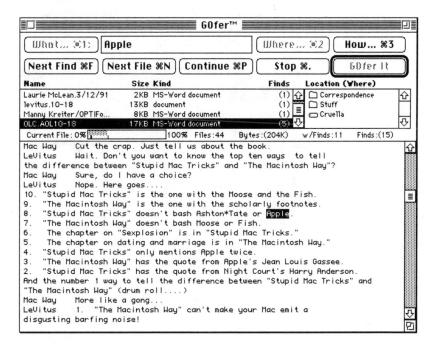

Figure B-8.   GOfer can find text within documents created by almost any application

Image Grabber
See Capture, in the "Control Panels" section of this chapter.

Key Caps
Apple System software.

miniWRITER

Text editing desk accessory. I keep it around mostly for its Stupefy feature, which removes all Macintosh-specific characters and replaces them with characters that can be read by other computers, such as the IBM PC. For example, it turns curly quotes (Option–Square Bracket/Option–Shift–Square Bracket) into straight quotes, bullets (Option–8) into asterisks, and em dashes (Option–Shift–Dash) into double dashes. This makes it easier to provide ASCII text files that can be read on computers other than the Mac. Shareware by David Dunham.

Phone Pad 3.1

Free-form multipage text database. Phrases can be entered in the Fast Find window (as shown on the right side of Figure B-9); when you double-click them, the page containing the first occurrence of that phrase appears. I use it to store pieces of text I think I'll be using again. Part of the File Director package. (Fifth Generation Systems; 504–291–7221)

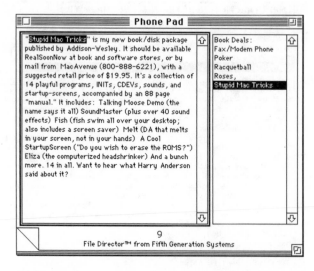

Figure B-9.   Phone Pad, a free-form multipage text storage system

Scrapbook

Apple System software.

TouchBASE

I use TouchBASE (shown in Figure B-10) to manage names and addresses of people I know. Though it's a desk accessory and uses only about 20K of RAM, it packs a lot of punch. It makes printing a batch of labels or a single envelope a breeze, and it has flexible options for exporting text for mail merge. I find it more than up to the task of managing my Contacts database.

Macintosh celebrity Guy Kawasaki says, "Dollar for dollar, TouchBASE is the most functional piece of Macintosh software I've ever seen." Guy knows. In fact, he likes this product so much he's an investor in the company.

Don't take our word for it, though. After Hours offers a free demo. Give 'em a call. (After Hours Software; 818–780–2220)

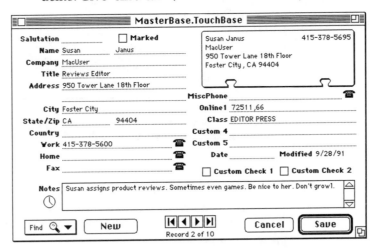

Figure B-10.   TouchBASE, an excellent contacts manager

Applications

Words and Numbers

I probably use more programs than I need to, but I enjoy pitting one against the next, and keeping the best of the bunch until something better comes along. Here are some that I find useful almost every day:

Acta 7

An outline processor, and a darn good one (see Figure B-11). Inexpensive, quick, and handy, it makes it easy to organize pieces of text, pictures, and/or sound. I use Acta for my to-do list. I also use it to organize my thoughts before I begin writing an article or book. (Symmetry; 602–998–9106)

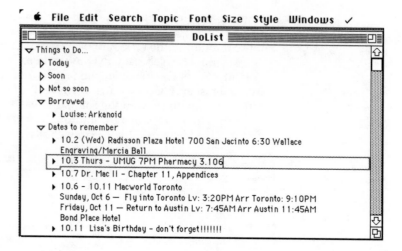

Figure B-11.   Acta, a superb outline processor that helps you organize your words (though it also works with pictures and sound)

Excel

I'm not much of a spreadsheet jockey, but when I need one, I usually turn to Excel. (Microsoft; 206–882–8080)

FileMaker Pro

When I need more database power than TouchBASE can provide, I use FileMaker Pro. It's intuitive and easy to use, yet powerful enough for most of my data management needs. (Claris; 408–727–8227)

HyperCard

Ah, HyperCard. The ubiquitous HyperCard. What is it? A programming environment? An application-building system? A hypertext tool? A picture storage device? Hypermedia? Or what?

I don't know. HyperCard sort of just . . . is. It's all of the above, and something more. I don't know how to describe it, but it's worth playing around with. Most Macs include a copy of it, so chances are you've got it laying around somewhere.

Unless you're really pressed for hard disk space, I suggest you keep it on your hard disk, for reading the occasional stack that sometimes comes with commercial software.

If programming HyperCard interests you, Claris sells a developer version with enough documentation to keep you busy for a month. (Claris; 408–727–8227)

Nisus

Nisus is not my everyday word processor, but it is still an excellent one. If it weren't for my reliance on Word's style sheets, and the way they import smoothly into PageMaker, I'd probably switch to Nisus full–time. Among its unique features are ten editable clipboards, virtually unlimited undos, integrated drawing, macros, a killer search and replace function, and the ability to find a text string in a file, even if it's not open. It's extremely capable, and it can be customized in many ways. Plus, it imports and exports to most other word-processor formats.

If you don't plan to use your word-processing documents with PageMaker, you should definitely take a look at Nisus. (Paragon Concepts; 619–481–1477)

Quicken

The perfect checkbook program for someone as accounting-impaired as me. Keeps track of inflow and outgo, generates reports even your CPA will love, and prints beautiful checks on the LaserWriter, to boot. Couldn't be easier to use. (Intuit; 415–322–0573)

PageMaker

The premier page-layout program. I've typeset several books (including the first edition of this book!), plus hundreds of fliers, pamphlets, booklets, directories, and advertisements with it; it's never let me down. It's expensive, but if you're going to be doing serious page-layout work, it's worth it. (Aldus; 206–622–5500)

Resolve

Claris' recent entry into the spreadsheet wars. Intuitive interface and cool charts make it a definite possibility. Also consider Lotus' 1-2-3 for Macintosh, which is reputed to be another serious competitor with Excel. I think Resolve is a particularly good choice for those just getting started with spreadsheets. The documentation is good, and Claris has always been known for above-average technical support. (Claris; 408–727–8227)

Retrospect

It's what I use for backing up and archiving. See Chapter 5.

Word

Industrial-strength word processor that just keeps getting better. Version 5.0, which I haven't used at this writing, adds page-layout features including drawing tools, a mail-merge helper, support for publish and subscribe, spelling and grammar checkers, and a thesaurus. More people use Word than all other word processors combined; I've used it every day for years. It's what I'm using right now. There must be a reason. . . (Microsoft; 206–882–8080)

Graphics

I'm not a very talented artist, but I do a lot of tinkering with graphics. In spite of my lack of artistic talent, I've designed a letterhead, logos, newsletters, and a lot more. Though I use programs such as Adobe Illustrator 3 or Aldus FreeHand 3.0 when I need to create color graphics for high-resolution output, I don't consider myself enough of an expert to give you a glowing recommendation. I also use Adobe Photoshop 2.0, but it's a sophisticated tool I don't think I use to its fullest. There are, however, three graphics programs I use often enough, and have acquired enough expertise with, that I feel qualified to recommend them to you. They are:

Amazing Paint

Simply put, the best black-and-white paint program around. It's what the original MacPaint should have been. Among its innovative features are multiple undos and redos, special effects such as Free Rotate, Slant, Distort, and Add Perspective, the ability to select more than one area of a document, and user-configurable everything.

The interface is sleek and uncluttered, and everything is easy to use. If you do a lot of black-and-white painting, you'll love this Amazing Paint.

Canvas

Canvas is the powerhouse of the color drawing programs. It's more powerful than a locomotive, yet its interface is so logically arranged that even a novice can master it quickly. With features galore, Canvas is often referred to as the Swiss Army knife of graphics programs.

If you need a powerful black-and-white, gray-scale, and full-color drawing program that you don't have to be a rocket scientist to use, this is it.

DeskDraw and DeskPaint

Though they're mentioned in the desk accessory section, I thought I'd point out that I use these two powerful desk accessories even more than Canvas or Amazing Paint. I like them a lot because they are desk accessories, so they open fast and don't use much RAM. Not only that, they're easy as pie to use. If you aren't a graphics heavyweight, or you don't have a lot of RAM to spare, DeskDraw and DeskPaint may well be the best (and least expensive) draw and paint products for you.

Persuasion

Not truly a graphics program, but rather, a presentation tool. With Persuasion, you can quickly and easily create on-screen presentations, or print a presentation on a laser printer, color printer, or 35mm slide printer. It comes with a lot of beautiful templates, making it even easier to produce a good-looking presentation. When I speak in public and a Mac projection system is available, I present with Persuasion. (Aldus; 206–622–5500)

Afterword

There you have it—the stuff I find myself using again and again. I'm very fortunate. My job as a columnist for *MacUser* means that I receive a lot of software and hardware for "evaluation." And evaluate them I do. The products I've lovingly described in this chapter are the tools I use every day—sometimes chosen from dozens of similar products.

All the products in this chapter are good ones. If I were awarding them mice, there's nothing less than a 4.5 (5 being the best rating *MacUser* gives—meaning that the product is truly excellent). Most of these products would receive 5 mice if it were up to me!

Whatever your software or hardware needs, these are products I find dependable, useful, and elegant each and every day. They are all solid choices; you won't be disappointed with any or all of them.

Appendix C

The Dr. Macintosh Dictionary

The words according to Dr. Macintosh.

accelerator card A type of card that contains a processor that shares computing tasks with the CPU of your Mac. It speeds up processing.

active window The frontmost, currently selected window. Only one window is active at any time. The active window's title bar is always highlighted.

ADB (Apple Desktop Bus) A low-speed input bus for input devices introduced with the SE and II and a part of every Mac since 1987. The ADB's main advantage is that you can daisy-chain up to sixteen devices (mice, keyboards, trackballs, graphics tablets, and the like) on the bus. Mac Plus and earlier Macs have separate mouse and keyboard ports, which means that keyboards and mice from earlier Macs don't work on the SE or II, and vice versa.

alert box The little message boxes that appear when your Mac has something to tell you. Examples include these always-popular messages: *An application can't be found for this document* and *Please insert the disk 'diskname.'* These messages are usually accompanied by a beep.

alias (System 7 only) A small (usually 2 or 3K) representation of a document, program, folder, or disk that you can use as if it were the original. When you double-click an alias, it locates the original and launches it. The name of an alias always appears in italic type.

Apple menu The menu from which you select desk accessories (or anything you place in your Apple Menu Items folder under System 7). It's the leftmost menu, called the *Apple menu* because it's represented in the menu bar by an Apple icon. Most programs support desk accessories or the Apple menu.

AppleShare Apple's file serving software. Requires a Macintosh Plus or higher as a dedicated server (that is, a machine that isn't used for anything else).

AppleTalk The network protocol built into every Mac. Allows Macs to communicate easily with other Macs and with AppleTalk-equipped printers (that is, many laser printers).

In the past, AppleTalk also referred to the cables and connectors used for connecting Macs, but the name of the hardware has since been changed to LocalTalk.

application Software that is used to accomplish tasks that would be necessary even if you had no computer: word processing, database manipulation, and so on. Applications are used to create files; they are the tools you use to accomplish most tasks on your Mac. Often called *programs*. Examples are MacWrite and MacPaint.

application menu (System 7 only) The menu at the far right of your screen. It shows which programs are currently open and lets you switch between them by choosing a menu item. It also has commands for hiding and showing the windows of open programs.

archive (archival backup) Copy of files stored in a safe place.

ASCII (American Standard Code for Information Interchange) A standard for assigning binary definitions to letters and numbers. Almost all computers can understand an ASCII file. On a Macintosh, ASCII files are usually saved as *text* or *text only*.

A/UX (Apple/UNIX) The Apple version of the UNIX operating system. UNIX is a multiuser, multitasking operating system developed by Bell Labs in the mid-1970s. It is popular among college networks, scientific laboratories, and the government for its sophisticated abilities in dealing with multiple users and tasks.

Available only for Mac II and later models.

background A phrase used to describe where a program is running (that is, actually doing something) under MultiFinder or System 7, when you are working in a different program in the foreground.

Most telecommunication programs (Red Ryder, MicroPhone II, SmartCom II) can run in the background. This means that they can log onto a remote computer via modem and upload or download information while you process words or crunch numbers in another program.

Some database and spreadsheet programs perform calculations, sort, and search in the background.

Background processing generally causes some negative effects in the foreground. If you're downloading a file in the background, you may notice that the performance of your foreground application is degraded somewhat—your cursor movement may become jerky, or menus may take longer to pull down. This is the price you pay for background processing.

background printing (spooling)   The ability to send a file to the printer while continuing your work. Printing in the background is often called *print-spooling*.

Without spooling, you usually have to wait several minutes while the file is being processed after you click the OK button in a print dialog. A spooler that allows background printing lets you get back to work in a lot less time. If you use MultiFinder or System 7, a spooler is built in. Or, several commercial products are available.

backup (back up)   A copy of a file, files, or the entire contents of a disk. Computers and hard disks break. A backup ensures you're never left without copies of important files. Don't shut down without a backup!

balloon   (System 7 only) Little pop-up descriptions of objects on the screen—icons, menu items, dialog box items, and so on—that appear when you point at the item if you have turned on Balloon Help in the Help menu (just to the left of the Application menu).

baud   Baud rate measures how fast your modem works. Higher means faster, but doubling baud rates doesn't double throughput. The speed of communication between any two modems cannot be faster than the slower of the pair. For example, if you have a 19,200-baud modem and your friend has a 2,400-baud modem, you'll communicate at 2,400 baud.

Baud describes the number of discrete signal events per second occurring on a communications channel. Though technically incorrect, *baud* is often used to refer to bits per second (bps),which isn't the same as discrete signal events per second.

BBS (bulletin board system; sometimes referred to as RBBS—remote bulletin board system)   An electronic communications center where users with modems can exchange notes and programs. You connect with a BBS by instructing your modem to dial its phone number. Some BBSs require payment before access is granted; others are free.

binary A numbering system that uses the powers of two. Computers use the binary system, which allows the use of only the numerals 1 and 0.

bit The smallest chunk of digital information, equal to a yes or no and represented by the numerals 0 or 1 in binary. All files are made up of bits. Lots of them.

bitmap (also bit map, BitMap, bit-map) Graphic format used by paint programs. Images consist of dots (pixels) on the screen. Most bitmapped graphics have a resolution of 72 dots per inch.

bomb The icon in the dialog box you see when your System crashes. Also used to refer to the crash itself: "I was working on my resumé when my Mac bombed." *See* crash.

boot (booting, boot up, booting up) In the old days, starting up a computer required you to toggle several switches on the front panel, which began an internal process that loaded the operating system. The process became known as *bootstrapping* (later shortened to *booting*), as a reference to "pulling yourself up by the bootstraps," which is what the computer would do when the right switches were toggled.

Today, *boot* refers to the process of starting up your computer. Some people also use it to indicate starting up an application: "So I booted up Excel and...."

boot blocks The first block of a file system, or the first two logical blocks of a volume. Boot blocks contain the system's startup instructions. Disk First Aid, Norton Utilities, and so on, can often detect and repair damaged boot blocks.

BPS (bits per second) *See* baud

bug In the old days, insects (yes, real bugs!) would fly into the guts of huge, refrigerator-size computers, which made for some spectacular system crashes. So things that caused crashes became known as bugs.

Today, *bug* refers to anything that makes your Mac act strangely and/or crash. Usually, a bug is attributable to sloppy programming. If you can duplicate a procedure that makes your Mac crash, you've found a bug. Report it to the software's publisher.

bulletin board *See* BBS

bundled software Software included with the purchase of other hardware or software.

bus The hardware used to connect peripherals or other computers. *Bus* also refers to hardware that transfers information between different components inside the computer. Common examples include SCSI Bus, NuBus (Mac II only).

byte A sequence of 8 bits. Represents a single alphanumeric character in most instances.

cache (pronounced "cash") A special area of memory (RAM) set aside for frequently accessed data. Because data can be read from RAM far faster than from disk, a cache can make your computer appear to be running faster.

The cache in your control panel (General control panel under System 6; Memory control panel under System 7) can improve performance significantly, but it can also cause trouble when used with certain applications. Unless you have more than a megabyte of RAM, set the cache to the lowest setting (32K) or turn it off. If you receive out-of-memory messages or your Mac starts to crash, turn the cache off. Also, don't use the cache on 1Mb machines with HyperCard, as HyperCard needs all of the available RAM on a 1Mb machine to operate properly.

If you have more than a megabyte of RAM, experiment with various settings to find one that suits you. Remember, the amount of RAM you allocate to the cache reduces the RAM available to run applications.

camera-ready copy A printing and publishing term used for output in final form, ready to be prepared for the printing press.

card A board that plugs into your SE or II and that implements specialized functions.

CD-ROM (compact disk–read-only memory) Optical storage medium that can hold up to 800Mb per disk. Data cannot be modified or deleted, though it can be copied. HyperCard is the most common software interface for accessing information on CD-ROMs.

CD-ROM players connect to the SCSI chain These players are similar to the popular audio CD players. Most CD-ROM players can read information into your computer *and* play your favorite Pink Floyd CD, though not at the same time.

CDEV (control *dev*ice; pronounced "see dev") Your System includes a modular control panel; CDEVs are the modules.

To install a CDEV, just drag it onto your System Folder. Some CDEVs require you to reboot before they take effect. To use a CDEV, choose Control Panel from the Apple menu and either select the specific one from the scrolling icons on the left side of the window or double-click its icon.

Apple-supplied CDEVs include General, Keyboard, Sound, Mouse, and Monitors. Some commercial utilities are also CDEVs, such as QuicKeys.

check box Control used in dialog boxes; an X in the box indicates that item is turned on. The Page Setup dialog box has several check boxes —Font Substitution, Text Smoothing, and so on.

Chooser Apple-supplied desk accessory that lets you choose among the devices, usually printers, that are connected to your Mac through the printer or modem ports.

Clipboard Special area of RAM set aside to hold text or graphics you cut or copy. The Clipboard can contain only one selection at a time: the last thing you cut or copied. When you use the Paste command, the current contents of the Clipboard are pasted. Because the Clipboard is in RAM, shutting down or crashing causes the loss of its contents.

close box Box in the upper left-hand corner of most Macintosh windows. Clicking in it closes that window.
    The close box is sometimes called the *go away box*.

Command key The key with the cloverleaf, just to the left of the space-bar on most keyboards. It is always used in conjunction with at least one other key, usually as a shortcut for a menu item. When instructed to type Command-p, for example, you would press the Command key and then the p key (without releasing the Command-key). Command-key shortcuts (sometimes called Command-key equivalents) are usually listed in menus.

Control key A modifier key found on some keyboards.

Control Panel An Apple-supplied desk accessory (it's a folder under System 7) that lets you control many of the ways your Mac responds to you. For example, you can adjust mouse speed, key repeat rate, delay until key repeat, the time on your Mac's internal clock, and much more from control panels.

coprocessor A chip other than the CPU that processes information. A Mac II has two processors: a Motorola 68020 and a 68881 math chip. The first processor is the CPU; the second handles only math, so it's called a math coprocessor.

copy protection Schemes that prevent unauthorized copying of software. Copy protection has unpleasant side effects. Copy-protected programs are harder to use with a hard disk, they wreak havoc with disk optimizers and backup utilities, and they can leave you without a usable copy of the program if the master disk is damaged or lost.
    If you have a choice between products, choose one without copy protection over one with it.

corruption (corrupt, corrupted) The term given to a file that has been damaged or scrambled in some way, and can no longer function properly. Corruption is usually the result of a crash (System error) or power interruption. Any file can become corrupted—documents, applications, System files, desk accessories, fonts, and so on, but the System and Finder are particularly susceptible to corruption since they are always running when you crash.

CPU (central processing unit) The chip that is the "brain" of your computer. The Macintosh uses the Motorola 68000 series of CPU chips: the Plus and SE have the 68000; the II has the 68020; the IIx, IIcx, IIci, IIfx, and SE/30 have the 68030; and the Quadras have the 68040. Power users call them by their last three digits: "It has an '040 and really screams."

Sometimes an entire computer is referred to as a CPU.

crash Unfortunate, unexpected occurrence in which you lose control of your Mac. Most crashes are the result of bugs in software. A crash generally forces you to restart your computer, which causes the loss of all work done since the last time you saved to disk.

creator Four-letter code your Macintosh uses to identify which application was used to create which document. Many applications and DAs allow you to view a file's creator and type (DiskTop, ResEdit, and 1st Aid Kit, for example).

The most common creator codes are: MACA (MacWrite), MSWD (Microsoft Word), WILD (HyperCard), and MPNT (MacPaint).

cursor The little pointer on the screen. The cursor almost always moves when you move the mouse or arrow keys. Cursors come in many shapes and sizes; the watch, arrow, and insertion point are all cursors.

DA (desk accessory) A program that resides under the Apple menu and is available no matter what application is currently running. DAs afford much of the functionality of MultiFinder to users with only 1Mb of RAM.

Under System 6, desk accessories can be installed as resources in your System with Font/DA Mover, or accessed without installing them with Suitcase II or MasterJuggler.

Under System 7, desk accessories act like little double-clickable applications and can be placed anywhere on your disk, though most people store them in the Apple Menu Items folder so they appear in the Apple menu.

Apple-supplied DAs include Alarm Clock, Calculator, and Puzzle. Commercial DAs include DiskTop, DeskDraw, and DeskPaint.

daisy-chain A series of peripheral devices connected to your computer, or the act of connecting peripherals in such a chain. A SCSI daisy-chain usually includes one or more hard disks and can also include a CD-ROM device, tape drive, scanner, or other hardware device.

The daisy-chain on the Apple Desktop Bus (ADB) always includes the keyboard and mouse but can also include a trackball or digitizing tablet.

In daisy-chains, devices are connected to each other in a series, and the last device in the chain is connected to your Mac.

data Information, usually stored on a computer in bits or bytes. More specifically, *data* usually refers to documents, especially database files, rather than to applications or programs.

data fork All Macintosh files have two forks: a data fork and a resource fork. The contents of each fork depend on what the file contains. Applications and System software store most of their information in the resource fork, and documents store most of their information in the data fork.

database Application (program) for storing, manipulating, and retrieving information (data). Most Macintosh databases allow data to consist of words and/or images.

    Also refers to the documents created by the application.

    A database program is sometimes called a DBMS (database management system).

DB-9 The connector that plugs into the serial or modem ports on older Macs.

DBMS (database management system) *See* database

decryption The process of decoding a document that has been encrypted for security reasons.

defragment The process of rewriting files on disks so that they reside on contiguous sectors, done with a specialized program such as DiskExpress.

desk accessory *See* DA

desktop The (usually) gray area in the Finder where the Trash and disk icons appear. Also refers to the entire Macintosh interface metaphor.

Desktop file An invisible file (meaning you can't see or modify it without special tools) on every Mac disk that contains important information for the Finder about the files on that disk.

dialog box The little message boxes that appear when your Mac needs you to make a decision. The boxes you see when you open or save are examples of dialog boxes, as is the one that says *Completely erase the disk....* Page Setup and Print are other commands that bring up a dialog box in most applications.

    Dialog boxes usually require input from the user—either typing or selecting a button.

DIN-8 The connector that plugs into the serial or modem ports of all Macs since the Mac Plus.

DIP SIMMs A SIMM (single in-line memory module) is a small board used to add RAM to your Mac (usually 1Mb). DIP SIMMs are slightly taller than low-profile SIMMs. If you intend to add other internal upgrades, such as an internal disk drive or an accelerator, you may have to use only low-profile SIMMs. Ask before you buy.

directory   Usually refers to one or both invisible directory files on every disk: the Volume directory, which contains information about the disk itself, and the File directory, which contains information about the files stored on the disk.

The message *This disk is damaged* usually indicates a damaged directory. Many types of directory damage can be fixed using Apple's Disk First Aid program.

disk   *See* floppy disk; hard disk

document   File created by an application. MacWrite is an application; Letter to Mom is a document.

double-click   Clicking the button on the mouse two times in rapid succession. In the Finder, this launches or opens an application, document, or folder. In most applications that use alphanumeric characters, double-clicking selects a single word. Double-click speed can be adjusted using the Control Panel DA.

download   To receive information from another computer on your computer. You can also download files from BBSs and on-line services. This is usually done with a modem, but you can now also hook up a Mac directly to a micro, mini, or mainframe and download via AppleTalk or Ethernet cable.

downloadable font   High-resolution fonts for use with PostScript printers. These fonts are usually stored on a hard disk. Printing is slower with downloadable fonts than with fonts that are resident in the printer.

dpi (dots per inch)   Measure of resolution for a screen, scanner, or printer. The higher the number, the sharper the type and images. Your Macintosh screen displays at 72dpi; the LaserWriter outputs 300dpi. A laser imagesetter (such as a Linotronic) outputs at resolutions as high as 2,540dpi.

driver   Software required for communication with a peripheral device. For example, printing requires that a driver be present in your System Folder. The ImageWriter and/or LaserWriter files you've probably noticed in your System Folder (if you've been able to print successfully) are these drivers. (Under System 7, printer drivers are stored in the Extensions folder, inside the System Folder.)

Another kind of driver is installed with the initialization application that came with a hard disk. This driver tells the disk how to interact with the Mac. If the driver becomes damaged, as it can from a crash or power interruption, it may cause your hard disk to crash or refuse to mount or boot.

Driver also refers to a type of resource stored in the resource fork of some DAs.

dual-page display A monitor large enough to show two 8½-by-11-inch pages side-by-side. (Dual-page displays are usually 19- or 21-inches, measured diagonally.)

8-bit color Able to display up to 256 colors at one time.

E-mail (also Email, electronic mail) Messages passed from computer user to computer user via modem and telephone lines or a local area network.

em dash A typesetter's term for a long dash, so named because it's approximately the same width as the capital letter M. In actuality, the width of an em dash is equal to the typeface's size in points. So an em dash in 12-point Helvetica is a dash 12 points wide.

In most Macintosh fonts, you can type an em dash by typing Option-Shift-hyphen. On a typewriter, an em dash is usually represented by a double hyphen.

em space A typesetter's term for a space as wide as the point size of the typeface being used. The em space is used in typesetting for indents.

en dash A typesetter's term for a dash longer than a hyphen but shorter than an em dash. An en dash is approximately the same width as the capital letter N and is used to separate numbers in a series (for example, 1988–1989, or 800–538–9696).

In most Macintosh fonts, you can type an en dash by typing Option-hyphen.

encryption A process that renders data unintelligible without the proper password. Requires special software.

EPS (also EPSF, encapsulated PostScript) A high-resolution file format for storing documents. This format essentially combines a PICT image, for high resolution on the screen, and a PostScript representation, for high-resolution output.

Programs that save EPS files include Adobe Illustrator and Aldus FreeHand. Most page-layout programs accept EPS files for placement within documents.

Ethernet High-speed network protocol. Ethernet can be two to five times as fast as LocalTalk, but it uses more expensive cable and requires a pricey hardware adapter for each Mac. (Quadras have built-in Ethernet connectors.)

expansion card A board that plugs into your SE or II and implements specialized functions not otherwise included on the Macintosh, such as video display and processing, a variety of coprocessors, peripheral devices such as modems, and network interfaces such as Ethernet.

file format (file type) The special way or ways in which an application stores information on disk. Many applications can read and write multiple file formats.

For example, MacWrite reads (opens) and writes (saves) files in the MacWrite and text file formats. SuperPaint reads and writes files in the PNTG (MacPaint), PICT (MacDraw), StartupScreen, and SuperPaint file formats.

file name (filename) The name of any file, application, or document. It can be up to thirty-one characters long and cannot contain a colon. The System software doesn't allow you to save a file name containing a colon; it either changes it to a dash or displays a dialog box that says there is a bad character in the file name.

file server A hard disk, usually dedicated to this single task, on a network that allows applications and documents to be shared by multiple users. Requires special software such as TOPS or AppleShare.

file transfer protocol A set of rules governing the exchange of information between computers and other computers or peripheral devices. SCSI, XMODEM, YMODEM, MacBinary, AppleTalk, Ethernet, and Kermit are examples of such protocols.

file-by-file (file-by-file backup) A method that backs up a disk one file at a time. It's more flexible than an image backup because it won't copy unused portions of the disk. On the other hand, it is often slower than an image backup because it reads the disk one file at a time.

filter Term used by backup programs to describe the ability to select (filter) what does or does not get backed up. Also: the term used to refer to certain file translation files.

Finder The Finder is part of the operating system. It's the System application that manages opening, closing, moving, renaming, and trashing files and folders. It also is in charge of ejecting, initializing, and erasing disks. The Finder is a special System file, and it can't be opened by double-clicking. It opens automatically every time you start up your Mac.

You must have a Finder and System file on any disk you use to start up a Mac.

FKEY (function key) A single-function program, accessed by pressing Command-shift and a number between 0 and 9.

FKEYs can be installed as resources in your System or added temporarily with Suitcase II or MasterJuggler.

Apple-supplied FKEYs include Screen dump to disk (Command-Shift-3) and Eject disk (Command-Shift-1 or 2).

There aren't many commercial FKEYs, but hundreds are available as public-domain software or shareware.

flat-file database A database management system that uses a single data file for all of the information. It cannot look up or utilize information stored in other data files.

floppy disk Macintoshes use a 3½-inch, hard-shell plastic diskette. A floppy disk drive reads and writes data to and from floppy disks. Older floppy disks had a capacity of 400K, but most recent models hold 800K, and the SuperDrive that comes with current models can hold up to 1.4Mb.

Interestingly, once initialized, an 800K floppy disk only has 779K of space on it. (The missing 21K is used by the invisible directory file and for formatting information.)

font A certain style of a set of characters, including letters, numbers, punctuation marks, and other symbols.

Font is often used to refer to a Macintosh typeface.

Font/DA Mover Apple-supplied application used prior to System 7 for installing fonts and desk accessories in your System file.

fragmentation Your Macintosh stores files in pieces on your hard disk. As your hard disk gets fuller, it writes files to any available space, even if that space is not contiguous. So as files are written, different parts are stored in different places on the drive. Fragmentation slows your hard disk down and can eventually cause data loss. Use a utility such as DiskExpress to periodically defragment your hard disks.

full-page display A monitor roughly the size of an 8½-by-11-inch page.

gigabyte 1,024 megabytes. Several hard disks can store over a gigabyte, and some tape backup systems—DAT and 8mm—can store that much or more on a single tape.

go away box *See* close box

gray-scale True gray displayed on the screen; not just a collection of black-and-white pixels (dots) cleverly arranged to simulate gray, as seen on Macs with built-in 9-inch screens. Requires either a gray-scale or a color monitor.

Most desktop publishing and graphics programs running on Macs that support color monitors can display gray-scale information on the screen. Gray-scale information is usually printed using a PostScript output device.

gray-scale monitor Able to display 8 or more shades of gray—most gray-scale monitors display 256 shades.

hard disk Mechanical, nonremovable, high-speed storage device capable of holding multiple (usually 20+) megabytes of data. Most connect through the SCSI port (internal drives are the exception) and are far faster than floppy disks.

HFS (hierarchical file system)   A filing system that allows you to arrange applications, documents, and folders in a hierarchy. Files and folders at the Finder (or Desktop) are said to be first-level files. Files within these first-level folders are second-level files. If any of these second-level files is a folder, the files inside it would be third-level files. And so on. You can *nest* (place files or folders within other folders) about twelve levels deep, depending on available RAM. (If you open more than twelve windows in the Finder, you may get an error message saying no more windows can be opened.)

HyperCard   A hypermedia application that allows storage and retrieval of text and bitmapped graphics. HyperCard files (called *stacks*) are easily configured by the user. Any piece of information in a HyperCard file can be linked to any other piece of information.

HyperCard has been bundled with every Macintosh since August 1987.

I-beam   The cursor you control with your mouse in most text-processing programs. It is called an *I-beam* because it resembles a cross-section of a steel beam.

icon   Icons are one of the things that make the Macintosh interface unique. An icon is a small picture that represents an object or action to your Mac. For example, disks are represented by icons that look like disks, folders by icons that look like folders, and documents by icons that look like a sheet of paper. All applications and most documents have distinctive icons when seen in the Finder (desktop).

To activate most icons, double-click on the icon.

image backup   Method of backing up a disk from beginning to end (sector by sector) without regard for files, folders, or the overall structure of the disk.

It does not distinguish between used and unused portions of the disk. An image backup of a 40Mb hard disk will take up 40Mb of backup media, even if only 10Mb of the hard disk contains files.

incremental backup   Backup in which only files that have been modified since the last backup session are copied.

information service   An information service is a large, commercial bulletin board system (BBS). Such services allow computer owners with modems to access an incredible range of services. You can make travel reservations, buy and sell stocks, download Macintosh software, and chat with other Macintosh owners.

All of the big services have local nodes in most cities, so logging on is not a long-distance call.

CompuServe has the most to offer and is reasonably priced. America Online offers a nicer Mac interface but has fewer services.

INIT (Startup Document) INITs (and many CDEVs) are small programs that you place in your System Folder and that are installed automatically at boot time. Suitcase II and MasterJuggler are examples. When you view By Kind in the Finder, INITs and CDEVs show up as Startup documents and Control Panel documents, respectively. In most cases, you can use quite a few of them simultaneously. Occasionally, a conflict will prevent your hard disk from booting.

initialize Erase a hard or floppy disk. Also called *formatting*.

insertion point Flashing vertical bar that indicates where characters will appear when you're typing in applications or the Finder (when naming or renaming an icon).

Installer Program that installs software. Most common is the Apple Installer, used for installing and updating the System software.

interleave The order in which your hard disk reads and writes sectors on the platter (disk). A 1:1 interleave reads every sector; 2:1 reads every second sector; 3:1 reads every third sector. Unless your manual tells you otherwise, use 1:1.

Interleave is usually specified when you initialize your hard disk for the first time. Some drives set it automatically. Using a drive formatted with the wrong interleave factor for your Mac will degrade performance.

invisible file Files that cannot be seen under ordinary circumstances. The Desktop is probably the invisible file you're most familiar with. Invisible files can be accessed only with special applications or DAs (ResEdit, SUM, DiskTop, and so on).

kerning Adjusting the space between characters to create a more pleasing effect. Kerning is usually measured in points or fractions of an em space. Kerning is a feature of most page-layout and some word-processing programs.

kilobyte (K, kbyte, or Kbyte) A kilobyte is equal to 1,000 bytes, and after bits and bytes, it is the smallest unit of measure for disk space or RAM.

kludge Not quite the best way of doing something. If a function could have been implemented in a better way, it's a kludge. Or kludgy. Kludges may not be elegant, but they usually work.

For example: Instead of purchasing an internal fan, you buy an oscillating fan at the corner store and aim it at your Mac. That's a kludge.

LAN (local area network)   A hardware and software setup that connects computers to other computers and peripheral devices such as printers. A LAN allows multiple computers to share files easily.

At the very least, a LAN consists of the physical cable and connectors (LocalTalk or Ethernet, for example) and file or disk serving hardware or software of some sort (TOPS, AppleShare, or MacServe, for instance). Other goodies such as multiuser database software and electronic mail (E-mail) are easily added.

landscape mode   Printing a page sideways—wider than it is long. Most programs allow you to select this option in the Page Setup dialog box. Landscape mode is often called *wide* (as opposed to the portrait mode, which is sometimes called *long*).

launch   To start up an application, such as "launch MacWrite."

leading   The amount of space between two lines of text, usually measured in points. Leading is a feature of most page-layout and word-processing programs.

Linotronic   Brand of high-resolution image-setting devices. Linotronic machines provide output from popular programs at resolutions up to 2,540dpi. Used for typesetting.

Lisa   The predecessor to the Macintosh. Reincarnated as the Macintosh XL; neither has been produced since 1985.

local area network   *See* LAN

LocalTalk   The name given to the cables and connectors sold by Apple for connecting Macs. LocalTalk cable and connectors used to be called AppleTalk cable and connectors. Today, *AppleTalk* refers to the network protocol, and *LocalTalk* refers to the wiring and connectors.

low-profile SIMMs   A SIMM (single in-line memory module) is a small board used to add RAM to your Mac (usually 1Mb). Functionally the same as DIP SIMMs, low-profile SIMMs are not as tall. This may be important if you intend to add other internal upgrades, such as an internal disk drive or an accelerator. DIP SIMMs may not leave sufficient clearance.

MacBinary   A standard for transferring Macintosh files from one computer to another. Always used in conjunction with an error-checking protocol such as XMODEM, MacBinary ensures that all the attributes (that is, both data and resource forks) are included when the file is transferred. Without it, files may become garbled and may be unable to be opened on the receiving Mac.

MacBinary is the preferred way to transfer files between two Macs. When sending files to be used by other computers, you should save them as text only and *not* use MacBinary.

macro A sequence of Macintosh keyboard or mouse events, programmed by the user to automate repetitive tasks. Creating macros requires additional software such as MacroMaker, Tempo, AutoMac, or QuicKeys. Certain programs have a built-in macro facility: Excel, Full Impact, and QUED-M are just a few.

math coprocessor A special chip designed to speed computation. The Mac II, IIx, IIcx, and SE/30 are equipped with math coprocessors. Most accelerator products also offer a math coprocessor as an option.

MAUG (micronetworked Apple user's group) A group of forums on CompuServe (an on-line service) dedicated to the sharing of information about Apple computers.

megabyte (Mb) 1,024 kilobytes (K). A megabyte is slightly more than an 800K double-sided floppy disk will hold. Megabytes are used to measure RAM; 1Mb is the standard amount in most Macintosh CPUs as of this writing.

memory Where computers store information. Comes in two types: volatile and nonvolatile, depending on whether the contents survive when the computer is turned off. RAM is volatile; ROM and hard and floppy disks are not. Memory is measured in bytes (and kilobytes, megabytes, gigabytes, and so on).

menu A list of commands that appears on the screen when you click on a menu title. You drag down to make a selection. Menus are found in the Finder as well as in most applications and desk accessories.

menu bar The strip of menu titles at the top of the screen.

menu title Word or phrase in the menu bar that designates it as a menu. Click on it to reveal the menu. Drag down to make a selection.

MFS (Macintosh filing system) An old system of storing files and folders. MFS was a flat, rather than hierarchical, filing system. It allowed storage one level deep—everything in every folder was stored at the same level.

MFS was replaced with the more efficient HFS when the Mac Plus was introduced in 1986.

MIDI (musical instrument digital interface) A protocol for exchange and storage of information between a computer and a musical instrument.

modem (*modulate/demodulate*) A modem is a device that allows your computer to communicate with the outside world via telephone lines.

Technically speaking, it converts digital information (bits and bytes) from your Mac into analog information (noise) that can be sent over standard phone lines, while converting incoming analog information into digital information your Mac can understand.

modifier key   Non-printing keys on the keyboard—Command, Option, Control, Shift, Tab—usually pressed in combination with one or more other keys.

monochrome monitor Displays only black and white.

motherboard The main circuit board in your Mac. It houses the most important chips, including the CPU. Macintosh motherboards are quickly and easily swapped (by an authorized dealer, of course) for upgrades and/or repairs.

mount The act that causes a disk's icon to appear on the desktop in the Finder. (It's automatic in most cases.) More specifically, a *mounted* disk is one that can be used at a given time.

   You can't use a disk before it's mounted. If you insert a disk, or boot with a hard disk turned on, and no icon appears on the desktop, the disk is refusing to mount.

MUG (Macintosh user group) A group of Macintosh enthusiasts who hold regular meetings, exchange shareware and public-domain stuff, publish informative newsletters, and generally provide an informative setting for anyone who uses a Mac. There are more than 1,000 user groups in the U.S. alone!

   If you want to know how to contact the user group nearest you, call 800–538–9696, extension 500.

MultiFinder   Apple's multitasking operating system option, only available in software versions prior to 7.0. Before System 7, Apple gave you a choice of single-tasking or multitasking—called Finder and MultiFinder, respectively. If you choose MultiFinder, you can open several applications simultaneously, some of which can run in the background. Only one window can be active at a time, though certain tasks (telecommunications, disk backup, and so on) can continue even if another application is active. (System 7 doesn't have a single-tasking mode like earlier system software; it's always in a multitasking mode.)

nesting Placing folders within folders.

network *See* LAN

NuBus A protocol used by the Mac II series (Mac II, IIx, and IIcx) that allows expansion cards to communicate at high speeds. The ability to add expansion cards easily is often called *open architecture*.

NuBus expansion slots The slots (ports) on the main circuit board of the Mac II series that allow you to add expansion cards (for example, cards for video display and processing, a variety of coprocessors, peripheral devices such as modems, and network interfaces such as Ethernet).

object-oriented graphics Graphics created by applications other than paint programs and usually stored as PICT or EPS files. An object-oriented graphics program lets you select and rearrange elements within your drawing. MacDraw is an object-oriented graphics program.

OCR (optical character recognition) The ability to convert scanned text into text files rather than pictures. Devices with OCR enable you to scan, for example, a typewritten report, and then use the resulting file with your favorite word processor.

Affordable systems that really work are just now becoming available.

on-line service *See* information service

optimizer An application that rearranges files on a disk for maximum speed.

Parameter RAM *See* PRAM

partition Division of a hard or floppy disk into multiple, separate virtual disks. You can use each partition as if it were a separate disk. Most software allows you to password-protect partitions.

Many hard disks include partitioning software; otherwise, you have to purchase it.

Partitions are a particularly useful organizational tool if you have a large hard disk with thousands of files and folders. Unless you require password protection, the benefit of partitioning is much reduced if your hard disk is less than 80Mb or has a small number of files.

PICT File format for object-oriented graphics (PICTures). PICT files can be written and read by many applications, and most page-layout programs import (place) PICT files.

In most applications that save a PICT file, you must select Save As and specify the PICT format. If not, your file will be stored in the program's native file format.

Programs that read and write PICT files include MacDraw and MacDraw II, Canvas, and SuperPaint.

pixel The dots that make up the image on a screen. A Macintosh screen displays 72 pixels (dots) per inch (or, you might say that a Macintosh screen pixel is $\frac{1}{72}$ of an inch).

When you print a document using a printer that supports resolutions above 72dpi, the screen pixels are converted to more densely packed pixels on the printed page. For example, most laser printers support 300dpi.

platen The rubber roller that serves as a backing for the paper during printing and paper loading on impact printers such as the ImageWriter.

pointer An arrow-shaped cursor used for selecting icons, graphic objects, and menus, and for double-clicking in the Finder.

pop-up menu A menu that appears in a place other than the menu bar. When you click on a pop-up, a menu appears. Pop-up menus usually appear in dialog boxes and are identified by a box with a shadowed outline.

port As a noun, *port* refers to a connection through which your Mac sends and receives data. Examples include the ADB, modem, printer, and SCSI ports.

When used as a verb, *port* means to convert a program to run on a different computer. Many games are ported from the IBM or Apple II to make them run on a Mac. This cannot be done by the user; the publisher must do the porting. Products ported from other computers usually stink.

portrait mode Printing a page with the usual orientation—longer than wide. Most programs allow you to select this option in the Page Setup dialog box; the other option is usually the landscape (or wide) mode.

PostScript A device-independent page-description language created by Adobe Systems and used by the LaserWriter and Linotronic. PostScript provides a way for files created on any computer to be output at the highest resolution the printer allows.

power user Someone who uses a Macintosh better, faster, or more elegantly than you. Or, someone who can answer Macintosh-related questions you can't.

PRAM (Parameter RAM) A small amount of internal RAM, maintained by battery, that keeps your Mac's clock running and stores such things as serial (modem and printer) port configurations.

Some of the more obvious signs of PRAM problems are when your Mac clock doesn't work correctly and when the Chooser forgets settings.

print spooler *See* background printing

printer driver *See* driver

processor A chip that processes information (as opposed to RAM, which only stores it). A Mac II has two processors: the 68020 CPU (central processing unit) and a 68881 math coprocessor.

program *See* application

programmer's switch Every Mac comes with a little piece of plastic called the programmer's switch. It is actually two switches: the front switch is the reset switch, and the rear switch is the interrupt switch.

The reset switch works the same as turning your Mac off and back on with the power switch. If you need to restart your Mac after a crash or freeze, you can push the reset button instead of turning the power off and on.

The rear switch, the interrupt switch, can sometimes return you to the Finder after a crash if you type the proper sequence (see Chapter 6).

protocol   A set of rules governing the exchange of information between computers and/or peripheral devices. Examples include SCSI, XMODEM, MacBinary, AppleTalk, and Ethernet.

public-domain software   Software to which the author retains no rights—it is available to anyone for free, usually through on-line services and user groups.

QuickDraw   Internal routines, built into the Mac ROM and System software, for drawing graphics to the screen or printer. These QuickDraw routines are responsible for almost everything you see on the screen; they allow the Macintosh desktop metaphor to work the way it does.

radio button   A type of button, usually found in dialog boxes or HyperCard, in which the user clicks to select one from two or more choices.

The Page Setup dialog box is a good example—there are usually four radio buttons for different paper sizes. Selecting one by clicking it deselects the other choices.

RAM (random access memory)   The temporary memory in which your Mac stores information while it's running. RAM is sometimes known as *volatile* memory, because its contents are lost whenever you power down or crash. The first Mac had 128K (kilobytes) of RAM. The Fat Mac had 512K and the Mac Plus, SE, and II all have at least 1,024K of RAM.

You can add RAM to most models of Macintosh.

RAM cache   *See* cache

RBBS   *See* BBS

Read Me (Read Me documents)   Plain text documents that provide late-breaking information about software. These files can be read with Apple's TeachText or any program or DA that reads text files.

If you purchase software that has a Read Me file on any of the disks, you should read the file before you install the software or use it. The file usually contains important information that doesn't appear in the documentation.

reboot Restart your Mac. Always use the Finder's Restart command. Flicking the power switch without using the Shut Down command is asking for trouble.

relational (relational database) A type of high-end database that can link information in various files. Relationships can be one-to-many, many-to-one, and one-to-one. This allows the database to look up information in other files and use it in the file currently being accessed.

Although some flat-file databases can perform a single lookup, relational databases allow you to link numerous files in various ways.

ResEdit (Resource Editor) Apple's resource-editing application. Almost everything in a Macintosh file is considered a *resource*; ResEdit gives you tools to modify (edit) them. If you know what you're doing, you can modify alert boxes, menus, dialog boxes, and much more.

ResEdit is a powerful tool. It can destroy your files. Never use ResEdit on a master or original file; *always* work on a copy.

Available from CompuServe, GEnie, America Online, most user groups, and some dealers.

resolution The term used to describe the number of dots per inch your printer or monitor produces. The Mac displays 72 dots per inch on the screen; the LaserWriter prints 300 dots per inch on paper. So the Mac has a screen resolution of 72dpi, and the LaserWriter has a printing resolution of 300dpi.

resource fork The part of a file that contains resources used by the application, such as menus, fonts, and icons.

RGB (RGB monitor) A model for displaying video images. RGB (which stands for red, green, blue) provides better resolution and color than conventional television, which uses a model known as composite video.

RGB monitors are commonly used with the Mac II series.

restore Opposite of backup. The process of moving files that were backed up previously to the disk from which they were originally backed up. Usually done only in emergencies.

ROM (read-only memory) Nonvolatile memory that resides on a chip inside your Mac. It contains parts of the Macintosh operating system. It can never be erased or changed.

SANE (standard Apple numerics environment) Apple's built-in implementation of the IEEE standard for computation. SANE utilizes a math coprocessor if one is available.

scanner A device that converts paper images (flat art) into graphics files (usually MacPaint or TIFF).

Scrapbook An Apple-supplied desk accessory that lets you store text or graphics. Text or graphics pasted into the Scrapbook remain there until removed. You can copy text or graphics from the Scrapbook and paste them into most applications.

screen dump A built-in method (FKEY) for capturing the image on your screen to a MacPaint file. Press Command-Shift-3, and the image on your screen at that moment will be saved as Screen 0. (It's called Picture 1 under System 7.) Under System 6 or earlier, the file can be viewed or modified with any program that will open a MacPaint file; under System 7 or later, it can be viewed or modified with any program that will open a PICT file. (The version of Apple's TeachText that comes with System 7 can open PICT files.)

script (scripting language) The instructions followed by a macro in either a stand-alone macro program (QuicKeys, MacroMaker) or a program equipped with its own internal macro facility (Excel, MicroPhone II).

SCSI (small computer system interface; pronounced "scuzzy") High-speed data port (bus) introduced with the Mac Plus and included with all current Mac models. The SCSI bus allows up to six devices to be daisy-chained to your Mac, communicating at speeds far faster than the modem, printer, or ADB ports allow.

SCSI bus *See* daisy-chain; SCSI; SCSI ID number

SCSI ID number The Macintosh allows you to connect up to six external or internal SCSI devices. Each must be assigned a different ID number (don't use 7 or 0; they're reserved for the Mac itself and an internal hard disk, respectively). Some devices allow you to select the ID number using software; others require you to set dip switches or thumb wheels.

    If you don't use the Startup Device selector in your control panel to select another device, your Mac will boot from the startup device (a device with a System Folder) that has the highest ID number.

sector A small portion of a floppy or hard disk.

selection rectangle The dotted box that results from clicking and dragging. Items within the box are selected when you release the mouse button.

serial (serial port) A port for connecting peripherals to your Mac. The printer and modem ports are serial ports. A serial port is slower than the SCSI port.

shareware Try-before-you-buy software. Some of it is incredible. Thousands of programs, DAs, INITs, and graphics are available as shareware. The easiest place to get ahold of it is from on-line services such as CompuServe, America Online, or GEnie. Most user groups have shareware libraries available to members.

Support shareware. If you use it, send the developer a check!

SIMM (single in-line memory module) A small board containing eight memory chips, usually totaling 1Mb, used for adding RAM to your Mac. You can have up to four SIMMs (4Mb) in an SE or Plus; up to eight in the II, IIx, IIcx, or SE/30.

size box The box at the lower right-hand corner of most active windows in which you can click and drag to resize the window.

spool (spooler, spooling) An acronym for store printed output online. A spooler is a device that allows printing to occur without tying up your Mac. A spooler prints your document to disk and then sends that file to the printer in the background while you continue working.

With System software releases, Apple supplies a laser spooler that works only under MultiFinder. Commercial spoolers include Super-LaserSpool and LaserSpeed.

stack A file created by and used with HyperCard.

standard directory dialog box The dialog box you use when you Open or Save a file. If you're hip you call them GetFile and PutFile.

suitcase (suitcase file) Slang for a font or DA file, so-called because their icons look like little suitcases.

sysop (*system operator*) The person who manages/operates a bulletin board (BBS).

System A file used by the Mac to start up and provide system-wide information. It can't be opened by double-clicking; it opens automatically every time you start up your Mac.

You must have a Finder and System file on any disk you use to start up a Mac.

System error   *See* crash; bomb

System heap The System heap is a special area of RAM set aside for things such as fonts and DAs. Increasing its size will help you if you have a large number of fonts and DAs.

If you ever see an error message with the number -108, it probably means you need more space in your System heap.

System 7-friendly System 7-friendly programs run perfectly under System 7. The majority of the programs you use under System 6 fall into this category. The coolest, though, are System 7-savvy programs.

System 7-savvy System 7-savvy programs not only run perfectly, but also take advantage of System 7.0-specific features like Interapplication Communication (IAC) and Apple Events.

System 6.0.x 0.x means any version of System 6—System 6.0. through System 6.0.8. If you are using System 6, you should be using version 6.0.4 or later, as these are generally regarded as more stable than earlier versions.

System software The System, Finder, and all related files and utilities supplied by Apple. System software is updated approximately twice a year. It is usually available from Apple dealers, on-line services, and user groups.

TeachText An Apple-supplied application that reads text files. The Read Me file on Apple System software updates is in the TeachText format.

telecommunication The exchange of information from computer to computer using phone lines and modems.

telecommunication software The software you use to control a modem.

terminator Terminators are little devices that help prevent noise and strange behavior on the SCSI bus. They look like the 25- or 50-pin plug you find on a SCSI cable, but they have no cable attached. Plug the terminator into the last unoccupied cable connector in the SCSI chain. External terminators should be available from your local dealer.

Some devices, including most internal hard disks, have their own internal terminators. Others, such as Apple's Tape Drive, require an external terminator.

text only File saved in ASCII format. Text files contain only letters and numbers; no graphics or formatting. Text files can be read by many applications and DAs and by almost every type of computer.

32-bit addressing (System 7 only) Some Macs can use very large amounts of RAM, usually 9 or more megabytes. In order to do so, you must turn 32-bit addressing (found in the Memory control panel) on.

throughput The amount of actual data transmitted per second. Used to measure data transfer speeds for modems and LANs.

thumb wheel A small wheel with numbers on it used by some SCSI devices to select the ID number. You turn it with your thumb to select the SCSI ID number you want to assign to that device.

TIFF (tagged image file format) A high-resolution bitmapped file format that can store gray-scale information. Most scanners save in the TIFF format. TIFF files can be opened and manipulated by many applications. Most page-layout programs import (place) TIFF files.

title bar The lined bar at the top of each window that contains the file or folder's name. Clicking and dragging the title bar moves the window. A highlighted title bar, one with black stripes showing, indicates that the window is active.

toner cartridge A plastic container for toner powder, which serves as the laser printer's "ink," used in the printing process.

Trash The icon in the Finder that looks like a garbage can. You drag files you no longer need to it. Files dragged in the Trash are deleted by using the Empty Trash command in the Special menu. If you don't use the Empty Trash command, files in the Trash are deleted when you next launch a program or eject a disk.

Under System 7, files are not deleted until you choose Empty Trash, even if you launch a program, eject a disk, restart, or shut down.

24-bit color Able to display over 16 million colors at one time.

type A four-letter code that your Macintosh uses to identify the application that created a particular document. Many applications and DAs allow you to view a file's creator and type (such as DiskTop, ResEdit, and First Aid Kit).

The most common types for documents are: WORD (MacWrite), WDBN (Microsoft Word), STAK (HyperCard), and PNTG (MacPaint). Most applications are of the type APPL.

upgrade (or update) A periodic improvement to hardware or software. Software upgrades (that is, new versions) are usually offered to existing owners at a reduced price. Hardware upgrades vary widely in pricing.

In general, *upgrade* refers to a major new version, and *update* refers to a minor bug-fix release. Unfortunately, there is no rule of thumb; many developers use these words interchangeably.

upload To send a document via modem (or local area network) to another computer.

user group A club or organization made up of people who use the Mac. Most user groups hold regularly scheduled meetings, demonstrate software, maintain public-domain and shareware libraries, and offer help to novices.

utility A program designed specifically for use with a computer. Backup programs, screen savers, and macro generators are examples of utility programs.

video card The interface between the monitor and your Mac—it goes inside your Mac.

virtual memory (System 7 only) Space on your hard disk that the Mac is tricked into thinking is RAM. Certain models of Mac allow you to use virtual memory (you'll find it in the Memory control panel if your Mac supports it).

So, for example, you can make a 4Mb Mac think it has 8Mb of RAM by turning on virtual memory.

Virtual memory is significantly slower than real memory.

volume A *volume* is the term used to refer to a storage device, such as a hard disk or a file server. Volume can refer to an entire disk or part of a disk. *See also* partition.

WORM (write once, read many) A type of removable optical drive with a capacity of better than 500Mb, written to and read by lasers. WORMs are nonerasable. When they get full, you just pop in a new WORM cartridge (about $200).

write-protect The little plastic tab in the upper right corner of a floppy disk (shutter-side down, label side facing you) that prevents the disk from being written to. If you can see light through the hole, the disk is write-protected.

XMODEM An error-correcting protocol for transferring files from one computer to another via modem.

YMODEM Another error-correcting protocol for transferring files from one computer to another via modem. YMODEM offers two benefits over XMODEM: You can send batches of files (XMODEM forces you to send them one at a time), and the name of the file is transmitted along with the file. XMODEM requires you to name the incoming file when you download it.

zone A *zone* is a small "subnetwork" within a larger network. Many large networks are divided into zones to enhance their performance.

zoom box The little box in the upper right-hand corner of most windows in which you can click to enlarge or shrink the window.

Index